UNITY OR SEPARATION

UNITY OR SEPARATION

Center-Periphery Relations in the Former Soviet Union

Edited by
Daniel R. Kempton and
Terry D. Clark

Westport, Connecticut
London

Library of Congress Cataloging-in-Publication Data

Unity or separation : center-periphery relations in the former Soviet Union / edited by Daniel R. Kempton and Terry D. Clark.

p. cm.

Includes bibliographical references and index.

ISBN 0–275–97011–6 (alk. paper).—ISBN 0–275–97306–9 (pbk. : alk. paper)

1. Central-local government relations—Russia (Federation) 2. Federal government—Russia (Federation) 3. Russia (Federation)—Ethnic relations. 4. Central-local government relations—Former Soviet republics—Case studies. I. Kempton, Daniel R. II. Clark, Terry D.

JN6693.5.S8U55 2002

320.4′049′0947—dc21 00–052865

British Library Cataloguing in Publication Data is available.

Library of Congress Catalog Card Number: 00–052865

ISBN: 0–275–97011–6

0–275–97306–9 (pbk)

First published in 2002

Praeger Publishers, 88 Post Road West, Westport, CT 06881

An imprint of Greenwood Publishing Group, Inc.

www.praeger.com

Printed in the United States of America

The paper used in this book complies with the Permanent Paper Standard issued by the National Information Standards Organization (Z39.48–1984).

10 9 8 7 6 5 4 3 2 1

Copyright Acknowledgments

The editors and publisher gratefully acknowledge permission for use of the following material:

Chapter 4, "The Case of Sakha: Bargaining with Moscow" by Daniel R. Kempton is based upon Daniel R. Kempton, "The Republic of Sakha (Yakutia): The Evolution of Centre-Periphery Relations in the Russian Republic," *Europe-Asia Studies* 48(2): 577–603; and Daniel R. Kempton, "Budgetary Politics in the Russian Federation: The Case of Sakha (Yakutia)," in *International Journal of Public Administration* 22(9–10), Marcel Dekker, Inc., N.Y., 1999, 1345–1385. Reprinted from *International Journal of Public Administration*, p. 1345–1385, courtesy of Marcel Dekker, Inc.

Contents

CHAPTER 1

AN INTRODUCTION TO CENTER-PERIPHERY RELATIONS

Daniel R. Kempton and Terry D. Clark

The book provides a preliminary, but exceptionally thorough, review of the emerging center-periphery relations in the states of the former Soviet Union. While this issue may seem a mundane one, in the former Soviet Union center-periphery problems threaten the territorial integrity of many of the Soviet successor states. Even in those cases where center-periphery conflicts do not pose a threat to the survival of the successor state, they are a matter for seemingly endless negotiation and renegotiations and are the focus of a crucial political debate. Yet, how these debates are resolved ultimately will have a significant effect on the economic and political shape of the Soviet successor states.

The 1991 collapse of the Soviet Union was an epic event. It resulted in the dismemberment of the Soviet Union and the less tangible, but nonetheless real, unleashing of centrifugal forces of ethnic nationalism, religious animosity, and regional self-interest. Once the twin principles of centralized rule and the immutability of borders were abandoned, a Pandora's box was opened. It unleashed centrifugal forces with no predetermined or natural endpoint. Like a Russian *matroishka* doll, a wide variety of ethnonationalist groups sought to carve out homelands from within the 15 designated successor states.[1] Ultimately, the validity of the successor states' claim to independence rested not on any objective criteria, but on the sometimes-whimsical Soviet system of rewarding and punishing ethnic groups as they historically fell into or out of favor with Moscow. For example, in May 1944 units of the Soviet secret police systematically rounded up and deported virtually the entire Crimean Tatar population. In June 1945 the Crimean ASSR (part of the Russian SSFR) was then abolished, although the decision was not announced until June 1946.

Then in February 1954, to mark the tercentenary of the union of Russia and the Ukraine, Nikita Khrushchev transferred the Crimea to the Ukraine as a present. The Ingush also lost their republic status after they were deported from the Caucasus to Central Asia in 1944. When they were allowed to return home after 1957, Ossetians inhabited much of their land. Thus they were resettled on the border of Chechnya and given a joint republic with the Chechen. In somewhat a reverse situation, Karelia was made a union republic in anticipation of the annexation of Finland, and the addition of more Finnish speakers. However, when Finland successfully resisted Soviet aggression, Karelia lost its union republic status. The Transcaucasian states were absorbed into the Soviet Union *en masse* and only later subdivided by Stalin. The borders he drew were a matter of controversy then, and are a matter of conflict today.

Thus, when the Soviet Union collapsed, the question of which components would be independent was largely a result of bad central planning, historical quirks, and whims. The Soviet components that held the status of "union republic" in 1991 received independence; the rest did not. Despite solid claims based on population size (the Tatars) or cultural uniqueness (the Chechens), these and other potentially deserving ethnonationalist groups were left frustrated.

The problems in center-periphery relations created by the breakup of the Soviet Union can be divided into four logically distinct, but empirically overlapping, categories. The first category is composed of cases in which ethnonationalist groups are actively seeking independence from the successor states in which they found themselves. Cases in this category have spawned a number of violent conflicts and as a result have attracted the most international attention. The bloodiest and best-known examples are Chechnya in Russia, Transcaucasia in Moldova, and Abkhazia in Georgia. Unfortunately, there are many cases in this category, which still threaten to become violent.

A second closely related category consists of those ethnonationalist groups and regions for whom the breakup of the Soviet Union brought what was perceived as political disassociation from the main part of their nation, which resided in a separate successor state. Examples include Uzbeks living in the other Central Asian states, Armenians in Nagorno-Karabakh, Ossetians in North Georgia and Russians living in regions of Latvia, Estonia, Moldova (Trans-Dneister), the Ukraine (Crimea), and Kazakhstan (the northern 40% of the state). While groups or regions in this category may consider independence (e.g., the Trans-Dneister Republic), the more typical goal is some form of increased association or even reunification with their kinsmen abroad. While problems in this category have received less public attention, they have generated more than their share of bloody conflicts (e.g., Nagorno-Karabakh and Ossetia) and may hold the greatest potential for mass violence (the Crimea).

A third category of problems includes those regions that, because of some combination of ethnic and economic issues, have sought a greater degree of autonomy within the successor states in which they now live. Among the many examples are Sakha, Tuva, and Crimea. These cases differ in that the regions or groups in question are not challenging the integrity of the successor states, but merely a redistribution of power. In this category many of the titular population groups are not a majority even within the particular region in which they reside.

A fourth category is the most basic and common problem. This category includes regions, cities, and other components that base their demands for greater autonomy on purely economic grounds. Most of Russia's oblasti, regions with no ethnic designation, fall into this category, as do nearly all of the cities of the former Soviet Union. Whether large cities like Moscow and Riga—which deal directly with their respective national governments—or small towns in Siberia—which deal with a regional government—every municipal government has its own opinions of which powers it should be allowed to exercise. Needless to say, the national governments also have their opinions as to which powers should be exercised by each level of government. In the Soviet Union there were few unresolved issues in center-periphery relations. Political decisions flowed from the capital down to the localities. Tax revenues went to Moscow and all capital for redistribution to local budgets came from Moscow. Today, the powers and resources that are granted to central, regional and local governments are a matter for seemingly endless renegotiation, and occasional struggle. Which level of government will create taxes and determine tax rates? Which level will collect the taxes? Which level of government will determine how revenues are spent? How is state property privatized, and who receives the revenues that accrue from such sales? Who owns natural resources that are regionally concentrated? Who sets educational and cultural policy? Each of the successor states has had to find its own answers to these and many other unsettled questions in center-periphery relations.

Although these problems have received less international publicity than the ethnic conflicts discussed above, in some ways they are the most important. How these problems are resolved will shape the distribution of power and resources throughout the successor states. Moreover, it will partially determine the economic fortunes of the successor states and even the depth of their democratization.

This book grapples with cases in center-periphery relations that are drawn from all four categories discussed above. It assumes that, for better or worse, center-periphery relations will partially shape the political dynamics of all the Soviet successor states. However, because the Soviet Union failed to bequeath the successor states with a viable blueprint for center-periphery relations, each of the successor states has had to create its own forms of center-periphery relations. That is not to say that the successor states have recreated *tabula rasa*. While they face a common dilemma, their emerging attempts to resolve the problem have varied. They range from the complex multi-tiered federal system emerging in Russia, to the Baltics, where regional governments in the French model are agents of the central government monitoring the activities of popularly elected local governments. But for all the successor states, center-periphery relations are a subject of constant negotiation and renegotiation and remain politically charged.

The question then is not so much what solutions have been adopted, as what solutions are emerging? That is to say, many of the successor governments have introduced constitutions or other legal frameworks to govern center-periphery relations. However, these frameworks have been subject to frequent revision, and practice often differs from the legal frameworks. Thus the only way to accurately understand center-periphery relations in the successor states is to examine specific relationships. Thus, the first task for our authors was to provide an accurate description of a specific set of center-periphery relations. This entailed answering a number of difficult questions. What powers are being distributed to the periphery, and what powers remain with the center? How secure and explicit are the powers given to each level of government? How are disputes resolved? Are the successor states adopting similar solutions to similar center-periphery problems? Answering these questions provides the best possible description of center-periphery relations in the successor states.

However, the authors do not stop at description. They also evaluate the effectiveness of the emerging solution, its appropriateness for the emerging state, and its ability to provide both long-term stability and a basis for lasting democracy. What they conclude is that in some cases, real progress has occurred. While the process is often messy and sometimes violent, workable solutions are being developed that are deciding the future distribution of power and resources in the successor states. Ultimately, these solutions may, or may not, prevent the further disintegration of the successor states. It is too early to draw long-term conclusions. However, it is not too early to conclude that some of the solutions adopted by the successor states have provided a modicum of political stability, have decelerated the process of *matroishka* nationalism, whereby it was feared the successor states would gradually shatter into smaller and smaller states. With the potential exception of Chechnya, since 1992 no new states have been carved out of the former Soviet Union. This record compares favorably with recent events in the Balkans and even in what was once Czechoslovakia.

CENTER-PERIPHERY RELATIONS

Use of the term center-periphery relations is increasingly commonplace among analysts of comparative politics and has already been introduced to the study of politics in the Soviet successor states.[2] The term, as used in this study, is closely related to the concept of intergovernmental relations (IGR) as used in the study of public administration. The concept originated in the United States and refers explicitly to the relationships between governments at various levels of the U.S. political system.[3] Despite the utility and richness of the concept of IGR, it is problematic for this study. First, IGR has not moved much beyond its American roots and has never been reformulated for comparative politics. Second, IGR is in sense too broad in that it includes the widest possible variety of intergovernmental relationships. In the American context, it deals not only with federal-state relations, but also, interstate relations, federal-local relations, local-state relations, county-state relations, and so on. While all of these relationships are potentially important in the Soviet successor states, they are beyond the context of our study. Instead, the chapters on Russia deal exclusively with the relations between Russia and its constituent republics and regions, or subjects (*subekty*) as they are called in the Constitution. Similarly the chapters in Part II deal primarily with relations between the national governments and local governments. In these cases there is no intervening level of government. When they do exist, they are essentially agents of the central government.

A final problem, for our purposes, is that because the study of IGR focuses on governmental relations and policy, it tends to ignore the cultural factors that are critical to center-periphery in many of our cases. The study of center-periphery relations is narrower in that it focuses only on the relationships between the central government and, depending on the case in question, the regional or municipal governments. Conversely it is a broader term in that it deals not only with relationships between governmental units, but also with the division of political, economic and social powers between various levels of government. Another advantage is that center-periphery relations is a term frequently used in comparative politics.[4] However, there are a few drawbacks to using the term that merit some attention. First, the term is used frequently by Marxists and neo-Marxists to describe both international relations and comparative politics. As an international relations term, it is used to describe the relations between the capitalist states at the center of the global economy and the poorer states at the periphery. In comparative politics it is used to describe the relations between the more developed, urbanized center of a single state and its less developed, less urbanized areas.[5] This leads to the connotation that the periphery is permanently weak, or in Frank's terms, underdeveloped, relative to the center.[6] Moreover, for most neo-Marxists, including Frank, the underdevelopment of the periphery is a direct result of the center's development. This book does not share these assumptions. To the contrary, it gives considerable attention to the disparate development levels of various parts of the periphery, and considers the relative power of the center and periphery to be open to political struggle.

A second problem with the concept of center-periphery relations is that center and periphery are not always geographically isolated. For example, Moscow and St. Petersburg are both subjects (*subekty*) of Russia and thus part of the Russian periphery. Conversely, both geographically and economically they are near to the center of Russia. Similarly, relations between the Lithuanian national government and the municipal government of Vilnius, its capital, are, in our view, a suitable topic for center-periphery relations even though both are located in the same city.

For our purposes, center-periphery relations will be defined as the relationship between national governments and lower levels of government that have specific, but smaller, geographic jurisdictions. The center is not presumed to be more powerful or more developed than the periphery. Instead, the distinction resides with the center's political jurisdiction, which extends to the entire state. Conversely the periphery is made up of those units of governments, and their supporters, that exercise jurisdiction over a geographically limited portion of the state.

CHAPTER SUMMARIES

This book contains eleven substantive studies of center-periphery relations, each of which was written specifically for this volume. The authors come from geographically diverse institutions in North America and Europe. The chapters are written by some of the leading scholars in this rapidly emerging field. Each chapter derives from extensive empirical research on the part of the authors, and each has undergone multiple drafts to improve its quality and increase the consistency in both subject matter and terminology. The original chapters for the volume came out of three panels at the 1997 meetings of the American Association for the Advancement of Slavic Studies, which were organized by the editors. Other chapters were subsequently solicited from leading experts in their respective fields in order to provide more comprehensive coverage and to include some critical individual cases.

This book is divided into two parts. Part I deals exclusively with Russia, which represents by far the greatest portion of the Soviet population and landmass. Russia is also a relatively unique case in that it maintains a separate level of regional government, which generally has considerably more power and legitimacy than the local level. Russia has also attempted to resolve the center-periphery problem with a unique form of asymmetrical federalism. The first chapter in the Russian part of the book is Daniel R. Kempton's discussion of the concept of federalism and its potential applicability to Russia. The chapter first suggests that the evolution of Russian federalism can be best understood in three institutional stages. The first stage lasted from the rise of Gorbachev, when the components first began to make unilateral claims against the center, until the collapse of the Soviet Union. During this phase many of Russia's components, or *subekty* as they are called in the Russian Constitution, began to make claims for greater autonomy and even sovereignty. As part of his competition with Gorbachev, Yeltsin was willing to grant numerous, but varied, concessions to many of Russia's components, primarily the republics. The second stage began with the collapse of the Soviet Union and ended with the implementation of the 1993 Russian Constitution. During this stage center-periphery relations fluctuated coterminously with the level of conflict at the center. When Yeltsin's conflict with the Supreme Soviet was greatest, he was impelled to make concessions to Russia's *subekty* in order to win their support.

Conversely, when the conflict at the center was diminished, particularly after Yeltsin's defeat of the Supreme Soviet, he generally took powers back from the *subekty*. The third stage of relations began with the implementation of the new Constitution, which set basic limitations on center-periphery relations, but left open the process of bilateral negotiations between the *subekty* and the center.

The chapter concludes that while federalism may exist in the Russian Constitution, Russia's components have received a dizzying variety of powers. However, it also raises a number of pertinent questions for analysis in the subsequent chapters. For example, will Russia's asymmetrical federalism, in which some *subekty* receive more powers and autonomy than others, provide Russia with the flexibility to maintain its territorial integrity throughout the difficult transitions to capitalism and democracy? Or, will the inequality between *subekty* the system creates be a source of destabilizing tension? The subsequent chapters provide mixed conclusions to these questions. Another important question is, does the current level of federalism provide a sufficient check to prevent governments at any level from backsliding into dictatorship?

Because of the asymmetrical nature of Russian federal relations—with each *subekt* having unique powers and responsibilities—the only viable way to assess the evolution of Russian federalism is to empirically examine individual cases. Thus, each of the subsequent substantive chapters deals with a specific region, or related regions, of Russia. Each chapter examines the unique characteristics of the region, the strategies it has pursued in its relations with the federal government, and the specific powers and responsibilities that it has received. In Chapter 3 James Alexander concludes that the Komi and Russian governments have established through their bilateral agreement, which supplements the vague parameters of the 1993 Constitution, a basic framework for center-periphery relations. Although both Komi and the federal government continue to violate, on occasion, the terms of this framework, he does find that Komi and the national government have developed a stable relationship, which he terms semi-federal.

In Chapter 4 Daniel Kempton concludes that Sakha (Yakutia) has won and lost considerable powers. Its power reached a zenith just before the implementation of the 1993 Constitution. Since then, the federal government has gradually stripped Sakha of some of its powers. However, the powers it lost were generally those that were unique to Sakha, and a few other republics, and were considered excessive both by the federal government and by many of the other *subekty*. Nonetheless, Kempton concludes that Sakha continues to exercise considerable political and economic autonomy.

In Chapter 5, Ann Robertson documents two very different strategies for maximizing regional autonomy. By adopting a highly conflictual strategy and insisting on absolute independence, Dudaev led Chechnya to war, and economic collapse. Conversely, by working with the national government, Shaimiev has negotiated considerable political and economic autonomy for Tatarstan.

Thus, while Chechnya's status remains in limbo, Tatarstan has developed a federal relationship with many benefits for the republic.

In Chapter 6, Ingmar Oldberg focuses on the economic accommodations Moscow has conceded to the Kaliningrad Oblast. Although these concessions appear to have brought a degree of stability to center-periphery relations, as is the case elsewhere, Oldberg notes that the failure of Moscow to live up to its financial obligations to the oblast is eroding the federal relationship. (As argued in Chapter 8, this is a problem for most Russian center-periphery relationships.)

In Chapter 7, Helge Blakkisrud's study of the Nenets Autonomous Okrug deals with nested relationships, in which one subekt is geographically contained within another subekt. Blakkisrud presents considerable evidence of the difficulties of these relationships. Unfortunately, the status of nested *subekty* is ambiguous since the Constitution at point refers to the equality of all *subekty*, and in other places implies regional governments have administrative control over the autonomous oblasty within their territory. On the positive side of the ledger, the federal government has largely allowed the *subekty* to resolve these issues through peaceful negotiations. On the negative side of the ledger, the federal government is presently ill-equipped to adjudicate these disputes when its intervention is needed.

In the concluding chapter to Part I, Daniel Kempton compares the evidence provided by the five substantive case studies against the necessary and beneficial conditions of federalism presented in Chapter 2. His conclusion is a mixed one. Russia has made remarkable progress in creating the necessary conditions for federalism. Many of the beneficial conditions are also growing. However, it is too early to claim that Russia has built a stable federation. Serious shortcomings include Russian political culture, which provides little active support for shared rule, and financial culture, in which both levels of government frequently fail to live up to their obligations to the other level. Thus while analysts should be impressed by Russia's progress, they cannot be sanguine about Russia's future success as a federal system.

Part II of the book looks at the evolution of center-periphery relations in the non-Russian successor states. In these newly emergent states, federalism is not an issue. Instead, the struggle to define the relations between central government on the one hand and regional and local governments on the other revolves around the issue of autonomy within the context of a unitary state and the challenges that this poses to the establishment of a national identity around which the emerging state can integrate. The opening chapter by Terry D. Clark provides a theoretical overview of center-periphery relations in these systems. It argues that idiosyncratic analyses of local governments treated in isolation will not help us to understand the trajectory of change, let alone the relationship between national governments and subnational units. Only a systemic approach that takes into consideration the constraints placed on local governments by market forces and the constitutional order will permit us to do so. Such an approach necessarily treats the evolution of center-periphery relations as the result of a bargaining process between local governments and the center.

Each subsequent chapter considers these and other issues in the context of a specific successor state. These chapters conclude with an assessment of the relative autonomy of local and regional governments within the successor state in question. Paul Kubicek argues that regionalism underlies virtually every aspect of politics in Ukraine. It is the defining characteristic of presidential and parliamentary elections. The state-building project has been complicated by the lack of a national identity capable of unifying the country's disparate regions. As a consequence, the center has been overtaxed by the demands of trying to pull the regions together. This is particularly evident in the relationship between Kiev and Crimea, the most explosive in the country. Nonetheless, the weakness of Ukrainian nationalism opens the possibility of an emerging concept of citizenship on a civic basis, vice ethnic. Hence, Ukraine may not be doomed to perpetual instability.

Terry D. Clark focuses on the importance of efficacious local government to the democratization project. The efforts by overzealous central governments in unitary systems can greatly undermine the capacity of local authorities. In Lithuania's unitary state the tendency has been toward increasing centralization. The central government's control over local budgets is particularly problematic. Nevertheless, local elites have managed to leverage their popular mandates to engage in protracted bargaining with Vilnius, the result of which will likely be decided by the ability of local governments to develop a professional administration and facilitate the emergence of a local civil society.

In Central Asia center-periphery relations are marked by the continued dominance of the center. Lawrence R. Robertson and Roger D. Kangas argue that local and regional governments in Uzbekistan are extraordinarily weak. Similar to the Soviet era, most decisions are made in the vertical structures of the executive branch under the President. Local governments and administrations are left with little to no room for discretion in executing the directives and programs of the center. Anthony Bichel's chapter on the role of a unique social institution, the *mahalla*, in Central Asia further questions the degree to which center-periphery relations is a salient political issue in the region. Indeed, it may well be the case that informal power structures actually engage in governance at all levels of the political system, constitutional structures being little more than a façade or vehicle for the more personalistic politics of the region.

The concluding chapter pulls together the conclusions from the individual chapters and assesses the extent to which the successor states have developed solutions to their shared problem. The book's unique comprehensiveness and comparative nature enable the authors to draw some tentative conclusions as to the relative success of the various strategies that have been adopted in solving the common problems of center-periphery relations. Finally, the editors return to the question of whether the varied solutions to the problem of center-periphery relations will provide the successor states a solid foundation for political stability and fertile ground for the growth of democracy.

NOTES

1. Ian Bremmer, "Reassessing Soviet Nationalities Theories," in Ian Bremmer & Ray Taras, eds., *Nations and Politics in the Soviet Successor States*, Cambridge: Cambridge University Press, 1993, p. 22.

2. Jeremy R. Azrael and Emil A. Payin, *Conflict and Consensus in Ethno-Political and Center-Periphery Relations in Russia*, Santa Monica, CA: Rand Center for Russian and Eurasian Studies, 1998.

3. Deil S. Wright, "Understanding Intergovernmental Relations," in Jay M. Shafritz & Albert C. Hyde, eds., *Classics of Public Administration*, California: Brooks/Cole Publishing, 1992, pp. 550–563; and Deil S. Wright, *Understanding Intergovernmental relations*, California: Brooks/Cole Publishing, 1982.

4. See for example, H. Daalder, "Consociationalism, center and periphery in the Neatherlands," in Per Tovsvik, ed., *Mobilization Center-Periphery Structures and Nation Building: A Volume in Commemoration of Stein Rokkan*, Bergen, Norway: Iniversitetforlaget, 1981, pp. 181–240; and H. Guillorel, "France: Relation, periphery, state and nation-building," in Per Tovsvik, ed., *Mobilization Center-Periphery Structures and Nation Building: A Volume in Commemoration of Stein Rokkan*, Bergen, Norway: Iniversitetforlaget, 1981, pp. 390–428.

5. Joel Samoff and Rachel Samoff, "The Local Politics of Underdevelopment," *American Review* VI (1), 1972, 69–97.

6. Frank actually refers to the center and periphery as metropole and satellite. Andre Gunder Frank, "The Development of Underdevelopment," *Monthly Review*, XCIII, September 1966, pp. 17–31.

PART I

Russian Center-Periphery Relations: A Federal Experiment

CHAPTER 2

THREE CHALLENGES TO ASSESSING RUSSIAN FEDERALISM

Daniel R. Kempton

> The Question of the relationship of the states to the federal government is the cardinal question of our constitutional system. At every turn of our national development we have been brought face to face with it and no definition either of statesmen or judges has ever decided it. It cannot, indeed, be settled by one generation because it is a question of growth, and every successive stage of our political and economic development gives it a new aspect, makes it a new question.
>
> Woodrow Wilson, 1911

Federalism is the most discussed solution to Russia's current center-periphery problems. While federalism is not a new concept, the way it is viewed has changed dramatically. Over the course of the twentieth century federalism has gone from being viewed as a weak and transitory form of government to being portrayed as a virtual panacea for states torn by ethnic conflict and even as a pattern for future regional integration. Early English constitutional authorities, such as Lord Bryce, commonly "viewed the classical federal system as no more than a transitory step on the way to constitutional-governmental unity."[1] In the 1930s, Laski saw federalism as a pragmatic but temporary way for Britain and other colonial authorities to shift power to more local authorities within their empires. Friedrich believed the process more frequently moved in the opposite direction, but portrayed federalism in a similar fashion. For him federalism arose when a group of previously autonomous states, typically driven by the defense imperative, formed a single central government. Thus, like Bryce, Friedrich saw federalism as a transitory step rather than as an end goal.[2] Today, however, federalism is considered the hallmark of a stable, ethnically diverse state. It is used in many modern democracies including Australia, Canada, Germany, Spain, Switzerland, and the United States. It has been adopted to manage ethnic tension in India, South Africa, Malaysia, and Russia. Moreover, in the minds of more optimistic scholars, Europe is creating a model for evolution to federalism that may someday be emulated by regional associations in Southeast Asia, Southern Africa, or in the former Soviet Union.

While there are many forms of center-periphery relations, the 1993 Russian Constitution explicitly commits Russia to federalism, hence creating the Russian Federation. As described in the 1993 Constitution, the Russian Federation is composed of 89 distinct *subekty* (component subjects). Like the former Soviet Union, the Russian Federation is a complex federal state, meaning that its components are not equal in status or power. Its *subekty* include: 21 republics, 49 *oblasti* (regions), 1 autonomous *oblast*, 6 *krai* (territories), 10 *okruga* (autonomous areas), and 2 federal cities (Moscow and St. Petersburg). But is Russia really an emerging federal state, or is it—like the Soviet Union—merely a unitary state in federal clothing? This is a fiercely debated issue among Russian politicians and among scholars both within and outside of Russia. It is also the purpose of Part I of this book to assess Russia's progress on the road to federalism.

There are three basic challenges to assessing the evolution of federalism in Russia. The first challenge arises from the idiosyncratic nature of Russian center-periphery relations. Put bluntly, Russia's 89 *subekty* have been allowed to negotiate with the center to determine the powers they will hold and the rights they will exercise. Thus, the only way to accurately assess Russian federalism is to focus on the relationships between the center and individual *subekty*. This book contains six such studies. Each of the following five chapters focuses on a specific *subekt*, or at most two such *subekty*, and examines their relationships with the center over time. Each of these studies was written specifically for this book and involved considerable research on the part of the scholars involved. Each addresses common issues. Most importantly, what strategies were adopted by the *subekt* government and by the federal government, and to what degree has this relationship evolved to a point at which the relationship might be labeled federal? A summation of the findings and overall conclusions will be discussed in Chapter 8.

The second challenge to assessing Russian federalism arises from the ambiguity of the concept itself. Precisely because federalism is such a popular idea it is a term that is often used but rarely defined. Fortunately there is extensive literature that discusses not only what federalism is, but also helps to establish the necessary and beneficial conditions for the establishment and maintenance of federalism.

The third challenge to assessing Russian federalism arises from the malleable and rapidly changing nature of Russian center-periphery relations. Russia has created new institutions, enacted new laws, and written a new constitution. These changes have altered the rules for Russian center-periphery relations.

They have created new opportunities for Russian federalism and erected new barriers to federalism. Thus one cannot accurately assess the evolution of Russian federalism without some notion of institutional change in Russia.

The purpose of this chapter is to help with the latter two challenges. It will first examine the definition of federalism and lay out its necessary and beneficial conditions. It will then lay out an institutional approach for dealing with change in Russian politics. However, before tackling these two tasks, it useful to first consider why federalism is so appealing to contemporary states, including Russia. Presumably, federalism has historically proven beneficial and these benefits are readily apparent to contemporary Russians.

THE BENEFITS OF FEDERALISM

In the twentieth century there has been an exponential proliferation of federal states. In 1987 Elazar reported that nearly 40 percent of the world's population lived in federal systems and concluded that the federalist revolution was "among the most widespread—if one of the most unnoticed—of the various revolutions that are changing the face of the globe."[3] In 1996 Watts reported 23 federal states and proclaimed "a paradigm shift from a world of sovereign nation-states to a world of diminished state sovereignty and increased interstate linkages of a constitutionally federal character."[4] What accounts for federalism's rising popularity in the twentieth century? The answer can be found in a brief consideration of the perceived benefits of federalism.

The first and most obvious benefit is an ancient one. The creation of a common defense was a key factor in the formation of both the Israelite Federation and the Greek Leagues. Both the Hanseatic League and the federal systems originating after the Reformation helped protect their constituent components in a dangerous world. Similarly, Merkl contends, "Most modern federations originated in response to extraordinary challenges from abroad and at home. They sought the greater security and international power of a larger state."[5] Modern federations—like formal alliances—allow their members to call on defensive capabilities far greater than they individually possess. This allows the components to protect their common borders, without significant loss of local autonomy.

For Russians, the security dilemma has always been more than a theoretical problem—it has been a historical reality. Russian history texts are filled with invasions by the Mongols, the Poles, the Lithuanians, the Turks, the French, and most recently twice by the Germans. Not surprisingly, therefore, many Russians believe that any further carving up of historic Russia will leave Russia even more vulnerable to foreign threats and domestic turmoil. Federalism is a way to keep Russia together in the absence of a powerful central government, thus preserving the enhanced security provided by the collective capabilities of all of Russia.

The second and most widely discussed benefit of federalism is that it can accommodate diverse minority groups within a single state. As a Canadian government commission concluded, "Only federalism as a political system permits two cultures to live and develop side by side within a single state."[6] Gagnon concludes, "Federalism is a process offering a variety of options to cope with many conflicting cleavages. It is also utilized as a political instrument for communities to express themselves and be included in the political process."[7] Thus federalism seems to offer weighty tools for dealing with the revival of global nationalism and the growth of cultural awareness.[8] First, it can lower the temperature of elite competition by multiplying the number of available bureaucratic and political posts. A political or ethnic group may be politically insignificant at the national level, but may be politically dominant within its territorial component. Second, federalism multiplies the arenas for negotiation. Third, federalism gives groups an institutional power base that may make it easier to defend their interests at the federal level. Finally, and most importantly, it gives a minority group the ability to preserve itself by allowing it control of cultural and educational policy within a set territory.

Despite the severing of the other 14 union republics, contemporary Russia remains a large and diverse multi-ethnic state. The Russian Federation is proportionately far more Russian than was the Soviet Union (approximately 80% as compared to just over 50%). Yet it still contains a sizable, diverse, and politically entrenched minority population. Of Russia's 89 *subekty* (components), 21 are ethnically defined as non-Russian. Together, the republics account for about 30 percent of Russia's territory and contain about 20 percent of its population. Each of these republics was designated as the homeland for a specific "titular" minority population. Although not all of these ethnic groups remain a majority within their own homeland, they continue to exercise special powers and enjoy special rights. In many cases these have been expanded, and the titular language has been raised to official status. To complicate matters, each of the republics also has a sizable Russian population, and in a number of cases Russians are now the most populous group. The other 68 *subekty* are territorially defined, and as such have no ethnic designation. While these *subekty* are presumed to be Russian, and indeed contain a Russian majority population, many of them contain sizable non-Russian minorities.

Many of Russia's minorities are culturally quite distinct, including numerous Turkish, Mongolian, and native populations. The religious practices of the peoples of the Russian Federation include Orthodoxy, Catholicism, various forms of Protestantism, Islam, Buddhism, and traditional ancestor worship. Instead of disappearing during the Soviet period, the cultural, linguistic and religious traditions that separate Russia's minorities from Russians have experienced a profound and widespread rebirth and renaissance. Since the collapse of the Soviet Union, these differences have spurred numerous declarations of sovereignty, two bids for independence (Tatarstan and Chechnya) and one civil war (Chechnya).

In the minds of many Russians, the collapse of the Soviet Union unleashed the powerful centrifugal forces of ethnic nationalism and regional self-determination. Once the principle of the immutability of borders was shattered, a Pandora's box had been opened, triggering a process that had neither a pre-determined end point nor a natural firebreak.[9] To illustrate this process Bremmer offers the term "*matrioshka* nationalism."[10] Just as ever smaller dolls emerge from a within a Russian *matrioshka* doll, ever smaller states would rip their independence from Russia and the other successor states. For Russia, federalism may provide a way to halt this process and reseal Pandora's box.

However, even supporters of federalism urge caution. As Watts argues, "The function of federations is not to eliminate internal differences but rather to preserve regional identities within a united framework. Their function is not to eliminate conflict, but to manage it in such a way that regional differences are accommodated."[11] Increasing a state's capacity to manage regional tension is no guarantee that these conflicts will be resolved, or even successfully managed. In one sense, federalism actually allows conflict to emerge and encourages the politicization of conflict. Ethno-linguistic issues that might otherwise be secondary tend to rise to the forefront of politics in a federal system. Federalism also creates a second tier of group conflict. Groups that may be cultural or ethnic majorities at the national level, and thus may be very happy within a unitary system, may be minorities within a given territorial component. In this way ethnic conflict at the territorial level is created or exacerbated. This leads some Russian analysts to claim that Russia's federalism is creating, rather than resolving, disunity and conflict.[12]

A federal system, therefore, offers no guarantees for successful conflict resolution. In the last 40 years federal systems have failed in the West Indies, Pakistan, Malaysia, Nigeria, Yugoslavia, and Czechoslovakia. Even long-established federal states—like Canada—have at times teetered on the brink of collapse. At the same time, federalism has proven successful in handling numerous problems of cultural and ethnic diversity.

A third widely perceived benefit of federalism is the contention that it promotes democracy. At a minimum, by institutionalizing competing groups of political elites and dividing power among them, federalism makes tyranny more difficult. But even more than this, federalism admits the legitimacy of conflicting interests and commits all sides to peaceful accommodation. In short, it accepts pluralism and breeds tolerance for diverse interests that are core requirements for the sustenance of democracy. It also creates a second level for citizen participation in governance. Elazar argues that federalism also tends to raise public attention to constitutional issues and "generates a continuing referendum on first principles."[13] Because the constitution serves as the demarcation of powers between the federal and component governments, it attracts greater attention. Despite the advantages federalism holds for democracy, there is no guarantee that the adoption of federalism will lead to democracy. (Whether democracy is itself a precondition for federalism will be addressed in a subsequent section.) While many Russians are desirous of democracy, somewhat surprisingly it is not one of the arguments commonly made in defense of Russian federalism.

A fourth alleged benefit of federalism is that it offers the economic advantages of larger markets, larger economies of scale, and more coordinated economic planning.[14] Although this is undoubtedly true, a sovereign state need not join a federation to increase its economic cooperation and coordination with its neighbors. While the EU may be moving toward a federal arrangement, the North American Free Trade Association and other groups have largely limited their cooperation to the economic sphere. Moreover, the uncertain and changing nature of federal relationships can undermine the stability—at least relative to unitary systems—that is often necessary for a united and productive economy.[15] It is also worth remembering that in any economic scheme for cooperation between two states there are both winners and losers in each affected sector of the economy.

Finally, federalism is regularly praised for its adaptability and flexibility. Because federalism is based on the assumption of constant negotiation and renegotiations between territorially defined groups, change and adaptation are an inherent part of every federal system. Because federalism at once encourages competition and compromise, it forces innovation. No federal state can be immutable or static.

In sum, politicians and academicians alike praise federalism for the benefits it is perceived to produce: security, accommodation of diversity, democracy, economic prosperity, and flexibility. Elazar goes one step further and argues that federalism is an end in itself that can be perceived of as the highest form of political and human relations.[16] Although, it is clear from this discussion that federalism provides many potential benefits, it is important to understand from the outset that these benefits are not always achieved. The multiple centers of political power in a federal state may serve as a target of opportunity for a threatening neighbor. It may provide a pretext for external intervention. While many federal states have succeeded in using federalism to satiate ethnic or cultural groups, others like Nigeria and Yugoslavia have failed. Federalism may promote democracy, economic development, and political flexibility, but it cannot guarantee them. Federal states are flexible, but they may actually encourage more demands than can be accommodated.

DEFINING FEDERALISM: NECESSARY AND BENEFICIAL CONDITIONS

In his 1946 consideration of federalism, we are warned, "Where common usage differs so much, the academic man must be careful not to adopt too rigid a definition."[17] In his classic text of 1950 Friedrich reported, "Federalism, when spoken of in general discussions, is used rather vaguely to mean any kind of association of autonomous units."[18] Thirteen years later Hicks complained,

"It is a major complication that federalism is not easy to define; it has meant many differing things to many people."[19] In 1968 Elazar reported, "no single definition of federalism has proven satisfactory to all students."[20] He notes that there are numerous reasons for the rather ambiguous use of the term "federalism." Only a few need be listed here. First, because of its flexibility the practice of federalism varies dramatically both between states and over time within states. Contemporary federalism in Germany differs from that of Canada, the United States, or Australia. The term has been used both by communist states—Yugoslavia and the Soviet Union—and by democracies. It is used by bureaucratized developed states as well as by underdeveloped states. Yet the term obviously had different meanings in these different circumstances. Similarly, the current distribution of federal and state powers in the United States would probably be unrecognizable to the authors of *The Federalist*. A second problem is that federalism is used for very different purposes. While it is used in Nigeria and Russia to maintain unity and prevent secession, it is a tool to promote economic integration in the European Union. Third, federalism can be both a means and an end. Fourth, federalism may alternatively be used to describe a political system or a social-cultural phenomenon. Finally, federalism is used to refer both to a structure and to a process. While it is impossible to resolve all of these ambiguities or to create a consistent usage, it is possible to simplify and clarify the use of the term for this study.

As a starting point, Elazar contends that "The simplest possible definition is *self rule plus shared rule*."[21] Elsewhere he elaborates, "In the broadest sense, federalism involves the linking of individuals, groups, and polities in lasting but limited union in such a way as to provide for the energetic pursuit of common ends while maintaining the respective integrities of the parties."[22] This basic definition, which is accepted by other modern experts on federalism,[23] suggests that federalism is actually a broad category of political arrangements, which include some degree of unity and some degree of territorially based autonomy. Conceptually, we might conclude—as Friedrich does—that federalism is anything between a loose association and a unitary state.[24] We might then conceive of a federal state as the middle ground on a long continuum with unitary states at one extreme and loose associations at the other end. As Elazar notes, federalism can then be considered a broad genus, within which there are several species: confederations, federations, federacies, associated states, common markets, consociational polities, unions, condominiums, and leagues. To some degree each of these adopts the federal principle. Although Elazar provides some discussion and examples of each, it is not always easy to distinguish between them in the real world.

In order to evaluate Russia's progress in the construction of federalism it is necessary to explicate Elazar's definition (self rule plus shared rule) by articulating the necessary and beneficial conditions for federalism.[25] Arend Lijphart lists five principal attributes of a federal state. Chapman refers to three essential elements. Lynn and Novikov identify two distinguishing features, while Watts list six common structural features. Rather than debating the appropriate number of necessary conditions, this chapter attempts to provide a relatively exhaustive list of the conditions of federalism and provide some consideration as to whether each condition is necessary, or merely beneficial.

The Necessary Conditions

Consensual Participation

A first necessary condition of federalism, as emphasized in Dicey's classic study of constitutional law, is that federalism is voluntary in nature. This same theme is apparent in Elazar's contention that federal states involve some form of voluntary covenant or contract among its components. More recently, Watts has argued "Federations are the consequence of reflection and choice by individuals endeavoring to facilitate through a working out of a mutually acceptable relationship within a family of independents."[26] While scholars of federalism agree that federal relations are in essence voluntary, they do not agree on what this entails.

Following Lord Bryce, many theorists have argued that given the consensual nature of federal states, they can only be formed by the voluntary joining of previously separate and sovereign entities, such as the formation of the United States from the original 13 colonies. Similarly Friedrich notes, "Historically speaking, federal governments often evolved out of leagues or confederations."[27] Merkl's argument that most modern federal states formed in response to security threats also presumes a contract among previously sovereign states.[28] Dicey goes further to argue that federalism is a stage in the transition from separate states to a unitary state.

Admittedly, many of the best-known modern federal states (e.g., the Netherlands, Switzerland, and the United Sates) emerged from previously autonomous components. Nonetheless, it is unhelpful to mingle the historical process that most frequently leads to federalism with the definition itself. Elazar, who identifies three basic methods by which polities come into existence, again clarifies this issue: conquest, organic evolution, and covenantal foundings.[29] He argues that each of these "tends" to lead to a particular form or type of polity. Federal states tend to be created by covenant or contract, rather than by organic growth or by conquest. However, he leaves open the possibility that any method of formation can lead to any type of policy.

Thus, while federal states are most frequently established through a contract among previously sovereign entities, other methods are possible. Laski argued that federalism was a way for the British Empire to gradually devolve power to local governments in its overseas territories. Historically a number of federal systems were created in the decolonization process in response to ethnic diversity. Australia, Canada, India, Pakistan, and Nigeria all devolved from imperial unity (the British Empire) into federal states. Other modern examples of unitary states that devolved into federal states include Belgium and Spain.

Belgium was founded as a unitary state in 1830 but has passed through four stages that culminated in federalism in 1993. Spain has devolved toward federalism since the implementation of its 1978 constitution.[30] Thus, the origin of a federal state will undoubtedly help shape its character, but federal states can emerge by various means.

What is necessary for all federal states is that the regional governments' continuing participation in the federal state is largely voluntary or consensual. This does not mean that the components provide an absolute right of secession. In fact, many federal states expressly prohibit secession. Canada, Nigeria, Pakistan, and the United States have all actively resisted secession, in the latter three cases militarily. Despite the horrific bloodshed of the American Civil War, the American states are still seen as consensual partners in the American system. What then does consensus entail? Simply put, consensus means that neither the federal government nor the component governments can dictate terms to the other. Instead, the federal government is required to build consensus among the component governments, particularly for policies that affect the components. As a number of contemporary theorists have argued, federal states are states in which the federal government cannot unilaterally implement a significant change in the powers, rights or borders of the federal components. One might say that the components hold a collective veto over the federal government on these issues.

A Written Constitution

This leads to the second necessary condition. Federal states must have a relatively rigid contract that specifies the rights and powers of the components. In the vast majority of cases this contract takes the form of a written constitution. (In some cases—like Canada and Russia—written constitutions are supplemented with negotiated agreements.) Typically, the constitution also provides a relatively rigid specification of the powers of each level of government.[31] Generally, those clauses of the constitution that affect the powers, rights, and borders of the components can only be amended with the consent of the components. In some cases this may require the support of a majority or a super majority of the component governments. In other cases the amendment process may require popular support in a majority or a super majority of the components. (The United States, as the classic model, incorporates both methods.) In many cases the constitution also institutionalizes the allocation of resources, by specifying ownership of resources and the power to collect taxes and other revenues. In general, it can be said that the constitution enshrines the contract or covenant between the levels of government.

While a written constitution appears to be a necessary condition for modern federal states, Watts' warning that there may be a gap between constitutional form and reality is worth heeding.[32] No federal state can from the outset fully anticipate the issues that will arise in the future, and thus cannot fully specify powers. For example, the American founders could not have anticipated the communications revolution (including radio, television, telephones, and the internet), and thus could not provide the same level of specification of powers in these areas that they provided for the oversight of commerce or the military. As a result, as Wilson's introductory quote suggests, federal states will be redefined as new powers are assigned and the distribution of old powers is reinterpreted. In this way the relative powers of each level of government evolve and develop. Unless the constitution is itself under constant revision, which would tend to undermine its rigidity, these changes are often not explicitly provided for in the constitution. This means that even with a written constitution, there tends to be considerable ambiguity over the rights and powers of each level, which leads not surprisingly to considerable political tension. Even in the U.S. case, an argument can be made that this process has been used to strip the states of their original powers and has been used to corrupt federalism.

Adjudication Between Levels

The third necessary condition is some form of adjudication between the levels of government.[33] Adjudication can be conducted by going directly to the population through the use of frequent referenda. However, the power to adjudicate constitutional disputes is more commonly given to a general supreme court (e.g., the United States, Canada, Australia, India, Malaysia, and Australia), a specific constitutional court (e.g., Belgium, Germany, Russia, and Spain), or a limited tribunal (e.g., Switzerland). Irrespective of form, what is required is some impartial and independent forum for settling the disputes between the levels of government. In the process of settling specific disputes, these courts or tribunals help the system adapt to changing circumstances.

Given the importance that federal states give to the judiciary, it is sometimes derogatorily labeled "government by the judiciary." Typically, however, this is checked by stripping the adjudicative body from the power to enforce its own decisions. Instead, the adjudicating court or tribunal must rely on its moral authority and integrity to ensure that its decisions are carried out. Thus the impartiality and independence of the adjudication mechanism is critical to the long-term success of the federation. To ensure the neutrality of the adjudicating body on federal issues, both the federal government and the components are sometimes given a role in the formation of the adjudicative body. The most common formula is for the federal government, in the form of the President or Prime Minister, to be allowed to nominate members. However, members often need to be confirmed by the components, typically through their representatives in the upper chamber of a bicameral parliament. While some federal systems allow representatives of the components on the adjudication body (e.g., Switzerland), this can undermine the perceived impartiality of the adjudicative body.

Federal Representation

The fourth necessary condition is some mechanism for the components to participate in politics at the federal level. There are many institutional arrangements that can provide component representation. (One of the most unique was the rotating presidency, which was used in Yugoslavia after Tito's death.) However, the most common locus of component representation is in the federal legislature. Friedrich, Lijphart, and Merkl all conclude that most modern, federal states have bicameral legislatures, in which the upper chamber contains representatives from the territorial components.[34] King calls this the most distinctive characteristic of a federal state.[35] The method by which these representatives are chosen varies dramatically. In Canada the federal government appoints them, while Switzerland leaves the method of selection up to the components in practice. In India representatives are elected by the state legislature. Similarly prior to 1913 in the United States the state legislatures selected their senators. (Practice, however, varied widely. Some states held officially non-binding popular votes, which effectively determined the legislature's selections.) In Russia the legislative and executive head of each component receive automatic seats in the Federation Council.

In fact, some federal states provide regional component representation in both chambers. For example, although the members of the U.S. Senate are not chosen by their states, each member is identified with a state, is considered part of a single state delegation, and no district is drawn across state boundaries. Thus while the U.S. Senate was designed to provide maximum representation to the small states, by providing equal representation for all states, the U.S. House of Representatives, where representation is based on population size, was to provide more effective representation for large states. For similar reasons, Russia's *subekty* have objected to the current system of electing one half of the members of the Duma, Russia's lower house, by proportional party vote.

Although the powers of the upper chamber vary greatly among federal states, the upper chamber generally possesses powers that give it a special role in areas of relatively greater concern to the components. These may include confirmation of constitutional or Supreme Court judges, approval of the federal budget, changes in tax laws effecting the components, territorial changes, education policy, language policy, and cultural policy. However, practice again varies.

A Division of Powers Between Levels of Government

Probably the most widely recognized necessary condition of federalism is a specified division of powers between at least two levels of government. In a sense, federal states contradict the nation-state conception of an indivisible sovereign state. In federal states the power for self-government is divided between two levels. This contradiction between shared powers and indivisible sovereignty was well understood by the American founders. They argued that while in a monarchy sovereignty was invested in the monarch, in a democracy sovereignty was invested in the people as whole. Thus, the people could disperse the power to govern between two levels without ever really dividing sovereignty, which remained with the people as a whole. As Madison argued in *The Federalist* (no. 46), "The federal and state governments are in fact but different agents and trustees of the people, constituted with different powers, and designed for different purposes." For this reason, Elazar argues that it is critical that each level of government administers some programs that serve the people directly.[36] This ensures that all governments have a direct tie to the people, the ultimate source of sovereignty.

There is no clear answer as to how much power or which specific powers must rest with the component governments. (This will be addressed in a subsequent section.) However, it is necessary that the division of powers cannot be unilaterally amended. Typically the powers granted to each level are specified in either a relatively rigid constitution, or in some cases, a negotiated contract with the government, which is not unilaterally alterable by either side. For Elazar, the inability of either side to alter the division of powers unilaterally is what separates a federal system from a decentralized unitary system. Both systems may grant considerable powers to the component governments, but only federal systems give their components the legal means to protect their powers. Elazar has conceptualized a federal system as being a matrix, as opposed to a hierarchical pyramid. Within the matrix, "there are no higher or lower power centers, only larger or smaller arenas of political decision making."[37] In such a system the powers assigned to different levels of government can be, and often are, overlapping. The amount of power necessary for each level of government to minimally possess, to prevent encroachment by other levels, is at once a function of the rigidity of the contract between them and the popular commitment to a federal division of powers.

A Federal Political Culture

Irrespective of the above structural characteristics, most scholars agree that federalism cannot survive without a supportive political culture.[38] Watts explains, "What we can learn from other federations that have succeeded is that even more important than their formal structures has been the public acceptance of the basic values and processes required for a federal system."[39] What values must a political culture inculcate in order to support federalism? Those most commonly mentioned include: (a) a tolerance of diversity, (b) the acceptance of multiple loyalties, (c) a mutual forbearance and self-restraint in the pursuit of goals, (d) a commitment to negotiations as a method for resolving disputes, and (e) a willingness to change. Numerous examples can be cited to illustrate the importance of political culture, but for our purposes a few will suffice. For federalism to succeed Americans have been forced to tolerate the practices of diverse religious and ethnic minorities. Thus, what is legal in Nevada (including prostitution and gambling) is strictly prohibited throughout the Mormon communities in neighboring Utah. For federalism to succeed in Spain, the federal government has had to accept the fact that most Basques owe their first loyalty to the region. For federalism to succeed, English-speaking Canadians have had to refrain from using their numerical superiority to pass laws and practices that threaten the language and cultural practices of

French speakers. Instead, they have accepted a seemingly endless process of renegotiating the terms of Quebec's participation in Canada.

The Beneficial Conditions

Obviously there are numerous discrepancies among scholars of federalism as to which conditions are necessary and which are merely beneficial. Thus there are many conditions that are considered necessary by some scholars, but are considered only helpful, or not even mentioned, by other scholars. For our purposes, these are labeled beneficial conditions. All of the following conditions were considered necessary, or at least very beneficial, by at least one major scholar of federalism. Because the purpose of this study is to produce a relatively exhaustive list of conditions that will determine Russia's success as a federal state, this paper has tried to err on the side of comprehensiveness, rather than exclusiveness. Nonetheless when the author could identify a clear reason for categorizing a particular condition as "beneficial" rather than as "necessary," this has been provided.

A Center-Periphery Balance

Some scholars have long-argued that an effective federal state requires not only a specific division of powers—as discussed above—but also a roughly equivalent balance between the powers of the federal government and the collective powers of the component governments. This balance provides each level with the institutional power base necessary to protect its powers and rights. As Watts argues, even in the extreme case the federal government must have the powers sufficient to resist balkanization.[40] At the other extreme, the component government must have the collective power to resist undesired centralization toward a unitary state. The fulfillment of these two conditions creates an equilibrium between the centrifugal demands of the components and the centripetal desires of the federal government. Along these lines, the authors of *The Federalist* (no. 51) argued that the U.S. federal system would have "a double security." Aside from the well-known separation of the departments of power into three branches, the division of power between the federal and state governments provided a second security. This line of argument has led some contemporary theorists to conclude that a federal state requires not just a division of powers that cannot be unilaterally amended, but a division of powers such that two levels must be relatively balanced in relation to one another. Some analysts have gone so far as to suggest that an indicator of the relative erosion of American federalism is the relative percentage of public expenditures controlled by the states relative to that controlled by the federal government.[41] (In fact the U.S. federal government's share of public expenditures greatly exceeded that of the states and local governments after the Second World War and the Korean Conflict, but is more nearly balanced today than in the 1930s, when the greatest inequity existed.)

Is relative equity or balance between the federal government and the component governments necessary for the success of federalism? First, unless balance is reduced to a measurable indicator—such as expenditures—it is almost impossible to measure. Second, there is tremendous variation in both the kinds of power and the relative degree of power granted to the components. Generally, the greater the degree of homogeneity in a state, the more the powers that have been allocated to the federal government.[42] However, even this is simply a trend, not a rule. Similarly, while customs and excise taxes almost always fall under federal jurisdiction, and personal income taxes are generally local, there are numerous exceptions. Third, federal systems are undergoing continual change. The powers of the levels frequently rise and fall depending on external and internal demands. Thus there does not seem to be a set level of power that must be held by each level. A balance is not only indefinable, it is unnecessary. A relatively equitable balance of power will help federalism, by further increasing the ability of each level of government to defend its powers. However, the ultimate guarantee of the division of power is that the division of power be clearly specified in a relatively rigid constitution or negotiated agreement, and that the political culture encourages respect for the contractual nature of the division of powers.

Symmetry Among the Components

A second beneficial condition, which is especially germane in the Russian context, is the symmetry among the components. It is generally agreed that asymmetry among the components of a federal state, particularly extreme asymmetry, is destructive. Elazar bluntly states that federal arrangements in which "one entity is clearly dominant" are likely to fail.[43] Conversely, he points out that for federal states to succeed, "The constituent polities in a federal system must be fairly equal in population and wealth or at least balanced geographically or numerically in their inequalities if noncentralization is to be maintained."[44] His argument can be supported by a wealth of historical data. In states like Nigeria and Pakistan (as originally constructed) asymmetries have helped provoke civil wars. In Czechoslovakia, it led to peaceful separation. Watts argues that wherever asymmetry has been extreme it has inevitably become a source of tension and instability. "Consequently, in many federations there have been efforts to reduce the corrosive effect on unity of such disparities and to enhance federal cohesion by formal schemes for the redistribution and equalization of resources among member states."[45] Not surprisingly, therefore, analysts of Russian federalism have warned that the asymmetry among Russia's components is destructive to federalism and "may destroy constitutional norms."[46]

It is appropriate to conclude that asymmetry can be corrosive to a federal state. However, reality is complex. Watts, for example, distinguishes between political asymmetry—which arises from differences in cultural, economic, social, and political conditions—and constitutional asymmetry, in which there are legal differences in the powers constitutionally granted to the varied component governments. Political asymmetry, as discussed above, can be detrimental or even damning to a federal state. However, the most dangerous situation—when one component has more than the rest of them combined—is quite rare and is not applicable to Russia. Moreover, all federal states have some degree of political asymmetry, and the asymmetry itself may be somewhat balanced. While one component may be economically dominant, another may be the most populous, and a third may contain the political capital.

Conversely, constitutional asymmetry can serve a constructive purpose in some federations. Spain, for example, has allowed asymmetry to exist in order to tailor the autonomy granted to each region according to their varied desires for and abilities to utilize greater autonomy.[47] (For similar reasons, the EU has allowed variation in the pace of integration.) In the Malaysian federation relatively greater autonomy has been granted to the two Borneo states as a means for safeguarding their special "non-Malayan" interests. Similarly in Canada Quebec has enjoyed a degree of legislative asymmetry deemed necessary to protect French-speakers and their culture. Even the United States, which seeks symmetry with its 50 states, continues to maintain very different relations with the Virgin Islands, Puerto Rico, and even Washington, D.C.

Many Russian analysts and politicians believe these cases offer sufficient precedents for Russia's multiple-level federalism, where the 21 ethnically defined republics are given different powers and rights than are the 68 territorially differentiated components. It also provides precedents for Russia's creation of federalism via a series of bilateral agreements.[48] Watts notes that the intergovernmental delegation of powers has proven an important tool for adding flexibility to federal states, and earlier federal systems that did not explicitly provide for this have sometimes added it.[49] Thus while extreme asymmetries, particularly political asymmetries, can be destructive or even fatal, some asymmetry is acceptable and may even be useful for dealing with components with varied capabilities and desires for autonomy.

Federal Political Parties

Many students of federalism discuss the potentially important role that can be played by political parties in the maintenance and sustenance of federalism. Ordeshook and Shvetsova argue that Madison and Hamilton's one "glaring omission in *The Federalist*, was their failure to provide a mechanism to coordinate the political sovereignty which the Constitution had itself divided."[50] In their defense they cite Schattschneider's argument that "political parties created modern democracy . . . and modern democracy is unthinkable save in terms of political parties."[51] Similarly, Riker singles out the party system as the institutional condition that sustains the federal bargain.[52] Also in the spirit of behavioralism, Grodzins argued that it was the American party system that preserved pluralism in America.[53] Elazar agrees that the existence of a non-centralized party system may be critical to the maintenance of federal noncentralization.[54] Finally, Watts warns that when parties operating at a federal level have become primarily regional in their focus, then federalism itself is endangered.[55]

The clear consensus then is that a non-centralized party system is beneficial in the sustenance of federalism. However, its status as a necessary condition is open to question. As Martin Diamond contended, the decentralized American party system exists in part because of the federal constitutional structure.[56] In all federal systems, the division of powers among the levels of government forces parties to coordinate their politics at the national level, while tailoring themselves to meet local demands. Moreover it does not appear that any particular form of party system exists in all federal states. Some federal states are two-party systems, others are multi-party systems. Some have a plethora of small regional parties, others do not.

A Non-centralized Bureaucracy

Of lesser importance than a decentralized party system, but still beneficial to the sustenance of a federal state is a decentralized bureaucracy. Elazar suggests that in highly centralized states it is necessary to examine how bureaucracies are organized. In highly bureaucratic federal states, he notes the tendency to operate almost exclusively through the bureaucracies of the constituent units.[57] Conversely, in the Soviet Union, which was federal in name only, the bureaucracy did much to subvert federalism. In the Soviet case, component bureaucracies were under the complete control of the central bureaucracy. Because Russia has inherited much of the Soviet bureaucracy, as well as some of its bureaucratic culture, the relationship between the two levels of bureaucracy could be of considerable importance to the working of federalism.

Democracy

The argument was made above that federalism helps to create and maintain democracy. The argument here is the reverse, that democracy is beneficial for the sustenance of federalism. First, democracy gives minority groups a relatively greater ability and right to protect their culture from encroachment by the majority culture. They are allowed to form parties, vote, organize themselves, and participate in the selection of leaders. These minorities frequently view federalism as a means to protect their cultural and political autonomy. Thus, in all states sizable minorities are a likely source of support for federalism, but in democracies they are typically more effective in their support. Second, building on the thoughts of the American founders, modern democracies typically look for ways to prevent a concentration of power, which may endanger democracy, and to protect the minority from tyranny by the majority. Federalism is a mechanism that historically has been successful in helping achieve both of these goals; in the latter case it has done particularly well when minorities are geographically concentrated. Thus democracies may view federalism as an important tool for preserving itself. Finally, the very argument that modern democracy allows for a division of powers, with ultimate sovereignty resting with the people, provides a theoretical justification for federalism. However, note that all three of these arguments suggest only that democracy helps sustain and justify federalism. They do not lead to the conclusion that democracy is a necessary precondition. For example, even in non-democratic systems significant minorities may provide significant support for federalism.

The extent to which ancient federal systems were democracies is not fully known. Certainly the selection of leaders among the tribes of ancient Israel was less than completely democratic by modern standards. Similarly, the federations of medieval Europe were formed by agreements among leaders from the nobility, often in conjunction with religious leaders, who sought to preserve their individual autonomy. A number of modern federal states also fail to meet democratic standards. The Malaysian federation is a federal state in that there is a real division of powers which is meaningful and constitutionally protected, but many of the component governments were once led by hereditary sultans. (Today most of their powers and privileges have been curtailed and passed to democratic rulers.) Similarly, the United Arab Emirates is composed of hereditary sheikhdoms that have federated together to share specific state powers. The Soviet Union did not fail the test of federalism because it was undemocratic. It failed because its components, however ruled, did not have the autonomy necessary to voluntarily participate in a truly federal state. It was not a federal state because the division of powers specified in its constitution was fraudulent.

Thus, there is a relationship between democracy and federalism. Federalism can help sustain liberty, and democracy can help sustain federalism. However, neither appears to be a necessary precondition for the other.

Economic Conditions

Brinkman and Bovt contend that Elazar, and other scholars, ignore the economic preconditions necessary for federalism.[58] They cite the work of Beard, Brown, and McDonald to contend that American democracy and federalism only succeeded because of preexisting economic conditions.[59] Similarly, Brinkman and Bovt point out that economic integration in Western Europe and the accompanying evolution of federalism have been closely tied to economic conditions in Europe. Their argument has merit in that economic incentives are undoubtedly an important factor in the support for federalism. Certainly the political commitment to federalism will be greatest when both the component governments and the people as a whole believe that economic cooperation will be of general benefit. Thus economic conditions can help to either maintain or erode federalism. Elazar himself included economic conditions, such as the lack of resources and the lack of common interests, as potential explanations for why federal states fail.[60] Certainly the inequitable distribution of resources has been a major factor in Nigeria's instability, including the Biafran Civil War. However, more important than actual economic conditions are the perceptions of those who commit to the federation. In a sense, if the people and the component leaders believe they will benefit from federalism (recollect that the potential benefits are not only economic), then economic conditions are clearly secondary to the political culture and its level of support for federalism.

THE INSTITUTIONAL EVOLUTION OF RUSSIAN FEDERALISM

The third challenge to assessing Russian federalism results from the malleable nature of Russian center-periphery relations. On one hand, because the evolution of Russian center-periphery relations is largely idiosyncratic to the individual *subekty*, it can only be assessed only through the evaluation of the evolution of the relationships between the center and specific *subekty*. This is done in the following five chapters. On the other hand, as John Slocum argues, key institutional changes in Russia have set common parameters for the overall development of Russian center-periphery relations.[61] In essence, Russian center-periphery relations have passed through several discrete stages of institutional arrangement, a different primary conflict between at least two federal institutions, and different sets of basic rules of the game for center-periphery relations that prevailed during each stage (see Table 2.1).[62]

On the surface using an institutional framework to examine the Russian transition might seem counter intuitive. After all, the Soviet Union was a state in which the actual functions of institutions bore little resemblance to their constitutionally defined roles. Similarly, during the early post-Soviet period, the Russian presidency and parliament were institutions whose occupants were elected during the Soviet era. Their powers were defined by a constitution which, despite more than a hundred amendments, was not designed for a democracy. Thus its relevance to Russian politics was questionable at best. While the 1993 Constitution helps to define the powers of Russia's political institutions, many gaps between the Constitution and reality remain. Moreover, Russia's institutions continue to undergo numerous substantive changes. Often, the institutions seem less important than the personalities that lead them. Despite these problems, an institutional perspective provides a useful framework for understanding many aspects of Russian politics, including center-periphery relations. This chapter provides some explication of the historical stages in Russian center-periphery relations.

STAGE 1: THE SOVIET COLLAPSE

The first stage in Russian center-periphery relations began with Yeltsin's election to the chairmanship of the Russian parliament in March 1990 and ended with the collapse of the Soviet Union in December 1991. During this period the Soviet Union was ruled by the 1977 Soviet Constitution (often

Table 2.1
Institutional Stages

Institutional Stage	Dates	Central Conflict	Rules of the Game
The Soviet Collapse	March 1990–September 1991	Gorbachev vs. Yeltsin	The 1977 Soviet Constitution had little formal legitimacy. The *subekty* used the conflict in Moscow to extract concessions from Yeltsin, which he was unable to implement.
The Battle for Russia	September 1991–December 1993	Yeltsin vs. The Supreme Soviet	The 1978 Russian Constitution was amended to provide greater presidential posers. Yeltsin needed the backing of the *subekty* to counter the Supreme Soviet. Yeltsin had the ability, but less desire, to implement his promised concessions.
The New Russia	December 1993–present	Yeltsin vs. The State Duma	The 1993 Constitution created a presidential system. Yeltin's need for an alliance with the subekty was diminished, and he has attempted to "retake" powers from the *subekty.*

called the Brezhnev Constitution). Ironically, this was an extremely democratic constitution, but was never meant as guide to working democracy. Instead it was a high-sounding collection of democratic platitudes that were meant to be superseded in the real world by the supremacy of the Communist Party, which it specifically enshrined. While the 1977 Constitution legally made the Soviet Union a federation and gave sweeping powers to the Union Republics, including Russia, it was largely discredited in the eyes of the vast majority of the population. In practice, the Constitution was largely irrelevant to center-periphery relations within Russia. The most that can really be said is that because there were no accepted legal parameters governing Russia's relations to its component parts, the relationships were left open to considerable bargaining between the center, or centers to be more precise, and Russia's components.

More important to the practice of federalism, the late Soviet period was characterized by an intense political battle between Mikhail Gorbachev's Soviet government (which sought to maintain the territorial integrity of the union and, as much as possible, the centralization of power in Moscow), and the 15 union republic governments on the other hand (which sought to maximize their political and economic autonomy). In theory Yeltsin's Russian government was simply one of 15 republican governments. In practice, however, the Russian government occupied the same capital as the Union government, Moscow, and was a claimant to the vast majority of Russian territory. In this sense the battle between the Soviet and Russian governments was not so much a center-periphery struggle, but a struggle between two contenders for the center.

The intensity of this conflict at the center gave Russia's component governments unprecedented, but undefined, political and economic autonomy. Many component governments used this autonomy to issue a cascade of legislation, decrees, and constitutions that unilaterally asserted local control over their natural resources, industry, agriculture and fiscal resources. Some even used the opportunity to unilaterally change the status of their component. Some lower-level components, like Sakha and Ingushetia, claimed republic status within Russia. Tatarstan, already a republic of Russia, claimed status as union republic of the Soviet Union, which would put it in line for independence. Chechnya skipped this step altogether, and after breaking from Ingushetia, also sought independence from Russia.

Gorbachev and Yeltsin, who were locked in a seemingly unrelenting battle for political power, both found it inopportune to react harshly to even the most radical demands issued by Russia's component governments. Sensing a political opportunity, Yeltsin tacitly endorsed these claims and even reached bilateral agreements with many component governments recognizing their claims. The cost to Yeltsin of doing so was minimized by the fact that he was not yet in a tangible position to live up to any of the commitments he made to the component governments. Thus he publicly welcomed the steps toward sovereignty taken by many of the *subekty*. Drawing on the arguments of some of Russia's leading democrats, he adopted the slogan of sovereignty from the ground up.[63] What this meant was that Soviet sovereignty had to be built on the consent and support of the federal republics and Russian sovereignty would be built on the consent of its *subekty*. Toward this end, he welcomed the *subekty*'s declarations of sovereignty, declaring in September 1990 that Russia's republics should "take all the sovereignty they could swallow." Shortly thereafter he supported the republics' claims to control their own resources.[64] Yeltsin's strategy, which was designed to win the support of Russia's republics in his battle with Gorbachev, was highly successful.

However the situation was not nearly as blissful for Russia's component governments as it might otherwise seem. The requisites of federalism, as discussed above, were notably lacking. While the components were apparently unrestrained in their ability to claim new powers in status, in most cases they had neither the resources nor the expertise to exercise the powers they had claimed. Moreover, despite Yeltsin's apparent support for their claims, there was no new constitution or federal legislation to institutionalize the myriad of gains claimed by Russia's individual components. As a result there was no clear division of powers and there was no institution tasked to adjudicate disputes between Russia and its components. Nor did the component governments have representation in the creation of federal policy. Their representatives in the Congress of People's Deputies, which was elected in March 1989, had no direct ties to the component governments and these governments had no powers over their representatives. Moreover, the functional legislature was really the Supreme Soviet, which was elected by and from the Congress with no guarantees for regional representation. In sum, the components' claims were left in an uneasy state of political limbo pending the result of the central struggle between the Soviet and Russian governments.

STAGE 2: THE BATTLE FOR RUSSIA

Gorbachev's resignation and the accompanying collapse of the Soviet Union dramatically altered the terms of center-periphery relations in Russia. On the one hand, Yeltsin's power was no longer contested by Gorbachev and thus, he was better able to deliver on the numerous promises that he had made to the *subekt* governments. On the other hand, with Gorbachev retired and the Soviet state fading into the pages of history, Yeltsin lost a key incentive for living up to his promises to the *subekty*. Moreover, with Russian independence any budgetary concessions or transfer of power to the *subekty* entailed a direct loss for Yeltsin and his government. Under these conditions, there was little reason to believe significant concessions to the *subekty* would be forthcoming.

Fortunately for the *subekty*, the conflict between Yeltsin and Gorbachev was soon replaced by an equally heated conflict between Yeltsin and his former supporters within the Russian Supreme Soviet. Yeltsin began this conflict with some key advantages. First, because of his populist resistance to Gorbachev and communism and because of his larger than life heroism during the tense days of the August 1991 Soviet coup, Yeltsin entered the fray with far greater notoriety and popularity. Second, Yeltsin's status as Russia's first popularly elected president gave him unparalleled legitimacy both domestically and internationally. However, the basic parameters for this conflict were set by a Soviet-era constitution, which made the parliament, not the president, the supreme authority. Although more than 100 amendments were made to the 1978 Russian Constitution, which markedly increased the powers of the presidency, the original document gave clear supremacy to the Russian Supreme Soviet. It also gave the Supreme Soviet ample tools for undermining and challenging the president.

As the struggle between the Soviet and the president intensified, the *subekt* governments soon recognized the opportunity to increase their autonomy. Thus the cascade of new unilateral declarations and bilateral agreements continued. At the same time, the *subekt* governments realized the tenuous nature of their gains. Their bilateral gains were envied by the less fortunate *subekty* and were resented by federal officials in both the Soviet and the government. They soon concluded that while their gains could be maximized through bilateral agreements, their gains could only be institutionalized in a multilateral agreement, which recast Russia as a truly consensual federation. These efforts culminated in the March 1992 signing of three separate treaties, one with the republics, one with the regions, and one with the other components. Collectively these treaties were known as the Federal Treaty. The Federal Treaty enumerated those powers granted to the federal government, those that fell under "joint" jurisdiction and a brief listing of those belonging to the *subekty* alone. The Treaty was not all that the *subekty* had wanted. The vast majority of powers were given to the federal government. Thus some of the republics only signed after receiving special assurances and considerable persuading.[65] (The Republic of Tatarstan and the Republic of Chechenya were the only two that refused at the time. Tatarstan later signed an agreement.)

The Federal Treaty also continued the asymmetrical nature of the Russian Federation. It affirmed the special "sovereign" status of the republics and gave them many new powers. These included the right to conduct their own foreign policy and foreign trade.[66] Of critical importance to the mineral producing republics, the Treaty said that the land and resources of the republics belonged to the people living there. However, ownership and use of the land, and its mineral resources, are subject to the regulations of both republican and federal law.

Despite the compromising nature of the Federal Treaty, the *subekty* spent the next 18 months trying to convince Moscow to institutionalize the Federal Treaty. This meant persuading the Supreme Soviet to pass the necessary enabling legislation and, more importantly, ensuring that the Federal Treaty was incorporated into any new Russian constitution. By spring 1993 the Supreme Soviet and the president had each developed their own draft constitutions. While neither draft formally included the Federal Treaty, Yeltsin pledged to honor the Federal Treaty and incorporated some of its principles into his draft.

During summer 1993 the conflict between the Soviet and Yeltsin continued to heat up. By early fall, Yeltsin made further concessions to the *subekty*. His draft constitution was amended to include the basic text of the Federal Treaty. In doing so it recognized the republics as "sovereign" within Russia. (It did not clarify how "sovereign" republics could exist within a "sovereign" Russia.)

The new draft also protected the bilateral concession won by the *subekty*. Finally, it promised the *subekty* a role in federal politics in the form of a bicameral parliament, the upper chamber of which (the Federation Council) would be composed of the executive and legislative heads of the *subekty*. The existing component government representation in federal policymaking, the fourth necessary condition of federalism, was not meaningful. The Russian legislative structure in place from 1990 until December 1993 duplicated the two-tier system Gorbachev created for the Soviet Union. The Russian Congress of People's Deputies was composed of 1,068 deputies, of which 168 were elected from national-territorial components and 900 from territorial components. However, the Congress elected a 268 member Supreme Soviet, which served as Russia's functional legislature. While all members of the Congress were to eventually have an opportunity to serve in the Supreme Soviet, this did not work in practice. Thus, the regional representation created in the Congress was severely mitigated by the election of the Soviet. Moreover, because the Congress was elected in the Soviet period, when the elections were still subject to considerable manipulation by local communist leaders, the *subekt* leaders never felt that those in the Supreme Soviet represented their interests. Toward this end, many *subekt* leaders actively supported the creation of a parliamentary house directly representative of the *subekty*.

In sum, during the second stage the center remained preoccupied with internal conflict. The new competing centers also tried to woo the *subekty*'s support in their internecine battle. Yeltsin's willingness to make concessions to the *subkety* was near endless. The one prominent demand Yeltsin would not concede was granting the republics the right to secede. At the same time, when it came to institutionalizing the powers and rights gained by the *subekty*, Yeltsin remained hesitant. While the Federal Treaty at first appeared to be a major gain for the *subekty*, its status remained in doubt throughout 1993.

STAGE 3: THE NEW RUSSIA

The introduction of the 1993 Russian Constitution marked the beginning of the third, and current, institutional stage in Russian center-periphery relations. This stage introduced three major institutional changes relevant to Russian center-periphery relations. First, by creating new institutions with new powers the Constitution shifted the balance of power between the federal executive and the federal legislature. Second, by reconfiguring the parliament the Constitution created new forms of representation for the *subekty* in federal politics. Finally, it set new constitutional parameters on center-periphery relations.

First, in terms of legislative-executive relations, the net effect of the new Constitution was undoubtedly to institutionalize the growing powers of the executive, while decreasing and constraining the powers of the parliament. It leaves intact and codifies the president's powers to issue decrees, which are roughly equivalent to parliamentary legislation. The only limitation on the scope of such decrees is that they may not contradict the Constitution or federal legislation. At the same time it gives the president the power to veto parliamentary legislation. A presidential veto can only be overridden by a two-thirds majority of both houses of the Federal Assembly. The likelihood of such a step is further diminished by the divided nature of the parliament itself. While the lower chamber, the State Duma, continues to represent a significant challenge to the president, the upper chamber has typically provided the president a second check on the Duma. Thus, the president can veto a bill that originates in the Duma and subsequently substitute his own decree for the failed bill.

On the surface the Constitution provides the Duma a significant check on the president in that it has the power to approve the government and its ministers and can hold a vote of "no confidence" in the government. However, the latter power is not nearly as significant as it might seem. In order to remove the Prime Minister the Duma must hold two successful votes of no confidence within a three-month period. In such instances, the president is given the option of either replacing the Prime Minister or disbanding the Duma and calling for new elections. In the unlikely event the president should consent to remove his chosen Prime Minister, at present he need not replace his other ministers or even the deputy prime ministers at the same time.[67]

The Federal Assembly's ability to remove the president is even more limited. Charges of impeachment can be made only in cases of "high treason or some other grave crime, confirmed by a ruling of the Supreme Court of the Russian Federation on the presence of indicators of crime in the President's actions and by a ruling of the Constitutional court of the Russian Federation confirming that the procedure of bringing charges has been observed" (Article 93). The charge for impeachment must be initiated by at least one-third of the deputies of the Duma and must receive the support of two-thirds of the deputies. The decision for impeachment must then receive two-thirds support in the Federation Council.

The marked shift toward a strong presidential system has considerable importance for center-periphery relations. As previously argued, during the previous two stages in Russian politics the *subekty* were able to extract major concessions from the center by playing off the conflict between Yeltsin and the parliament. (This assertion will be documented in the subsequent substantive chapters.) To the extent that the conflict at the center dissipates or disappears entirely, this would leave the *subekty* less leverage to pursue their goals. To the contrary, the center would be unencumbered in any attempts to "retake" the *subekty.*

In December 1993 the central conflict in federal politics appeared to have been resolved. The Russian Supreme Soviet was disbanded and its leaders were in jail or politically marginalized. With the Supreme Soviet defeated, there was no central conflict. Yeltsin's primary reason for an alliance with the *subekty* was at least temporarily removed. He was free to launch a program to "retake" the *subekty.*[68] A number of regional and local executives who had opposed Yeltsin were removed or pushed into retirement. Yeltsin also issued a decree mandating new elections for all regional soviets, many of which had sided with the Russian Supreme Soviet during the October conflict. For republican legislatures this step was merely "recommended." Even still, many obliged. Most importantly, many of the rights and powers the *subekty* had persuaded Yeltsin to place into his July draft of the Constitution were removed from the draft issued in late November, which was enacted after the December plebiscite.

Despite the imbalance the new Constitution created in favor of the president, it did not completely eliminate the inherent tension of executive-legislative relations. In the same elections in which the Constitution was approved, voters elected a State Duma inimical to Yeltsin. Although far from a majority, Valdimir Zhirinovskii's ultra-nationalist Liberal Democratic Party (LDP) received the most seats in the December 1993 Duma elections. The results of the 1995 and 1997 Duma elections, which gave the communists the largest number of seats, were no more heartening to Yeltsin. When Yeltsin's position was most secure (such as immediately following the promulgation of the Constitution and after his 1996 reelection), he was both more willing and more able to challenge the *subekty*. At other times, such as when he faced organized opposition in the Duma from first the nationalists and more recently from the communists, his need for an alliance was relatively greater. While executive-legislative conflict thus remains a central and distinguishing component of Russian politics, its effect on center-periphery relations has been markedly reduced by the lopsided nature of the new presidential system. More succinctly, because the Duma is a much lesser threat to Yeltsin than its more powerful predecessor, the Supreme Soviet, his need for an alliance with the *subekty* is proportionately reduced.

The second significant institutional change was the creation of a new bicameral legislature, the Federal Assembly. As previously noted, a hallmark of many federal systems is a bicameral legislature, in which the upper house is designed to maximize the representation of the component governments. The 1993 Constitution created a bicameral parliament, known collectively as the Federal Assembly. The lower chamber, the State Duma, was to have a mix of single member district seats and proportional party representation. The upper chamber, the Federation Council, was to provide *subekty* representation. However, since the promulgation of the Constitution the *subekty* have sought to increase the regional affiliation of the Duma, while increasing the directness of their representation in the Federation Council.

The State Duma elected in 1993 had 225 members elected by party lists and 225 members elected from single member districts. The *subekty* complained that most of those elected by party lists came from Moscow and St. Petersburg and had no real affiliation with or loyalty to any of the *subekty*. Their leaders in the Federation Council felt that this formula did not give the *subekty* a real role in federal politics. Thus, in spring 1995 they twice rejected the Duma's draft law on parliamentary elections because it provided for a 225/225 split. After a presidential veto and two unsuccessful Duma attempts to override the veto, a compromise was struck. The compromise provided the same split, but limited each party to 12 candidates on their list without a regional affiliation. In December 1995 four parties won seats by proportional representation. This meant that only 48 of the members lack any regional affiliation. However, the *subekty* were disappointed by the compromise. The parties determine the 225 deputies elected by party list and play a key role in nominating and funding those elected by district. Thus, the primary loyalty of nearly all deputies will continue to be to their party rather than to the *subekty* in which they reside.

Even more controversial was the method for electing the Federation Council. Although Yeltsin had promised the *subekty* representation in the Federation Council, the Constitution did not specify the form of representation. *Subekty* leaders wanted automatic representation for the legislative and executive heads of each of the *subekty*. In the 1993 elections, however, Yeltsin required direct election of Federation Council members, or senators, as they soon became known. As a last minute concession to the *subekty*, Yeltsin agreed to let governmental officials serve as senators without resigning their positions at home. As a result, many *subekty* leaders were elected to the Federation Council. Of the 175 senators, 40 were governors of their territories, 16 were republican heads, 13 were heads or deputy heads of their local Soviets and seven were mayors.[69]

As the December 1995 parliamentary elections approached, the debate over the selection of the Federation Council was rekindled. A majority in the Duma believed that the Federation Council should be elected directly. Their only concession was to suggest that the *subekty* be given a role in the nomination process. The *subekty*, however, wanted the legislative and executive heads of the *subekty* to either receive automatic appointment to the Federation Council, or be allowed to select their representation. Yeltsin was generally sympathetic to the *subekty*'s position. While most republican leaders were popularly elected, the governors of most of the regions were handpicked by Yeltsin and were subject to removal by Yeltsin. In September 1996, 99 of the 178 senators were considered Yeltsin loyalists.[70] After Yeltsin vetoed a number of draft laws from the Duma, a compromise was reached. The executive and legislative heads of each of the 89 *subekty* would continue to serve in the Federation Council, but all appointed *subekt* executive heads were required to stand for election no later than December 1996.[71] The Federation Council rejected the compromise, but the State Duma overrode the Federation Council and Yeltsin signed the bill into law.[72]

The results of the *subekt* elections were somewhat disappointing to Yeltsin in that more than half of the governors that he had previously appointed were voted out of office. Even those who remain, now have an independent source of legitimacy and are thus considerably less dependent on Yeltsin. Conversely, the communist governors that now serve in the Federation Council are more independent of the national parties to which they belong. Moreover, irrespective of their party affiliation, the new governors need cordial relations with the federal government, which provides them necessary subsidies and helps them attract foreign investment. Thus, government officials predicted that the new Federation Council would continue to be a source of support for Yeltsin and the government.[73]

The new Federation Council, which first convened in January 1996, has continued to be considerably more supportive of both Yeltsin and the government than the Duma. The logic behind Yeltsin's previous alliance with the *subekty* remains. Yeltsin needs the *subekty* to counter the Duma and the *subekty* still depend on Yeltsin to give them greater economic sovereignty than the Duma would provide. Increasingly the *subekty* also need Yeltsin to limit the growing demands they face from local governments.[74] However, because the senators all have significant duties within their individual *subekty*, it is not possible for them to focus on federal issues to the same extent as their colleagues in the Duma. As a consequence the Federation Council is in session only a few days each month.[75] While certain categories of bills require consideration by the Federation Council, particularly those relating to the budget, others can go to the president for signing if the Federation Council does not act within 14 days.[76]

Yeltsin and the *subekty* have a shared interest in increasing the power and role of the Federation Council. In particular, many senators have argued that the Federation Council should play a direct role in the preparation of the budget and in personnel issues at the federal level.[77] As a practical step toward this end, Yeltsin increased the size of professional staff available to the Federation Council.[78]

The third change introduced by the 1993 Constitution set the first clear parameters on center-periphery relations. Despite the widespread criticism of the Constitution and the lingering doubts about the legality of the constitutional plebiscite that brought it into operation, the Constitution is considered binding. Those who oppose the Constitution generally seek to amend or rewrite it; they do not disregard it. At the same time, the parameters set by the Constitution are quite general and purposely leave much for future negotiation.[79]

Critics of the new Constitution within the *subekty* portrayed it as a betrayal. More specifically, they charged that the Constitution: (a) invalidated the Federal Treaty; (b) entailed a mechanical leveling of all *subekty*; and (c) provided for a unitary state, rather than a federal one. Each of these charges is serious enough to merit further consideration. With respect to the first charge, the Constitution does not contain the text of the Federal Treaty, the alternative preferred by the *subekty*. In fact, it contains only one specific reference to the Federal Treaty. Article 1 Section 2 states that "In the event of nonconformity between the Constitution and the Russian Federal Treaty . . . the Constitution of the Federation shall apply."[80] Thus clearly the Constitution has supremacy. By implication, however, the Federal Treaty is binding in all cases in which there is no actual contradiction.

The second charge, that the Constitution entails some equalization of the status of *subekty*, also has some validity. It twice alleges that "All *subekty* of the Russian Federation shall be equal (*ravnopravny*) among themselves" (Articles 5.1 and 5.4). Moreover, the republics lost their status as "sovereign states within the Russian Federation" as granted by the Federal Treaty. Instead, Article 4.1 affirms that "The sovereignty of the Russian Federation shall apply to its entire territory." And, Article 4.2 says that federal laws shall have supremacy throughout the entire territory of the federation. Yet, there are numerous exceptions to this allegedly equal status. While the republics are allowed constitutions (Article 66.2), the other *subekty* have charters (Article 68.3). Republics alone are given the right to establish their own state language—which may coexist with but not replace Russian (Article 68.3). More importantly, the Constitution allows for "other treaties on the delimitation of scopes of authority and powers" (Article 11.3). This means that the all the bilateral agreements signed by the *subekty* are valid, except when they contradict the Constitution. Historically, the republics were in a much better position than the regions (*oblasty*) to force such concessions from the center. Thus while the Constitution set forth the equality of all *subekty* as a philosophical goal, it simultaneously validates the methodology for introducing tremendous inequality among the *subekty*.

The final charge, that the Constitution provides for a unitary state, is harder to reject. A cursory analysis of the Constitution suggests that—despite its name—the Russian Federation remains a highly centralized state. Article 71 lists 18 powers that are granted to the federal government. These include:

a. the adoption and amendment of the Constitution and federal law and compliance with them;
b. determining the federal structure and territory of the Russian Federation;
c. the regulation and protection of human and citizen rights and liberties;
d. the establishment of the system of federal bodies of legislative, executive and judiciary power;
e. the control and management of state property;
f. determining the basic principles of federal policy and programs;
g. establishment of the legal framework for a single market; financial, monetary, credit, and customs regulation, emission of money and guidelines for price policy; federal economic services, including federal banks;
h. the federal budget; federal taxes and levies; federal funds of regional development; federal power grids, nuclear energy, fissionable materials, federal transport, railways, information and communications, space activities; and
i. foreign trade relations of the Russian Federation.

Article 72.1 then lists 14 issues that are placed under "The joint jurisdiction of the Russian Federation and the subjects of the Russian Federation." These include:

a. ensuring the compliance of the republican constitutions and laws and charters and laws of the other components with the Federal Constitution and federal laws;
b. the protection of human and citizen rights and ensuring the rights of ethnic minorities;
c. issues of the possession, use and management of the land, mineral resources, water and other natural resources;

d. delimitation of state property;
e. management of natural resources, protection of the environment and ecological safety; specially protected natural reserves;
f. general questions of upbringing, education, science, culture, physical and cultural monuments; and
g. establishment of the general guidelines for taxation and levies in the Russian Federation.

Article 73 then explains that any areas not specified as under federal jurisdiction or under joint jurisdiction of the federal government and the *subekty* belong exclusively to the *subekty*.

The list of powers included in Articles 71 and 72 is so extensive that the obvious question is what meaningful powers are left for the *subekty*? Probably very few. Federal taxation is wholly within federal jurisdiction and the federal government even has the power to set guidelines for taxation policy at other levels. While the Federal Treaty's promise of republican ownership of natural resources may remain operative, the Constitution gives the federal government joint jurisdiction over the use and management of natural resources. Subsequent passages of the Constitution (Article 75) also established clear federal control over monetary policy, the banking system, and state loans. In practice, however, the federal government's role in the so-called shared powers may be more one of oversight than of actual control.

What makes the Constitution far more acceptable to the republics is Article 78.2, which states: By agreement with the organs of executive power of the *subekty* of the Russian Federation, the federal organs of executive power may delegate to them part of their powers provided this does not contravene the Constitution of the Russian Federation or federal laws. In short this opens up a huge loophole, legalizing bilateral agreements between each *subekt* and the federal government. The contents and implementation of these bilateral treaties will ultimately determine the extent of federalism in Russia. Thus they will receive considerable attention in the following chapters.

NOTES

1. Edward McWhinney, *Constitution-making: Principles, Process, Practice*, Toronto: University of Toronto Press, 1981.
2. Carl J. Friedrich, *Constitutional Government and Democracy*, Boston: Ginn and Company, 1950, pp. 189–90.
3. Elazar, 1987, p. 6.
4. Watts, 1996, p. xi.
5. Peter H. Merkl, *Modern Comparative Politics*, New York: Holt, Rinehart and Winston, 1970, p. 247.
6. David Kwavnick, ed., *The Tremblay Report: Report of the Royal Commission of Inquiry on Constitutional Problems,* Ottawa: McClelland and Stewart, 1973, p. 209.

7. Alain-G. Gagnon, "The Political Uses of Federalism," in Michael Burgess and Alain-G. Gagnon, *Comparative Federalism and Federation*, Toronto: University of Toronto Press, 1993, p. 38.

8. Alain-G. Gagnon, "The Political Uses of Federalism," in Michael Burgess and Alain-G. Gagnon, *Comparative Federalism and Federation*, Toronto: University of Toronto Press, 1993, pp. 18–19.

9. Daniel R. Kempton, "The Republic of Sakha (Yakutia): The Evolution of Centre-Periphery Relations in the Russian Federation," *Europe-Asia Studies*, v. 48, no. 4, 1996, pp. 587–89.

10. Ian Bremmer, "Reassessing Soviet Nationalities Theories," in Ian Bremmer & Ray Taras, eds., *Nations and Politics in the Soviet Successor States*, Cambridge: Cambridge University Press, 1993, p. 22.

11. Ronald L. Watts, *Comparing Federal Systems in the 1990s*, Kingston, Ontario: Queen's University, 1996, p. 103.

12. Elana Oracheva, IEWS, *RRR*, vol. 3, no. 9, p. 5 March 1998.

13. Elazar, 1987, p. 86.

14. Ralph J. K. Chapman, "Structure, Process and the Federal Factor: Complexity and Entanglement in Federations," in Michael Burgess and Alain-G. Gagnon, *Comparative Federalism and Federation*, Toronto: University of Toronto Press, 1993, p. 69.

15. Watts, 1996, p. 99.

16. Elazar, 1987, p. 81.

17. Kenneth C. Wheare, *Federal Government*, 1946, p. 1, cited in Richard L. Brinkman and Georgy Bovt, "Russian Federalism: An American and West European Comparison," *International Journal of Social Economics*, v. 21, n. 10–12, 1994, p. 137.

18. Carl J. Friedrich, *Constitutional Government and Democracy*, Boston: Ginn and Company, 1950, pp. 189–221.

19. Hicks, 1963, p. 16, in Brinkman & Bovt, 1994, p. 137.

20. Brinkman & Bovt, 1994, p. 137.

21. Elazar, 1987, p. 12 (italics in the original).

22. Elazar, 1987, p. 5.

23. Michael Burgess, "Federalism and Federation: A Reappraisal," in Michael Burgess and Alain-G. Gagnon, *Comparative Federalism and Federation*, Toronto: University of Toronto Press, 1993, p. 5; Preston King, *Federalism and Federation*, London: Croom Helm, 1982, p. 91; and Ronald L. Watts, *Comparing Federal Systems in the 1990s*, Kingston, Ontario: Queen's University, 1996, p. 6.

24. Carl J. Friedrich, *Constitutional Government and Democracy*, Boston: Ginn and Company, 1950, pp. 189–221.

25. Arend Lijphart, "Non-Majoritarian Democracy: A Comparison of Federal and Consociational Themes," *Publius*, 1988; Ralph F. K. Chapman, "Structure, Process and the Federal Factor: Complexity and Entanglement in Federations," in Michael Burgess and Alain-G. Gagnon, *Comparative Federalism and Federation*, Toronto: University of Toronto Press, 1993, p. 86; Nichols J. Lynn and Alexei V. Novikov, "Refederalizing Russia: Debates on the Idea of Federalism in Russia," *Publius: The Journal of Federalism*, v. 21, no. 2, 1997, p. 188; and Watts, 1996, p. 7.

26. Ralph J. K. Chapman, "Structure, Process and the Federal Factor: Complexity and Entanglement in Federations," in Michael Burgess and Alain-G. Gagnon, *Com-*

parative Federalism and Federation, Toronto: University of Toronto Press, 1993, p. 72.

27. Carl J. Friedrich, *Constitutional Government and Democracy*, Boston: Ginn and Company, 1950, p. 191.

28. Peter H. Merkl, *Modern Comparative Politics*, New York: Holt, Rinehart and Winston, 1970, p. 247.

29. Elazar, 1987, p. 4.

30. Watts, pp. 26–27.

31. Watts, 1996, p. 53.

32. Watts, 1996, p. 14.

33. Watts, 1996, pp. 91–93.

34. Peter H. Merkl, *Modern Comparative Politics*, New York: Holt, Rinehart and Winston, 1970, p. 248; Arend Lijphart, "Non-Majoritarian Democracy: A Comparison of Federal and Consociational Themes," *Publius*, 1988; and Carl J. Friedrich, *Constitutional Government and Democracy*, Boston: Ginn and Company, 1950, p. 198.

35. Preston King, "Federation and Representation," in Michael Burgess and Alain-G. Gagnon, *Comparative Federalism and Federation*, Toronto: University of Toronto Press, 1993, p. 95.

36. Elazar, 2987, p. 202.

37. Elazar, 1987, p. 37.

38. Elazar, 1987, pp. 18, 79, 154; Burgess, "Federalism and Federation: A Reappraisal," in Michael Burgess and Alain-G. Gagnon, *Comparative Federalism and Federation*, Toronto: University of Toronto Press, 1993, p. 17; Lynn & Novikov, 1997, p. 188; Watts, 1996, pp. 112–113; and Brinkman and Bovt, 1994, pp. 133–136.

39. Watts, 1996, pp. 112–113.

40. Watts, 1996, p. 31.

41. Peter C. Ordeshook and Olga Shvetsova, "If Hamilton and Madison Were Merely Lucky, What Hope Is There for Russian Federalism," *Constitutional Political Economy*, n. 6, 1995, p. 116.

42. Watts, 1996, p. 31, 39–40.

43. Elazar, 1987, p. 244.

44. Elazar, 1987, p. 170.

45. Watts, 1996, pp. xiii, 59, and 62.

46. IEWS, *Russia Regional Report*, Special Supplement, v. 3, n. 16, p. 23 April 1998.

47. Watts, 1996, pp. 6, 21–22, 26.

48. IEWS, *Russia Regional Report*, Special Supplement, v. 3, n. 9, p. 5 March 1998; IEWS, *Russia Regional Report*, Special Supplement, v. 3, n. 14, p. 9 April 1998.

49. Watts, 1996, p. 3.

50. Peter C. Ordeshook and Olga Shvetsova, "If Hamilton and Madison Were Merely Lucky, What Hope Is There for Russian Federalism," *Constitutional Political Economy*, n. 6, 1995, p. 113.

51. E. E. Schattschneider, *Party Government*, New York: Holt, Rinehart, and Winston, 1941, p. 1.

52. William H. Riker, *Federalism: Origin, Operation, Significance*, Boston: Little, Brown, 1964, p. 136.

53. Morton Grodzins, "The Future of American Federalism," in Daniel J. Elazar, ed., *Cooperation and Conflict: Readings in American Federalism*, Itasca, IL: F.E. Peacock, 1969, pp. 61–71.

54. Elazar, 1987, p. 178.

55. Watts, 1996, p. 112.

56. Martin Diamond, "On the Relationship of Federalism and Decentralization," in Daniel J. Elazar, ed., *Cooperation and Conflict: Readings in American Federalism*, Itasca, IL: F.E. Peacock, 1969, pp. 72–81.

57. Elazar, 1987, pp. 172–173.

58. Richard L. Brinkman and Georgy Bovt, "Russian Federalism: An American and West European Comparison," *International Journal of Social Economics*, v. 21, n. 10–12, 1994, pp. 1133–1161.

59. Charles A. Beard, *An Economic Interpretation of the Constitution*, New York: Macmillan, 1913; Robert E. Brown, *Charles E. Beard and the Constitution*, Princeton: Princeton University Press, 1956; and F. McDonald, *We the People,* Chicago: Chicago University Press, 1958.

60. Elazar, 1987, p. 240.

61. Rogers Brubaker, "Nationhood and the National Question in the Soviet Union and Post-Soviet Eurasia: An Instrumentalist Account," *Theory and Society* 23, 1994, and John W. Slocum, *Disintegration and Consolidation: National Separatism and the Evolution of Center-Periphery Relations in the Russian Federation.* Ithaca, NY: Cornell University Peace Studies Program, Occasional Paper, p. 19, 1995.

62. Slocum, ibid., p. 2.

63. Gail W. Lapidus & Edward W. Walker, "Nationalism, Regionalism, and Federalism: Center-Periphery Relations in Post-Communist Russia," in Gail W. Lapidus, ed., *The New Russia: Troubled Transformation*, Boulder: Westview Press, 1995, p. 82.

64. B. Keller, *The New York Times Sunday Magazine,* (1993 September 23).

65. Elizabeth Teague, "Russian and Tatarstan Sign Power-Sharing Treaty," *RFE/RL Research Reports* 3(14) (8 April 1994): 19–27.

66. Tolz, op. cit., p. 4.

67. This issue is currently under negotiations as the communists have offered to suspend a planned vote of no confidence if Yeltsin will accept a change to the effect that the dismissal of the government would mean replacing all major ministers.

68. Dwight Semler, "Focus: Crisis in Russia," *East European Constitutional Review* 3(1), (1993/94): 113.

69. Darrell Slider, Vladimir Gimpel'son and Sergei Chugrov, "Political Tendencies in Russia's Regions: Evidence from the 1993 Parliamentary Elections," *Slavic Review* 53(3), (1994): 713.

70. OMRI, *Russian Regional Report*, vol. 1, no. 2, p. 4 September 1996.

71. Yeltsin reportedly timed the decree so that his appointees would still be in charge during the summer 1996 elections. OMRI, *Daily Digest,* 28 August 1996.

72. Ironically the Duma later challenged the procedure in the Constitutional Court on the grounds that the process violated the Constitutional principle of the separation of powers. OMRI, *Daily Digest*, no. 31, p. 13 February 1997.

73. IEWS, *Russian Regional Report*, vol. 2, no. 16, p. 8 May 1997.

74. IEWS, *Russian Regional Report*, vol. 2, no. 13, p. 17 April 1997; and IEWS, *Russian Regional Report*, vol. 2, no. 22, p. 19 June 1997.

75. OMRI, *Russian Regional Report*, 1(2), (4 September 1996); and IEWS, *Russian Regional Report*, 22 January 1997.

76. IEWS, *Russian Regional Report*, p. 4 September 1996.

77. Maria Balynina, *RIA Novosti* (10 April 1997).

78. OMRI, *Russian Regional Report*, 2(13), (17 April 1997).

79. Edward W. Walker, "Designing Center-Region Relations in the New Russia," *East European Constitutional Review*, 4(1), (1995): 54–60.

80. This and other quotes from the Constitution use the translation found in Albert P. Blaustein, *Constitutions of the Countries of the World*, New York: Oceana Publications, Doubleday Ferry, May 1994, pp. 1–42.

Chapter 3

Komi and the Center: Developing Federalism in an Era of Socioeconomic Crisis

James Alexander

Frequently portrayed as an ideal balance between centrifugal and centripetal forces,[1] federalism has been widely discussed as a vital organizing principle for the development of democracy in Russia. While striving to achieve this balance, Russia has swung from side-to-side, at one time threatening the very dissolution of the Russian Federation and at another threatening the restoration of centralized control. Still striving for the appropriate balance, contemporary Russian federalism continues its uncertain development.

A part of the federal development process has been the signing of bilateral treaties defining the rights and responsibilities of the federal center, or Kremlin, and the individual governments of each *subekty*. This process has led to an asymmetric federalism based on the uneven nature of these agreements, among both the various signatories and those *subekty* that have not yet completed such an agreement. While it is uncertain why particular *subekty* were able to sign such agreements while others were not, there is speculation that then-President Yeltsin was simply rewarding regional leadership that had pledged its support of the center.[2] This led some to claim that the imbalance of relations creates a basic inequality between subject governments that threatens stability in Russia.[3] Nevertheless, it has also been argued that an accumulation of bilateral treaties actually promotes greater stability in the system, particularly if the most disruptive *subekty* are brought into these treaties first. In this way, the most significant forces working against federalism are being "co-opted" into the system; those *subekty* that are least threatening to the union are brought in later at less favorable terms.

In March 1996, the Komi Republic became one of the early signatories in a series of *subekty* entering into a treaty with federal authorities. The treaty also included eight separate agreements dividing broad economic, political and social responsibilities between the two levels of government. In several ways, the document simply placed a legal stamp, and certain federal guidelines, on several years of independent behavior in Komi's capital, Syktyvkar. Yet, even in signing the agreement, the difficulties for officials in contemporary Russia to follow legal directions has continued on both sides of the treaty. When not to their convenience, Komi authorities have continued to resist, even ignore, political directives emanating from the center. Meanwhile, in asserting its authority throughout Russia, the Kremlin has attempted to reduce the local powers of regional leaders such as the Head of the Komi Republic, Yuri Spiridonov.

The dynamic relationship between Komi and the center raises questions as to the efficacy of the bilateral treaty itself. Yet, it will be shown that many of the difficulties implementing the treaty and establishing a functioning federal relationship between these levels of governments emerge—whether directly or indirectly—from the continuing Russian economic crisis. Although not the only factor influencing this relationship, I find that the inability of both sides to meet their fiscal obligations (in terms of federal revenue transfers and the republic's tax collection practices) limits the necessary habituation of interaction across levels, the building of trust that comes from long-term reliable exchange. Truthfully, there has been some degree of regularization in this relationship—in fact, there have been numerous instances where the treaty is observed outside the fiscal relationship—yet the most significant factor driving Komi's relationship with the center is the presence/absence of "real" money. It is only intuitively obvious to note that a central edict proffering funding for the development of a particular program is much more likely to be observed than one that requires expenditure, but does not include the necessary funding.

Located in the far north of Russia and bordering the western Ural Mountains, the Komi Republic is most identifiable by its history as a location for Stalinist state labor camps (gulags), its ethnic divisions, and abundant natural resources. As for Sakha's diamond deposits described in Daniel Kempton's chapter, the potential wealth associated with this last characteristic further helps to explain any advantages that Komi might have had in negotiating a favorable bilateral treaty. On the political front, Spiridonov has been a strong figure in Komi politics since the mid-1980s when he served as the second secretary of the Komi Communist Party before being elevated as the first secretary. He was elected chairman of the Komi Supreme Soviet in 1990 and is currently serving his second term as Head of the Komi Republic. He is an independent-minded leader, who has been willing to resist central Russian directives, in the interests of both the republic and his own political future. He has also played a strong role in limiting the development of a political opposition in Komi. As the republic's chief executive, Spiridonov is a member of the Federation Council and has been active in pursuing the interests of Russia's Northern Regions.

Komi is a multi-ethnic territory in which Russians comprise over half of the population (Spiridonov is Russian), while the indigenous Komi are about 25 percent. While ethnicity issues are important in Komi, they do not threaten to destabilize the republic. Overall, an already declining population of 1,163,000 is expected to decline further to 1,034,00 by 2015.[4] While the declining population might have a negative effect on the republic's development, it would seem that Komi has a bright economic future. Fuel (oil, coal, and gas) is the largest industry in the region, making up approximately 50 percent of Komi's GDP. Oil is the main export, providing 63 percent of total export revenue, followed by wood-related products (16 percent) and coal (11 percent). Komi has trade relationships with over 40 foreign countries and has been actively expanding its ties with other regions in Russia.[5]

The research presented in this chapter is grounded in fieldwork carried out in 1993–1994 and during the summer of 1997, although the discussion extends to include developments through early 1999. The first section brings this chapter into the overall framework of this book, briefly examining theories of federalism and actual federal development in Russia, before focusing on Komi's place in this development. The second section examines Komi relations with the center from late 1990 until early 1995. The third and fourth sections carry the discussion forward. The third section employs several theoretical issues deemed important to the development of federal systems to examine developments in Komi. These issues include Komi political culture and views of the state, and the local development of civil society and political parties. The fourth section details the important provisions of the bilateral treaty. The chapter concludes with an assessment of the treaty's influence, particularly these several provisions, and explores the general evolution of federal relations between Komi and the center.

FEDERALISM AND RUSSIA

Federalism is a means for distributing authority among diverse bodies over an otherwise unified territory.[6] It is a form of government through which rule is divided between regional and national government as a means for encouraging self-rule within the regions and shared rule across the entire state. In dividing responsibilities across levels of government, the popular attention is also divided: "Federalism encourages competition between orders of government for popular support."[7] In this way, a population can grow to identify with both the nation-state and the region.

The Soviet Union was a self-described federal system divided along the lines of ethnonational identity into 15 union republics, which were further subdivided. As described in the introduction to this volume, while the self-determination of each union republic was theoretically recognized in the Soviet system, reality was much different. In general, totalitarian states employed federalism as a means to consolidate their rule, only permitting a minimal degree of cultural autonomy to ethnic groups concentrated within a particular region.[8] For the Soviet Union, the little regional autonomy that existed under Stalin became even more limited during the Khrushchev era with the elimination of regional economic councils and a greater push toward russification through language policy.[9]

Russia's lack of experience with substantive federalism raises important questions about the country's ability to develop a functioning federal system. Such uncertainties were borne out during the early- and mid-1990s as centrifugal forces seemed to dominate Russian politics as several *subekty* attempted to pull away from central control. Most notable among these struggles have been the public feud between Tatarstan and the center and the disastrous civil war fought in Chechnya. While most center-periphery struggles were in the shadows of these two major confrontations, the combination of attempts by other *subekty* to declare their sovereignty from Moscow's control (to varying degrees) threatened to undermine the authority of the Russian state. In 1992, this threat led to the approval of the Federal Treaty. In this document the Russian *subekty*, in particular the national republics, were given a degree of independence that placed Russia perilously close to the formation of a centrally weak confederation.[10] The life of this treaty was particularly short, however, as the rising struggle between President Boris Yeltsin and the Supreme Soviet eventually culminated in the violent events of early October 1993 and led to presidential attempts to reassert central authority.[11] This process was best exemplified by the new Russian Constitution, which focused national authority on the president (Article 4) and set up equal relations for all levels of the territory (Article 5). Nevertheless, this equality was immediately muddied by the second clause of Article 5, providing republics the right to their own constitutions, while all other entities were limited to a charter. Yet, the federal constitution appeared to reduce the advantages long held by the republics that had been codified in the Federal Treaty.

Following the December 1993 popular ratification of the Constitution, centripetal forces have been "held at bay" by a number of *subekty* administrations insistent on protecting the measure of sovereignty already acquired. As discussed in the introduction—and various chapters—to this volume, this process has been most evident in the numerous bilateral treaties signed between Moscow and the majority of Russia's regions. Although many of the treaties following the first such agreement with Tatarstan in 1994 have been more guarded in their allocation of authority to each particular region, Moscow has nonetheless recognized the signatory regions' right to greater control over their respective territories. As will be shown in the case of Komi, this has been particularly notable as pertains to provisions for "ownership of natural resources and land, wider budgetary and tax powers, and the right to engage directly in foreign economic relations."[12] In this fashion, the centripetal forces of the Yeltsin Constitution have been diminished.

A number of scholars examining Russian politics are dismayed with the manner in which federalism is developing. A clear critique leveled against the bilateral treaties lies in the fact that many of the terms of these treaties actually contradict the Constitution, particularly where the elevation of some regions violates the equality clause of Article 4.[13] How these contradictions will be resolved is as yet unclear. As pertains to the unequal treatment of regions, however, Sergei Valenti argues,

> Everyone knows what separating one's children into favorites and non-favorites leads to. The result [in Russia] has been analogous—a total lack of respect on the part of the children (the RF subjects) toward the parents (the state) and toward each other. This lack of respect was manifested both in the multitude of instances when the subjects of the Federation refused to execute the decisions of the federal center, and in the adoption by a number of regions of constitutions and individual legislative acts whose basic provisions contradict the RF Constitution.[14]

Valenti argues that the early treaties, often involving economically important *subekty* (such as Komi), placed socioeconomic expediency over a normative-legal principle of state-building.[15] This uneven development of society carries even greater threats. On one level, the uneven nature of federal development can but lead to greater complications in the already challenging task of making and enforcing legislation across Russia. On another, this process breeds corruption across levels of government as local elites and federal bureaucrats take advantage of unmonitored relations.[16]

While there is ample room to criticize the unevenness of the division of powers among *subekty*, some scholars are less concerned. While acknowledging that the developing asymmetries in federal policy do create risks, James Hughes argues that such may be the result of pragmatic policymaking. The asymmetric nature of center-periphery relations has actually "restrained secessionist tendencies, allowing Moscow to negotiate on the basis of the particular interests of each republic and region."[17] Such reasoning has mixed theoretical backing. While Canadian concessions to Quebec have not proven to be particularly successful, the Spaniards have experienced a greater degree of success in mollifying the separatist elements in the Catalan and Basque regions of northern Spain. In the case of Catalonia, broader autonomy has significantly reduced secessionist demands and eliminated terrorist acts. Although the degree of success is not the same for the Basque region, there has been an overall decline in its secessionist movement as well.[18]

No matter the correct interpretation of the bilateral phenomenon, this process has not been accompanied by the development of a federal political party system, described in the introduction as a beneficial condition for the maintenance of a successful federal system. In the Russian case, the underdevelopment of political parties is a byproduct of the electoral structure. Because party list voting for the State Duma is founded on national lists, centered on Moscow, there is no means for regional parties to develop. To promote this, a system like the German system of regional party lists is needed. Although deputies emerging from single-member districts often join a party or bloc in the Duma, candidates for these positions have been largely independent. Furthermore, the staggered scheduling of elections (1995 and 1999 Duma elections, 1996 and 2000 presidential elections, and varying regional elections) has further kept candidates and officials from coalescing around common interests at a single moment in time.[19] As described in the introduction, political party development is often seen as a measure for democracy. If such is the case, Russia and Komi have a long way to go.

The introduction depicts the six necessary and six beneficial conditions for federalism. In examining the relationship of the Komi Republic with the center, I find that the majority of the necessary conditions are met to a large degree, particularly conditions one (consensual participation), two (written constitution) and four (federal representation), and will not be focused on, although aspects of the latter arise in the general discussion of Komi politics. Conditions three (adjudication between governmental levels) and five (a division of powers between levels of government) are partially met and will receive greater discussion below. Condition six (a federal political culture) is one of those characteristics that Elazar identifies as closely associated with successful federalist development and receives extended treatment here.[20] An important issue for understanding developments in Komi, the existence of a federal political culture is important for strong federal systems to have meaningful public support. Closely linked to this idea is the existence of a popular will to federate. In neither case is it clear that these qualities exist in contemporary Russia, particularly given the lack of popular experience with federalism[21] and the current economic and social difficulties that are drawing the popular attention away from political reforms.[22]

Elazar makes an important observation in his studies of federal systems that have developed in the English-speaking world: there is no real concept of the state, for it emerges from popular sovereignty. In this sense, for citizens of these societies, there is no central focal point of power because it is dispersed throughout the population.[23] A tradition of popular sovereignty makes identification with two (or more) centers of authority an easier prospect for people living in systems based on the contractarian philosophies of Thomas Hobbes and John Locke; with such a background, the development of federal systems appears "natural." This is in contrast to the centralization found in Russian history. In the Soviet and Russian past the state takes on almost mythic proportions as the focal point of power, sparking sovietologist Robert Tucker to describe "Russia as a double entity: Russian state and Russian society."[24] Although weaker than its predecessors, the contemporary Russian state continues to draw popular attention as a leader and provider of social goods.[25] In Komi, this aspect of Russian political culture is detrimental to the development of a successful federal system, unless expectations can come to focus on the "sovereignties" of both levels of government.

Of the beneficial conditions to federalism, conditions one (balance of power between the center and its components) and two (symmetry among the components) are somewhat beyond the purview of this chapter as they deal with system-wide issues. Elazar is particularly concerned with the former, however. As discussed below, whether this has been achieved in Russia is particularly doubtful. While relations may have calmed over the past several years, the center-periphery dynamic reflects a continuing antagonism that is unlikely to be solved soon. This antagonism is evident in Komi-Kremlin relations. Thus, condition one will be examined specifically as concerns Komi, rather than all of Russia, particularly in regard to the 1996 bilateral treaty.

Conditions three thru six (federal political parties, a non-centralized bureaucracy, democracy, and economic conditions, respectively) will be examined throughout the coming discussion. Elazar is particularly concerned with the existence of a civil society as a vital means for overlapping and participating in the *subekty*-national competition. The same may be said for the development of a party system to act as a linking mechanism across levels of society and to ameliorate the center-region conflict.[26] Other than Communist Party activities, neither sector of society was active during the Soviet era, nor have they made particular inroads into contemporary Russia either.[27]

DEVELOPMENTS IN THE KOMI REPUBLIC

In 1990 Komi was one of the first Autonomous Soviet Socialist Republics to declare sovereignty from the dictates of the Soviet Union.[28] This move was followed by similar dramatic assertions over the next several years. For example, when faced with a severe food shortage in early 1991, the Komi Supreme Soviet passed a law to withhold raw material "exports" if Soviet and Russian authorities did not meet the plan for food deliveries to the republic.[29] Two months following the aborted putsch in August 1991, the Komi legislature amended its Constitution to allow itself the authority to "veto decisions by the presidents of the USSR and the Russian Soviet Federated Socialist Republic."[30] It even went so far as to declare all mineral resources its exclusive property.[31] Despite these threatening actions, however, a Komi drive for independence never truly materialized. In fact, the 1992 Federal Treaty, which recognized national republics as state entities and provided the republics with complete legislative and executive authority over their territories,[32] was approved by the Komi Supreme Soviet by an overwhelming margin (103 to 15 with seven abstentions).[33]

Komi efforts at developing a semi-autonomous niche within the Russian political system continue, however. With the events of October 1993, the tack of Komi leadership for developing the republic's sovereignty was redirected by Yeltsin's call for the dissolution of all regional soviets (including the Komi Supreme Soviet) and the eventual publication of the draft Russian Constitution in November 1993. In a losing effort, the *de facto* Komi leader, Spiridonov (then Chairman of the Komi Supreme Soviet), quite vocally opposed passage of the Constitution for it did not include the Federal Treaty, particularly those provisions providing advantages to the Russian republics.

Further attempts to assert federal control over the *subekty* led Spiridonov to delay implementation of Yeltsin's intended program for regional political reform and set up his own power base. This lasted until January 1995, when the new Komi State Council was chosen by popular vote. In the interim, Spiridonov shrugged off the electoral defeat of a Komi referendum to create a Komi presidency by legislatively including the position (re-named Head of the Republic) in the February 1994 Komi Constitution. In this way, Spiridonov followed Article 5 of the Russian Constitution, which allows national republics to form their own constitutions, while continuing to ignore federal supremacy. On May 8, 1994, Spiridonov's election as Head largely eliminated the power base of his main opposition (Chairman of the Komi Council of Ministers Viacheslav Khudiaev) and placed Spiridonov in a strong position to centralize Komi politics around his leadership.

Drawing on the Komi Constitution and the Komi Law on Executive Authority passed by the still existing Supreme Soviet in October 1994, Spiridonov ensured the election of a State Council largely dependent on his rule. The Constitution identifies 20 districts in Komi of regional/territorial importance (Article 70). Additionally, the leadership position of each district is included in the executive branch (Article 94) under the direction of the Head. Until recently, these 20 Heads of Administration have been appointed by the Head of the Republic (Komi Law on Executive Authority, Article 32). In turn, these Heads of Administration have been in the position to appoint local administration heads in towns and villages, thus ensuring vertical control of the region. Overall, the 20 regional/territorial districts overlap with 30 electoral districts based on population to comprise[34] the 50 electoral districts of the current State Council (Komi Constitution, Article 71).

With an inherent advantage in January 1995 elections, 13 of the administrative heads were elected to the State Council along with others who were, or would become, beholden to the Head through ministerial appointments to the executive branch. Furthermore, although not as beholden to Spiridonov's rule, 16 of the "generals" of Komi industry (oil, timber, gas, etc.) were elected to the Council as well.[35] In a seemingly corporatist arrangement that has been exhibited across Russia in various forms,[36] this group has been generally supportive of the Head in a mutually beneficial alliance.[37] In this fashion, Spiridonov created a dependent, rather than independent legislative branch. As one local reporter claimed, one-half of the State Council is in the "pocket" of the Head.[38] Thus, in resisting Yeltsin's directive from October 1993 for 15 months, Spiridonov had positioned himself and future Heads close to being the sole political influence on Komi policy toward Moscow.

Having emerged from the period of internal "reconstruction," Komi has begun to play a notable role in federal politics. Spiridonov and his ally, State

Council Chairman Vladimir Torlopov, have actively pursued Komi and regional interests writ large as representatives to the Federation Council. Torlopov serves as the chairman of the Committee on Social Policy.[39] Shortly after the formation of the Federation Council, Spiridonov began to actively advocate the interests of Komi and lobby for the creation of a bilateral treaty with the federal government. Additionally, he became one of the leaders of the Council of the Heads of Republic along with the leaders of Karelia, Tatarstan, Sakha, and Bashkiria. Early on, this body determined the republics' policy toward the center.[40]

Spiridonov actively strives to represent the interests of the Russian North. In fact, during 1997 Syktyvkar hosted two conferences searching for solutions to developing the North's economy and finding a place for the region in the larger Russian economy.[41] Spiridonov has consistently proclaimed the importance of the North to Russia and Russia's obligation to the region:

> [A] state program for the development of the northern regions is absolutely necessary today. After all, more than 90 percent of all of the mineral-raw material potential of Russia is concentrated in them.[42]

To Komi's advantage, Spiridonov had a strong working relationship with former Prime Minister Chernomyrdin, actually turning down an offer to be the "first deputy in charge of fuel and energy questions."[43] What this relationship ultimately meant in policymaking is difficult to determine. Yet, as discussed below, Spiridonov's unwillingness to work with local civic organizations changed soon after Chernomyrdin's dismissal in spring 1998, perhaps a sign that he was "circling his wagons" after having lost his patron. When asked what he believed to be the most positive and negative events affecting Russian life in 1998, Spiridonov responded:

> The most negative is the change of Chernomyrdin's government. When Chernomyrdin was changed for Kirienko, life for Russians and their well-being was threatened. This came to pass in the August financial crisis, the after effects of which both the center and the regions are still disentangling.[44]

POLITICAL CULTURE AND THE STATE: LIMITED SUPPORT FOR FEDERALISM

Komi's political culture provides limited support for the development of federalism in Russia. This view is supported by history. For centuries Russia was dominated by the *de facto* centralized state of the Tsar that was only reinforced by the centralizing, unitary nature of the Communist Party of the Soviet Union. Under Soviet leadership, Russians became accustomed to central state guidance across the political, economic, and social spheres of society. Fundamental to the state's leading role was its responsibility for the social safety net of Soviet society, a support system that has declined dramatically in its effectiveness in the post-Soviet era. Based on fieldwork in 1993–1994, the population of Syktyvkar reacted to rising instability in all spheres of life to "support the concept of a leading state: a state that requires social order and discipline while providing focused guidance to the populace."[45] In looking to the state for guidance, people were looking past local authorities for the solution to Russian turmoil. In part, this arose because many people did not view local political figures as politicians with independent political agendas for the Komi Republic.[46] In essence, they viewed their officials more as bureaucrats: the implementers of central directives, rather than the makers of policy.

While the majority of interviewees in 1994 supported the "leading state," there was a minority view that supported a diminished state role in society. Rather than focus on the state's responsibility to provide the positive rights of a guaranteed job, medical care, and education, a more reform-oriented populace focused on negative rights, or freedom from state control.[47] This small portion of the population saw the state fulfilling a regulatory, rather than intrusive role in guiding Russian society. While the lines were not clearly drawn between these groups, as the minority group also favored state provision of social supports, there appeared to be a strain of opinion in Syktyvkar that could lend its support to expanded local responsibilities across a spectrum of state and private concerns.

An aspect of that perspective that overlapped conservative- and reform-oriented opinions lay in support for the expansion of local control of Komi economic relations. Thus, while there was majority support for centrally-directed economic reform, there was also support, at times internally contradictory, for federal relations in the economic sphere.[48] Furthermore, as codified in the bilateral treaty, this support has blossomed into central recognition of the Komi right to direct much of local economic development. Nevertheless, in summer 1997, Komi's leaders were deflecting popular attention away from developing a separate sphere of local responsibility for economic development toward the reform failures (late wage payments, tax burdens, etc.) of the government in Moscow. Blaming the national government placed local leaders in a strong position to take personal advantage of the public's lack of attention on local affairs. Whereas Komi officials had expanded authority over regional affairs, the people of Komi continued to discount the possibility for local political independence. In November 1997, a Syktykvar resident described the situation as follows,

> Maybe something has changed for functionaries. Maybe their hands are less tied. But as I understand it, there has been little change in the economy. All the money used to go to Moscow and it still does. Clearly, [President Yeltsin's] aides are misinforming him. Take the new budget for example. After all it should be coordinated with the territories. This is described as a positive achievement. But from the local press and interviews with our leaders I discover that this year there has been no discussion with the territories for the first time. . . . [T]he main issues are still decided in Moscow. So it is too early to talk about profound changes in relations between Moscow and the Republic of Komi.[49]

In muddying the water of responsibility (regional or national), local political and economic officials have been able to "catch a lot of fish" through unethical and corrupt practices.[50]

Civil Society and Political Parties

The development of a political culture supportive of Russian federalism has been further hindered by the slow, seemingly retrograde, development of civil society and political parties in the Komi Republic. Rather than helping develop popular loyalty across levels of government, the weaknesses of Russia's political parties and civil society give certain centrifugal forces the upper hand. While there was some evidence of the development of a politically aware and participatory population in Syktyvkar in 1993–1994, conditions in Russia during that period mitigated against further development. In a society suffering from comprehensive trauma, the fact that people were focusing on their private lives rather than becoming involved in public affairs was not unexpected. At the same time, however, there was little optimism among respondents that civic involvement in public affairs would have any sort of effect.[51] As a result, civil society was comprised of a few small, extremely ineffective groups that was mirrored by a lack of local party development. In 1997, the situation was much the same. Although they had agitated for more access to the policymaking process, the leaders of these groups were not optimistic that their voices carried more weight than three years before.

Initial limitations went beyond simple developmental inadequacies to the juridical basis of Komi politics. First, Article 7 of the Komi Law on Executive Authority requires the Head of the Republic to suspend all membership in political parties or other socio-political organizations. Second, the Head's initial authority to appoint 20 Heads of Administration, who had a natural advantage in election to the State Council, led to a system based on personality rather than pluralism. Pluralist development has been further dampened by the election of various government officials (under Spiridonov's authority) to seats in the State Council. Through the Komi Constitution, Spiridonov was able to limit the development of healthy political competition by insisting that the State Council (which only meets twice a month[52]) not be a professional legislature. Coupled with the allegiance of Heads of Administration to the Head of the Republic, until 1998 there were several deputies who also worked in governmental ministries. This fact further created the image of a dependent legislature, while undermining the development of pluralism in the republic.

Another politico-institutional hindrance to the development of political parties and, hence, the strengthening of federal relations has been the irregular schedule for elections.[53] The first election for the Head was in May 1994 and is scheduled to occur at four-year intervals (1998, 2002, etc.), although Spiridonov forced early elections in November 1997. The first elections to the State Council occurred in January 1995 and are also scheduled at four-year intervals (1999, 2003, etc.). Furthermore, neither of these elections coincides with the federal elections to either the presidency or the State Duma. In this way, there is little ability for political parties to develop a base and/or momentum for development in Komi. In essence, a single date for elections to various levels of government would allow candidates from individual parties to work together. Beyond simply the disconnected activities of certain candidate activists, a unified election date could mobilize these individuals into a more coherent party mass with a greater chance for long-term development over a series of elections.

As for much of Russia, under these conditions there is little concrete development in Komi political parties.[54] Discussions with the local leadership of the political party Democratic Choice of Russia, Igor Bobrakov, and the socio-political movement Women of Russia, Olga Savast'ianova, made it clear that both organizations lacked local membership. During summer 1997, each organization had approximately 30 members in Syktyvkar. Bobrakov argued that years of Communist Party rule meant that many people continued to fear the development of new parties, democratic or not. Furthermore, democratic parties were particularly underdeveloped in Komi because of the lack of party competition in the republic at any level. Also, few of the local political leaders belong to parties. Explaining a certain degree of low party competition, the Komi Constitution prohibits the Head from belonging to a political party. Thus, there is "no lightning rod" for political alliance or opposition. Bobrakov further claimed that although the Communist Party had the strongest local organization, the fact that it was not in power in Komi helped explain the lack of a developed democratic opposition. He perceived that underlying popular antipathy for the Communists would spur increased opposition activities if the Party were in power.[55]

The local affiliate of Women of Russia carried greater promise for the development of civil society. Founded in February of 1997, by summer the group already had 400 members spread among 18 of the republic's 21 regions. The organization is concerned with four issues: economics, public health, public security, and politics. The fact that the organization is not solely political may partially explain the support provided by the Komi authorities, including a two-room office in a government building.[56] This is contrasted with Russia's Democratic Choice, which received no support from local government. Furthermore, local officials link Bobrakov's leadership of an "opposition" party to his affiliation with the local opposition newspaper *Molodesh Severa*. On two occasions the Komi government revoked his journalist's accreditation. In both cases, however, a campaign by the newspaper led to his reinstatement.[57]

The Division of Power: The Balancing Act

This section examines the juridical basis of the federal balance exhibited in the bilateral treaty signed by former Prime Minister Viktor Chernomyrdin and Head Yuri Spiridonov in March 1996. Many issues in Kremlin-Syktyvkar relations that were not discussed in the Constitution of the Russian Federation were later raised in the Komi Constitution. The bilateral treaty provides a mutually agreed on codification of the federal relationship. Ultimately, many practices (i.e., tax collection, environmental regulation, etc.) that were already in effect in Komi were recognized by federal authorities.[58] As regional political authorities had little say in drafting the 1993 Russian Constitution—an aspect in Spiridonov's opposition to its electoral approval—the treaty outlines mutually recognized roles for each level of government. In this way, the legal basis for Komi's relations with Moscow comes to approximate the balance between center and periphery that is considered vital for the development of effective federalism.[59]

The bilateral treaty signed on March 20, 1996, between the government of the Russian Federation and the government of the Komi Republic concerns the "demarcation of authority" of each governmental entity. The treaty itself is a general political guidepost for Komi-Kremlin relations. The most weighty aspect of the document, however, involves a series of eight agreements (*soglashenie*) that append the treaty and that specifically define the roles of each level of government. These agreements vary across a spectrum of issues, primarily focusing on economic development (Table 3.1).

Most aspects of the agreements, particularly the first three, describe the mutual responsibilities of both levels of government for the development of these various sectors of society. Still, there are clearly some areas where Komi authorities received greater responsibilities than they carried before. This is notable in areas related to the development of the Komi economy and the production of Komi's natural resources.

Table 3.1
Outline of Agreements[60]

Agreement(s) Nos. *1-8* Between the Government of the Russian Federation and Government of the Republic of Komi about the demarcation of authority in . . .

1. the area of socio-economic development
2. the area of international and foreign trade ties
3. the branches of the fuel-energy complex
4. the solution of socio-labor questions, the provision of employment for the population and regulation of migratory processes
5. the area of the agro-industrial complex
6. in the area of public secondary, primary professional and secondary professional (pedagogical) education
7. in the area of the protection of the surrounding environment and use of natural resources
8. in budget (inter)relations

Of special interest are the second, third, and eighth of these agreements. The second agreement is an example of Russia attempting to reassert some measure of control over the international policies of its *subekty.* This agreement recognizes the *de facto* Komi practice of carrying out independent trade policy in the international arena. Rather than follow past practice of controlling international business relations through the Ministry of International Affairs and the Ministry of Foreign Economic Relations, the Russian Federation only asks that Komi cooperate with these two ministries in implementing its policies. The most stringent aspect of the agreement requires Komi to inform these ministries at least one month prior to the establishment of formal ties. Furthermore, if the Russian Federation comes to an international agreement concerning the fuel-energy complex, the Komi Republic must abstain from making an agreement of its own.

In return for Komi participation with federal authorities, the Russian Federation has agreed to direct interested international parties toward the Komi Republic for potential investment in the fuel-energy complex. The agreement further allows Komi representatives to participate on Russian international trade missions affecting the interests of Komi in this economic area. Finally, Komi is legally allowed to act in its own interests to attract international investment and the representatives of foreign companies to the Komi Republic.

Moving from issues of trade policy, the third agreement focuses on the development of natural resources in the republic. It calls for expanded collaboration across levels of government in the search for natural resources and in attracting investors to help develop oil production. Komi is required to privatize the oil industry along the line of the privatization program implemented by the Russian Federation. Additionally, the Komi Head has been allowed to represent the local oil companies in setting a quota for the export of oil and oil by-products outside of Russia. Komi in turn receives a guaranteed equal position in competing to sell its oil production to the Russian state.

Along with several of the other agreements, the third agreement deals with the difficulties of providing for a shifting employment base in a transition economy. More specifically, it provides for federal aid in transferring workers out of the harsh environmental and working conditions of the far north to better climes. This is particularly important in consideration of the declining profitability of the coalmines stretching as far north as Vorkuta in the Arctic Circle. With mines closing, and others threatening to close, a potentially productive population needed aid in moving to areas of greater opportunity in Russia. Moreover, as also described in agreements four and five, the federal government agrees to continue the Soviet provision of subsidies and bonuses to those working in industry and agriculture (and other fields) in the difficult conditions of a northern region.

Finally, the eighth agreement requires Komi to pay its share of taxes as determined under federal law and the budget for any particular year. In return, the Russian government is to provide monthly payments for the realization of an economic development program in Komi. Furthermore, Komi is to be classified under federal revenue distribution categories as either "a region in need of help" or "a region especially in need of help." Federal law concerning the federal budget will determine the size of such aid. This classification is designed to ensure Komi a larger share of the revenue distributed by the federal government. Finally, as part of the return for guaranteeing to pay its taxes, the Komi government, in agreement with the Russian Ministry of Finance, is allowed to determine the amount of taxes to be levied against local enterprises and other contributors to the federal budget.

The Practice of Federalism in the Komi Republic

When emerging from field research in summer 1997, I was quite skeptical about the prospects for meaningful federal developments in Komi relations with the center. This skepticism was founded on the almost universal pessimism of local commentators about the effectiveness of the bilateral treaty, especially those parts that required specific financial responsibilities from federal authorities. Moreover, Igor Bobrakov was concerned that the federal structure lay behind the rise of political corruption in Komi, particularly the rise of Spiridonov and his cohort. He argued that provisions for regional autonomy underlying federalism had facilitated the creation of an authoritarian regime within the republic itself. Along with Shumeiko, Bobrakov noted the absence of any significant level of regional government autonomy in Russian tradition.[61] Bobrakov argued that more appropriate structures might mimic the unitary French political system. In addition to the historical argument, however, Bobrakov's position rested on two basic issues: (1) he believed that successful, radical economic reform can best be carried out from the center, and (2) he did not trust Komi's political leadership, especially because opposition groups were effectively barred from participating in local decisionmaking.[61] Other commentators in 1997 expressed similar reservations, although generally with less ideological and/or political content.

With another two years of perspective, it is easier to assess the effects of the bilateral treaty and the development of the federal relationship between Komi and the center. In some ways, the concerns of the activists and officials raised here were overstated: the treaty does in fact provide a basic, if not effective, framework within which relations across the governmental levels are managed. In other ways, however, they seemed right on track. Bobrakov's concerns, which were often so tied to his own political goals, seemed to lose a little force by late 1998 as Spiridonov made efforts to include competing political movements in making Komi policy. Essentially aiming outward, toward federal and international relations, there have been two collective organizations formed with Spiridonov's blessing. Forming just after the dismissal of Prime Minister Chernomyrdin in March, the first group brought together 14 regional organizations into a consultative body to the Head.[62] The second group, "Transformation of the North," brings together eight reform-oriented political parties/ movements following the leadership of the local "party of power," Our Home Is Russia. With Spiridonov in attendance, this movement's founding conference was held in October 1998.[63]

While the latter group appears to have been the most durable, both groups have been founded with the general goal of a unified defense of Komi (even the entire northern region) in the face of anti-reformist elements in the national government. When asked what he felt was the most positive event in 1998, Spiridonov was most pleased with the

> union of socio-political forces in the republic, guaranteeing [fewer] political shocks in our northern region, and the possibility of more quickly emerging from the economic crisis where we were thrown by the political games at the level of the federal structure.[64]

While there continues to be skepticism following failed agreements in the past,[65] the external focus of the movement goes beyond earlier attempts by political organizations to expand their roles in Komi's internal affairs. Thus, there seems to be a rising consensus that has not been seen in Komi since before the events of October 1993 and the assertion of Russian executive power. When examined in the face of events concerning the three agreements discussed in the previous section, however, this type of unity may be more a sign of difficulties in the federal relationship than a positive sign for the democratization of Komi.

Skepticism voiced by State Council Deputy and Deputy Agriculture Minister Sergei Gusiatnikov in 1997 concerning the areas of international trade covered by the second agreement focused squarely on Komi's relationship with the center. Gusiatnikov specifically pointed to central interference in trade with Belarus. Because the center had consistently failed to meet its fiscal transfer obligations, Komi had used barter to acquire tractors produced in the former all Union Republic. While the bilateral treaty had yet to effect noticeable positive changes, he argued that prior to the treaty signing in March 1996, local gas company *Severgazprom* had been more independent, allowing natural gas to be the bartering instrument in trade relations with Belarus.[66] Gusiatnikov's contention that Moscow was being obstructionist in international trade relations underlines Spiridonov's contention in May 1997 that "federal ministries and departments vary in their adherence [to the treaty]. They are fulfilling mostly that which does not require any money."[67] While the problem of fiscal transfers will be discussed below, the question of central interference in areas of international trade falls into the category Spiridonov describes.

While it is difficult to assess the several aspects discussed above concerning the second agreement, trade with Belarus does not seem to have suffered unduly since summer 1997. Spiridonov visited Belarus in December 1997 and had productive talks with Belarusian President Aleksandr Lukashenka concerning trade in the machine building industry and the production of fuel resources. In signing an intergovernmental cooperation agreement between

Komi and Belarus, it was expected that future relations would bring an expansion in trade beyond the $300,000 worth of light-industry products sent to Komi in 1997.[68] In March 1998 Spiridonov followed protocol by requesting and receiving Yeltsin's approval to invite Lukashenka to visit the republic. While various internal Belarusian issues kept Lukashenka from visiting that year, he eventually signed an agreement focusing on economic cooperation between the two regions in February 1999. Further evidence that this aspect of the treaty might be functioning as planned, particularly as relates to the aspect requiring the center to help attract foreign business interests to the region, foreign investments in the Komi economy had increased from $116 million in 1995 to $200 million in 1996 and may have increased to as much as $355 million in 1997.[69]

Just as certain aspects of the second agreement appear to be functioning, so too is the case with the third agreement. Yet, here the results are more mixed, again pointing to the distinction between provisions requiring funding and those that do not. As some actors had commented earlier, some of these provisions had largely been implemented prior to the treaty signing. In April 1996, Komi was among a handful of regions that had met their state privatization assignments in full.[70] Thus, the treaty requirement that the Komi oil industry be privatized along federal guidelines was well on its way to being fulfilled if it had not been done already. Unfortunately, much of the remainder of this particular agreement has not been fulfilled, in this case by the center. This is exemplified by a meeting Spiridonov and other regional leaders had with President Yeltsin in February 1998 to discuss the renegotiation of the "power-sharing agreements" to make both sides more accountable. In raising this issue, Spiridonov aimed specifically at the Russian Ministry of Finance which was not providing needed financial aid for the joint development of natural resources (in this particular instance, bauxite was the resource discussed) as per the eighth agreement.[71] Potentially addressing this issue, Prime Minister Primakov eventually signed a law providing federal support for bauxite and manganese extraction in December 1998.[72]

In 1997 a number of commentators independently identified federal transfer of payment problems as the underlying difficulties in Komi.[73] In keeping with the financial crisis that exploded onto the scene in August 1998 through early 1999, the situation eventually worsened. The central failure to meet many of its fiscal obligations violates aspects of a number of the agreements, including the provisions of agreements three thru five as concerns payments and subsidies for workers in the republic, some of which have long been part of a policy to pro-rate payments to take into account the harsh conditions and higher expenses of the Far North. As for many regions, a central and regional inability to pay workers for several months at a time has led to significant strike activity. This is particularly the case in the coal industry. In order to meet obligations, Komi officials have periodically taken out prohibitively expensive loans to pay back wages.[74]

Probably one of the clearest ways of solving the payments problem for miners in the declining coal industry is the provision in agreement three for federal aid to help transfer workers from the north to better climates with greater career perspectives. Although there has been some movement out of Komi and the population has definitely been declining, difficulties receiving promised payments has complicated the process of worker resettlement.[75] All these difficulties are exacerbated, if not caused, by the persistent difficulties of both levels of government to achieve their payment obligations: tax collection in Komi and revenue transfer from the center.

The economic difficulties in contemporary Russia are a play on the old Soviet labor joke: "They pretend to pay us, so we pretend to work." In this case, however, the "joke" can be updated: "They pretend to transfer central revenues, we pretend to collect our taxes." The failure on the part of both levels to fulfill their obligations in the revenue arena is the most serious threat to developing a strong federal relationship. It is also a long-term problem that has not been solved by the bilateral treaty.[76] Unfortunately, there is somewhat of a vicious cycle that develops in which revenues that are not transferred cannot be taxed, taxes that are not collected cannot be transferred to the center, central revenues cannot be sent to the regions, and so on. While this is an oversimplification, the reality is that both sides are often functioning with a paucity of real currency, a by-product of IMF-driven monetary policy. In essence, the federal government has often simply failed to meet its wage obligations, payments for programs serving veterans and invalids and used various mechanisms of accounting that wiped out mutual debts, yet still left Komi with no concrete currency to fulfill its obligations.[77]

As the federal authorities failed to fulfill their responsibilities, so too have Komi authorities. Frustrated with relations with the center, Spiridonov has been willing to violate the law over issues about which he disagrees. Just before the devaluation of the ruble in mid-August 1998, Spiridonov complained that Komi had contributed 1.4 billion rubles ($222 million) to the federal budget over the previous two years, yet had received nothing in return.[78] For its part, Komi has been collecting taxes in the form of barter and other mutual agreements, even going so far as to ignore a Yeltsin decree barring regions from collecting taxes in kind. [79] Of course, if firms lack the currency to pay taxes, they also lack the currency to pay wages. Thus, it has not been unusual to see workers standing on street corners selling their "wages," from furniture to vodka to toilet paper.

The end of 1998 brought an interesting accomplishment in Komi tax collection. Collecting taxes at a feverish pace, the republican tax service collected almost 40 percent of the entire year's taxes in November and December. This relative success made the Komi government optimistic that it would meet its obligations over the following year. Whether the tax service can continue to collect taxes at this rate is uncertain, but meeting financial goals may have been dealt a blow when the federal government removed Komi from the "needy regions" list. Explicitly mentioned in the eighth agreement, this classification had provided Komi certain subsidies. Given Komi's general economic condition, it may be the case that other *subekty* are simply doing worse. Komi has had somewhat of an advantage for acquiring foreign currency earnings through natural resource exports.[80] Oddly, the republican leadership did not object, perhaps less a sign of optimism than a sign of resignation that they would ever get the subsidies following the August crisis. Going somewhat further, this action could also signify that the accumulation of negative experiences in dealing with federal funding issues may lead to a more self-reliant Komi government. Still, Gusiatnikov's 1997 contention would seem true: developments in federal relations exhibiting greater juridical independence at the regional level mean little if the payment crisis continues.

Nevertheless, *de jure* evidence of regional autonomy was at the heart of a struggle between the center and Komi over the implementation of the 1995 Law on the Establishment of Local Self-government. A subject that I have written about extensively elsewhere,[81] this struggle gets at several of the conditions for federalism: the division of power between levels of government, recognition of the final adjudicator across levels, a balance of power between the center and its components, and the development of democracy. Komi resistance to implementing the 1995 law exhibits Spiridonov's opinion that the federal government already carries—and may be strengthening—its grip on Komi, arguing that Russia is reverting to a more unitary system.[82] Ironically, development of independent, local self-government entities in the republic is a direct threat to the vertical authority structure that Spiridonov has maintained since 1994.

Local political movements see the local self-government issues as the key to Komi's democratization and have been quite active in striving to implement the law. One such approach has been the communist-affiliated People's Patriotic Alliance of Russia's (NPSR) willingness to employ variously the Komi Supreme Court, the Komi Constitutional Court, the Russian Constitutional Court and the Russian Supreme Court to force Spiridonov to implement the law. Following losses at each level (March 1997, January 1998, and January 1999), Spiridonov has employed various semantic and administrative maneuvers to delay, avoid, and/or undermine compliance with the courts. With the Russian Constitutional Court and Russian Supreme Court decisions of January 1998 and January 1999, respectively, Spiridonov was seemingly forced to institute the law. Nevertheless, just before February 7, 1999, elections, maneuvers by the Head continuc to raise doubts almost two years later about the eventual development of Komi local self-government.[83]

CONCLUSION

The broad politico-legal framework for the federal relationship between Komi and the center has been established. In a slow process of development, the outlines of that framework are becoming clearer. Unfortunately, the incentive for both sides to adhere to this developing framework does not always exist. While the tradition of centralized authority acts as a significant obstacle to federalism's maturation, constantly retarding the process is the economic crisis that has dogged independent Russia since its inception. Because much of government involves the transfer of revenue across levels of authority, inconsistent tax collection and sporadic budgetary redistribution clearly hinder the habituation process that is necessary for the evolution of a workable system. Without the trust that comes from a cooperative relationship established over time, there is as much temptation for federal authorities to mandate compliance as there is for Komi authorities to ignore directives with no teeth or reward.

In the United States' developed federal system, access to budgetary funds is a powerful tool for implementing national policy. One need only examine how the 50 states complied with the federal order to raise the legal drinking age to 21 during the 1980s when the distribution of federal highway funds were tied to compliance. Nevertheless, the U.S. system has developed to a point in which budgetary transfers need not be involved for states to comply with national laws, Supreme Court rulings, and presidential orders. In fact, it is a normal process for states to implement national policies that require local expenditure without accompanying federal funds. While such unfunded mandates have become a battle line in the United States, the requisite trust that has developed from years of practicing federalism generally leads dissatisfied states to employ the system to address their concerns rather than simply ignore the order. Without such well-founded practices, Russian *subekty* are just as likely to avoid complying. Ultimately, until the trust is developed that the federal authorities will meet their obligations, authorities in the *subekty* will find ways to avoid central policies that appear inconvenient.

As demonstrated above, the economic future of the Komi Republic is bright. In this respect, working with federal authorities, particularly concerning international trade and investment, would seem to be in the republic's interest. Unfortunately, Komi is afflicted with symptoms of "Dutch Disease," or an overdependence on natural resources for the republic's economic well-being.[84] As mentioned at the outset, Komi receives 63 percent of its export income through oil sales. This, of course, makes Komi particularly vulnerable to the international market. With oil prices at an all-time low in early 1999, the prospects for Komi economic growth in the short term were not particularly good; of course, oil-based revenues flowed into the region throughout 2000 as prices soared. This boom-or-bust type of economic opportunity can only increase the tendency for Komi authorities to "defect" from the federal system when to their advantage.

Even under conditions of constant disruption, however, Komi is slowly becoming habituated to federal practices. Head Spiridonov has publicly declared his loyalty to Russia and recognizes the republic's position as an integral part of the federation. In that vein, he has been willing to use national legislative, executive, and legal institutions to fight for Komi's interests. Contradicting these participatory practices is the Head's inclination to ignore and/or delay rulings that are not in *his* interest. This pattern is exemplified by Komi's delayed implementation of the 1995 law on local self-government, a delay that Komi's opposition groups claim limits the evolution of civil society and retards the democratization of the republic. Nevertheless, this law and others are slowly being incorporated into the Komi legal framework. Thus, amid these contradictions, Komi and central authorities have developed a system that might best be termed "semi-federalism."

In the eternal pregnancy that is Russian reform, the bilateral treaty between Komi and the center is a step toward developing a functioning federal system. Hampered by constant socioeconomic crisis, many of the provisions of the treaty have only been slowly implemented. Whether a healthy federal system can be delivered from the ongoing crisis has yet to be seen. Yet, the fact that the treaty is implemented at all under such trying conditions would seem to indicate that it is an important step toward establishing the balance of sovereignties that will allow functional federal relations to take hold.[85]

NOTES

Support for this project was received from the Faculty Research Committee, Northeastern State University, Tahlequah, OK, 74464.

1. Alain-G. Gagnon, "The Political Uses of Federalism," in Michael Burgess and Alain-G. Gagnon (Eds.), *Comparative Federalism and Federation* (Toronto: University of Toronto Press, 1993), p. 26.
2. James Hughes, "Moscow's Bilateral Treaties Add to Confusion," *Transition* (September 20, 1996).
3. Sergei Valenti, "Russian Reforms and Russian Federalism," *Anthropology & Archaeology of Eurasia*, vol. 36, no. 1 (1997): 73–85.
4. "*K 2015 gody respublika 'postareet' na vocem' protsentov*," *Molodesh severa*, 9 July 1998, p. 2.
5. The majority of this information on Komi comes from "Regional Profile: Komi Republic," *IEWS Russian Regional Report* (Executive Edition), 2 April, 1998.
6. I would like to thank Tamara Resler for helping me formulate the ideas for this section.
7. Gagnon,"The Political Uses of Federalism," p. 37.
8. Daniel Elazar, "International and Comparative Federalism," *PS: Political Science and Politics* (June 1993): 191.
9. Zvi Gitleman, "Federalism and Multiculturalism in Socialist Systems," in Daniel Elazar (Ed.), *Federalism and Political Integration* (Tel Aviv, Israel: Turtledove Publishing, 1979): 162–163.
10. Vladimir Lysenko, "*Problemy Razvitiia Federativnykh Otnoshenii v Sovremennoi Rossii*," *Kentavr* (March-April 1995): 24.
11. Ibid., p. 25.
12. Hughes, "Moscow's Bilateral Treaties," p. 41.

13. Vladimir Lysenko, "How Strong Are the Treaty Foundations of Federative Relations," *Anthropology & Archeology of Eurasia*, vol. 36, no. 1 (1997): 33–55. For a similar discussion in the same journal, see Egor Stroev, "Rossiiskii Federalism," pp. 86–93.

14. Valenti, "Russian Reforms," pp. 78–79.

15. Ibid., p. 79.

16. Lysenko, "How Strong Are the Treaty Foundations," p. 52.

17. Hughes, "Moscow's Bilateral Treaties," p. 43.

18. Elazar, "International and Comparative Federalism," p. 193. Also, see Juan Linz and Alfred Stepan, *Problems of Democratic Transition and Consolidation: Southern Europe, South America, and Post-Communist Europe* (Baltimore: Johns Hopkins University Press, 1996).

19. This discussion is drawn from Peter Ordeshook, "Russia's Party System: Is Russian Federalism Viable," *Post-Soviet Affairs*, vol. 12, no. 3 (1996): 195–217, and Peter Ordeshook and Olga Shvetsova, "Federalism and Constitutional Design," *Journal of Democracy*, vol. 8, no. 1 (January 1997).

20. Elazar, "International and Comparative Federalism," p. 193.

21. Vladimir Shumeiko, "Real Federalism as the Basis for the State Organization of Russia," *Anthropology & Archaeology of Eurasia*, vol. 36, no. 1 (1997): 29.

22. James Alexander, "Uncertain Conditions in the Russian Transition: The Popular Drive Toward Stability in a "Stateless" Environment," *Europe-Asia Studies*, vol. 50, no. 3 (1998): 415–443.

23. Elazar, "International and Comparative Federalism," p. 192.

24. Robert W. Tucker, *The Soviet Political Mind* (New York: Frederick A. Praeger, 1963): 70.

25. Robert Brym, "Re-evaluating Mass Support for Political and Economic Change in Russia," *Europe-Asia Studies*, vol. 48, no. 5 (1996): 751–766; James Alexander, *Political Culture in Post-communist Russia: Formlessness and Recreation in a Traumatic Transition* (New York: St. Martin's Press, 2000).

26. Michael Burgess, "Federalism as Political Ideology: Interests, Benefits and Beneficiaries in Federalism and Federation," in Burgess and Alain-G. Gagnon (Eds.), *Comparative Federalism and Federation* (Toronto: University of Toronto Press, 1993), p. 107. See also, Ordeshook and Shvetsova, "Federalism and Constitutional Design," p. 28.

27. Ordeshook, "Russia's Party System." See also, John T. Ishiyama, "The Russian Proto-parties and the National Republics: Integrative Organizations in a Disintegrating World," *Communist and Post-Communist Studies*, vol. 29, no. 4 (1996): 395–411.

28. Interview with Valerii Potolitsin (Director for the Committee on Legislation and Deputy Ethics), July 1, 1997.

29. *TASS* (March 19, 1991) in *FBIS-SOV-91–055* (March 21, 1991); and *Radio Rossii* (March 25, 1991) in *FBIS-SOV-91–58* (March 26, 1991).

30. *Vesti* (October 24, 1991) in *FBIS-SOV* 91–208 (October 28, 1991).

31. Moscow Russian Television Network (February 15, 1992) in *FBIS-SOV-92–032* (February 18, 1992).

32. Vladimir Shlapentokh, *From Submission to Rebellion* (Boulder: Westview Press, 1997), pp. 99–100.

33. *POSTFACTUM* (March 20, 1992) in *FBIS-SOV-92–056* (March 23, 1992).

34. Igor Bobrakov, "*Partiia vlasti zakonchila reformu vlasti*," *Molodesh severa*, 2 February 1995, 4.

35. Igor Bobrakov, "*Partiia vlasti zakonchila reformu vlasti*," *Molodesh severa*, 2 February 1995, 4.

36. Peter Kirkow, "Regional Warlordism in Russia: The Case of Primorskii *Krai*," *Europe-Asia Studies*, vol. 47, no. 6 (1995), pp. 926, 940; James Hughes, "Sub-national Elites and Post-communist Transformation in Russia: A Reply to Kryshtanovskaya & White," *Europe-Asia Studies*, vol. 49, no. 6 (1997), p. 1031; Neil J. Melvin, "The Consolidation of a New Regional Elite: The Case of Omsk 1987–1995," *Europe-Asia Studies*, vol. 50, no. 4 (1998), p. 627; and, D. V. Badovskii and A. Iu. Shutov, "Regional Elites in Post-Soviet Russia: Aspects of Political Involvement," *Russian Social Science Review*, vol. 38, no. 3 (May-June 1997), p. 33; and Darrel Slider, "Privatization in Russia's Regions," *Post-Soviet Affairs*, vol. 10, no. 4 (1994), p. 377.

37. Interview with Sergei Gusiatnikov, State Council Deputy and Deputy Agriculture Minister, July 4, 1997.

38. Interview with Igor Bobrakov, Assistant Editor (*Molodesh Severa*), July 4 1997.

39. ITAR-TASS (November 25, 1997) in *FBIS-SOV-97–329* (November 27, 1997).

40. ROSSIYA (May 4, 1994) in *FBIS-USR-94–055* (May 25, 1994), p. 27.

41. Rossiyskaya Gazeta (May 17–23, 1997) in *FBIS-SOV-97–120* (May 23, 1997).

42. ROSSIYA (May 4, 1994) in *FBIS-USR-94–055* (May 25, 1994), p. 27.

43. Ibid.

44. "Ekho Moskvy," *Molodesh Severa*, January 1, 1999, p. 3.

45. James Alexander, *Political Culture in Post-communist Russia*, p. 196.

46. Ibid., p. 88.

47. Ibid., p. 197.

48. Ibid., pp. 94–95.

49. *Rossiyskiye Vesti* (November 4, 1997) in *FBIS-SOV-97–310* (November 6, 1997).

50. Interview with Vasilii Kuznetsov, Director of the Committee for the Budget, Taxes and Economic Policy (State Council of the Komi Republic), July 14, 1997. Alleged corrupt practices being discussed in Komi in 1997 burst onto the national scene in February 1997. See, S. Sorokin, "Korruptsiyu v Komi obsudiat v Moskve," *Molodesh Severa* (February 11, 1999), p. 2.

51. Alexander, *Political Culture in Post-communist Russia*, p. 175.

52. Interview with Valerii Potolitsin, Director of the Committee for Legislation and Deputy Ethics (State Council of the Komi Republic), July 1, 1997.

53. Ordeshook, "Russia's Party System."

54. Ishiyama, "Russian Proto-parties."

55. Bobrakov interview, July 4, 1997.

56. Interview with Olga Savast'ianova, Director Komi Division of Women of Russia, July 7, 1997.

57. Bobrakov interview, July 4, 1997.

58. Ibid.

59. *Gagnon*, "The Political Uses of Federalism."

60. Bobrakov interview, July 4, 1997.

61. Shumeiko, "Real Federalism as a Basis."

62. Yurii Shabaev, "Komi Republic Concerned Over Russian Government Reshuffle," *IEWS Russian Regional Report* (Internet Edition), vol. 3, no. 14 (9 April, 1998).

63. Natal'ia Melnikova, *"Zashchita regiona - v edinstve i soglasii," Respublika*, 20 October 1998, p. 3. With changes in Spiridonov's leadership, Bobrakov showed that political allegiances are far from permanent. By summer 1999 he had been partially coopted into Spiridonov's circle. In addition to participating actively in Transformation of the North, Bobrakov had been hired as a correspondent for the republic's official newspaper, *Respublika*.

64. "Ekho Moskvy," p. 3.

65. A. Lisov, *Demokraticheskii blok: tret'ia popytka," Molodesh Severa*, October 22, 1998, p. 2.

66. Gusiatnikov interview, July 4, 1997. The discussion concerning trade with Belarus occurred in the presence of an assenting trade representative from the former Soviet republic.

67. *Rossiyskaya Gazeta* (May 23, 1997) in *FBIS-SOV-97–120* (June 24, 1997).

68. Radio Rossii network (December 16, 1997) in *FBIS-SOV-97–350* (December 18, 1997) and INTERFAX Belarus Business Report (December 22, 1997) in *FBIS-SOV-97–356* (December 29, 1997.

69. Trud (May 29, 1997).

70. EKONOMIKA I ZHIZN (April 18, 1996) in *FBIS-SOV-96–076–S* (April 19, 1996).

71. Yuri Shabaev, "Komi President Seeks Better Deal from Moscow," *IEWS Russian Regional Report* (Internet Edition), vol. 3, no. 6 (February 12, 1998).

72. Yuri Shabaev, "Komi's Chief Lobbies for Subsidies, Tax Breaks," *EWI Russian Regional Report* (Internet Edition), vol. 3, no. 51 (December 22, 1998). While a good sign for a deepening federal relationship, at the time of this article's completion, it was still too early to assess the new law's effectiveness.

73. Savast'ianova interview, July 7, 1997; Interview with Lutsia Viter (Director of the Komi Republic's Union Committee for Health Workers), July 7, 1997; and, Andrei Borodikin (Chief of the Mayor's Press Center), July 14, 1997.

74. Yuri Shabaev, "Komi Struggles with Financial Crisis," *IEWS Russian Regional Report* (Internet Edition), vol. 3, no. 26 (July 2, 1998).

75. ITAR-TASS (October 7, 1997), in *FBIS-SOV-97–280* (October 8, 1997) and Rossiyskaya Gazeta (May 23, 1997).

76. During 1994–1995, Komi under-received about 250 billion rubles from the federal budget. In turn, during the first six months of the following year only 48 percent of taxes paid into the federal budget were received. See Rossiyskiye Vesti (July 12, 1996) in *FBIS-SOV-96–187–S* (September 27, 1996) and Rossiyskiye Vesti (July 25, 1996) in *FBIS-SOV-96–147* (July 31, 1996).

77. Rossiyskaya Gazeta (May 23, 1997).

78. "Komi Leader Speaks Out," *IEWS Russian Regional Report* (Internet Edition), vol. 3, no. 31 (August 13, 1998).

79. NTV (October 18, 1997) in *FBIS-SOV-97–291* (October 22, 1997).

80. Yuri Shabaev, "Komi Must Live Without Federal Aid in 1999," *EWI Russian Regional Report*, vol. 4, no. 3 (January 28, 1999).

81. See James Alexander, "Pluralism in the Komi Republic? Overcoming Executive Resistance," *Demokratizatsiya*, vol. 7, no. 3 (Summer 1999): 370–382.

82. Yuri Shabaev, "Komi Chief Speaks out on Relations with Center," *EWI Russian Regional Report* (Internet Edition), vol. 3, no. 26 (July 2, 1998).

83. Yuri Shabaev, "Party of Power Dominates in Komi State Council Elections," *EWI Russian Regional Report*, vol. 4, no. 5 (February 11, 1999). Even though they are often resistant, Komi officials are willing to recognize federal court decisions. For example, in September 1998 the State Council complied with a spring 1998 Russian Constitutional Court ruling that employees in state service cannot simultaneously hold a legislative position. See Yuri Shabaev, "Komi Parliament Loses Some Civil Servant Members," *EWI Russian Regional Report* (Internet Edition), vol. 3, no. 44 (November 5, 1998).

84. Pavel Krotov, "Simptomy 'Gollandskoi bolezni' naidetsia li lekarstvo? Bozmozhnosti ekonomicheskoi stabilizatsii resursnogo regiona," *Respublika Komi: vlast,' biznes, politika* (Syktyvkar: Institut regional'nykh sotsial'nykh issledovanii Respubliki Komi, 1998), pp. 8–29.

85. The resignation of Boris Yeltsin and accession of Vladimir Putin to the presidency in winter 1999–2000 implants more uncertainty into the development of Russian federalism. This is most evident in Putin's 2000 reforms of the Federation Council and the creation of seven "super" regions to simplify and further centralize Kremlin control over Russia's 89 regions. While it is difficult to forecast the results of these reforms, they do not necessarily undermine the development of Russian federalism, although they could well change the direction.

CHAPTER 4

THE CASE OF SAKHA: BARGAINING WITH MOSCOW

Daniel R. Kempton

This chapter uses the institutional framework laid out in Chapter 2 to trace the evolution of the relations between the Republic of Sakha (Yakutia) and the Russian center. It accepts the basic premise that Russian center-periphery relations have passed through several discrete stages of institutional change. Each stage is demarcated by a unique constitutional arrangement, which determined the basic roles of the game for political conflict during that stage. Each stage is also characterized by a primary conflict between at least two federal institutions. Finally, the constitutional arrangements combined with the primary conflict helped to set basic rules of the game for center-periphery relations during each stage.[1]

The first stage began with Boris Yeltsin's election to the chairmanship of the Russian Supreme Soviet and ended with the collapse of the Soviet Union in December 1991. During this stage the discredited 1977 Constitution still formally guided the Soviet Union. The central political dynamic in Soviet politics throughout this period was the struggle between the Soviet government and the governments of Russia and the other union republics. The second stage began with Russian independence and ended with the promulgation of the new Constitution in December 1993. The rules of the game, while rather loosely defined, were set by the often-amended Russian Constitution of 1978. While this Constitution was given some legitimacy, it was considered unworkable by most, and bore little similarity to the real practice of power in Russia. For example, while the 1978 Constitution made the parliament supreme, it was clearly the president who dominated the political process. During this period the central institutional conflict was between the Russian president and the Soviet-era Russian parliament. Yeltsin's October 1993 coup against the Russian parliament and subsequent promulgation of the new Constitution opened the third and present stage of center-periphery relations. The central political conflict of this period continues to be a parliamentary-presidential struggle. However, the current system—as defined by the new Constitution—is a presidential system. It provides for an elected but relatively weak parliament, the bicameral Federal Assembly. The powers given to the president, however, are much greater than in most western systems, parliamentary or presidential. The remainder of this chapter traces the evolving powers and responsibilities of one *subekt* of the Russian Federation, the Republic of Sakha (Yakutia), through these three stages.

STAGE 1: THE SOVIET COLLAPSE

The Republic of Sakha is vast frozen land in central Siberia. It contains approximately one fifth of Russia's total land area, but is sparsely populated with just over a million people inhabiting more than 1.2 million square miles. Most of the population resides in a relatively few large cities. The obvious reason for the discrepancy is climate. Nearly a third of Sakha lies north of the Arctic Circle. It is the coldest region of the world inhabited by people year around. What compensates for the harshness of life in Sakha is that it is one of Russia's most richly endowed *subekty*. It produces 97 percent of Russia's diamonds, 21 percent of its gold and 100 percent of its antimony.[2] It also holds a seemingly inexhaustible supply of coal, tin, fish, timber, furs, and a variety of other resources.

Life in Sakha during the Soviet period was extremely harsh. It was difficult, therefore, to attract the necessary labor to extract raw materials from Sakha and the rest of Siberia. To meet this shortage two basic methods were used. First, following Tsarist tradition, but on a grander and more horrific scale, the Soviets sent prisoners to extract Siberia's resources. Millions died in the Soviet *gulag archipelago* before Khrushchev began dismantling the system in the mid-1950s. The second method was to attract volunteers to Siberia with special incentives and higher wages. As thousands of *prishlie* (newcomers) flowed into Sakha they gradually surpassed the native population. The Sakha (or Yakut as the Russians called them) are not technically native to the region. They are a pastoral people of Turkic origin that gradually migrated from the southwest some seven centuries ago.[3] The Sakha, who comprised 80 percent of the population in 1922, dropped to approximately 33 percent by the close of the Soviet period. Most of the *prishlie* are of Slavic origin including: Russians, Belorussians, and Ukrainians. At the time of the last census (1989), the Russians alone comprised approximately 50 percent of the population. Since the collapse of the Union, many Russians have left. As a result, the Sakha people now comprise closer to 38 percent of the population.[4]

Gorbachev's reforms brought both new opportunities and serious problems for Sakha. In the latter category, Gorbachev's *perestroika* (restructuring) of the Soviet economy consumed vast capital resources both for the retooling of the decrepit Soviet industry and for the importation of the foreign consumer goods necessary to maintain the support of the Soviet people. As Bradshaw reminds us, "*perestroika* was an emphasis on the modernization of the existing industrial facilities rather than the development of new ones."[5] Thus the policy tended to favor the European regions of the Soviet Union, where the existing industries were located. The big losers in these budgetary reallocations were large-scale, capital-intensive projects, such as those necessary to open new mines and to extend existing transportation routes into remote regions throughout Siberia. Sakha was particularly plagued by serious transportation problems. Sakha's economy depended on a few key transportation routes to export its raw materials and import its industrial goods, fuel, and foodstuffs. Three-fifths of these goods were shipped by way of the Lena River and its tributaries, which were only navigable for half the year. Its only potential major year-round transportation links are the Baykal-Amur Mainline (BAM) and the Trans-Siberian Railroads. Unfortunately, funding for the planned Amur-Yakutsk Mainline (designed to link Sakha to the above railroads) evaporated during *perestroika*. Most of Sakha's goods had to be shipped to the mouth of the Lena River and then traverse down the river during the short summer season while the river was still navigable. The industrial and consumer goods necessary during the long winter had to be purchased in advance. Concurrently, Sakha's exports were sent north up the Lena during the same period. However, Sakha was not paid for its exports until after they reached Moscow and were sold. Thus, Sakha's winter economy survived largely on the availability of summer credit. However, with *perestroika* vast sums of capital were absorbed in the importation of consumer goods and the amount of credit available to Sakha and other regions decreased dramatically.

A collateral effect of Sakha's transportation problems was the inflated prices its consumers paid to offset the high transportation costs. With *perestroika* the manufactured goods and foodstuffs Sakha imported were both scarcer and dramatically more expensive. While past Soviet regimes compensated for Siberia's inflated prices and scarcities with premium pay, during the Gorbachev years inflation overwhelmed the meager pay increases approved to offset the inflated prices paid by Siberians.

The Siberian governments and state industries were similarly harmed by the pricing policies of the *perestroika* years. While the state allowed dramatic inflation in both transportation costs and consumer goods, it refused to raise the price of the raw materials produced by Sakha. Even when Sakha's raw materials were sold on the international market for hard currency, the amount received by Sakha was unaffected. This led Mikhail Nikolayev, then Chairman of Sakha's Supreme Soviet, to conclude that the central government was "robbing" Sakha of its raw materials.[6] He claimed that every year Sakha gave the Soviet government about $1.5 billion in foreign currency earnings and Sakha received only about four percent of that sum for itself.

On the positive side of the ledger *perestroika*, and the *glasnost* (openness) which accompanied it, allowed Sakha to pursue its political and economic concerns in ways theretofore unimaginable. Beginning in 1989 a number of organizations were formed or revived to promote the political, cultural, and economic rights of the Sakha people. While these organizations initially focused on cultural issues, such as the restoration of native languages, they soon edged into more political issues, such as granting the local people a greater share of the wealth from the resources extracted from their lands. Their arguments found ready support within the political hierarchy, which was disproportionately staffed by ethnic Sakhas. (Russians tend to dominate in the economic hierarchy of the republic.)

A second early source of political initiative was the mining industry. In 1989 and 1990 a large number of mining unions—frustrated by their low wages, poor living conditions and lack of safe working conditions—began addressing their complaints to the Soviet government and the increasingly independent Russian government. When public appeals and protests failed to prompt a satisfactory response, the miners turned to more forceful methods. Led by the more militant coal miners, the mining unions began a wave of work stoppages and strikes throughout the Soviet Union. By the summer of 1991 many of Sakha's gold miners had joined the unrest.[7] They were infuriated that Gorbachev was selling the gold they mined on the world market to subsidize his reforms, while they were paid only a fraction of market prices. Many gold mining operations, particularly the independent *artely*, either joined the strike or simply stopped shipping gold to Moscow. While Gorbachev saw the miners as a threat, Yeltsin looked on their unrest as an opportunity. He promised the miners higher wages and better conditions if they transferred their production to the Russian government.

The combined pressure from the miners and the newly formed cultural organizations prompted Sakha's government to action. In September 1990 Sakha sought to raise its status within the Soviet Union and changed its name from the Yakut Autonomous Soviet Socialist Republic (ASSR) to the Yakut-Sakha Soviet Socialist Republic (SSR). It then issued a declaration of state sovereignty, which asserted that all natural resources on its territory, including its rich deposits of gold and diamonds, were the property of the people of Sakha. There was even talk of charging Moscow for the right to extract Sakha's resources. When Gorbachev refused to accept Sakha's claims, the flow of diamonds to Moscow was temporarily severed.

Preoccupied with his battle against Gorbachev's government, Yeltsin welcomed the steps toward sovereignty taken by Sakha and Russia's other republics. Drawing on the arguments of some of Russia's leading democrats, he adopted the slogan of sovereignty from the ground up.[8] What this meant was that Soviet sovereignty had to be built on the consent and support of the federal republics and Russian sovereignty would be built on the consent of its *subekty*. Toward this end, he welcomed the *subekty*'s declarations of sovereignty, declaring in September 1990 that Russia's republics should "take all the sovereignty they could swallow." Shortly thereafter he supported the republics' claims to control their own resources.[9] Yeltsin's strategy, which was designed to win the support of Russia's republics in his battle with Gorbachev, was highly successful.

Nikolayev, the chairman of Sakha's Supreme Soviet and Sakha's elected president after December 1991, became one of Yeltsin's most dependable supporters. Nikolayev and Yeltsin reached a number of early understandings. They agreed in principle that after Russian independence, Sakha would be granted a much greater role in the extraction, development and sale of its resources. In particular Sakha would be allowed to keep all or most of its locally generated tax revenues. Yeltsin also promised that Sakha would be allowed to independently sell and receive the profits from at least 10 percent of its diamond sales.[10] (This was later increased to 20%.) While 20 percent might seem small, the value of Sakha's annual diamond sales was estimated at between $1 billion and $1.5 billion.[11] To symbolize the new relationship, in early December 1991 Nikolayev presented Yeltsin with a 241.7 carat diamond named "Free Russia." The ceremony marked Russia's impending independence and Sakha's transfer of control over its diamonds, and other natural resources, to the Russian government.

Even before Gorbachev's resignation was operative, Sakha began employing the powers it had claimed and those specifically promised by Yeltsin. In taking more control of the diamond industry, Sakha's Council of Ministers decided to close down one of its giant diamond plants because of the extensive damage it was causing to the local environment.[12] At the same time, Sakha's leaders were eager to increase the percentage of its diamonds cut locally. Although Sakha produces more than 98 percent of Russia's diamonds, only a small percentage was cut in Sakha. Yet the cutting and processing of diamonds adds more than 15 percent to their total value. The Soviet Union (and Russia as its successor) was contractually bound to sell its uncut diamonds at a set price via De Beers, but it could sell cut diamonds directly to the highest bidder.[13] Moreover, while diamond mining provides relatively little employment, the cutting and processing of diamonds is quite labor intensive. Thus, in 1991 Sakha's government launched a new firm, *Tuymaada* Diamond—a joint stock company, with the express purpose of expanding secondary diamond industries in Sakha. *Tuymaada* then signed agreements with firms from Belgium, Japan, and South Korea to build 16 new cutting factories and a host of related industries. De Beers itself agreed to become a partner in the construction of a major cutting plant with the capacity to cut 100,000 carats per year. These plants are expected to ultimately employ approximately 2,000 cutters, many of whom have now completed their training.[14] By 1994 *Tuymaada* had opened six plants, with more than 900 employees, and had increased its capital from 10 million rubles to 1.837 billion rubles.[15]

Finally, Sakha followed Russia's lead and signed an agreement allowing De Beers' Central Selling Organization to market its allotted independent diamond sales. To develop its tremendous natural gas reserves, Sakha also signed an agreement with a South Korean consortium to explore the possibility of building a gas pipeline to South Korea in order to export gas throughout the Pacific Rim.[16]

In sum, the late Soviet period was characterized by an intense political battle at the center, which Sakha exploited to extract concessions from both sides. During this period Nikolayev received numerous promises of greater economic and political autonomy from Yeltsin. In exchange, Yeltsin received Sakha's political support. While Yeltsin had not specifically approved of many of Sakha's self-declarations regarding its sovereignty and right to the ownership of its natural resources, he supported these rights in principle. Moreover, Nikolayev received specific promises from Yeltsin regarding the ownership and sale of some of its resources. Because the 1977 Soviet Constitution provided little specifics as to the powers of the *subekty* within Russia, which was then itself a federal republic of the Soviet Union, both Yeltsin and Gorbachev were relatively unconstrained in their commitments to the *subekty*. Moreover, because of the institutional ambiguity as to the powers of Russia and the Soviet government, the *subekty* were able to make fairly radical demands for sovereignty and economic autonomy with little fear of harsh reactions from Moscow.

Sakha's relationship with the federal government during this first stage was clearly marked by at least one of the necessary characteristics of federalism discussed in Chapter 2. Although Sakha was not truly a "voluntary" member of the Soviet state, the division of powers was voluntary to the extent that Sakha was free to unilaterally claim many powers and rights. At the same time, Sakha had little ability to exercise the powers it claimed. Yeltsin sought to build consensus with the *subekty*; Gorbachev did not feel similarly compelled. Yet, it was Gorbachev who controlled the central government. Unlike the *subekty* that sought independence (Tatarstan and Chechnya), Sakha successfully upgraded its status within the Soviet Union. While neither Gorbachev nor Yeltsin challenged Sakha's declarations, they were not institutionalized in a written constitution. And, there were many in Moscow, particularly in the Supreme Soviet, who recognized neither Sakha's claims nor Yeltsin's assurances. In reality, there was no clear division of powers, nor was there an institution or mechanism to adjudicate disputes and Russian political culture never accepted the legitimacy of Sakha's claims. Finally, while Sakha was free to claim whatever powers it liked, it had no formal or meaningful voice in the creation of federal policy. Its representatives in the Congress of People's Deputies, elected in March 1989, had no direct ties to Sakha's government and Sakha had no power over them. Moreover, the functional legislature was really the Supreme Soviet, which was elected by and from the Congress with no guarantees for regional representation.

STAGE 2: THE BATTLE FOR RUSSIA

As discussed in Chapter 2, after Russian independence Yeltsin was more able to deliver on his promises to Sakha, but much less inclined to do so. Not surprisingly, therefore, Russian independence was accompanied by rumors that the center would renege on many of its promised concessions. By January 1992 Sakha still was not being allowed to independently sell 10 percent of its diamonds as promised and there was no change in its taxes. In fact, officials in the Russian government were suggesting that Sakha should contribute at least 65 percent of its revenues to the federal government. Moreover, opposition to giving Sakha a large portion of the diamond profits was building within the Russian Supreme Soviet. The government of Sakha, however, insisted that all promises be kept without compromise.

During this stage Sakha simultaneously sought redress for its concerns along two distinct tracks. First, beginning in January it entered bilateral negotiations with Moscow on the taxation issue and on sharing control of and revenues from the diamond industry. These negotiations were in a sense competitive in that whatever concessions Sakha extracted from the center would not automatically be granted to the other *subekty*. If Moscow signed bilateral agreements with the wealthier and more powerful *subekty* limiting their contribution to federal revenues, this would reduce the concessions Moscow could afford to make to the remaining *subekty*. Second, Nikolayev increasingly became a major player in the effort to sign a comprehensive agreement between all the *subekty* and Moscow, which would specify a clear division of powers between the *subekty* and the federal government as required by our first characteristic of federalism. While both sets of negotiations were to prove exceptionally difficult and laden with pitfalls, both brought tangible results.

In the bilateral negotiations, Ruslan Khasbulatov (Chairman of the Russian Supreme Soviet) and his parliamentary supporters initially sought to outbid Yeltsin for the support of Sakha and the other *subekty*. During a January tour of Siberia, Khasbulatov pledged parliamentary support for both Sakha's right to a share of the diamond revenues and for Nikolayev's call for a bilateral agreement delineating Sakha's economic and political rights within the Russian Federation.[17] He warned, however, that the government (particularly Yeltsin) could not be trusted to fully understand and take into account the peculiarities of each region. In February the Supreme Soviet passed an ambiguous "Law on Mineral Resources," which promised the *subekty* and the local governments each one-third of the profits from minerals mined from their lands.[18] Later it enacted legislation giving the *subekty* a greater oversight role in mining decisions.[19]

Yeltsin's offers, however, proved more substantive and more reliable. On March 31 an agreement was signed that gave Sakha a major role in the diamond industry and raised its share of independent diamond sales to 20 percent of all diamonds mined in the republic. The centerpiece of the agreement was the formation of a new diamond firm called *Almazy Rossii-Sakha* (Diamonds of Russia and Sakha, henceforth ARS). ARS was created as a joint stock corporation with shares assigned: 32 percent to the Russian Federation, 32 percent to the government of Sakha, 23 percent to workers' groups, five percent to a retirement fund, and one percent to each of eight local governments.[20] Profits are shared accordingly. While the details have never been made public, Sakha was also given control of 11.5 percent of all the gold mined in the republic.[21]

The legality and prudence of ARS's formation were repeatedly and vociferously challenged in the Supreme Soviet. Critics contended that Sakha was given far too great a role in the diamond industry, which it might use to increase revenues even beyond the generous allotment the agreement provided for, or to destroy the cutting industry outside Sakha by denying it access to profitable stones for finishing. They also argued that without strong parliamentary oversight, *Almazy Rossii-Sakha* would be subject to manipulation by De Beers and its international diamond cartel.[22]

Yeltsin ignored his parliamentary critics. When they refused to pass the legislation creating *Almazy Rossii-Sakha*, in December 1992 he issued a presidential decree to provide a legal basis for the firm. While Sakha's leaders still complained about the slowness with which Sakha was paid for its diamonds, they were generally pleased. By 1994 payments from ARS comprised about one-half of Sakha's budget.[23]

Concomitant to ARS's formation, Nikolayev and Yeltsin came to terms on an innovative agreement on Sakha's taxes. The agreement allowed Sakha to use the federal taxes it collected to pay for all federal personnel and programs on its territory. Only after these obligations were met were the remaining revenues sent to Moscow.[24] While this process did not allow Sakha to evade its tax commitment to Moscow, it did ensure that federal programs in Sakha were fully funded (a growing problem elsewhere), before any revenues were sent to Moscow.

In March 1992 the multilateral negotiations culminated in the signing the Federal Treaty. Although Nikolayev had played a key role in the negotiations, the treaty fell far short of his expectation. Thus Sakha signed the treaty only after special assurances and considerable persuading.[25] Ultimately, the Federal Treaty affirmed the special "sovereign" status of the republics and gave them many new powers. These included the right to conduct their own foreign policy and foreign trade.[26] Of critical importance to Sakha and the other mineral-producing republics, the Treaty said that the land and resources of the republics belonged to the people living there. However, ownership and use of the land, and its mineral resources, are subject to the regulations of both republican and federal law.

Despite the compromising nature of the Federal Treaty and its ambiguous status, Nikolayev continued to back Yeltsin in the struggle for the center. In April when Yeltsin called a referendum to break the deadlock he received the enthusiastic support of a few select republican leaders. Among his staunchest supporters was Nikolayev, who boasted that some 70 percent of Sakha's population backed Yeltsin.[27] That summer Yeltsin rewarded Nikolayev's support with a presidential decree that, if implemented, would have repealed the necessity of preliminary payments for shipments to Sakha.[28] Nikolayev also received Yeltsin's promise to deal personally with Sakha's shipping problems.[29] However, Nikolayev still refused to unequivocally endorse Yeltsin's draft constitution because it did not incorporate the Federal Treaty.

By the end of that summer, Yeltsin amended his draft constitution to include the basic text of the Federal Treaty. In doing so it recognized the republics as "sovereign" within Russia. (It did not clarify how "sovereign" republics could exist within a "sovereign" Russia.) The new draft also protected the bilateral concession won by Sakha and others. Finally, it promised the *subekty* a role in federal politics in the upper chamber of a new bicameral parliament. However, Sakha's parliamentary leaders saw these concessions as insufficient. In a meeting of the Presidium of the Supreme Soviet of Sakha, members argued that the draft constitution's articles on Russia's federal system called for an equalization of the status of all the *subekty*.[30] They contended that the principal of "territorial *guberniyazation*" elaborated in Yeltsin's draft constitution provided for a unitary state and "a mechanical leveling" of all *subekty*. Thus, they refused to even submit the draft for consideration by Sakha's full Soviet.

Nikolayev, however, continued his by then well-established strategy of trading political support for Yeltsin for economic and political rewards.[31] He publicly backed Yeltsin and his revised draft constitution. When relations between Yeltsin and the Russian Supreme Soviet continued to erode, Nikolayev endorsed Yeltsin's call for parliamentary elections. In August 1993, Yeltsin rewarded him with a presidential decree creating a program for social and economic development in Sakha, which was billed as a measure for implementing the Federal Treaty.[32] A development fund was to be created as a joint stock company with funds coming from the federal government, Sakha, and, in some cases, foreign investors. Capital from the fund would then be invested in programs to improve Sakha's housing, transportation, and agriculture.

During the crisis of October 1993 Nikolayev remained one of Yeltsin's most stalwart supporters. In late September, when many *subekty* leaders endorsed the parliament or refused to back either side, Nikolayev called a special session of the Supreme Soviet of Sakha, which expressed its unequivocal support for the president. Even after Yeltsin ordered the troops to take the parliament by force, Nikolayev continued to blame the parliament and endorse Yeltsin.[33] This time his reward was a presidential decree promising Sakha interest-free credit until 1998.[34]

The toughest decision for Nikolayev, however, was whether to endorse Yeltsin's final draft constitution, scheduled for approval on the same ballot as the December 1993 parliamentary elections. The final draft, which was unveiled just weeks before the constitutional plebiscite, contained numerous setbacks for the *subekty*, and the republics in particular. Nikolayev could not, therefore, endorse the draft. But by then Nikolayev had invested too heavily in Yeltsin to risk the numerous bilateral concessions Sakha had received. Nikolayev outlined his position artfully. He argued that no one believed that this was Russia's final constitution.[35] However, he suggested that it could be "strengthened" after the plebiscite by explicitly guaranteeing the sovereignty of the republics or by incorporating the Federal Treaty into its text. At the same time, Nikolayev argued that Russia could no longer function normally without a new constitution.[36] Thus, without endorsing the Constitution itself, he campaigned for its adoption in the plebiscite. Although Nikolayev's own vice president, Vyacheslav Shtyrov, refused to vote for the Constitution, Nikolayev's efforts were successful. Despite frigid temperatures, Sakha produced a 65 percent turnout, and more critically, 53 percent support for the Constitution.[37]

By the end of the second stage, Sakha's relations with Russia exhibited more of the necessary conditions of federalism than in the first stage. Most importantly, there was a clearer division of powers between Sakha and the federal government. Sakha's struggles had brought explicit and significant concessions. Sakha was able to keep a large portion of the profits from the diamond industry and had the discretionary powers to use those profits however its leaders saw fit. Also of great importance were the powers over taxation that Sakha's bilateral treaty granted it. With respect to federalism, more important than the right to keep federal tax rubles at home, was the Sakha's right to select which federal institutions would be paid. During this stage Sakha also gained considerable autonomy at home, which was specified both in the Federal Treaty and its numerous bilateral agreements with Moscow.

The way in which Sakha gained these rights was largely consensual, as required by the first necessary condition of federalism. Although Sakha had not gained all the rights and powers it sought, the ones it was given were derived from "consensual" negotiations. Sakha's leaders played a major role both in the development of its bilateral treaties and in the evolution and passage of the multilateral Federal Treaty.

On one hand, a significant barrier to stable federal relations was that the rights gained by Sakha were not enshrined in the Russian Constitution during the second stage. On the other hand, unlike during the first stage, the division of powers between Sakha and the federal government was made explicit through a series of bilateral agreement. Moreover, the legality of such agreements had been confirmed by the Federal Treaty. However, whether or not the Federal Treaty would be incorporated into the forthcoming constitution became a major subject of controversy between the federal government and many of the *subekty*. Thus, while stage two brought a clearer division of powers, it was not an unambiguous division. Federal representation for Sakha, the fourth necessary precondition, technically existed, but was not particularly meaningful. Thus, Nikolayev actively supported the creation of a parliamentary house directly representative of the *subekty*. Russia also lacked a formal mechanism for adjudicating disagreements of interpretation as to the division of powers. Nor was there a national political culture that would support Sakha's claims against the center. To the contrary, many of the other *subekty*, republics and territories alike, resented the impressive powers that Sakha and a few other republics were able to accrue.

In sum, during the second stage Sakha succeeded in institutionalizing many of the powers it gained, but Sakha's relations with the Russian center entailed too few of the necessary conditions for federalism to comfortably refer to the relationship as a federal one. Moreover, the lack of some of the beneficial conditions was also beginning to cause problems. In particular, the asymmetry between the *subekty* was becoming a point of considerable tension.

STAGE 3: THE NEW RUSSIA

The introduction of the 1993 Russian Constitution ushered in a new stage in Russian center-periphery relations. For Sakha, this was undoubtedly a mixed blessing. On the one hand, many of the bilateral agreements Sakha had negotiated were granted far more secure legal status by the Constitution's explicit acceptance of bilateral treaties as the mode of conducting center-periphery relations. On June 29, 1995, Nikolayev and Yeltsin signed a bilateral agreement that affirmed and codified 15 previous bilateral agreements.[38] (Independent gold sales apparently increased from 12 to 15%.) In the assessment of Blazer and Vinokurova, the agreement granted Sakha:

> Unprecedented economic leeway in making foreign contact, distributing profits and allocating taxes. Republic jurisdiction extends to internal districting, as well as health, education, science and cultural policy.[39]

On the other hand, the absence of a clear competitor to Yeltsin, at least initially, and the strength of the new presidential powers left Yeltsin freer to conduct a campaign to "retake" the *subekty*. This effort was also support by many regions, and other *subekty*, that believed that some republics had grabbed too much autonomy.

A number of the general attempt to retake the *subekty* had a direct affect on Sakha. First, after the defeat of the Supreme Soviet Yeltsin issued a decree mandating new elections for all regional soviets, many of which had sided with the Supreme Soviet. Although this decree was merely "recommended" for Sakha, it complied without delay. Second, in July 1997 Yeltsin issued a decree that dramatically increased the powers of his presidential representative, an institution that he then proposed extending to the republics as well as to the regions. According to the decree, the presidential representatives would oversee the use of federal funds by the *subekty* and would coordinate the activities of federal agencies functioning in their respective *subekty*. A third challenge to the *subekty* was an effort to bring the constitutions, charters, and laws of the *subekty* into conformity with the federal Constitution and federal law. According to Anatoly Chubais, then Presidential Chief of Staff, the laws of about one-third of all of the *subekty* violated the federal Constitution, including those of all but two of the republics.[40] A specific but relatively minor issue is illustrative. In October 1996, the Central Electoral Commission found that the electoral laws of about 25 *subekty* violated the federal electoral laws by illegally including residence and language requirements in their electoral laws.[41] (Sakha is among these.) While Chubais was afraid that such a direct attack on the *subekty* would "threaten the disentegration of Russia," he continued to support efforts to force conformity even after becoming prime minister in 1997.[42]

Sakha was also affected by the general efforts to bring the finances of the *subekty* under closer federal supervision. During a spring 1997 trip to Sakha, Chubais criticized the *subekty* in general, but implicitly Sakha in particular, for demanding ever more subsidies, without even trying to raise capital through privatization.[43] Shortly thereafter, Sakha's government announced its intent to sell 49 percent of its stock in Sakhazoloto (Sakha Gold). The federal government also criticized Sakha and other *subekty* for their failure to make their payments to the center, particularly to the federal pension fund.[44] By March 1997, the *subekty*'s debt to the federal budget was in excess of 35 trillion rubles. According to one government spokesman, delays in payments from the *subekty* were leading to delays in pension payments nationwide. Allegedly, some *subekty*, including Sakha, had unilaterally reduced their payments by as much as 40–50 percent. Sakha was also singled out for particular scorn for its failure to transfer tax dollars to the federal budget. According to Deputy Finance Minister Vladimir Petrov, by May 1997 Sakha, Tatarstan and Bashkortostan—all of which had signed special bilateral treaties with the federal government to keep a greater portion of their taxes at home—owed the federal budget a combined one trillion rubles in back taxes in the first quarter of 1997.[45] Analysts speculated that the divisions within the federal government that Sakha had once exploited no longer existed. Thus Sakha would now have to meet its debts.[46] The message apparently struck home in Sakha and elsewhere. By the end of June the chairman of the federal pension plan reported that 90 percent of the *subekty* had now paid their debts to pension earners.[47]

The most significant and direct attack on Sakha came in the form of a renewed struggle for control over the diamond industry. In the period before the promulgation of the new Constitution, Sakha successfully fought to gain greater control of its diamond wealth (see above). Institutionally, this was accomplished through the creation of *Almazy Rossii-Sakha* (ARS), a firm jointly controlled by Russia and Sakha and designed to provide each a major share of the diamond profits. For Sakha ARS's creation was a tremendous success. By 1994 payments from ARS comprised about one-half of Sakha's budget. In 1995 ARS generated returns of $721 million and its net profits were estimated to be $250–$330 million.[48] The taxes and profits it paid to Sakha comprised 80 percent of Sakha's 1995 budget. In 1996 ARS allegedly made $1.4 billion, $600 million from its exports through De Beers.[49]

ARS worked, at least for Sakha. The relationship between ARS and the government of Sakha was exceptionally close. It was somewhat difficult to see where one organization began and the other ended. The president of ARS, Vyacheslav Shtyrov, was also Sakha's vice-president. An insightful journalist reported that Russia was evolving into an oligopoly in which big businesses dominated in specific regions.[50] In this case, there was a virtual merger of the regional government and a single business. Stoner-Weiss argues that the close cooperation between economic and political elites is an important and increasingly common phenomenon at the *subekt* levels. She contends that this cooperation accounts for the relatively greater economic success of some of the *subekty*.[51] Although Sakha was not one of her test cases, her thesis offers an excellent explanation for Sakha's economic gains from 1991 through 1996.

Despite ARS's obvious success, its critics in Moscow remained active. Nikolayev complained that a small clique in Moscow was interfering in the republic's affairs. Shtyrov claimed political and financial circles in Moscow were trying to gain control of ARS. In spring 1996 ARS's opponents precipitated a second major struggle over the diamond industry. ARS's critics at *Roskomdragmet* had never accepted the desirability of cooperation with De Beers. Thus, when the Russo-De Beers agreement expired in December 1995, they vocally opposed renewing the agreement with the existing terms. In February 1996 the Russian Finance Ministry and De Beers signed a framework for renewing their cooperation that appeared on the surface quite similar to their past arrangement. De Beers would sell 95 percent of Russia's first $550 million worth of rough diamond exports, and 80 percent of all stones above that.[52] The Finance Ministry officials who helped negotiate the framework argued that the resulting final agreement would not hurt Russia's indigenous cutting industry because it pertained only to stones exported abroad. However, it was precisely on these grounds that officials at *Roskomdragmet* attacked the framework.

Acting in conjunction with the Russian Association of Diamond Producers (RADP) *Roskomdragmet* launched an attack on ARS. Acting chairman of *Roskomdragmet* Kotliar and Ararat Evoyan, executive director RADP, raised three basic problems with the framework. First, they argued that the cutting industry, which was based largely outside of Sakha, could not survive without the right to export uncut diamonds abroad for cutting on consignment.[53] The Russian diamond cutting business largely utilizes the so-called classic method for cutting diamonds, which wastes up to 63 percent of the uncut diamond.[54] Many gem diamonds can not be profitably cut using this method. Unfortunately, the discovery of which diamonds can be profitably cut using the classic method is made at a variety of stages in the cutting process. Since 1991 Russian cutters had regularly sent these unprofitable diamonds abroad for cutting on consignment. After being cut in Israel or Belgium, the cut diamonds were returned to Russia and sold as Russian-cut diamonds. De Beers considered this practice cheating on their agreement and had insisted that it be stopped. The new framework would do exactly that.

A second criticism of the framework was that Russian cutters could conceivably run out of diamonds. The point is a difficult one to understand, since in 1995 ARS extracted $1.3 billion in diamonds and the Russian cutting industry was only able to process $1 billion.[55] However, in 1994 Russian cutters purchased nearly all of their stones not from ARS, but from *Roskomdragmet*, which bore responsibility for distributing diamonds from the State Diamond Fund. In 1995 sales from the State Fund stockpile could meet only 50 percent of the demand from the domestic cutting industry, and in the first five months of 1996 there were no deliveries from the State Fund.[56] The most logical explanation is that the once legendary Soviet (now Russian) State Fund is running out of diamonds. If this is the case, then the domestic cutting industry is going to become increasingly dependent on ARS to meet its needs. The question thus became whether under the new agreement ARS would be able and willing to fully meet the needs of the domestic cutting industry, even at the risk of angering De Beers. RADP officials did not think so. ARS had made its record profits because of its cooperation with De Beers and because of its participation in the cartel. Moreover, ARS had already borrowed $800 million from commercial banks to finance the expansion of the diamond mining industry, and its receipt of the next $200 million loan, which it now needed, was being made dependent on its conclusion of a new trade agreement with De Beers.[57]

A third criticism of the framework was that RADP believed its members were already paying too high a price for the diamonds they received from ARS.[58] They claimed that the markup for diamonds from *Roskomdragmet* was only 4.5 percent, but it was eight percent for those from ARS. Allegedly RADP members paid more for ARS diamonds than did De Beers. Conversely, De Beers complained that the Russian diamond cutting industry was getting the cream of the Russian diamond crop. The domestic industry was largely cutting stones valued at over $300 per carat, while the mix being sent to De Beers had to be seeded with a few large stones.[59] The new framework guaranteed De Beers a random mix of the run of ARS's production. It did not change the price RADP members paid for ARS diamonds.

To avoid the alleged threat to the Russian cutting industry, *Roskomdragmet* and RADP offered two possible solutions. First, they suggested that RADP could itself purchase the entire run of diamonds from ARS. The diamonds that could not be profitably cut with the classic cutting method would then be sold abroad, possibly even to De Beers. Evoyan even suggested that RADP members might be able to make payments three or four months in advance, which would help Sakha with its seasonal transportation problems. Despite its superficial appeal, ARS found this offer both undesirable and infeasible. It was undesirable because it would have destroyed the single channel marketing system, which accounted for De Beers' success in maintaining artificially high prices for diamonds. These high profits were a direct cause of ARS's phenomenal profits. The proposal was infeasible because the Russian cutting industry was itself heavily in debt and it was doubtful it could provide the promised cash up front. ARS suggested that the only way to meet both the needs of the diamond industry and the cutting industry was to expand production and this could be best accomplished by maintaining its ties to De Beers.[60] Implicitly this would maintain ARS's access to new capital and allow it to expand production. In the meantime Russian cutters could buy some of their stones from ARS and some from De Beers at market prices.

The attack on ARS came to a dramatic head during a series of highly publicized and politically charged hearings on the diamond industry in May and June 1997. While many of the above arguments were aired publicly, the real battle focused on the statute "On Precious Metals and Precious Minerals." The implications of the law for the diamond industry were extremely controversial in that it appeared to give ARS the exclusive right to export uncut gem diamonds, despite attempts by *Roskomdragmet* and RADP to alter the law in order to create a state monopoly on diamond sales.[61] The law was approved by the Duma, but was initially rejected by the Federation Council. By the end of June the Federation Council also passed the law.

Much to the surprise of ARS and Sakha, President Yeltsin, their previously reliable ally, vetoed the law.[62] This was especially mystifying in that Yeltsin had backed the government memorandum of the previous winter, which first created ARS's exclusive right to export uncut diamonds. Had Yeltsin turned against Sakha? A better explanation for Yeltsin's behavior can be found in a statement by one of ARS's directors, Leonid Tolpezhnikov.[63] He said,

> in order to protect Russia's national interest in the area of uncut and cut diamonds, it is necessary to get rid of the conflict between the ARS company and the former *Roskomdragmet*, between the center and the territories, and between the government and the [diamond] sector, to get rid of the contradictions within the government and, finally, to look at the problem as a whole as well.

Tolpezhnikov was likely hoping for the evolution of a negotiated consensus and cooperation among the elements of the Russian diamond industry. The strategy implemented by Yeltsin, or more precisely by his government, was to force consolidation on the diamond industry through a simultaneous attack on both sides. With Yeltsin's position solidified by his reelection to the presidency, he was well positioned to impose consolidation.

The attack on *Roskomdragmet* was quick and decisive. In August 1996 Yeltsin signed a presidential decree disbanding *Roskomdragmet*.[64] Its replacement *Gokhran* (State Fund for Precious Metals and Gems) was made directly subordinate to the Ministry of Finance, which was firmly under the control of Yeltsin's young reformers. Bichkov, already suspended and under investigation for illegally exporting diamonds, was sacked.[65] Instead of replacing Bichkov with one of his deputies, such as *Roskomdragmet*'s acting Chairman Kotliar, Chernomyrdin appointed Deputy Finance Minister German Kuznetsov to head *Gokhran*.

The attack on ARS and Sakha was more drawn out and less effective, but equally tenacious. In November 1996 the Temporary Extraordinary Commission accused ARS of "concealing profits and therefore not paying $8.2 million taxes, and of conducting illegal foreign operations with currency and precious stones from which it received nearly $87 million."[66] ARS Chairman Shtyrov vehemently denied the charges and threatened to sue the federal government.[67] Recall that similar charges were made against *Roskomdragmet* officials. Moreover, according to many industry insiders, Yeltsin himself had heavily raided the State Diamond Fund to raise money for his reelection bid.

An equally serious problem for ARS and Sakha was the government's failure to sign a new agreement with De Beers. The previous agreement with De Beers expired on December 30, 1995, but De Beers had allowed Russia to continue to export some diamonds under the terms of the agreement during 1996. However, De Beers lost patience. In December it issued an ultimatum: unless a new agreement was signed by January 1, 1997, De Beers would no longer purchase Russian diamonds under the old terms. De Beers was reportedly responding to a statement from Russian Foreign Minister Alexander Livshits, who had said that De Beers should pay more attention to the interests of Russia's extracting and cutting industries.[68] Despite his previous support for the February 1996 framework for renewing the trading relationship, Livshits now demanded a renegotiation of the terms of the relationship. Meanwhile De Beers officials complained that Chernomyrdin would not even respond to their letters.[69]

Despite considerable public pressure from nearly every top official in ARS and the government of Sakha, the federal government continued to drag its feet. True to its word, De Beers suspended its purchases of Russian diamonds on January 1, 1997. Nevertheless, throughout the winter and spring of 1997 Russia's position remained unchanged. In April, Deputy Prime Minister Chubais replaced Livshits, by adding Finance Minister to his own title. Chubais was extremely critical of the privileges Sakha and other republics had obtained from their bilateral agreements with Yeltsin. In May he openly criticized Sakha's minimal contribution to the federal government.[70] He also complained that while Russia was a 32 percent owner of ARS—the federal government had not received a single diamond from the company. Moreover, ARS had failed to pay its large tax debt to the federal government. Conversely, Sakha—also an owner of 32 percent of ARS, received 20 percent of all diamonds mined in Sakha. Reportedly, Sakha purchased diamonds from ARS at a significant discount and resold them for a hefty profit.

In May *Izvestiya* reported that Moscow's strategy was forcing Sakha to its knees.[71] Without new sales, ARS could not afford either to pay its workers or to invest in new diamond production. Similarly, Sakha's infrastructure reportedly was collapsing, and it could not find the credit necessary to import goods for the following winter. Sakha soon conceded to a reorganization of the diamond trade. After months of extensive discussion and protracted negotiations, on July 22 Yeltsin signed a presidential decree that dramatically reformed the Russian diamond industry. [72] It stripped Sakha of the right to independently sell 20 percent of the diamonds mined on its territory. It removed ARS's monopoly on the export of diamonds. ARS was prohibited from selling diamonds at a discount to the government of Sakha, Nikolayev, or his associates. Finance

Ministry controls were placed on all aspects of the diamond industry, including the placement of federal government inspectors inside ARS's operations. The Russian cutting industry was given the right to import diamonds from abroad without exorbitant duties, thus creating price competition with ARS.

On July 25 Nikolayev flew to Moscow in the hope of again using his personal ties to Yeltsin to have the decree revoked. Reportedly, Yeltsin, who had played little role in Chubais' attack, agreed to many of Nikolayev's demands. Sakha was given the right to purchase diamonds from ARS at a price that Nikolayev told Yeltsin was cost. Presumably, Sakha could then resell these diamonds at a considerable profit. Yet, the decree Yeltsin had signed just five days earlier declared that Sakha could buy diamonds only on terms and prices that were fixed by the Russian Ministry of Finance. Nikolayev's appeal to Yeltsin would have worked, except that Chubais had prepared for just such a possibility. During Yeltsin's illness of the previous year, Chubais had authored a decree according to which future presidential decrees would only become valid after official publication, which remained under Chubais' control. Thus getting Yeltsin's signature on a piece of paper, as Nikolayev had done, was no longer tantamount to a presidential decree. Nikolayev's agreement with Yeltsin disappeared, and the original decree on reforming the diamond industry was published.

With *Roskomdragmet* gone, and the concessions to Sakha reversed, the diamond industry was now firmly in the hands of the federal government. Rapid progress on the signing of a new agreement with De Beers was now possible. Under the new agreement, signed on October 21, 1997, ARS must sell between $550 million and $1.2 billion in uncut gems to De Beers between December 1, 1997, and the end of 1998. Diamond exports that circumvent De Beers are strictly limited.[73]

The attack on Sakha's control of the diamond industry is best understood as an integral part of the aforementioned larger attempt to retake the powers that passed to specific *subekty*, particularly to many of the republics. The evidence suggests that from 1965 until the collapse of the Soviet Union there had been a gradual convergence of economic life in Russia's components.[74] They were becoming more and more alike in terms of indicators like infant mortality, economic productivity, standard of living, and crime. Since Russian independence the gap between the poorest and the richest *subekty* has grown rapidly.

The chairman of the Federation Council Committee on Constitutional Legislation and Legal Issues said the inequality of the *subekty* was one of the most pressing issues facing Russia.[75] He pointed out that the vast inequality was in direct contradiction to the promise of equal treatment contained in the Constitution. Yeltsin himself argued in his radio address that the unevenness of economic development among the *subekty* was the most acute problem Russia faced.[76]

Federal leaders inevitably blame the inequality on the bilateral agreements. While railing against the "double standards" among the treatment of Russia's *subekty*, Federation Council Chairman Yegor Stroev criticized the highly favorable terms received by a select group of *subekty*.[77] Sakha was singled out for special mention. Similarly, Valerii Zubov, the Governor of Krasnoyarsk, said that the leaders of the 17-member Siberian Accord opposed the special privileges granted to some *subekty*; again Sakha was used as an example.[78] Luzhkov himself once joked that maybe Moscow should join Tatarstan or Sakha, in order to take advantage of their deal.

The impression that Sakha and others had used their bilateral agreement to comparative advantage is an accurate one. Despite being one of Russia's most resource rich republics, in 1993 Sakha was partially subsidized by many of the poorer *subekty*, particularly the regions. According to Hughes, Sakha's budgetary subvention from the federal government was then 59,034 rubles per person, while the less well endowed Novosibirsk *oblast* received only 5,397 per person.[79] Presumably the agreement allowing Sakha to use its federal tax revenues at home has further widened this relative disparity since 1993. Since independence industrial production had decreased in nearly every *subekty*.[80] Sakha is one of four *subekty* in which industrial production has actually increased. As a result, during the past three or four years it had jumped from 43rd place to 21st place in Russia's ranking of regions by industrial production.[81] While Sakha was not without its problems, such relative gains inevitably generated considerable antagonism.

To rectify the inequity, the Duma sought a general law delimiting the division of power between the federal government and the *subekty*. However, the law they passed in April 1997 would have voided all existing bilateral agreements.[82] Thus it was not acceptable to the Federation Council or the government. Because of the opposition of the *subekty* leaders in the Federation Council, and their allies in the government, the bill was defeated. The *subekty* had the ability to defend themselves, at least collectively, against attempts by the center to unilaterally alter the balance of power. Instead, the government's effort, spearheaded by Chubais, was to gradually curb the most obvious excesses on a case by case basis.

Yet as witnessed above, even the attempt to strip Sakha of its rights and powers was only partially successful. Although the federal government reestablished control over the direction of the diamond industry, much of the profit remained in Sakha. When the flow of diamond sales cut off, in the summer of 1997 Chubais coerced Sakha to sign an agreement in which it agreed to again pay its taxes like other *subekty*.[83] Yet collectively, the *subekty* have gained greater control over their own budgets.

Admittedly, greater regional budgeting powers may be a mixed blessing. Simultaneously with its efforts to force the subekty to pay taxes, Moscow has reduced the subsidies to the *subekty*. The 1997 budget left the *subekty* responsible for financing 80 percent of all education; 88 percent of healthcare costs; 80 percent of social spending; and 70 percent of all major projects.[84] The 1998 budget proposed by Yeltsin was to make even more dramatic cuts in the level of subsidies, from 66.0 trillion rubles to 38.5 trillion rubles.[85] (Some of this appears likely to be restored in the budget negotiations.)

The most dramatic cuts in recent years have come in spending to the so-called north, including Sakha. The 1994 transportation season in Sakha was even worse than in previous years. Nikolayev repeatedly urged Yeltsin to provide the promised 2.8 million rubles. Noting that the republic had only received 10–15 percent of the goods received in the previous summer, Sakha's parliament declared an economic emergency and threatened to withhold the shipment of diamonds and other resources. While Yeltsin repeated his promises for aid and interest-free credit, then Finance Minister Panskov alleged that funds for the North had been diverted illegally to private accounts.[86] While the political turmoil this caused was considerable, the practical results were negligible. When winter arrived, Sakha and the other northernmost *subekty* had received only about half of their needed supply of oil.[87] The 1995 and 1996 transportation seasons were apparently only marginally better. In 1994–1995, the Far North was budgeted 8.5 trillion rubles of credits to stock up for the 1996 season; however, the amount was still insufficient. In 1996, the government spent 4.2 trillion rubles (about $769 million) on supplies to the north; of that sum 3.6 trillion rubles was subsidies compensating for transportation costs.[88] Thus while the northern *subekty* requested more emergency credit, the federal government wanted to investigate the possible misuse of the original funding.[89] In 1997 the federal government budgeted $919 billion rubles to support federal programs in the north, but by September it had spent only $24 billion.[90] The Children of the North Fund had received only 23 percent of its allotted funding. But according to the Chairman of the Duma's Committee on the Problems of the North, it is the 1998 budget which could "create economic catastrophe in the North." Reportedly, with the strategic food supply nearly depleted, the new budget was bereft of funds to subsidize food for the North.

The financial crisis that rocked Russia beginning in the fall of 1998 demonstrated that the increased economic autonomy of the *subekty* also has some benefits. While all of Russia was hurt by the crisis, many regional governments were able to weather the crisis much better than the center and were able to use their resources to help their constituents through the worst of the crisis.

CONCLUSIONS

Since Yeltsin's arrival on the political scene Sakha's relations with Moscow have passed through the three distinct institutional stages outlined in Chapter 2. During these stages Sakha's objectives have evolved. In Stage 1 Sakha sought to claim as many powers and rights as it could. More specifically it pursued an increased share of the revenues accrued from the sale of its vast mineral resources. It also sought to decrease its federal tax burden, while increasing the subsidies it receives from the center. In Stage 2 Sakha sought to have these powers institutionalized, first through bilateral agreements and then through the Federal Treaty and ultimately in the Constitution. In Stage 3 many basic powers were guaranteed to the *subekty* by the Constitution, but Sakha was forced into a defensive struggle to maintain some of the special powers it had acquired through the bilateral agreements. Throughout all three stages strategy remained relatively constant. Sakha sought, through Nikolayev, to trade its political support for Yeltsin for support for its political agenda. The success of this strategy varied with conditions.

During the first stage of Russian politics, Sakha claimed a greater share of its resource revenues, a reduced tax burden, and more political autonomy. Because of the intensity of his conflict with the Soviet regime, and the relative institutional vulnerability of his position, Yeltsin acceded seemingly to all of Sakha's demands. He recognized Sakha's higher status within Russia and made numerous promises on taxes and resource revenues. However, during this period, Yeltsin was not in a position to deliver on his promises. Thus, Sakha's victories were largely on paper. To the extent that there was a division of powers, the fifth necessary condition, it was both ambiguous and contested. While Yeltsin sought to build consensus with the *subekty*, Gorbachev did not feel similarly compelled. Yet, it was Gorbachev who controlled the central government. Although Sakha's acquisition of new powers was consensual, the first necessary condition of federalism, its overall participation in the Soviet Union was not. Similarly, while Yeltsin actively sought the support of the *subekty* in his contest with Gorbachev, they had only indirect representation in the Soviet Congress of People's Deputies and none in the Supreme Soviet, the functional legislature. At best Sakha's representation in federal policymaking, the fourth condition, was minimal. Finally, the written constitution was considered invalid by most, did not provide a clear division of power, and provided no effective mechanism for adjudicating center-periphery disputes.

By the end of the second stage, many of the rights and powers Sakha had claimed were finally codified in bilateral agreements. Sakha was able to keep a large portion of the profits from the diamond industry and had the discretionary powers to use those profits however its leaders saw fit. Also of great importance were the powers over taxation that Sakha's bilateral treaty granted it. With respect to federalism, more important than the right to keep federal tax rubles at home was the right Sakha acquired to select which federal institutions would be paid.

On the negative side of the ledger, the status of the bilateral agreements remained unclear. The Federal Treaty initially appeared to guarantee both a clear division of powers and the credibility of the bilateral agreements. However, whether the Federal Treaty would be incorporated into the new Constitution soon became the new focus of dispute. Thus, while the division of powers had become clearer, it was still ambiguous. The way in which Sakha gained these rights was consensual. Both the bilateral agreements and the Federal Treaty were the direct result of hard negotiations. As to the fourth necessary condition, Sakha technically had representation in federal policymaking but it was no more meaningful in the Russian Supreme Soviet than it had been in the Soviet Union's Supreme Soviet.

The dissolution of the Russian Supreme Soviet and the promulgation of the new Constitution marked the beginning of the third institutional stage in Russian politics. In terms of establishing a clear division of powers, this third phase has been a mixed blessing for the *subekty*. On the one hand, the third and current stage is marked by a much lower intensity executive-legislative conflict. Because the constitutional powers of the president are so great, the Duma is much less of a threat to the President's ability to govern than was the Russian Supreme Soviet. As a result, Yeltsin's need for an alliance with the *subekty* has been dramatically reduced, but certainly not eliminated. Particularly after his reelection, Yeltsin has been relatively unencumbered to launch attempts to retake powers from the *subekty*. Yeltsin has been modestly successful in this area, and Sakha has lost significant powers as a result. However, the attack has largely been to retake the special privileges Sakha and the other republics gained from their bilateral agreements. On the other hand, the Constitution now gives specific, albeit limited, powers to all *subekty*. It also gives legal status to the basic elements of self-rule provided for in the Federal Treaty. Thus, while the rights and power Sakha possesses today are less than in the second stage, they are now more secure. Having these powers institutionalized in the Constitution for all *subekty* is a positive step toward a stable federal system.

In terms of the consensual nature of Sakha's relationship with the center, the record of the third stage is also mixed. Yeltsin was in a position to dictate terms to the *subekty* in the new Constitution and has pressured Sakha into surrendering some powers. However, since then the Duma and the Federation Council have emerged as a meaningful—albeit weakened—check on the president. Thus the president and his government have had the upper hand in their relations with the *subekty* and have gained many concessions; they have not completely dictated terms. Instead they have had to negotiate, pressure, and bully Sakha into concessions. Moreover, to make dramatic constitutional changes affecting all the *subekty* now requires the cooperation of the *subekty* through their representatives in the Federation Council.

Along these lines, the third stage has brought a dramatic change in terms of the effectiveness of Sakha's federal representation. With the creation of the Federation Council the *subekty* now have a permanent and credible role in federal politics. President Nikolayev himself holds one of these seats. Since the bilateral agreements are a divisive issue among the Federation Council, it has not given Sakha any protection against the government's attack on its special privileges. However, it does give the *subekty* collectively a tangible defense against any constitutional amendments or federal laws to significantly diminish the autonomy of the *subekty* as a group.

Is Sakha's relationship with Moscow really a federal relationship? This chapter leads to three conclusions. First, the relationship has become progressively more federal since the collapse of the Soviet Union. Second, while Sakha has fewer powers than it did just before the promulgation, it is now more able to defend the powers it has. Sakha now has meaningful federal representation and the federal nature of Russian center-periphery relations without the "collective" support of the subekty. Third, Russia is an asymmetrical federation because of the legality of bilateral agreements. However, the asymmetry, at least in terms of the unique powers and rights Sakha possesses, has diminished since 1993.

NOTES

This paper builds on the research presented in two previous articles on Sakha. Daniel R. Kempton, "The Republic of Sakha (Yakutia): The Evolution of Centre-Periphery Relations in the Russian Federation," *Europe-Asia Studies*, 48(2): 577–603; and Daniel R. Kempton, "Budgetary Politics in the Russian Federation: The Case of Sakha (Yakutia)," *International Journal of Public Administration* 22(9–10), (1999): 1345–1385.

1. Slocum, ibid., p. 2.
2. Mikhail Nikolayev, *Nezavisimaya gazeta* (21 January 1995): 3.
3. Gail Fondahl, "Siberia: Native Peoples and Newcomers in Collision," in Ian Bremmer and Ray Taras, eds., *Nations and Politics in the Soviet Successor States*, Cambridge University Press, Cambridge, 1993, pp. 477–510.
4. Marjorie Mandelstam Blazer & Uliana Alekseevna Vinokurova, "Nationalism, Interethnic Relations and Federalism: The Case of the Sakha Republic (Yakutia)," *Europe-Asia Studies* 48(1), (1996): 101–120.
5. Michael J. Bradshaw, "Siberia Poses a Challenge to Federalism," *RFE/RL Research Reports* 1 (41), (16 October 1992): 6–14.
6. Mikhail Nikolayev, *Literaturnaya gazeta* (1 December 1993): 11.
7. Daniel R. Kempton with Richard M. Levine, "Soviet and Russian Relations with Foreign Corporations: The Case of Gold and Diamonds," *Slavic Review* 54(1), (1995): 80–110.
8. Gail W. Lapidus & Edward W. Walker, "Nationalism, Regionalism, and Federalism: Center-Periphery Relations in Post-Communist Russia," in Gail W. Lapidus, ed., *The New Russia: Troubled Transformation* (Boulder: Westview Press, Boulder, 1995), p. 82.
9. B. Keller, *The New York Times Sunday Magazine* (1993 September 23).
10. Daniel R. Kempton, op. cit. (1996).
11. E. Rubinfien, *Wall Street Journal* (29 January 1994): A-11.
12. INTERFAX, 28 August 1991, in *FBIS-SOV*-91–169 (30 August 1991): 109.
13. Kempton with Levine, op. cit.: 80–110; and Andrew R. Bond, Richard M. Levine, & Gordon T. Austin (1992), "Russian Diamond Industry in State of Flux," *Post-Soviet Geography*, 33(10), (1992): 635–644.
14. Kempton, op. cit. (1996).
15. Author interview with Evgeny Matveevich Bichkov, chairman, *Roskomdgramet*, Yuri A. Kotliar, first deputy chairman, *Roskomdgramet*, Moscow, 27 May, 1994; *Ekonomika i zhizn* (27 May 1994): 17; and *Vostochnyy express* 1(28 January 1994): 11.
16. INTERFAX (1991, Janauary 19), in *FBIS-SOV*-91–119 (20 June 1991): 11.
17. TASS (27 January 1992) in *FBIS-SOV*-92–018 (28 January 1992): 54; and TASS (28 January 1992) in *FBIS-SOV*-92–020 (30 January 1992): 46.

18. TASS (21 February 1992) in *FBIS-SOV*-92–37 (25 February 1992): 50.

19. *Kommersant*, 29 (13–20 July 1992): 4, in *FBIS-USR*-92–100 (7 August 1992): 46–48; INTERFAX (27 January 1993) in *FBIS-SOV*-93–017 (18 January 1993): 29; and *Kommersant* (16 July 1993): 2, in *FBIS-SOV*-93–135 (6 July 1993): 33.

20. Author interview with Sergei Aramovich Oulin, Director, *Almazy Rossii-Sakha*, Moscow, 23 May 1994.

21. Vera Tolz, "Regionalism in Russia: The Case of Siberia," *RFE/RL Research Reports* 2(9), (26 February 1993): 1–9.

22. Kempton with Levine, op. cit., 1995.

23. Author interview with Sergei Aramovich Oulin, Director, *Almazy Rossii-Sakha*, Moscow, 23 May 1994.

24. *Federatsiya*, no. 12 (2 February 1993): 2, in *FBIS-USR*-93–026 (6 March 1993): 52–53.

25. Elizabeth Teague, "Russian and Tatarstan Sign Power-Sharing Treaty," *RFE/RL Research Reports* 3(14), (8 April 1994): 19–27.

26. Tolz, *op. cit.*, p. 4.

27. Mikhail Nikolayev, *Literaturnaya gazeta* (1 December 1993): 11.

28.*ITAR-TASS* (19 June 1993) in *FBIS-SOV*-93–117 (21 June 1993): 44.

29. *Izvestiya* (22 June 1993): 2.

30. *Kommersant* (3 August 1993): 3, in *FBIS-SOV*-93–150 (6 August 1993): 29.

31. Kempton, op. cit., 1996.

32. *ITAR-TASS* (18 August 1993), in *FBIS-SOV*-93–159 (19 August, 1993): 25–26.

33. *INTERFAX* (4 October 1993) in *FBIS-SOV*-93–190–S (4 October 1993): 79–80.

34. *INTERFAX* (1 November 1993) in *FBIS-SOV*-93–210 (2 November 1993): 25–26.

35. Nikolayev, *Literaturnaya gazeta* (1 December 1993): 11, in *FBIS-USR*-93–161 (18 December 1993): 23–28.

36. *Rossiyskiye vesti* (4 December 1993): 1.

37. *Nezavisimaya gazeta* (16 December 1993): 3.

38. *Jamestown Monitor* 1(44), (1 July 1995).

39. Blazer & Vinokurova, 1996, p. 108.

40. RIA Novosti, 27 December 1996; and OMRI, *Russian Regional Report*, 2(13), (17 April 1997).

41. OMRI, *Daily Digest*, 24 October 1996.

42. *Kommersant-Daily*, 30 October 1996.

43. IEWS, *Russian Regional Report*, 2(22), 19 June 1997.

44. IEWS, *Russian Regional Report*, 2(9), 6 March 1997; and IEWS, *Russian Regional Report*, 2(10), 13 March 1997.

45. RFE/RL, *Newsline*, 55, 21 May 1997.

46. IEWS, *Russian Regional Report*, 2(18), 22 May 1997.

47. RIA, *Novosti*, 28 June 1997.

48. OMRI, *Daily Digest*, 14 November 1996; and IEWS, *Russian Regional Report*, 2(18), 22 May 1997.

49. IEWS, *Russian Regional Report*, 2(18), 22 May 1997.

50. *The Globe & Mail*, 10 July 1997.

51. Kathryn Stoner-Weiss, "Why Are Some Regions Doing Better Than Others," in IEWS, *Russian Regional Report*, 2(18), 22 May 1997; and Kathryn Stoner-Weiss, *Local Heroes: The Political Economy of Regional Government Performance* (Princeton: Princeton University Press, 1997).

52. OMRI, *Daily Digest*, 65, 1 April 1996.

53. *Kommersant-Daily*, 13 April 1996.

54. *Ekspert*, 32, 26 August 1996.

55. *Segodnya*, 27 July 1996, p. 3.

56. *Ekspert,* 22, 10 June 1996.

57. *Ekspert,* 22, 10 June 1996.

58. *Kommersant-Daily*, 13 April 1996.

59. *Delovoy mir*, 25 May 1996, p. 7.

60. *Delovoy mir*, 25 May 1996, p. 7.

61. *Ekspert,* 22, 10 June 1996; and *Delovoy mir*, 18 June 1996.

62. *Delovoy mir*, 2, 26 July–1 August 1996, p. 5.

63. *Delovoy mir*, 17 December 1996, p. 5.

64. *Delovoy mir*, 17 December 1996, p. 5; and ORMI, *Daily Digest*, 244, 19 December 1996.

65. Bichkov subsequently resurfaced as the president of the Russian Diamond Producers Association, an organization whose cause he had championed while head of *Roskomdragmet.*

66. OMRI, *Russian Regional Report*, 1(17), 18 December 1996.

67. OMRI, *Russian Regional Report*, 14 November 1996.

68. OMRI, *Daily Digest*, 19 December 1996.

69. *Kommersant-Daily*, 19 December 1996, 1, 8.

70. *Izvestiya,* 16 May 1997; and IEWS, *Russian Regional Report*, 2(18), 22 May 1997.

71. *Izvestiya,* 16 May 1997

72. IEWS, *Russian Regional Report*, 2(26), 17 July 1997; RFE/RL, *Newsline*, 1(78), 22 July 1997; and John Helmer, "Diamond in the Rough: How Yeltsin Decides," RFE/RL, *Newsline*, August 1997.

73. RFE/RL, *Newsline*, 1(144), 22 October 1997.

74. *Rossiyskiye gazeta*, 20 May 1997.

75. OMRI, *Daily Digest*, 17 January 1997.

76. RIA, *Novosti*, 8 June 1997.

77. IEWS, *Russian Regional Report*, 2(31), 18 September 1997.

78. RFE/RL, *Newsline*, 1(29), 13 May 1997.

79. Hughes, op. cit., p. 1147.

80. *Rossiyskiye vesti*, 20 May 1997.

81. *Rossiyskiye vesti*, 20 May 1997.

82. *Kommersant-Daily*, 26 April 1997.

83. IEWS, *Russian Regional Report*, 2(26), 17 July 1997; and IEWS, *Russian Regional Report*, 2(27), 21 August 1997.

84. OMRI, *Daily Digest*, 24 October 1996.

85. Irina Demchenko, Reuters, 20 August 1997.

86. *Izvestiya* (1 July 1994): 1; *Nezavisimaya gazeta* (20 October 1994): 5; OMRI, *Daily Digest* 102, Part I (26 May 1995); *Segodnya* (5 July 1994): 2, in *FBIS-SOV*-94–129 (6 July 1994): 33.

87. *INTERFAX* (20 October 1994), in *FBIS-SOV*-94–204 (21 October 1994): 37.

88. IEWS, *Russian Regional Report,* 2(4), (29 January 1997).

89. OMRI, *Daily Digest*, no. 184, Part I (23 September 1996); and IEWS, *Russian Regional Report,* 2(4), (29 January 1997).

90. IEWS, *Russian Regional Report*, 2(31), 18 September 1997.

CHAPTER 5

YELTSIN, SHAIMIEV, AND DUDAEV: NEGOTIATING AUTONOMY FOR TATARSTAN AND CHECHNYA

Ann E. Robertson

On August 31, 1996, Russian National Security Advisor Aleksandr Lebed negotiated the Khasavyurt accords, bringing an end to Russia's first war in Chechnya. The text of the document seemed to recognize Chechnya as an independent country, the status proclaimed by Chechen leader Dzhokar Dudaev in November 1991, and the provisions strongly resembled the requirements of Mikhail Gorbachev's April 1990 law on secession, including a five-year transition period and popular referendum. Although Boris Yeltsin's December 1994 decision to invade Chechnya was initially denounced by most Russian democrats and communists, both groups eventually supported the war. They feared Chechen secession would lead to the breakup of the Russian Federation.[1]

Following the collapse of the USSR, there was repeated speculation that the Russian Federation would also dissolve, as non-Russian regions proclaimed their autonomy or outright independence.[2] In April 1993, Boris Yeltsin himself told the Russian Council of Ministers, "It is no secret that the country is gripped by a feeling of anxiety about the [territorial] integrity of the Russian state. Will it share the same fate as the USSR?"[3] Much as the Baltic declarations of independence in 1991 triggered similar movements in other Union republics, the intransigence of a handful of Russian constituent parts could produce a destabilizing demonstration effect. Two Russian autonomous republics, Tatarstan and Chechnya, seemed the most likely catalysts for Russian disintegration.

On August 30, 1990, before the demise of the USSR, Tatarstan party secretary Mintimir Shaimiev proclaimed Tatarstan's sovereignty and indicated his interest in making his region the sixteenth union republic of the USSR. During the waning days of the Soviet Union, Shaimiev demanded that Tatarstan be admitted to the Commonwealth of Independent States (CIS) in its own right. In the Chechen-Ingush Autonomous Republic, retired air force general Dzhokar Dudaev seized power in September 1991 and proclaimed his republic's independence on November 2, 1991. The republic eventually split in half, with Ingushetia becoming a Russian republic in its own right, and Chechnya severing its ties with Moscow.

Chechnya and Tatarstan may have conducted similar campaigns to redefine their status vis-à-vis Moscow, but the comparison ends there. Though pursuing similar goals, their leaders adopted far different strategies for maximizing their autonomy. They also differ on a variety of measures, including size, ethnic Russian population, economy, and natural resources. Chechnya borders non-Russian states, while Tatarstan is completely surrounded by Russia (see Table 5.1). Most striking, however, is the different outcomes of these two campaigns. While Chechnya was obliterated by war, Tatarstan signed a unique power-sharing agreement with Moscow in early 1994.

Table 5.1
Basic Facts about Chechnya and Tatarstan

	Chechnya	**Tatarstan**
Incorporated into Russia	1859	1552
Land Area	7,800 square miles	68,000 square miles
Population	1.3 million	3.7 million
Ethnic Divisions	Chechen 52% Russian 29% Ingush 12%	Tatar 48.5% Russian 43.3%
Sovereignty	—	August 30, 1990
Independence	November 2, 1991	—
Treaty with Russia	August 31, 1996	February 15, 1994
Exports	oil, chemicals, food, timber, furniture	oil, automobiles, military production, agriculture
President	Dzhokar Dudaev (1991–96) Zelimkhan Yandarbiev (1996) Asian Maskhadov (1997–)	Mintimir Shaimiev

Note: figures based on 1989 census and include what is now the separate Ingush republic.

Why the separate outcomes to the Tatar and Chechen sovereignty movements? The answer lies in their leaders' differing appetites for formal ties with Moscow and their abilities to compromise. Shaimiev sought a voluntary power-sharing agreement with Moscow, while Dudaev proclaimed Chechnya's outright independence from both the USSR and Russia. A newcomer to politics, Dudaev used Chechen nationalism for personal gain. Shaimiev, in contrast, is a shrewd, experienced politician who capitalized on the uncertainties of the transition to seize control of his republic's resources, both natural and institutional.

Tatarstan and Chechnya illustrate the peculiarities of Russian federalism. In theory, political federations have four distinguishing characteristics.[4] First, each level of government has specifically reserved powers. Second, regional governments are composed independent of the center. Third, the center-periphery division of powers is consensual or volitional. Fourth, the regional governments have representation at the federal level. Federations may be symmetrical or asymmetrical, depending on whether all constituent components have equal rights and responsibilities. The 1993 Russian constitution created at least two categories of federal subjects and even within categories some subjects are more equal than others. After Boris Yeltsin dissolved the Russian parliament in October 1993, he used his newly strengthened personal authority to force his own highly centralized Constitution on the federation. He also ordered new regional elections and installed his personal representatives at the local level. Russian federalism, then, appears to little resemble the ideal model.

This chapter examines the nature of Tatarstan's and Chechnya's ties with Soviet Moscow and Russian Moscow from 1989 to 1994. Three distinct phases occurred: the perestroika era (1989–1991); professed independence (1991–1993); and eventual showdown with Yeltsin (1994). These phases will be examined from three perspectives: Moscow (both Soviet and Russian), Kazan, and Grozny. During each phase, the balance of center-periphery power was challenged and eventually revised. As that relationship changed, so too did the domestic political situation in each republic, necessitating an examination of the domestic level.

In Robert Putnam's terminology, Shaimiev and Dudaev were involved in a two-level game, each trying to reach an agreement with Moscow that would also satisfy their constituents at home.[5] Shaimiev's success resulted from his broader "win-set," a collection of the possible solutions acceptable at both the republic and federal levels. Dudaev's options were so narrow that his stance was a non-starter.

THE SOVIET EXPERIENCE

Phase One: Institutions Built on Hollow Ideas

The Soviet Union was a unique experiment in governance. When the core ideas of Leninism were proven hollow, the institutions built upon them collapsed. According to Galina Starovoitova: "the unity of any state is dependent on two basic factors: an integrated economic system (market or command) and a uniform ideological system, whether political, nationalist, or religious"; both were destroyed by glasnost and perestroika.[6] Similarly, in *Lenin's Tomb: The Last Days of the Soviet Empire*, David Remnick argues that opening the archives brought about the end of the USSR. "When history was no longer an instrument of the Party, the Party was doomed to failure. For history proved precisely that: the Party was rotten at its core."[7] Stephan Kux has noted that the concept of federalism is contrary to Soviet political culture, which has no tradition of tolerance, compromise, consensus, or power-sharing, all key features of federalism.[8]

Glasnost and perestroika brought challenges to the principles surrounding the shape and purpose of the Union. Gorbachev's willingness to reform was constrained by his insistence that the Union must stay whole and the Communist Party must stay in control. Compounding the uncertainty was Gorbachev himself, who had only a vague understanding of the nationalities problems in the USSR and consequently worsened tensions with nearly every policy he offered.[9] Chechnya and Tatarstan were not the only regions searching for a new form of political relations with Moscow. The first serious threats to the Union came from the Baltic republics, which had the advantage of law on their side.

On August 23, 1939, Nazi Germany and the Soviet Union had signed the Molotov-Ribbentrop pact, pledging neutrality in the event of attack by third parties. The pact included a secret protocol, which ceded Estonia, Latvia, and Lithuania to the Soviet Union. Although Moscow always claimed that the three Baltic states formally requested to become part of the USSR in 1940, Baltic citizens never accepted this argument and viewed the Red Army as an occupying force. Despite the spirit of glasnost, the Kremlin only reluctantly admitted to the existence of the secret protocols of the Molotov-Ribbentrop Pact in July 1989. Baltic leaders assumed they had a good case for leaving the USSR. Secession wasn't an issue, because the incorporation had been illegal, a fact long recognized by the United States and other countries.[10]

Secession was legally permitted in the USSR, at least in theory. According to Article 72 of the 1977 Soviet Constitution, "Every Union Republic shall retain the right freely to secede from the USSR." In reality, the centralized structure of the CPSU—not to mention widespread deployment of the Red Army—effectively prevented any region from exercising this right. Constituent units of republics, such as autonomous republics Chechen-Ingushetia and Tataria, did not have the right to secede. Instead of waiting for permission from Moscow, Estonia, Latvia, and Lithuania took the initiative. In March 1990 Lithuania announced that as it had never really been a part of the USSR, it would no longer observe the Soviet Constitution. Estonia and Latvia followed suit, but agreed to a negotiated withdrawal from Moscow.

Reconfiguring the union was a key topic at the September 1989 CPSU plenum on nationality questions. Speaking to the delegates, the Tatar first secretary, Gumer S. Usmanov, revealed that a local poll indicated that 67 percent of the residents of Tataria wanted to be elevated from an ASSR to full union-republic status.[11] Other Tatar delegates complained that Tatarstan had twice as many residents as Estonia, but many fewer rights.[12] The draft documents for the plenum proposed a variety of new configurations for the USSR, including dividing the RSFSR into autonomous economic regions[13] or the whole USSR into 50 or more American-style states.[14] According to the plenum platform a "completely new federation" was needed to address ethnic concerns.[15] The result, however, was a policy that emphasized the rights of the Soviet state over the rights of ethnic groups or individuals. Gorbachev also rejected requests to upgrade the status of several Russian autonomous republics.[16]

The outlines of a new union were debated throughout 1990. Gorbachev offered to let Lithuania leave the USSR, so long as it repaid Moscow for its "investment" in the region. The phenomenal price quoted, $33 billion in hard currency, made the offer impossible to accept.[17] The USSR Supreme Soviet adopted Gorbachev's *On the Procedure for Dealing with Matters Connected with the Secession of a Union Republic from the USSR* in April 1990. The law required that two-thirds of a republic approve secession in a referendum, a five-year transition period, and endorsement by the Soviet Congress of People's Deputies. Furthermore, the law allowed autonomous regions within republics, such as Tataria, to "raise the question of their own state-legal status," implying that an ASSR could upgrade itself to an SSR, or perhaps exit altogether.[18]

Three weeks later, the Supreme Soviet adopted the law, *On the Delineation of Powers Between the USSR and the Subjects of the Federation*, which redefined the 15 union republics as "subjects of the federation," like the autonomous republics already were. This appeared to downgrade the Union republics from voluntary, founding members of the Soviet federation to integral parts, and Gorbachev appeared to be reaching around Yeltsin to appeal to the autonomous republics in Russia. While apparently intended to damper the independence-minded Union republics, it instead encouraged the ASSRs and the remaining SSRs to declare their sovereignty.[19]

By this time, numerous parts of the USSR had taken up Lithuania's case. The Moscow City Soviet was backing the Lithuanian nationalists, thousands of people rallied on their behalf in Lvov and Tbilisi, and Rukh, the Ukrainian nationalist movement, passed a resolution supporting Lithuania.[20] Informal opposition groups in Azerbaijan, Uzbekistan, Kazakhstan, Tatarstan, Kyrgyzia, and Belorussia sided with Lithuania. Numerous groups banded together against Moscow; the Baltic states formed the Council of Baltic States and joined with other popular fronts from across the USSR into the Union of Democratic Forces.[21] Russia signed treaties and mutual recognition pacts with all three Baltic states.[22] A May 1990 Soviet public opinion poll of urban Russians revealed that 52.5 percent supported giving Union republics the right to secede while only seven percent opposed the idea.[23]

Even the CPSU was dividing along ethnic lines. At the 1988 Nineteenth Party Conference, republic party leaders spoke on behalf of their constituencies.[24] Following the March 1989 elections to the new Congress of People's Deputies, Lithuanian party leaders saw a need to ally with nationalism if they were to survive challenges from the increasingly strong Sajudis national movement. Realizing he could no longer could balance Moscow's demands for control and Lithuanians' wish for independence, Lithuanian communist party first secretary Algirdas Brazauskas sanctioned the establishment of a Lithuanian Communist Party independent from Moscow.[25] More importantly, a Russian Communist Party was finally created in June 1990.

Beginning in 1989 Russia steadily created its own complement of institutions, which had been prohibited since Lenin's time. These included trade unions, a Russian Komsomol, and eventually a popularly elected presidency. John Dunlop argues that Yeltsin's use of the "Russia card" was the key to undermining the predominance of the CPSU and the unity of the USSR.[26] The RSFSR Congress proclaimed Russian sovereignty on June 10, 1990, launching the so-called "parade of sovereignties" whereby almost every union republic and many subordinate unions declared their emancipation from Gorbachev.[27] Thus began a "war of laws" over whether USSR or RSFSR laws had primacy. Gorbachev encouraged the Russian autonomous republics against Yeltsin, offering them the possibility of upgrading their status in future union treaties.[28] Though encouraging the periphery to revolt proved advantageous against Gorbachev, Yeltsin saw his strategy backfire when the Russian periphery later turned on him. During an April 1990 trip to Kazan, when he told the autonomous republics to "take as much independence as you can swallow," Yeltsin didn't realize that it would be at his expense as well as Gorbachev's.

Throughout the first half of 1991, Gorbachev worked to formulate a new union treaty. On March 17, 1991, a referendum was held on the question of continuing the USSR as a "renewed federation of sovereign republics." The three Baltic republics plus Georgia, Armenia, and Moldova refused to participate in the vote. The six republics also refused to sign the April 23 "Nine-Plus-One" treaty, "effectively" ending their participation in the Soviet Union. At least in theory, the new treaty returned the Union republics to a higher status than the ASSRs.[29] Hours before the new union treaty was to be implemented, hard-liners staged a coup against Gorbachev. Court documents and testimony have since revealed that the preservation of the Union was a direct precipitant of the coup.[30] The plotters' "Appeal to the Soviet People" was full of warnings about the imminent demise of the USSR.[31]

The perestroika era demonstrates the weakness of Soviet federalism and the glaring lack of institutional options to address ethnic grievances. The Soviet "Union" proved to be a centralized state behind a federal veneer. Republic- and lower-level governments had few powers of their own and instead took their orders from the center. The center could also recast the original agreement as voluntary or involuntary with the stroke of a pen. Local party organizations were also subordinated to Moscow, which made sure that a Moscow-chosen ethnic Russian always stood looking over the shoulder of native local first secretaries. Existing federal institutions were unable to satisfy demands from below. Indeed, when republics began claiming the rights enumerated in the Constitution—namely the right to secede—the USSR began to crumble.

Phase Two: Reorganizing Russia

When Gorbachev's Soviet Union collapsed, leaders within Russia expected Yeltsin to deliver on his promises of economic and political autonomy. Instead, his proposed tax breaks and various concessions only served to anger everyone concerned: the republics for broken promises and the regions for discrimination. Ethnically defined republics had been privileged members of the Soviet Union; and ethnic regions within Russia presumed they would similarly receive special treatment in contrast to the predominantly ethnic-Russian regions. Some wanted still more. Yeltsin, like Gorbachev, had little experience with non-Russians nor had he given much thought to a nationalities policy.[32]

Just as Landsbergis and Brazauskas had grown impatient with Gorbachev and taken matters into their own hands, so too did local leaders within the Russian Federation. Tatarstan, Chechnya, Bashkortostan, Sakha, and Karelia individually announced their intentions to impose their own taxes and issue their own currencies, plans denounced by Deputy Prime Minister Boris Fedorov as unacceptable.[33]

Throughout 1992 and early 1993 Moscow and Russia's constituent parts battled over revenue distribution and the outlines of power. The main battlefield in this conflict was the process for drafting a new Russian constitution. The republics rejected any preliminary draft that threatened their privileges and as the Duma debated, proceeded to declare themselves independent and to search for various regional groupings, such as a pan-Caucasus group, a Pan-Turkic Assembly, a Urals Republic, or a Volga confederation. An interim agreement, the Federal Treaty, was signed in March 1992 by all components except Chechnya and Tatarstan.

In time, center-periphery relations were subordinated to the ongoing power struggle between Yeltsin and the communist-dominated Russian Duma. Key Moscow officials offered inducements to peripheral leaders in return for their support.[34] When Yeltsin defeated the communists, he won the right to send his version of the constitution for referendum. The final constitution, approved in the December 1993 referendum, conflicted with many of the bilateral agreements and with the Federal Treaty, which had clearly specified the powers given to the regions and republics.

The "federalness" of the 1993 Russian Constitution has been analyzed, debated, and defended by many scholars.[35] What is important here is how the Constitution was received in Tatarstan and Chechnya. Both republics objected to being listed as subjects of the federation and rejected the document as it had neither secession nor association mechanisms. Furthermore, leaders of both republics had already produced their own constitutions, which conflicted with the new Russian charter. How were conflicting distributions of power reconciled? Tatarstan and Chechnya were the only "parts" of the Russian Federation to balk at signing the 1992 Federal Treaty and the 1993 Constitution. This chapter examines how these two autonomous republics came to feel confined by Soviet and Russian institutions, leading them to demand reappraisal and reformulation. Retelling the events leading up to the Tatar treaty of February 1994 and the Chechen war later that year also highlights the differences between Mintimir Shaimiev and Dzhokar Dudaev and their contrasting political positions at home.

Tatarstan: Willing to Compromise

The Tatarstani sovereignty movement benefited from consistent, moderate policy statements, which offered the possibility of a compromise solution. Furthermore, the movement was aided by a respected leader, policy legitimacy, and a considerable effort to promote ethnic tolerance. Geography and economics also proved to be factors; Tatarstan simply proved too strategically important for Moscow to surrender. Tatarstani leaders recognized and accepted the limited reality of their situation.

Tatarstan came under Russian control relatively early, and centuries of interaction between Russians and Tatars facilitated ethnic tolerance in the region. The Muscovy state of Tsar Ivan IV was almost entirely Russian until the incorporation of Tatarstan in 1552, following the defeat of the Kazan Khanate. Today, Tatars are the second largest ethnic group in Russia, but they are spread across Russian territory. Within Tatarstan, ethnic Tatars are a plurality (48.5%). Some three-quarters of ethnic Tatars, however, live outside Tatarstan proper.[36] Tatars have long complained that only their region's lack of international borders kept it from being a union republic, a status denied in both the 1936 and 1977 Soviet constitutions. That same geographic fact, ironically, worked to Kazan's favor in the post-Soviet era.

Perestroika spawned an ethnic renaissance in Tatarstan, which focused on the Tatar language and spiritual culture. Efforts were made to increase knowledge of Tatar, including classes for adults, changing the language of instruction for schoolchildren, and increasing Tatar-language radio broadcasts. In 1990 Tatar was upgraded to official status, equal with the Russian language. Interest in religious rituals increased, though Kazan-based ethnologist Roza N. Musina is quick to deny that there was an increase in religiosity; this was not a case of rising Muslim fundamentalism. Rather:

> the increasingly frequent displays of overtly religious consciousness and conduct should be seen as an expression of a growing interest in ethnic identity. It appears that at a certain stage in an ethnic group's development, when its ethnically specific way of life is vanishing and its language atrophying, the ethnically distinctive components of its spiritual culture, such as its religion, play a compensatory role in the development of ethnic consciousness. It can fulfill both a protective function by preserving the ethnic

group from further erosion and a developmental role through promoting the processes of ethnic consolidation.[37]

Phase One: Why Can't We Be More Like a Union Republic?

As Gorbachev investigated new ways of defining the Union, Tatarstan sought to upgrade its status to Union-republic level. As mentioned above, Tatar delegates raised this issue at the September 1989 plenum on nationalities questions. Like Kosovo in Yugoslavia, Tatarstan originally did not want out of the union, but instead a more advantageous standing within the existing arrangement.[38] Tatarstan had a larger geographical area, population, and GNP than did several Union republics, but fewer rights.

Tatar leaders also were interested in *khozraschet*, *perestroika*'s move to shift budgeting responsibility to the republics. A November 1989 law had allowed the Baltic republics to create their own economic systems. Estonia was allowed to implement a one-channel tax system, while Latvia and Lithuania were granted more modest tax revisions.[39] In his memoirs, conservative Politburo member Egor Ligachev condemns these developments, arguing that the Baltics' embrace of *khozraschet* fueled their eventual secession.[40] Though the Council of Ministers began work to grant limited cost-accounting along with Moscow and Sverdlovsk oblast, Tatarstan's citizens still resented that their economy remained largely subservient to Russian or all-Union control.[41] This sentiment was found among both ethnic Tatars and ethnic Russians.[42]

The Tatarstan movement was not for national self-determination. Its leaders often cited the successful multi-ethnic culture of the republic. For example, with the July 30, 1992, *Joint Declaration of the Political Organizations of the Republic of Tatarstan*, 17 political and cultural groups pledged to work together for the benefit of Tatarstan. Similarly, "Christian and Muslim clergymen have made frequent joint appearances on television programs, at assemblies, and at ceremonial meetings, preaching peace and tolerance."[43] Shaimiev has refused to be a "standard-bearer of the national movement," stressing that the "slightest deviations" from Tatarstan's inclusive citizenship policy "are fraught with serious losses."[44]

Instead, the movement was for autonomy, particularly control over Tatarstan's lucrative natural resources. Locals believed their financial contribution to Moscow was not recognized with appropriate educational, cultural, social services, and broadcast funding. According to Aleksandr Lozovoi, vice chair of the Tatar parliament, "The Russian Federation and the Kremlin must understand that this is not only a matter of national reawakening, it's also a matter of economics. We want to control what we produce."[45] Tatarstan surpassed other Union republics in many ways. Its population was larger than that of Estonia, Latvia, Lithuania, Turkmenistan, and Armenia. Its territory was larger than the three Baltic republics combined.[46] Tatarstan was the second largest oil producer in the USSR and the home of the KamAZ auto plant, which produced some 25 percent of all Soviet vehicles. The KamAZ plant's output alone was larger than Estonia's entire economy.[47] Yet in 1989, for example, though Tatarstan's enterprises made a 3.7 billion-ruble profit, the region received only 2.5 billion back from Moscow.[48] Of Tatarstan's enterprises, the USSR controlled 80 percent and the RSFSR 18 percent, leaving only two percent to Kazan. "How can I explain to our taxpayers," asked Shaimiev, "that we are donors, the money has been given away in taxes, and I cannot get anything back? Is that logical? No!"[49] Even *Pravda* sanctioned Tatarstan's demands for more influence: "the autonomous republic's desire for real sovereignty is not a concession to fashion, but the conscious manifestation—forged through suffering, you might say—of its national dignity."[50]

Phase Two: How Much Sovereignty Is Enough?

On August 30, 1990, Tatarstani leaders seized control of their destiny. With only one abstention, the local Supreme Soviet, elected in 1989 and predominantly Communist, declared sovereignty, claimed responsibility for their natural resources, and changed the autonomous republic's name from Tataria to Tatarstan. Henceforth, they declared, local laws would take precedence over Russian and Soviet legislation.

Sovereignty was assigned to the Tatarstani people, not any particular political party, institution, or person.[51] Citizenship was to be granted on a civic, not ethnic basis. All nationalities were declared equal and Tatar and Russian became official state languages. Interestingly, the declaration of sovereignty made no mention of Tatarstan being part of the RSFSR. Instead, future relations with both Russia and the USSR were to be determined by treaty. Tatarstani leaders were inflexible on this point: Yeltsin failed to persuade Tatarstani leaders to sign the 1991 Union treaty as part of the Russian contingent.[52] Instead, Gorbachev had invited Tatar representatives to sign as a full-fledged union republic.[53]

Mintimir Shaimiev, chair of Tatarstan Supreme Soviet and first secretary of the republic branch of the CPSU, led Tatarstan's independence drive. He had been elected president of Tatarstan in June 1991, at the same time Yeltsin was elected Russia's president. Having initially voiced support for the August 1991 putsch, Shaimiev quickly resigned from the CPSU Central Committee and suspended his party membership following the hard-liners' defeat.[54] The Tatar party chief was traditionally a first among equals within the regional party hierarchy. Tatarstan had a reserved seat in the CPSU Central Committee and the USSR Supreme Soviet Presidium, a status similar to the Moscow and Leningrad party organizations.[55] Later, attempts to form a Urals or Siberian regional confederation were hampered by other republics' fear that Kazan would try to dominate the process.[56]

Unlike the erratic, capricious nature of Chechnya's Dzhokar Dudaev, Shaimiev has been notable for his consistent, non-hostile approach toward Moscow and for his firm insistence on multinationalism. While Dudaev's pronouncements varied daily in their content and credibility, Shaimiev's statements on Kazan's relations with Moscow remained nearly identical from the August 1990 declaration to the February 1994 bilateral treaty. Shaimiev shrewdly realized the symbiotic relationship between Tatarstan and Russia (e.g., Tatarstan's oil was worthless without Russia's pipelines and refineries, Tatarstan's truck and helicopter factories needed Russian customers) and understood that declaring independence would likely mean war. Noting that "independent" Chechnya had not been recognized by any state, Shaimiev commented, "I couldn't support this idea of independence before the people, knowing in advance that it couldn't be realized."[57]

Throughout the battles with Moscow, Tatarstan's leaders have waged a war of semantics. They have tirelessly insisted that they were not seeking independence or secession, but rather to have Moscow ratify Tatarstan's declaration of sovereignty. As Peter Rutland commented, Tatar leaders "finessed the controversial subject of 'independence' by the simple expedient of not using that loaded word."[58] Tatarstan made no territorial claims against the Russian Federation and stood willing to jointly own property with Russia.[59] Tatarstani leaders took the allowed policies to their full, logical conclusion—taking as much as they could swallow.

After the Soviet collapse, Tatarstan's economic position continued to give it leverage against Moscow. Tatarstan was one of the few net contributors to the federal budget, if it remitted taxes to Moscow. As the site of important industries and, perhaps more importantly, key military facilities, Tatarstan was too valuable and strategic for Russia to lose. Tatarstan had a virtual monopoly on the production of military aircraft and helicopters, particularly since that many Soviet military factories now lie in independent Ukraine.[60]

Tatarstani leaders successfully took advantage of the confusion of early 1992 to wrest control of their economy away from Moscow.[61] Kazan declared fiscal sovereignty on May 21, 1992, claiming control over all local tax revenue and refusing automatic remittances to Moscow. Tatarstan soon became an attractive investment opportunity and was visited by government and private representatives from Bulgaria, Canada, and Germany to explore possible joint ventures; trade agreements were signed with Turkey, Austria, and Greece.[62] The Hungarian branch of the European Economics Institute paid for Prime Minister Mukhammad Sabirov to visit Singapore, Taiwan, and South Korea in February 1993.[63] Tatarstan also signed inter-governmental economic agreements with Uzbekistan and Lithuania.[64]

On the Home Front: Shaimiev and His Constituents

Shaimiev chose a middle ground in the race to "take as much autonomy as you can swallow." As political discourse in the republic increased, some nationalist groups thought the president had not taken enough. Several leading Tatar nationalists accused Shaimiev of failing to fulfill the potential of the August 1990 proclamation. Instead of gaining independence, Shaimiev may have been more concerned about losing power. His adroit maneuvering during the

August 1991 putsch and rumors of ballot stuffing for Yeltsin's 1996 reelection suggest this is a man who can follow the prevailing political winds.[65]

In Tatarstan as throughout the USSR, numerous nationalist groups emerged in the perestroika era. Around three dozen political and social movements have emerged in Tatarstan; about half have an ethnic component to their charter.[66] Most prominent among these was the Tatar Public Center (TPC).[67]

The Tatar Public Center dates to late 1988 and held its founding Congress February 17–18, 1989. TPC's original platform called for elevating Tatarstan to Union-republic status, making Tatar the republic's official language, obtaining economic sovereignty, and promoting ethnic and cultural consolidation of Tatars living across the USSR. Tatarstan would thus be made an equal of the RSFSR. This agenda was largely adopted in the 1990 sovereignty declaration. Roza Musina depicts the TPC as a largely urban, intelligentsia organization:

> Although the TPC was founded as an essentially Tatar association, it rapidly expanded to include both a Jewish and a Crimean Tatar section and admitted several representatives of the Russian population. The majority of TPC members were intellectuals, primarily scholars, professors, and administrative personnel. A small number of former military personnel and university students also joined the Center, and a special committee for youth affairs was set up to work with the latter group. Very few workers, urban or agricultural, were attracted to the organization, and while a number of artists participated in events staged by the TPC, very few joined the organization.[68]

The TPC split in 1990, with its more radical wing forming the Tatar Party of National Independence, Ittifak (Alliance) National Party, and the Azatlyk (Freedom) Tatar Youth League. Another radical group, the Islamic Democratic Party of Tatarstan, was founded in 1991. All these groups advocated independence, and they criticized Shaimiev for kowtowing to Moscow. Fauziia Bairamova of Ittifak would later denounce Shaimiev for taking his seat in the Russian Federation Council, a parliament of a foreign state in her estimation.[69] By its second congress in February 1991, the TPC had achieved many of its original goals and turned its attention from cultural issues to more concrete political changes. With the 1994 bilateral treaty, detailed below, the nationalist movement split again. Ittifak became a leading member of the Milli Mejilis/All-Tatar Assembly movement, while the TPC, the Youth League, and other groups refused to participate.[70]

Tatar nationalists outside the ruling echelon attempted to create their own set of parallel institutions. The Milli Mejilis was established in February 1992 to serve as a national-ethnic parliament, representing Tatars throughout the former USSR. The Ministry of Justice questioned the legitimacy of the group, noting "state bodies cannot be formed on an ethnic basis."[71] In 1994, this charter was ruled "anti-constitutional" by a Kazan court, because it claimed jurisdiction over Tatars outside of Russia and because it was attempting to overturn rulings of the Tatarstan parliament.[72] Though Shaimiev was willing to cooperate with the Milli Mejilis on cultural development issues, he refused to sanction any rival to the elected republic parliament.[73] The Milli Mejilis advocates a more confrontational approach to Russia than Shaimiev's cautious strategy. Attending celebrations marking the first anniversary of Chechnya's independence, Milli Mejilis deputy chair Zaki Zainulli announced his group's intention "to achieve true independence by using almost the same means as the Chechen republic used."[74]

Following the 1994 agreement, Tatarstani political discourse began to turn from issues of sovereignty to socio-economic problems. With the ethnic Tatar and ethnic Russian populations nearly the same size, Shaimiev took pains to avoid framing his dispute with Moscow in ethnic terms. According to a pamphlet released by Shaimiev's office, three general political movements were present in the republic: pro-Russian, radical nationalists, and moderates. The beginnings of a multi-party system could be seen, with four Tatarstani parties, six branches of Russian parties, and a dozen political movements.[75] Shaimiev was strong enough and popular enough to ignore the more extreme of these groups. When nationalists declared Yeltsin *persona non grata* for his post-treaty visit in May 1994, Shaimiev dismissed the protestors, saying "Nothing ever pleases them."[76]

Phase Three: Institutionalizing a Unilateral Upgrade

Shaimiev and his followers initially tried to work within the existing political system, specifically seeking a higher legal status within the Soviet Union. When the USSR collapsed, Tatarstani leaders decided that the Soviet-era RSFSR Constitution had been voided. A new relationship with Russia had to be built; the old one could not be modified. This would take place in several stages. Shaimiev declared five principles for creating a renewed federation, principles which underscored his concern with the consensual aspect of the process: all federation components are equal, are sovereign on their own territory, voluntarily transfer powers to the center, and are the source of the Federation's sovereignty. Fifth and most importantly, the treaty process was to proceed from the bottom up, with regions voluntarily ceding powers to the center; this was not to be an instance of devolution.[77] In the interim, Tatarstan withheld federal taxes, only submitting enough to cover functions Kazan intended to delegate to the center. As Shaimiev explained,

> it would be stupid to transfer money to the center only to then sit around in the Russian Federation ministries' reception rooms and beg for your own money.[78]

Instead of sitting around, Shaimiev crafted a three-pronged strategy. First, his sovereignty policy would gain legitimacy by a public referendum. Second, he would move beyond traditional center-periphery arrangements to find entirely new concepts for bilateral relations. Third, he would keep a polite distance from the political activities of Russia proper.

Legitimate Policy. On March 21, 1992, Tatarstan held a referendum to confirm the continued validity of the 1990 sovereignty proclamation, given the new context resulting from the collapse of the Soviet Union. Voters were asked, "Do you agree that the republic of Tatarstan is a sovereign state, a subject of international law, building its relations with the Russian Federation and other republics and states on the basis of treaties between equal partners?" Some observers thought the wording cumbersome and obfuscatory, but parliament refused to heed the Russian Constitutional Court's ruling that the ballot was unconstitutional. Instead, it stuck to its position that the referendum was not a bid to sneak through secession. Yeltsin even made personal appeals to Tatarstan residents, asking them first to cancel the referendum and then to vote against the question.[79]

The measure passed with 61.4 percent of the vote in a turnout of 82 percent. Dudaev congratulated Tatarstan for the referendum, citing it as "the first tangible victory on the road to sovereignty and state independence."[80] Although the referendum results were not broken down by ethnicity, a December 1990 opinion poll conducted by the Public Opinion Research Center and the Sociology Laboratory at Kazan University revealed a split: 74 percent of Tatars and 51 percent of Russians supported the sovereignty declaration. One year later the figures had become more polarized: Tatars 84 percent and Russians 23 percent.[81] Tatarstan's cleavages may be more regional than ethnic. Rural areas tended to vote for independence, while urban areas, with larger Russian populations, opposed it.[82] The results strengthened Shaimiev's standing and confirmed his intent to abstain from the Federation Treaty.

Conceptual Innovation. Drawing on the work of constitutional scholar Oleg Rumiantsev, Tatarstani leaders created their own formula for relations with Moscow. Tatarstan adopted a new constitution on November 6, 1992. The document largely enshrined the principles of the 1990 sovereignty declaration. Briefly, "the republic of Tatarstan is a sovereign state with international rights which is associated with the Russian Federation on the basis of a treaty of mutually delegated authority."[83] Tatar citizenship was granted on a civic, rather than ethnic basis, and dual citizenship was allowed. All ethnic groups were made equal. Other articles stressed the supremacy of the republic's laws, claimed title to the region's natural and cultural resources, and made Tatarstan a nuclear-free zone.[84]

The Tatar Constitution proclaimed a new, "associated" status, similar to a Rumiantsev proposal for the 1993 Russian constitution.[85] Shaimiev hailed "this flexible formula [which] allows the situation to develop naturally and does not violate Russian territorial integrity" and indicated that Tatarstani leaders would be satisfied if such a provision were included in the preamble to the new Russian constitution.[86] It would also serve to protect Tatarstan from once again coming under "a center as rigid as the one we have only recently gotten rid of."[87]

Moscow understandably objected to the constitutional text, as did the federalist Citizens of the Russian Federation and Accord and Equality and Legality political movements. The Tatar nationalist groups argued that Tatarstan must first provide legal protection to its ethnic Russian population, failure to do so would violate standards of human rights.[88] Kazan had one last advantage: Moscow could not reasonably complain that Tatarstan was violating the existing Soviet-era Russian Constitution, as Yeltsin had been doing so for years.

In addition to declaring sovereignty, Tatarstan and neighboring republics considered a variety of possible regional arrangements as alternatives to the current system. The Bolsheviks had briefly considered a Tatar-Bashkir republic, but later relegated both to "second-tier" status. Should the RSFSR disintegrate, a Volga-Urals Federation of six autonomous Russian republics might result.[89] Tatar nationalists considered reviving the idea of Idel Ural Republic as well as creating Tatar-Bashkir Volga-Ural Confederation to be a Commonwealth of Independent States (CIS) member.[90] Shaimiev wanted to join the CIS as a founding member on par with independent republics, but his application was rejected because it would entail *de facto* recognition of Tatarstan's independence. Shaimiev then complained, "it is as if perestroika has affected only the peoples of the Union republics without affecting the others—the former autonomous entities—at all."[91]

Polite Indifference. While waiting for recognition from Moscow, Tatarstan stood aloof from Russian political processes. Its leaders boycotted the June 1991 presidential election, and Yeltsin received less than half the votes cast there.[92] Yeltsin "may become president of the Russian Federation, but he won't be our president," declared Ittifak leader Fauziia Bairamova. "We in Tatarstan want the same thing that those in union republics are fighting for: independence."[93]

Low turnouts for the April 1993 referendum and the December 1993 elections invalidated the results for Tatarstan. Shaimiev initially refused to hold the April 1993 referendum on the Russian constitution's framework until Tatarstan-Russia relations were clarified.[94] His national pride was still smarting from the "ham-handed pressure" and "vicious, massive propaganda campaign" Moscow waged to halt the 1992 Tatarstan referendum on sovereignty.[95] Shaimiev's sudden about-face to participate in drafting the new Russian constitution raised speculation that Yeltsin had made a secret deal to recognize Tatarstan's sovereignty if it would participate.[96] As for the December 1993 elections, Tatarstan refused to participate so long as the draft constitution denied the republics' sovereignty.[97]

Tatarstan also refused to follow Moscow's shock-therapy program. Instead it adopted a more humane reform program tailored to local needs. Yeltsin's government tacitly approved such an approach, by signing agreements on economic cooperation with Tatarstan leaders. The Kazan government subsidized food prices, delayed privatization, and undertook other "cushioning" measures to ease the transition.[98] Tatarstan also willingly shouldered its share of Soviet debt, an issue that had proved to be highly contentious in the Yugoslav breakup.[99]

Throughout 1992–1994, Moscow and Kazan quietly, slowly began to reach agreement on some matters. These included: economic cooperation (January 22, 1992); oil and petrochemicals (June 5, 1993); property and customs (June 22, 1993). A host of agreements were signed in February 1994, including banking, credit, and foreign exchange; foreign trade; the budget; defense industries; law enforcement; and the military. Further agreements on the environment and higher education have been mentioned, but no details given.[100] The published texts explicitly recognized the sovereignty of both Russia and Tatarstan. University of Kazan professor Mikhail Gershaft argues that the texts to the February 1994 agreements were never published to conceal the concessions made by both parties.[101] Gershaft also suggests that Tatarstan's foreign investors pressured Shaimiev to clear up the jurisdictional confusion before it harmed their interests. In any case, compromise had been reached.

In early 1994, Tatarstan became the first subject of the Russian Federation to sign a bilateral treaty with Moscow. Though it appeared to be a positive step toward formalizing a federal relationship, it probably resulted from changing center-periphery politics. Shaimiev apparently had been surprised at Zhirinovskii's showing in December 1993 elections and wanted to cast his lot with Yeltsin.[102] Following Yeltsin's October 1993 defeat of parliament, Shaimiev likely concluded that the bargaining advantage now lay with Yeltsin.[103] Tatar Prime Minister Mukhammed Sabirov claimed to have signed under duress brought on by a Russian threat to close a major oil pipeline.[104]

Under the bilateral treaty Tatarstan retains ownership of all its natural resources and may conduct its own foreign relations, including trade agreements. Its international legal status, however, remains cloudy and it is unclear whether Tatarstan could join any international organizations, such as the World Trade Organization. Defense is delegated to Moscow, as is the right to impose customs duties on trade outside of the Russian Federation. Tatarstan remains a net budget contributor, but negotiates with Moscow on its contribution level and handles many aspects on its own.[105] Tatarstani leaders would finally take their seats in the Federation Council. Tatarstan would use the Russian ruble, Russian passports, and Russian stamps, but would fly its own flag and open its own central bank. Most important to Moscow, Kazan acknowledges Russia's sovereignty and the 1993 constitution. Tatarstan also agreed to again hold elections to the Russian Duma, following the insufficient turnout for the December 1993 balloting. Recalling his controversial statement in Kazan in 1990, Yeltsin believed his stance had been vindicated by the bilateral agreement: Tatarstan "has taken on as much responsibilities as it can cope with," he said. "As for what is beyond its capabilities, it has delegated that to the federal authorities."[106]

Shaimiev had criticized the Russian Constitution for not incorporating the Federal Treaty, so he successfully pushed for the Tatar-Russo Treaty to be backed-up by a dozen agreements which provided implementation mechanisms for a variety of issues.[107] Shaimiev encouraged numerous amendments to the Tatarstan Constitution to resolve the contradictions with the Russian Constitution.[108]

Through consistent policies and conceptual innovation, Shaimiev successfully extracted a measure of independence from Moscow. His considerable strength and legitimacy within the republic helped to ensure that he could deliver any deal made with Moscow.

Chechnya: All or Nothing

The Chechen independence movement was handicapped by its leader's refusal to compromise, the near total destruction of Soviet-era institutions, and the region's relative insignificance to Moscow. The movement's leader, Dzhokar Dudaev, only compounded these difficulties. Ruling under questionable legitimacy, Dudaev would often resort to fantastic charges and to ancient grievances when conventional diplomacy failed. His total focus on nationalism produced a minuscule win-set—there was no solution that would satisfy both Moscow and Chechnya. Dudaev's ethnic rhetoric may have been a calculated move to unite his disparate constituency, but if so, his strategy failed miserably.[109]

Compared to Tatarstan, Chechnya came under Russian control relatively late and brought with it a legacy of armed resistance. Following a series of wars that began in 1817, the Russian tsars finally conquered Chechnya in 1859. In the aftermath of the Bolshevik Revolution, the Chechens and other Caucasus peoples founded an independent North Caucasian Federation, which lasted from 1918 until 1921, when it was annexed by the new Soviet state. Once a major oil producer, the Chechen oil industry has much less potential now.[110] The Chechen-Ingush Autonomous Soviet Socialist Republic (CI ASSR) was created in 1936 only to be abolished by Stalin in 1944. Fearing their collaboration with Hitler, Stalin brutally deported some 800,000 Chechens and Ingush to Siberia; approximately 240,000 died in the process. The CI ASSR was reestablished in 1957, though with changed borders.[111]

The Stalin era is key to understanding Chechen attitudes towards Moscow. Chechens were the largest single ethnic group deported under Stalin.[112] "Virtually every Chechen adult over the age of thirty-two was born in exile," noted relief worker Fred Cuny. "Perhaps this accounts for the high percentage of hardened, dedicated Chechen fighters in their thirties and forties."[113]

After proclaiming independence, Dudaev always portrayed Russian actions as imperialist interference in Chechen affairs. Yeltsin's policies were depicted as yet another manifestation of Russian imperial tendencies. Conversely, sovereignty was the only protection against a repeat of Stalin's effort to exterminate the Chechens.[114] Dudaev claimed that the events of 1991 were "the culmination of 300 years of expectations . . . Three centuries of struggle by the Chechen people" against Russia.[115] According to Dudaev, "The Chechens were never a part of Russia and, therefore, they are not seceding from it."[116] He chose the occasion of the fiftieth anniversary of Stalin's deportations of the Chechens and Ingush to reiterate his accusations of Russian interference and provocation.[117] Then-Russian minister of nationalities Nikolai Egorov refused to dispatch Russian troops to Chechnya during the August 1994 putsch, so that he could "deprive Dudaev of his main propaganda trump card—the threat of a Russian military intervention."[118]

Phase One: National Awakening in the Caucasus

With perestroika, new regional bodies emerged in the Caucasus, following the precedent set in the western regions of the USSR. The nationalist *Bart* (Harmony) Party, led by poet and future Chechen vice-president Zelimkhan Yandarbiev, emerged in July 1989, later changing its name to the Vainakh Democratic Party in 1990.[119] In November 1990, the All-National Congress of the Chechen People (OKChN) was founded.[120] OKChN was a component of the Assembly of the Mountain Peoples of the Caucasus, which aimed to create a trans-Caucasian federation, but early realized that Moscow would oppose such a development. Like the contemporary Baltic National Fronts, the Chechen National Congress proclaimed local sovereignty and sought to establish a secular Chechen state independent of the Russian Federation; independence from the USSR was still negotiable.

General Dzhokar Dudaev was elected chair at its founding Congress. Dudaev had most recently served as commander of a Soviet Air Force base in Tartu, where he had witnessed the Estonian national movement firsthand. While Soviet special forces intervened to suppress nationalist uprisings in Lithuania and Latvia in January 1991, Dudaev has been credited with blocking a similar maneuver in the Estonian capital.[121] Having spent his military career outside Chechnya, Dudaev had not been compromised by local clan politics.[122] Dudaev retired in March 1991 and returned to Chechnya.

Even prior to August 1991, the nationalist OKChN and Dudaev challenged the old-style local communists, led by Doku Zavgaev. When the Chechen-Ingush Supreme Soviet refused to recognize the OKChN's November 1990 declaration of sovereignty, low-level conflict between the two groups ensued. Initially this consisted mostly of harassment: the OKChN had to have its newspaper printed in Georgia and Baltic republics due to local censorship. But at a June 8, 1991, meeting the OKChN Executive Committee proclaimed the Chechen-Ingush Republic extinct, asserted their authority over the Chechen region, and dismissed the possibility of signing treaties with either the Russian Federation or the USSR. Furthermore, the Executive Committee called for elections for a Chechen president and parliament and for forming a Chechen national guard.

A Chechen-Ingush cleavage developed during this period. In mid-1991 Ingush leaders were working to reclaim historically Ingush territory now assigned to North Ossetia. The Chechen-Ingush government, in fact, announced it would not sign Gorbachev's 1991 Union Treaty until it could resolve the border issue.[123] While Russian officials visited the region to forestall an Ingush-Ossetian war, a June 20, 1991, congress of Ingush deputies proclaimed an Ingush republic within RSFSR but separate from Chechnya.[124] Dudaev did not try to persuade them to remain. By the time Dudaev's regime issued new passport stamps in mid-October 1991, the word "Ingushetia" had been dropped from the region's official name.[125] In June 1992, the Russian Duma formally approved the creation of a separate Ingush republic.

Phase Two: Dudaev Declares Independence

During the August 1991 putsch, the Chechen-Ingush Supreme Soviet supported the anti-Gorbachev State Committee for the State of Emergency. When the hard-liners were defeated, Dudaev demanded that the local Supreme Soviet be replaced. He seemed to have some popular backing; a *Golos Checheno-Ingushetii* poll revealed that 44 percent of respondents supported the OKChN as the legitimate authority, compared to only 29 percent for the local Supreme Soviet.[126] Boris Yeltsin and the Russian government also agreed on the need to replace the Chechen-Ingush Supreme Soviet—as well as others that had supported the coup—but insisted on elections first.

Impatient, Dudaev grabbed for power, seizing government buildings in Grozny. Party secretary Zavgaev fled to Moscow, eventually becoming Russia's ambassador to Tanzania.[127] When the local Supreme Soviet agreed to dissolve itself, RSFSR authorities established an interim 32–person Provisional Supreme Council to be the lawful government until elections could be held. When Dudaev refused to acknowledge the Council's authority, an impasse resulted.[128] TASS correctly labeled the situation a crisis of legitimacy: "official powers do not have any real strength, yet the victorious forces have not yet received legal authority."[129] *Rossiiskaia gazeta* noted that the situation was "not so much dual power as of a power vacuum."[130]

While Yeltsin was on holiday in Sochi, Russian Vice President Aleksandr Rutskoi attempted to defuse the situation.[131] At least a half-dozen parliamentary delegations were dispatched to Grozny and parliamentary speaker Ruslan Khasbulatov, an ethnic Chechen himself, condemned Dudaev's unconstitutional actions. Decrees ordering Chechens to vacate occupied buildings and disband paramilitary organizations were issued and ignored. Unable to contact Yeltsin, Rutskoi consulted with Soviet president Gorbachev.[132] Meanwhile, Chechnya elected its own president and parliament on October 27. Dudaev claimed to have won the presidency with some 90 percent, though Moscow denounced the elections as fraudulent and unconstitutional. Estonia and Georgia provided election observers, but reports suggested that few polling places were actually open.[133]

Dudaev's November 2, 1991, declaration of independence came when the division of authority between Russia and the USSR was fluid and contested. The Chechen crisis became both a symptom of and a key battle in the ongoing jurisdictional war in Moscow. Yeltsin imposed a state of emergency, halted ruble payments to Chechnya, and dispatched Russian Interior Ministry troops to the region, which were quickly repelled by Chechen forces. Still trying to assert his influence and undermine Yeltsin, Soviet leader Mikhail Gorbachev intervened, encouraging Rutskoi to introduce a motion in the Russian Duma to declare Yeltsin's decree invalid. After two days of debate, the Duma annulled Yeltsin's decree, saying that while constitutional, it was unenforceable.[134] The pro-Yeltsin Democratic Russia movement split over Chechen issue, with members divided over whether Yeltsin should use force to prevent the Russian Federation from disintegrating.[135] According to Gorbachev's last press secretary, Andrei Grachev, Yeltsin found Gorbachev's interference to be intolerable and this episode cemented his break with the Soviet leader.[136] Dudaev, however, praised Gorbachev for his reform efforts.[137]

The Chechens ignored the contradictory decrees from Moscow, and Dudaev took the oath of office on November 9, ironically wearing his Soviet dress uniform. In his inaugural address, Dudaev proclaimed martial law to ward off Russian provocation. "Now we can speak only about complete secession and the beginning of building our relations as equals . . . This, however, does not mean breaking relations between us and Russia."[138] Independence was confirmed by referendum on December 1, with 97.4 of voters in favor, though considerable voting irregularities were reported.[139]

Chechnya adopted a new constitution on March 12, 1992, one day before the first signatories to the Russian Federation Treaty. In line with previous Dudaev statements, the charter proclaimed Chechnya to be an independent, secular, sovereign state. The constitution provides for many of the trappings of statehood: insignia, revenue collection, a national bank, a diplomatic corps, border posts and customs, law enforcement, and armed forces. All ethnic groups are to be treated equally and both Chechen and Russia are state languages.[140]

Phase Three: Turning His Back on Moscow

From then on, Dudaev acted as though he ruled an independent state. Chechnya refused to participate in Russian referenda or elections and severed its fiscal ties with Moscow. Dudaev began to establish his own armed forces—subordinated to him, not parliament—assembled a national Olympic committee, and offered political asylum to both Erich Honecker and Zviad Gamsakhurdia.[141] First Deputy Prime Minister Yaragi Mamodaev visited Japan and Turkey in spring 1992, though foreign officials stressed that the trips were unofficial.[142] Dudaev himself traveled to Lithuania in January 1993 and Turkey, Jordan, Sudan, and Iraq in autumn 1993 in hopes of establishing economic links with these countries.[143]

Chechnya received some support from other peripheral parts of Russia and the former USSR, particularly Georgia. As early as April 1991, Dudaev found an ally in Georgian President Zviad Gamsakhurdia; the two leaders apparently shared a common fear of Russian imperialism. Rutskoi, among others, even accused Gamsakhurdia of egging on Dudaev in hopes of forming a Caucasian confederation. The Georgian leader appealed to all Georgians living in

Chechnya to vote for Dudaev in the 1991 Chechen presidential election.[144] The Abkhaz, Dagestani, and Avar national movements also backed Dudaev, and in mid-1994 the Confederation of the Peoples of the Caucasus warned that Russia was preparing to forcibly intervene in Chechnya.[145] Unlike the Tatars, who had ethnic kin elsewhere in Russia, and the Balts, who had émigré friends in Washington, the Chechens were largely on their own. The small Chechen Diaspora in Moscow cast their lot with Khasbulatov and issued a plea for Dudaev to leave.[146]

Like Tatarstan's Shaimiev, Dudaev was particularly interested in joining the Commonwealth of Independent States. But instead of waiting for an invitation, Dudaev set his own conditions: Chechnya would only join the CIS if Russia recognized its sovereignty.[147] If he couldn't join the CIS, Dudaev threatened to form a trans-Caucasian union, which would include Stavropol krai and other parts of southern Russia, in addition to Georgia, Armenia, and Azerbaijan.[148] "Unification of the entire Caucasus on a confederative basis," he told *Rossiia*, "will give the right and the opportunity to any people on this territory to choose the only correct way to a future without interference from third parties, especially Russia."[149] Following Gamsakhurdia's suicide—and coinciding with negotiation overtures from Moscow—Dudaev later argued for strengthening the CIS and restoring Russia to great-power status.[150]

In early 1992, Dudaev sent written appeals to Tatarstan, Bashkortostan, Azerbaijan, and Turkmenistan seeking to create a united front against Moscow's economic blockade.[151] Contacts between Chechnya and Azerbaijan increased in 1992, leading to speculation that a pan-Caucasian bloc was imminent.[152] Dudaev particularly sought recognition from Ukraine and Belarus—Russia's partners in dissolving the USSR. "Recognition could become the factor on the basis of which we could coordinate our actions," he argued. "Then the world would be able to see that peoples can really unite instead of looking up to Russia and the apologists of the former empire."[153] The Tatarstan parliament invited and received a delegation of Chechen parliamentarians in October 1992, though the Chechens concluded that their all-or-nothing approach was "more realistic" than Tatarstan's middle-range strategy.[154] For Chechnya's first anniversary of independence, Gamsakhurdia and representatives of Tatarstan, Israel, and Jordan attended the festivities.[155]

Few former Soviet republics expressed concern over the December 1994 Russian invasion of Chechnya, agreeing it was an internal Russian problem. Not too long ago many republic leaders and their nationalist movements had received support from Yeltsin's Russia against Gorbachev, and they were not going to abandon their ally now. Though Lithuanian nationalist leader Vytautus Landsbergis attempted to mediate in the matter, the Lithuanian government merely issued a reminder that it had not recognized Chechnya's independence.[156] Landsbergis eventually criticized both the Lithuanian government for bowing to Russia and the world community for their indifference to the Chechen invasion.[157] Estonia offered "moral support" to the cause of Chechen self-determination, and the Estonian parliament issued an official statement of protest. Pro-Chechnya rallies were held throughout all three Baltic states.[158] President Nursultan Nazarbaev of Kazakhstan, which has a sizeable Chechen Diaspora population, did telephone Yeltsin to express his desire for peaceful resolution of the conflict.[159] Kyrgyzstan agreed Chechnya was an internal Russian problem, while Tajik opposition leader Zafar Rakhmonov denied his group's involvement in Chechnya as mercenaries, noting "we have enough conflicts of our own."[160]

As the leader of an "independent" country, Dudaev refused to sign the 1992 Russian Federation Treaty. When opposition forces attempted to seize control of key Grozny communication facilities on the day of the Treaty's signing ceremony, Dudaev portrayed the events as a Moscow-backed coup attempt.[161] He also refused to hold the April 1993 referendum on Yeltsin's performance. Dudaev saw himself as creating a precedent for other non-Russian peoples long under Russian domination. "I think that we are a proving ground," he commented, "for testing the right of small groups to exist and develop independently."[162] He denounced the 1993 Russian constitution as "a concentration camp charter for small nationalities."[163]

However, the extent of Chechnya's independence from Moscow seemed flexible. In particular, Chechen leaders wanted to stay in the ruble zone.[164] "Today virtually all of Chechnya's leaders are declaring that they are prepared to have a common economic, information, and—more importantly—military space with Russia," Russian television reported in April 1992.[165] Foreign Minister Shamseddin Yuself noted that if Russia would only recognize Chechnya's independence, the two states "shall remain good friends."[166] Chechnya created its own currency, the tyum (banknotes) and the nakhar (coins), in September 1994, but has not issued them as Grozny cannot back the notes with gold.[167]

On the Home Front

While Dudaev sparred with Yeltsin, Chechnya began to crumble. Economic decline brought poverty, crime, and an atmosphere of lawlessness. Complaints about the situation led to political infighting in Grozny and competing claims of power. Unlike Shaimiev, Dudaev faced a formidable and growing opposition movement.

Economic Collapse. Dudaev voluntarily severed Chechnya's fiscal links with Moscow, neither collecting federal taxes nor accepting subsidies from the center. Local leaders seemed to think they could survive without Moscow. The economy was only lightly industrialized; with few factories there would be no need to rely on Russia for spare parts.[168] The region had proven oil reserves and prospects for more, though to date oil profits had gone straight to Moscow. More importantly, Chechnya was also a natural transit route for the rich Caspian oil fields. Dudaev argued that Chechnya's oil resources could turn the region into a "Kuwait of the Caucasus" and formulated an elaborate plan in which each Chechen family would be allotted 300 liters a month, to be sold or saved.[169]

In reality, the economy collapsed, while mafia-types grew wealthy from black market trading and arms trafficking. As Dudaev seemed unconcerned about the increase in mafia dealings, many observers assumed he was an active participant. Rumors circulated that Dudaev and his cronies had appropriated some Aeroflot planes and launched their own smuggling business with neighboring CIS members Turkey and Iran. Chechnya also became the primary source of counterfeiting in Russia.[170] Ruslan Khasbulatov claimed that by mid-1993, unemployment in Chechnya had reached 30 percent, industrial production had dropped 60 percent, and Dudaev's cronies had stolen more than 70 billion rubles. Without wages for at least three years, the Chechen militia was forced to fend for itself, partly by seizing hostages in order to collect ransom money.[171] Noting the rise in crime, Khasbulatov accused Dudaev of turning Chechnya into a "criminal cesspool and a staging post for international drug trafficking."[172]

When the economy collapsed, so too did Dudaev's popular support. As the dispute with Russia continued, inflation soared, food became scarce, and wages were at least six months in arrears. Russia had ceased sending rubles to Chechnya in 1992, meaning that salaries, benefits, and pensions went unpaid.[173] While common folks and presidential rhetoric blamed Moscow, informed Chechens blamed Dudaev. Journalist Anatol Lieven commented that during his visits to Chechnya in August and September 1994, "It was apparent that . . . Dudaev was extremely unpopular with much of the population, that ordinary people were infuriated by the collapse of wages, public services, and public order, and that his support was now largely based on the more conservative mountain areas and on his own presidential guard."[174] *Moscow News* later speculated that his own men, who resented his growing wealth, killed Dudaev.[175]

Back Channels and Power Struggles. From the early days of "independent" Chechnya, public support for Dudaev was not wholesale. As early as October 1991, in the midst of a prison mutiny, members of the intelligentsia staged rival public rallies, calling for new parliamentary elections to be followed by a referendum on whether to even have a presidency.[176] In the spring of 1993, pro- and anti-Dudaev groups staged parallel, permanent rallies in downtown Grozny.[177] When Dudaev attempted to dissolve parliament in April 1993, the parliamentarians joined the opposition rallies in downtown Grozny.[178] A serious attempt to assassinate Dudaev occurred in May 1994.

Members of Dudaev's government took initiatives independent of the president, creating confusion as they issued contradictory statements. In December 1992, First Deputy Prime Minister Yaragi Mamodaev undertook negotiations with Russia on the issue of power sharing. Mamodaev and Ramazan Abdulatipov, chair of the Russian Council for Nationalities, reached a tentative accord, much like the eventual Tatarstan agreement, whereby Chechnya would voluntarily delegate some of its powers to Russian institutions.[179] The

Chechen parliament and government quickly repudiated Mamodaev's statements, and it was strongly implied that he was acting without Dudaev's blessing.[180] When a Kremlin delegate came to Grozny to negotiate with Dudaev, his own parliament accused him of blocking progress—Dudaev had refused to allow the delegation's plane to land.[181] Mamodaev's negotiations resulted in Moscow lifting its economic blockade of Chechnya and remitting some 3 billion rubles in pension payments.[182] Yet so long as Dudaev remained in power, the agreement would not be instituted.

Throughout 1993, Dudaev faced consistent attacks from his parliament. The first phase of this power struggle came in February, when Dudaev had attempted to unilaterally impose presidential rule, only to be blocked by parliament.[183] In June 1993, the Chechen Cabinet of Ministers issued a global appeal to UN and CIS members, denouncing Dudaev for violence against his people. The cabinet then declared a traditional blood feud against Dudaev.[184] By April, Dudaev would attempt to dissolve the parliament—the same solution Yeltsin would try on his legislature later in the year—while the parliament began impeachment proceedings against him. The Chechen Supreme Court ruled that Dudaev's decrees changing the government structure were "anti-constitutional," and some 75,000 people rallied in downtown Grozny, demanding Dudaev's resignation.[185] The president eventually prevailed, dissolving parliament in June, but the incident revealed the divisions within the Chechen government. As parliament's newly appointed prime minister in the opposition "government of popular confidence," Mamodaev wasted no time in blaming the president for the economic chaos. Claiming that four million tons of oil products had been diverted from Chechnya in 1992, Mamodaev commented "I wonder why not all Chechen citizens took to the street."[186]

A 1994 round of inter-governmental talks, this time between Yeltsin chief of staff Sergei Filatov and Chechen state secretary Aslambek Akbulatov, was never recognized by Dudaev. In those talks Russia put forth two conditions. First, Chechnya must remain part of the Russian Federation. Second, Chechnya must conduct democratic elections; in the immediate future this meant rescheduling the unsuccessful December 1993 balloting.[187] The latter provision was a non-starter for Dudaev, as no sovereign state has representatives sitting in the legislature of another state.

Despite Dudaev's anti-Russia rhetoric, ethnic Russians did not openly oppose his actions much, at least prior to the 1994–1996 war. There were an estimated 300,000 ethnic Russians in Chechnya in 1992, though only one Russian deputy among the forty-one parliamentarians.[188] Soon after assuming power, Dudaev had decreed that all ethnic groups would be equal in Chechnya and made both Chechen and Russian official state languages.[189] While Dudaev concerned himself with the treatment of ethnic Chechens in Russia, he considered ethnic Russians living in Chechnya to be Moscow's problem.[190] Apprehensive of the increasing influence of Islam, many ethnic Russians simply left, an estimated 19,000 in 1991 alone.[191] Sergei Shakrai told the Russian constitutional court that some 250,000 persons had emigrated from Chechnya in the early 1990s.[192]

Regional challenges to Dudaev soon emerged. The Tbilisi newspaper *Svobodnaia gruziia* reported the existence of at least three opposition movements. An article entitled, "The Chechen Opposition: Who's Who?" profiled the three leading anti-Dudaev movements. *Daymokh* (Fatherland) was made up of intellectuals who believed Dudaev came to power illegally, but they support Dudaev's foreign policy. The pro-Russia, mostly communist *Marsho* (Freedom) cultivated ties with Russian Duma chair Ruslan Khasbulatov. Led by Leche Saligov, *Yso* (Justice) consisted of people shut out of Dudaev's personal spoils system and who wanted Russia to exert extreme pressure on the Dudaev regime.[193] These factions opposed Dudaev, but supported independence. *Marsho* leader Abdulla Bugaev complained that: "The people of Chechnya are tired both of the tyrannical regime of Dudaev and of the inconsistent and uncertain position of Moscow."[194] During July 1994, Ruslan Labazanov's unregistered Justice Party *Misso* (also rendered as *Nesso* or *Niiso*) surrounded the town of Argun and demanded Dudaev's resignation and that "all the money belonging to the people be returned."[195]

Another three anti-Dudaev factions had particularly strong popular followings.[196] Umar Avturkhanov, a former Soviet interior police major and Zavgaev protégé, led the Chechen Provisional Council, which was based in the Upper Terek district. In August 1994, with Russia's blessing, the Council tried to topple Dudaev, citing Dudaev's ruining of the Chechen economy and pledging to normalize relations with Russia. The Russian government recognized Avturkhanov as the legitimate leader of Chechnya.[197] Maria Eismont claims the FSK then undertook supplying the Provisional Council, uniting the opposition forces, and making Khasbulatov understand that Moscow did not welcome his presence.[198]

Moscow sided with Avturkhanov over the other opposition groups. Yaragi Mamodaev, the former leader of the Chechen state construction company, headed the "Government of Popular Trust," essentially the parliament Dudaev had dissolved in April 1993.[199] Under Dudaev Mamodaev had served as prime minister and parliamentary speaker. In fall 1994, Ruslan Khasbulatov, an ethnic Chechen who had led the 1993 parliamentary revolt against Yeltsin, established his own base in Tolstoi Yurt following his amnesty from prison. Dudaev seemed particularly threatened by Khasbulatov, who had proven his willingness to challenge Yeltsin.[200] Khasbulatov unsuccessfully tried to invade Grozny on October 15, 1994. These groups objected not to Chechen independence, but to Dudaev and his ruinous economic policies.

In addition, exiled leader Zavgaev had taken up residence in Moscow, where he ran a puppet government supported by Yeltsin and Interior Minister Anatolii Kulikov.[201] Zavgaev occupied the Chechen seat in the Russian Federation Council until November 1996, when he finally accepted his government-in-exile's resignation.[202]

The Problem Was Dudaev. As often happens in politics, one man came to personify a specific policy. Dudaev became synonymous with Chechen national independence and corruption. The *Segodnia* newspaper concurred, noting "it is this 'symbolic' aspect . . . that allows the president of Chechnya to be a geopolitical figure of the Caucasus as well."[203] From spring 1992, Dudaev's regime came under severe criticism, not for seeking independence, but for the declining economy, rising crime, and Dudaev's personal style. A *Rossiiskaia gazeta* correspondent, for example, criticized Dudaev for his "neo-bolshevism, intolerance toward different thinking—precisely that against which the current leaders of Chechnya themselves fought so fiercely."[204] *Pravda* described Dudaev as "a web of contradictions . . . impulsive and emotional."[205] Dudaev himself claimed to only be working for his country; he repeatedly stated he would voluntarily retire if only the world would recognize his state's independence.[206]

Instead, Dudaev may have harmed his country's international image and chances for reconciliation with Russia. His actions alternately confused and antagonized Moscow. One day he would advocate a common economic zone, the next day he would see conspiracies all around. For example, on February 23, 1992, Dudaev told a rally in Grozny that he had evidence of an impending "provocative attack" by the Russian military, communists, mafia, and/or secret services. However, he was still amenable to close political and economic ties with Moscow.[207] Eventually, the Kremlin decided it would be futile to negotiate with Dudaev. Russian political analyst Andrei Kortunov described Dudaev as "the incarnation of the irrational, fanatic, uncontrolled, maverick, loose-cannon-type politician."[208]

Many of Dudaev's allegations about Russian actions were fanciful at minimum, if not outright paranoia. In an October 15, 1991, radio broadcast, he claimed to have scientific evidence that Russia was about to trigger an earthquake in Chechnya, and in 1994 he announced Moscow was planning to explode a nuclear device on Chechen soil.[209] He claimed Rutskoi was training drug addicts to launch a *kamikaze* assassination plot against him.[210] Western journalists and OSCE observers agreed he was psychologically unstable—a paranoid megalomaniac.[211] Tatar President Shaimiev told prominent Russian ethnologist Valerii Tishkov that Yeltsin's advisors were repeating insults that Dudaev had allegedly made against the Russian president.[212] A president-to-president meeting between Dudaev and Yeltsin might have satisfied Dudaev's need for recognition and led to a treaty on the Tatarstan model.[213]

Dudaev's assassination by Russian forces in April 1996 made him a martyr to the Chechen cause. Many Chechens refused to believe he was dead, particularly since no body was ever found. Sightings were common and he was expected to attend Independence Day celebrations in September. Some Chechens even indicated they would vote for Dudaev in the January 1997 presidential elections.[214] Russian intelligence forces reported that Dudaev's supporters were preparing to produce a Dudaev double to bolster support.[215]

Women began to name their babies "Dzhokar" and the casualties from the 1944 deportations acquired the designation "Dzhokar's children."[216]

Yeltsin Reins in the Wayward Republics

By 1994 Yeltsin had dissolved the communist-era Congress of People's Deputies and imposed his own super-presidential constitution. Now his attention turned to the obstinate republics. His government had competing suggestions for how best to accomplish this. Tatarstan proved to be the easier case.

Russian officials hailed the Russian-Tatarstan agreement as a possible model for other recalcitrant parts of the Federation. Soon after the agreement's completion, Tatarstani Deputy Prime Minister Vasilii Likhachev offered to help mediate the Russian-Chechen conflict, and Russian Deputy Prime Minister Sergei Shakhrai suggested using the Tatar model to settle the issue of Crimean separatism.[217] Similar treaties have since been signed with other republics: Chuvashia, Kabardino-Balkaria, North Ossetia, Sakha, Udmurtia, Burtiatia, and Bashkortostan.

The treaty was not without its critics in Moscow. Sergei Baburin complained that it was nonsense for a state to "sign a treaty with part of itself."[218] Russian Deputy Prime Minister Sergei Shakhrai dismissed such objections for their logical and factual errors, noting precedents set by other federations, particularly Spain. He further stressed the uniqueness of the Tatarstan situation, and defended Moscow for "choosing the lesser of two evils" in trying to stabilize the federation.[219] The ethnic-Russian regions also were not happy with Tatarstan's special status. Sverdlovsk Governor Eduard Rossel declared that he and other members of the Federation Council would never permit Chechnya to receive such special treatment.[220]

Kremlin Conflict over Chechnya

Yeltsin was involved in his own two-level game, facing criticism from his cabinet over the Chechen situation. The various factions opposed to Dudaev each found allies in the Kremlin. One puzzle in the Chechen crisis is that it was virtually ignored by Moscow in 1992 and 1993. *Izvestiia* went so far as to accuse Yeltsin of de facto recognizing Chechen independence.[221] But in late 1994, Dudaev's insubordination became so intolerable that the Kremlin decided he had to be removed by force. Why the turnaround? Michael McFaul believes that Yeltsin ordered the invasion not to save the Federation, but to save his presidency. McFaul points to three consequences of the 1993 parliamentary elections as forcing Yeltsin to change his political orientation. First, the success of Vladimir Zhirinovskii demonstrated the electoral value of Russian nationalism. Second, the campaign revealed the incohesiveness of the democratic reformers. Third, and most important, the simultaneous referendum ratified the new Russian constitution. "In 1994, therefore, Chechnya's independence became the exception rather than the rule—and was a major eyesore for a Russian president seeking to consolidate and strengthen state power."[222] McFaul's theory is supported by reports that Russian Foreign Minister Andrei Kozyrev has admitted, "We all know that we messed up in Chechnya . . . But if we admit the mistake, it means that someone has to be responsible for it. Then the President [Yeltsin] will head the guilty list, and no one will reelect him, and then Zhirinovskii will come."[223]

Yeltsin's cabinet appears to have been divided over how to handle the Chechen crisis. Prior to the 1994 invasion, Yeltsin's pointman on Chechnya was Sergei Shakhrai, who held a deep disdain for the Chechen leader.[224] Shakhrai had long advocated overthrowing Dudaev, and his actions led Chechen State Secretary Aslanbek Akbulatov to accuse Shakhrai of meddling in Chechen affairs to advance his own political image.[225] When Russo-Chechen talks appeared ready to begin in May 1994, Yeltsin removed Shakhrai from his posts as minister of nationalities and lead negotiator, bringing cries of protest from the Chechen opposition forces, who believed him to be more sympathetic to the anti-Dudaev cause.[226]

In the summer of 1994, the Russian government declared the Chechen situation to be a destabilizing factor in the region, specifically noting Chechen-rebel actions, which crossed into Russian territory, such as a hijacking in Mineralnye Vody. The statement also noted that Moscow might be "forced to protect Russian citizens [from Chechen attacks] in full accordance with the Russian Constitutions and other laws."[227]

Though the Russian Security Council vote to invade Chechnya was unanimous, opinion was in fact divided. Individual members had their own motives to either support or oppose the fight. Russian Counter-Intelligence Service chief Sergei Stepashin, who provided the intelligence for the debate, had previously made known his desire for "tough" talks with Dudaev to protect railway lines in Chechnya, insisting that the region was still part of Russia.[228] Defense Minister Pavel Grachev thought a quick campaign could improve his public standing, tarnished with charges of corruption. National Security Advisor Iurii Baturin was known to oppose invasion, but was conveniently out of town when the vote was taken.[229] Amy Knight believes "the assault on Chechnya represented a gain for the security services, the FSK in particular, because . . . they were the mastermind behind it."[230] In time, Russian leaders accused of betraying Russia in the process of marketization turned the Chechen conflict into a test case of Russian statehood. The fact that Lebed, a political outsider, got credit for brokering peace only served to further anger the inner circle of power.[231]

Intrigue was so widespread and convoluted that various factions even accused Yeltsin and Dudaev of collusion. Noting the parallel paths of the two presidents in early 1993, Mamodaev accused Yeltsin of whipping up the "Chechen question" when he needed to consolidate support. Yeltsin's declaration of a state of emergency in regions bordering Russia, for example, handed Dudaev evidence of an external threat that could serve to unite squabbling

Chechens.[232] Khasbulatov argued that without Russian support, Dudaev "never would have remained in power for three years."[233] Dudaev himself took to depicting Yeltsin as being deceived by his staff and prevented from working on his own due to factional power struggles within the Kremlin, a position re-emphasized by Dudaev's widow, who claims her husband tried to contact Yeltsin four times.[234] Barely a month before his death, Dudaev told journalists that he believed Yeltsin had ordered his assassination to bolster his own chances for re-election.[235]

Did They Take More Than They Could Handle?

In the years since the bilateral treaty, Tatarstan has exercised its autonomy on several issues. Tatarstan had been repeatedly granted exceptions to Russian federal legislation. For example, they were allowed to increase their 1994 oil export quota and to use the hard currency revenue to build a medical complex.[236] The republic has adopted the most liberal land ownership law in the entire Federation, even allowing purchases by foreigners.[237] Kazan has also legislated alternative service for Tatarstani citizens called by the Russian draft.[238]

The most contentious issue with Moscow has concerned dual citizenship and passports. The Kremlin has repeatedly called Tatarstan's citizenship law unconstitutional, pointing out that individuals, such as fugitives, could renounce their Russian citizenship while still claiming Tatarstani citizenship.[239] Kazan, in turn, has bitterly complained that Russia's new passports no longer indicate the holder's nationality and demanded that the passports be printed in both the Tatar and Russian languages.[240] Ultimately, an agreement was reached allowing Tatarstan (and Bashkortostan) to modify Russian passports with local languages and symbols.[241]

Incoming Russian President Vladimir Putin initially tried to rein in the republics by subordinating them to seven new federal districts in May 2000. Still, however, Shaimiev was able to wrangle concessions for Tatarstan. He has been allowed to run for a third term as president—allowed under the Tatarstani Constitution, but not the Russian one—and Tatarstan has become the only republic other than Chechnya to switch from Cyrillic to Latin script. [242]

In return, Tatarstan has agreed to start paying its federal taxes in full.[243]

By the time Russia invaded Chechnya in 1994, the breakaway republic had established precious little independence. Fearing Moscow's wrath, no state had recognized the Dudaev regime, which was widely seen as illegitimate. No country has recognized Chechnya's passports, as Moscow would interpret such action as tacit recognition of Chechen independence.[244]

Russia launched a second war against Chechnya in 1999, largely to shore up the Kremlin in advance of the December 1999 parliamentary elections and the 2000 presidential elections.[245] Even before this second war, Chechnya desperately needed cash to rebuild its war-ravaged capital. Of Moscow's promised

$138 million for 1997, only $21 million made it to the National Bank of Chechnya.[246] Chechens have turned to extreme measures to raise cash. At least $10 million has been raised from kidnapping Westerners, and some $10 billion in currency forged.[247] The devastation has only increased with the second war.

Revisiting the four characteristics of federalism highlights how Russia has bent the rules for Tatarstan and Chechnya. First, while the Russian constitution does delineate a center-periphery division of power, it also has flexibility. Article 78 allows the center to devolve some powers to the republics and likewise the republics can assign some of their responsibilities upward. Moscow has demonstrated a willingness to use this article on an ad hoc basis, resulting in a hodgepodge of agreements with various subjects of the federation, beginning with the 1994 treaty with Tatarstan. A highly asymmetrical federation has resulted.

The Khasavyurt accords particularly stood out from Moscow's collection of bilateral agreements. The agreement has no standing in Russian law. Lebed signed it as the chair of the Russian Security Council, a body not mentioned in the 1993 constitution. The document was not ratified by parliament, as required for international agreements, nor could it be classified as an inter-governmental agreement as Lebed was not a government minister. Both Yeltsin and Chernomyrdin distanced themselves from the document, and Lebed was fired shortly after.[248] Nearly a year later, the two sides still could not even agree on what to call the document. Chechnya's president Aslan Maskhadov, elected in January 1997, has rejected associated status, but as late as 1998 was willing to establish a common economic and defense zone.[249]

Second, the current Chechen and Tatarstani regional governments were elected without interference from Moscow. The 1997 Chechen elections were funded by the Organization for Security and Cooperation in Europe, much to the dismay of Russian foreign minister Evgenii Primakov.[250] Both presidents were elected by comfortable margins (Maskhadov with 59.3% and an unopposed Shaimiev 97.5%) in elections generally regarded as fair. Their respective stances toward Russia were popularly endorsed. Tatarstan's March 1992 referendum was viewed as fairly conducted—if possibly unconstitutional under Russia's Soviet-era document—and validated Shaimiev's stance toward Moscow. Sovereignty was a non-issue in the January 1997 Chechen presidential election; all sixteen candidates advocated independence from Russia.

Third, the current center-periphery division of powers was jointly developed. Yeltsin's government was able to constitutionally accommodate the Tatarstani autonomy demands and even appropriated Kazan's model for use in other situations. With Chechnya, Yeltsin urgently needed to end the war for domestic reasons, principally his 1996 re-election. By mutual agreement, the specifics of power sharing were put off for five years—conveniently after Yeltsin's second term of office was scheduled to end.

Fourth, the constituent parts of the Russian Federation are represented in Moscow through the Federation Council. Shaimiev agreed to take his seat only after the bilateral treaty was signed. The Chechen seat was occupied by government-in-exile leader Zavgaev until November 1996. Maskhadov has refused to sit in a "foreign" assembly. The republic leaders had highly different receptions in Moscow. While he and his representatives were willing to meet and negotiate face-to-face with Shaimiev, Yeltsin never met Dudaev and preferred to work through back channels and rival claimants for power. Although Yeltsin received Maskhadov in Moscow during his peace-maker phase, Putin refuses to negotiate with the "war criminals" in Grozny. [251]

The two cases here have had very different outcomes to date: the Chechen conflict has twice led to war, while Tatarstan has been rewarded special privileges and exemptions. Why the different outcomes?

The answer comes in the "win-sets" proposed by Dudaev and Shaimiev, to return to Putnam's language. Shaimiev was consistent, even adamant, in his belief that because of changed circumstances, Kazan's relationship with Moscow had to be renegotiated. Though his fundamental position was inflexible, it offered room for Russia; the game had a positive-sum outcome. His idea of building new institutions explicitly assigned some areas of responsibility to the Russian Federation, it just did not wait for Kazan's powers to be handed down from above. In consequence, Shaimiev ultimately was able to find common ground with Yeltsin, though the process required several years of negotiations.

Dudaev, in contrast, quickly enunciated an extreme policy—independence—and never was clearly in a position to negotiate on Chechnya's behalf. Unable to control rivals for power at home, Dudaev saw more flexible political rivals return from Moscow with offers for limited autonomy. His anti-Russian imperialism rhetoric had found a responsive audience at home, however, and Dudaev found himself unable to find a compromise palatable to both Moscow and Chechens. He became bound up in his own image as the liberator of Chechnya, perhaps of the entire Caucasus. As Shaimiev astutely noted just one week before Dudaev's assassination, "He stands at the head of the banner of independence. The people believed him . . . therefore there will be no easy path."[252] Though Dudaev is gone, Moscow has found the Chechen problem a convenient pot to stir or settle as domestic circumstances warrant. But with Maskhadov unable to control all the Chechen guerrilla units, it will be exceedingly difficult to find a solution acceptable to Russians and Chechens alike.

NOTES

Ann Robertson would like to thank Peter Reddaway and Carl Linden for their comments on earlier versions of this chapter and Karen Zietlow and Andrew Howard for their research assistance.

1. Peter Rutland, "A Fragile Peace," *Transition* (November 15, 1996): 49–50. The text of the Khasavyurt accords states that the treaty has been reached based on

the norms of international law (*mezhdunarodnogo prava*), *Izvestiia* (September 3, 1996): 1.

2. See, for example, Jessica Eve Stern, "Moscow Meltdown: Can Russia Survive?" *International Security* 18.4 (Spring 1994): 40–65. For an alternative view, see Allen Lynch and Reneo Lukic, "The Russian Federation Will Remain United," *Transition* (January 12, 1996): 14–17.

3. Quoted in Ann Sheehy, "Russia's Republics: A Threat to Its Territorial Integrity?" *RFE/RL Report on the USSR* 2.20 (May 14, 1993): 34.

4. Daniel R. Kempton, "Bargaining with Moscow: The Case of Sakha," Chapter 4, in this volume.

5. Putnam's original work appeared in the summer 1988 issue of *International Organization*. It was expanded in an edited volume which appeared as "Diplomacy and Domestic Politics: The Logic of Two-Level Games," in *Double-Edged Diplomacy: International Bargaining and Domestic Politics*, ed. Peter B. Evans, Harold K. Jacobson, and Robert D. Putnam (Berkeley: University of California Press, 1993), 431–468.

6. Galina Starovoitova, "Nationality Policies in the Period of Perestroika: Some Comments from a Political Actor," in *From Union to Commonwealth: Nationalism and Separatism in the Soviet Republics*, ed. Gail Lapidus and Victor Zaslavsky (New York: Cambridge University Press, 1992): p. 116.

7. David Remnick, *Lenin's Tomb: The Last Days of the Soviet Empire* (New York: Random House, 1993): 7.

8. Stephan Kux, "Soviet Federalism," *Problems of Communism* 39.2 (March/April 1990): 20.

9. Lengthy treatments of Gorbachev's ignorance in this area include Bohdan Nahaylo and Victor Swoboda, *Soviet Disunion: A History of the Nationalities Problem in the USSR* (New York: Free Press, 1990), especially Chapter 15; Gail W. Lapidus, "Gorbachev's Nationalities Problem," *Foreign Affairs* 68, no. 4 (fall 1989): 92–108; and Paul Goble, "Ethnic Politics in the USSR," *Problems of Communism* 38, no. 4 (July/August 1989): 1–14.

10. See Robert A. Vitas, "The Recognition of Lithuania: The Completion of a Legal Circle," *Journal of Baltic Studies* 24, no. 3 (fall 1993), 247–262. A much longer analysis is Vitas's *The United States and Lithuania: The Stimson Doctrine of Nonrecognition* (New York: Praeger, 1990).

11. *Pravda* (September 22, 1989), in *Current Digest of the Soviet Press* [hereafter CDSP] 41.40 (November 1, 1989): 14.

12. Elizabeth Teague, "Center-Periphery Relations in the Russian Federation," in *National Identity and Ethnicity in Russia and the New States of Eurasia*, ed. Roman Szporluk (Armonk: M.E. Sharpe, 1994): 29.

13. John B. Dunlop, *The Rise of Russia and the Fall of the Soviet Empire* (Princeton: Princeton University Press, 1993): 17 citing: *Pravda* August 17, 1989.

14. Dunlop, p. 18n. 58.

15. Kux, op. cit.

16. Starovoitova, p. 117. Ann Sheehy, "Gorbachev Addresses Central Committee Plenum on Nationalities Question," *RFE/RL Report on the USSR* (September 29, 1989): 1–4.

17. Bill Keller, "Gorbachev Wants Lithuania to Pay Billions to Secede," *New York Times* (March 8, 1990): A1; and "Lithuania: What Price Freedom?" *Newsweek*

(March 19, 1990): 31. [On USSR Secession Law]: Ann Sheehy, "Gorbachev's Arguments Cut Little Ice with Lithuanians," *RFE/RL Report on the USSR* (February 9, 1990): 33–35.

18. Ann Sheehy, "Supreme Soviet Adopts Law on Mechanics of Secession," *RFE/RL Report on the USSR* 2.17 (April 27, 1990): 2–5.

19. Roman Solchanyk, "The Draft Union Treaty and the "Big Five,'" *RFE/RL Report on the USSR* (May 3, 1991): 16–18.

20. Suzanne Crow, "Support within USSR for Lithuania's Independence Drive," *RFE/RL Report on the USSR* (April 13, 1990): 3–4.

21. Yasin Aslan, "Muslim Support for Baltic Independence," *RFE/RL Report on the USSR*, (May 25, 1990): 16; Kathleen Mihalisko, "*'For Our Freedom and Yours': Support among Slavs for Baltic Independence, "RFE/RL Report on the USSR*, (May 25, 1990): 17–19.

22. Jan Arveds Trapans, "Averting Moscow's Baltic Coup," *Orbis*, 35.3 (summer 1991): 431; Riina Kionka, "Russia Recognizes Estonia's Independence," *RFE/RL Report on the USSR* (February 1, 1991): 14–16; Gytis Sulevicius, "Lithuania Signs Treaty with Russia," *RFE/RL Report on the USSR* (August 23, 1991): 19–21; and Will Englund, "Bypassing Gorbachev, Yeltsin signs pact recognizing Lithuania," *Baltimore Sun* (July 30, 1991): A4.

23. Paul Goble, "Gorbachev's Baltic Policy Backfires," *RFE/RL Report on the USSR* (May 25, 1990): 1–3. For poll see Adrian Karatnycky, "Their Empire Crumbling, Russians Turn Inward," *Wall Street Journal*, European edition (May 15, 1990): A8.

24. Nahaylo and Swoboda, p. 305.

25. Kestutis Girnius, "Lithuanian Communist Party Edges toward Independence," *RFE/RL Report on the USSR* (October 6, 1989): 15–17; Francis X. Clines, "Lithuanians Resist Pressure from Moscow on New Party," *New York Times* (November 18, 1989): A3; Saulius Girnius, "Lithuanian Communists Deny Gorbachev's Request," *RFE/RL Report on the USSR* (November 3, 1989): 29–30; Esther B. Fein, "Gorbachev Voices 'Alarm' on Lithuanian Party Split," *New York Times* (December 22, 1989): A12; and Saulius Girnius, "Lithuania," *RFE/RL Report on the USSR* (December 29, 1989): 23–26.

26. John B. Dunlop, *The Rise of Russia and the Fall of the Soviet Empire* (Princeton: Princeton University Press, 1993).

27. See summary in Ann Sheehy, "Fact Sheet on Declarations of Sovereignty," *RFE/RL Report on the USSR* (November 9, 1990): 23–25.

28. Ann Sheehy, "Russia's Republics."

29. Roman Solchanyk, "The Draft Union Treaty and the 'Big Five,'" *RFE/RL Report on the USSR* (May 3, 1991): 16–18 and "The Gorbachev-El'tsin Pact and the New Union Treaty," *RFE/RL Report on the USSR* (May 10, 1991): 1–3.

30. Dunlop, pp. 195–99. Mark R. Beissinger, "The Deconstruction of the USSR and the Search for a Post-Soviet Community," *Problems of Communism* 40.6 (November/December 1991): 27–35. Also see Boris Yeltsin, *The Struggle for Russia* (New York: Times Books, 1994): 39.

31. Dawn Mann, "The Circumstances Surrounding the Conservative Putsch," *RFE/RL Report on the USSR* (September 6, 1991): 1–5.

32. Parallels are noted in Vera Tolz, "The Role of the Republics and Regions," *RFE/RL Research Report* 2.15 (April 9, 1993): 8–13; Dunlop, p. 61.

33. OMRI Daily Report (June 4, 1993).

34. Edward W. Walker, "Federalism—Russian Style: The Federation Provisions in Russia's New Constitutions," *Problems of Post-Communism* 42.4 (July/August 1995): 3–12; Gail W. Lapidus and Edward W. Walker, "Nationalism, Regionalism, and Federalism: Center-Periphery Relations in Post-Post-Communist Russia," in *The New Russia: Troubled Transformation*, ed. Gail Lapidus (Boulder: Westview, 1995).

35. See, for example, Elizabeth Teague, "Center-Periphery Relations," Lapidus and Walker; Walker, "Federalism—Russian Style"; Darrell Slider, "Federalism, Discord, and Accommodation: Intergovernmental Relations in Post-Soviet Russia," in *Local Power and Post-Soviet Politics*, ed. Theodore H. Friedgut and Jeffrey Hahn (Armonk: M.E. Sharpe, 1994); Steve Solnick, "Federal Bargaining in Russia," *East European Constitutional Review* 4.4 (Fall 1995); and Solnick, "The Political Economy of Russian Federalism: A Framework for Analysis," *Problems of Post-Communism* 43.6 (November/December 1996): 13–25.

36. Roza N. Musina, "Contemporary Ethnosocial and Ethnopolitical Processes in Tatarstan." In *Ethnic Conflict in the Post-Soviet World: Case Studies and Analysis*, ed. Leokadia Drobizheva et al. (Armonk, NY: M.E. Sharpe, 1996): 197; Katherine E. Graney, "The Volga Tatars: Diasporas and the Politics of Federalism." In *Nations Abroad: Diaspora Politics and International Relations in the Former Soviet Union*, ed. Charles King and Neil J. Melvin (Boulder: Westview, 1998): 153–178.

37. Musina, p. 201.

38. For Kosovo, see Milan Andrejevich, "Serbs Crack Down on Kosovo," *Radio Free Europe Report on Eastern Europe* (July 27, 1990): 48–52 and Fabian Schmidt, "Kosovo: The Time Bomb That Has Not Gone Off," *RFE/RL Research Report* 2.39 (October 1, 1993): 21–29.

39. See, for example, Donna Bahry, "The Union Republics and Contradictions in Gorbachev's Economic Reform," *Soviet Economy* 7.3 (1991): 238–239.

40. Egor Ligachev, *Inside Gorbachev's Kremlin* (New York: Pantheon, 1993): 173–174.

41. Gertrude E. Schroeder, "Nationalities and the Soviet Economy," in *The Nationalities Factor in Soviet Politics and Society*, ed. Lubomyr Hajda and Mark Beissinger (Boulder: Westview, 1990): 63. It is unclear whether the policy was enacted, as the issue eventually was eclipsed by Union-Treaty discussions.

42. Ann Sheehy, "Tatarstan Asserts Its Sovereignty," *RFE/RL Research Report* 1.14 (April 3, 1992): 2.

43. Musina, p. 202.

44. Moscow News Fax (April 20, 1992) in FBIS-SOV (April 23, 1992): 32–33.

45. Cited in Justin Burke, "Yeltsin Faces Nationalist Protest," *Christian Science Monitor* (April 23, 1991): 6.

46. Edward W. Walker, "The Dog That Didn't Bark: Tatarstan and Asymmetrical Federalism in Russia," *Harriman Review* 9.4 (Winter 1996): p. 4.

47. Uli Schamiloglu, "The Tatar Public Center and Current Tatar Concerns," *Report on the USSR* (December 22, 1989): 12, citing *Politicheskoe obrazovanie* 8 (1989): 99.

48. Carroll Bogert, "Wanting Out of Russia," *Newsweek* (November 12, 1990): 40–41.

49. Quoted in Hoffman, "Artful Regional Leader."

50. *Pravda* (September 1, 1990): 3 in FBIS-SOV (September 1, 1990): 115–116.

51. *Pravda* (September 1, 1990): 3 and Moscow Domestic Service (September 1, 1990) in FBIS-SOV (September 5, 1990): 115–116.

52. Sheehy, "Tatarstan Asserts."

53. Walker, "Dog," p. 14.

54. *Pravda* (August 31, 1991): 2 and TASS (September 3, 1991) in FBIS-SOV (September 4, 1991): 98.

55. *Segodnia* (February 22, 1994): 4–5 in FBIS-SOV (March 16, 1994): 19–26.

56. Lisa M. LeMair, "A Regional Approach to Russian Federalism? IREX Seminar in Kazan," *IREX News in Brief* 5.6 (November/December 1994): 22.

57. Quoted in David Hoffman, "Artful Regional Leader Slips Moscow's Grip," *Washington Post* (June 16, 1997): A1.

58. Peter Rutland, "Tatarstan: A Sovereign Republic Within the Russian Federation," *OMRI Russian Regional Report* 1.5 (September 25, 1996).

59. INTERFAX (November 24, 1992) in FBIS-SOV (November 25, 1992): 46.

60. *Kommersant-Daily* (February 5, 1994): 3 in FBIS-SOV (February 7, 1994): 35–36.

61. Robert J. Osborn has called 1992 the year of "regional economic autonomy by default." See his "Russia: Federalism, Regionalism, and Nationality Claims," in *Russia and America: From Rivalry to Reconciliation*, ed. George Ginsburg, Alvin Z. Rubinstein, and Oles Smolansky (Armonk: M.E. Sharpe, 1993).

62. *Rossiiskaia gazeta* (December 24, 1992): 2 in FBIS-SOV (January 5, 1993): 35; *Rossiiskaia gazeta* (February 8, 1994): 3 in FBIS-SOV (February 10, 1994): 36.

63. *Kommersant-Daily* (February 11, 1993): 9 in FBIS-SOV (February 12, 1993): 40–41.

64. *Nezavisimaia gazeta* (February 25, 1993): 1 in FBIS-SOV (February 25, 1993): 49–50.

65. Hoffman, "Artful Regional Leader."

66. Musina, p. 200. Schamiloglu notes that as minority, ethnic Tatars did not win seats in USSR Congress of People's Deputies. Tufan Mingullin, an ethnic Tatar deputy, did attend TPC meetings.

67. See Schamiloglu.

68. Musina, pp. 201–202.

69. *Rossiiskaia gazeta* (October 14, 1992): 2 in FBIS-SOV (October 16, 1992): 40; *Segodnia* (March 17, 1994): 3 in FBIS-SOV (April 6, 1994): 34–35.

70. *Kommersant-Daily* (July 8, 1994): 15 in FBIS-SOV (July 19, 1994): 43–44.

71. INTERFAX (July 30, 1992) in FBIS-SOV (July 31, 1992): 38.

72. *Kommersant-Daily* (July 8, 1994): 15 in FBIS-SOV (July 19, 1994): 43–44.

73. *Komsomolskaia pravda* (January 16, 1992): 1 in FBIS-SOV (January 22, 1991): 65; Maiak Radio Network interview with Shaimiev (August 30, 1992) in FBIS-SOV (August 31, 1992): 28–29.

74. INTERFAX (November 9, 1992) in FBIS-SOV (November 10, 1992): 51–52.

75. *Kazanskie vedomosti* (August 3, 1994): 4 in FBIS-SOV (August 8, 1994): 33.

76. *Izvestiia* (June 1, 1994): 1 in FBIS-SOV (June 1, 1994): 29–30.

77. *Pravda* (September 8, 1993): 4 in FBIS-SOV (September 13, 1993): 42.

78. *Nezavisimaia gazeta* (August 24, 1993): 3 in FBIS-SOV (August 24, 1993): 31.

79. TASS March 25, 1992, in FBIS-SOV (March 25, 1992): 54. Sheehy covers the ballot wording in "Tatarstan Asserts Its Sovereignty."

80. INTERFAX (March 22, 1992) in FBIS-SOV (March 23, 1992): 52.

81. POSTFACTUM (April 29, 1992) in FBIS-SOV (April 29, 1992): 45.

82. Walker, "Dog," p. 18; Sheehy, "Tatarstan Asserts," p. 3.

83. INTERFAX (November 6, 1992) in FBIS-SOV (November 10, 1992): 51.

84. See summary of constitution in Walker, "The Dog That Didn't Bark," p. 21. Shaimiev's comments on the document were reported in *Rossiiskie vesti* (November 21, 1992): in FBIS-SOV (November 25, 1992): 46–47.

85. RFE/RL Daily Digest (March 25, 1992) based on Novosti reports from March 24, 1992.

86. ITAR-TASS (April 23, 1992) in FBIS-SOV (April 24, 1992): 34–35.

87. Moscow Television (January 8, 1993): in FBIS-SOV (January 12, 1993): 34–37.

88. INTERFAX (November 21, 1992): in FBIS-SOV (November 24, 1992): 39.

89. *Nezavisimaia gazeta* (November 26, 1991) in CDSP 43.47 (December 25, 1991): 2.

90. Ann Sheehy, "Tatarstan and Bashkiria: Obstacles to Confederation," *RFE/RL Research Report* 1.22 (May 29, 1992): 33–37; Stern 60; Musina 197, 205.

91. *Komsomolskaia pravda* (January 16, 1992): 1 in FBIS-SOV (January 22, 1991): 65.

92. Justin Burke, "Yeltsin Faces Nationalist Protest," *Christian Science Monitor* (April 23, 1991): 6; Dunlop, p. 63.

93. Ibid.

94. ITAR-TASS (January 27, 1993) in FBIS-SOV (January 27, 1993): 39.

95. *Nezavisimaia gazeta* (April 1, 1993): 1 in FBIS-SOV (April 2, 1993): 39–41.

96. *Nezavisimaia gazeta* (May 20, 1993): 1 in FBIS-SOV (May 21, 1993): 49–50.

97. *Izvestiia* (October 30, 1993): 2 in FBIS-SOV (November 3, 1993): 54.

98. Radio Rossii (May 19, 1992) in FBIS-SOV (May 21, 1992): 76. *Federatsiia* (March 16, 1993): 3 in FBIS-SOV (March 18, 1993): 41–42.

99. INTERFAX (June 14, 1992) in FBIS-SOV (June 16, 1992): 49–50; Ann E. Robertson, "Suffering for Their Cause: The Merits of Dissolution versus Secession," presented at the Georgetown University Center for German and European Studies Conference, "Toward a New Europe: A Continent in Transition," Washington, DC (November 9–10, 1996). Dane Rowlands, "International Aspects of the Division of Debt Under Secession: The Case of Quebec and Canada," *Canadian Public Policy* 23.1 (1997): 40–54.

100. "Agreements Signed by the Government of the Russian Federation and the Republic of Tatarstan, 1992–1994," sidebar in Teague, "Russia and Tatarstan," pp. 22–23.

101. Mikhail Gershaft, "Tatarstan Helps to Define a New Federalism for Russia," *Prism* 1.17 (August 25, 1995). Gershaft's actual text says February 1993, but context and additional facts suggest that it must be a typographical error.

102. Elizabeth Teague, "Russia and Tatarstan"; ITAR-TASS (December 15, 1993) in FBIS-SOV (December 16, 1993): 15.

103. Lapidus and Walker, "Nationalism, Regionalism, and Federalism," pp. 99–102.

104. Teague, "Russia and Tatarstan," p. 20.

105. Rutland, "Tatarstan," OMRI Russian Regional Report. Treaty text available in *Rossiiskaia gazeta* (February 18, 1994): 5 in FBIS-SOV (February 23, 1994): 34–36.

106. ITAR-TASS (May 30, 1994): 1 in FBIS-SOV (June 1, 1994): 28.

107. *Literaturnaia gazeta* (March 30, 1994): 12 in FBIS-SOV (April 13, 1994): 29–32.

108. For an itemized list of amendments, see *Respublika Tatarstan* [Kazan] (December 15, 1994): 2 in FBIS-SOV (December 27, 1994): 24–27.

109. Anatol Lieven suggests this crazy-like-a-fox strategy in *Chechnya: Tombstone of Russian Power* (New Haven: Yale University Press, 1998): Chapter 2, esp. p. 76.

110. Robert Ebel, "The History and Politics of Chechen Oil," *Post-Soviet Prospects* 3.1 (January 1995).

111. "Russia: Partisan War in Chechnya on the Eve of the WWII Commemoration," *Human Rights Watch/Helsinki* 7.8 (May 1995).

112. Robert Conquest, *The Soviet Deportation of Nationalities* (New York: St. Martin's, 1960): 54.

113. Frederick C. Cuny, "Killing Chechnya," *New York Review of Books* (April 15, 1995): 15. Cuny disappeared in Chechnya and is presumed dead.

114. Chechen Secretary of State Aslambek Akbulatov made the sovereignty—extermination connection during an INTERFAX interview on March 25, 1994; see FBIS-SOV (March 28, 1994): 32–33.

115. Russian Television Network (December 29, 1991): in FBIS-SOV (January 2, 1992): 73–74.

116. *Za Vilnu Ukraiinu* [Lvov] (February 22, 1992): 1 in FBIS-SOV (March 18, 1992): 43–46.

117. INTERFAX (February 24, 1994) in FBIS-SOV (February 25, 1994): 26–27.

118. *Kommersant-Daily* (August 13, 1994): 3 in FBIS-SOV (August 15, 1994): 27–28.

119. Lieven, pp. 58, 59, 60, 70. Liz Fuller, "Chechnya after Dudayev," *OMRI Analytical Brief* 1.81 (April 26, 1996).

120. There are few accounts of the early days of Dudaev and the OKChN. This section relies heavily on Ann Sheehy, "Power Struggle in Checheno-Ingushetia," *Report on the USSR* (November 15, 1991): 20–26.

121. Paul Goble, "Chechnya and Its Consequences: A Preliminary Report," *Post-Soviet Affairs* 11 (1995): 24; Adrian Bridge, "Estonia Holds on to Dudaev Legend," *Independent* [London] (April 27, 1996): 9; John B. Dunlop, *Russia Confronts Chechnya: Roots of a Separatist Conflict* (New York: Cambridge University Press, 1998): 97–99.

122. Lieven, pp. 58–59.

123. TASS (August 15, 1991) in FBIS-SOV (August 16, 1991): 39.

124. Galina U. Soldatova, "The Former Checheno-Ingushetia: Interethnic Relations and Ethnic Conflicts," In *Ethnic Conflict in the Post-Soviet World: Case Studies and Analysis* ed. Leokadia Drobizheva et al. (Armonk, NY: M.E. Sharpe, 1996); Jane Ormrod, "North Caucasus: Fragmentation or Federation?" in *Nation and Politics in*

the Soviet Successor States ed. Ian Bremmer and Ray Taras (New York: Cambridge University Press, 1993): 457; Sheehy, "Power Struggle," p. 22; see, for example, Vremia newscast of September 14, 1991, in FBIS-SOV (September 16, 1991): 76–77; TASS September 16, 1991, in FBIS-SOV (September 17, 1991): 48–49. Ingush leaders have publicly declared that they have no intention of rejoining Chechnya, RFE/RL Newsline (January 17, 2001).

125. Moscow Central Television, October 16, 1991, in FBIS-SOV (October 17, 1991): 66.

126. *Pravda* (September 13, 1991): 6. LEXIS/NEXIS Russian Press Digest (September 13, 1991).

127. Aleksei Malashenko, "Chechnya: The War Is Over, But the Situation Remains Complex," *Prism* 3.5 (April 18, 1997).

128. TASS, September 15, 1991, in FBIS-SOV (September 16, 1991): 77–78.

129. TASS, September 13, 1991, in FBIS-SOV (September 17, 1991): 48.

130. *Rossiiskaia gazeta* (September 14, 1991): 1 in FBIS-SOV (September 24, 1991): 65–66.

131. Russian Television (October 9, 1991): in BBC Summary of World Broadcasts (October 11, 1991) via LEXIS/NEXIS. Also see "Session Discusses Chechen-Ingush Situation" in FBIS-SOV (October 11, 1991): 40–44.

132. See Rutskoi's interview with Moscow Radio-1 in FBIS-SOV (October 11, 1991): 40–43. The October 16, 1991, *Vesti* newscast also mentioned the telephone conversation between Rutskoi and Gorbachev. FBIS-SOV (October 17, 1991): 65.

133. Moscow Radio Rossii (October 27, 1991) in FBIS-SOV (October 28, 1991): 67.

134. Elizabeth Shogren, "Strongman Demands Full Secession for Russia's Chechen-Ingush Region," *Los Angeles Times* (November 11, 1991): A6; Susan Viets and Peter Pringle, "Veto on Yeltsin Gives Heart to Chechen Rebels," *Independent* [London] (November 12, 1991): 11; Emil A. Payin and Arkady A. Popov, "Chechnya: From Past to Present." In *U.S. and Russian Policymaking with Respect to the Use of Force* (Santa Monica: RAND, 1996), available at www.amina.com/article/history.html.

135. Daniel Sneider, "Yeltsin Runs into Test of Authority over Insurgency," *Christian Science Monitor* (November 12, 1991): 1.

136. Andrei Grachev, *Dalshe bez menia . . . : Ukhod Prezidenta* (Moscow: Izdatelskaia Gruppa Progress, 1994): 134 cited by Jack Matlock, *Autopsy on an Empire* (New York: Random House, 1995): 809n. 46. Yeltsin does not mention the incident in his autobiography for this period.

137. INTERFAX (January 26, 1992) in FBIS-SOV (January 28, 1992): 56–57.

138. Quoted in Elizabeth Shogren, "Strongman Demands Full Secession for Russia's Chechen-Ingush Region," *Los Angeles Times* (November 11, 1991): A6; martial law was lifted on November 21; Dunlop, *Russia Confronts Chechnya*, p. 122.

139. TASS, December 2, 1991, in FBIS-SOV (December 3, 1991): 72.

140. The Chechen Constitution is reprinted in Diane Curran, Fiona Hill, and Elena Kostritsyna, *The Search for Peace in Chechnya: A Sourcebook 1994–1996* (Cambridge: Harvard University Strengthening Democratic Institutions Project, March 1997).

141. See reportage in FBIS-SOV (January13, 1992): 43–44. For Honecker, see Moscow Radio Rossii (December 15, 1991) in FBIS-SOV (December 17, 1991): 50.

142. *Izvestiia* (March 25, 1992): 6 in FBIS-SOV (March 27, 1992): 21–22; *Rossiiskaia gazeta* (April 11, 1992): 1 in FBIS-SOV (April 13, 1992): 34.

143. *Izvestiia* (February 2, 1993): 2 in FBIS-SOV (February 4, 1993): 30; ITAR-TASS (October 1, 1993) in FBIS-SOV (October 4, 1993): 11; INTERFAX (November 21, 1993) in FBIS-SOV (November 22, 1993): 41.

144. INTERFAX (October 17, 1991): in FBIS-SOV (October 18, 1991): 63–64.

145. Sheehy, "Power Struggle," p. 25; INTERFAX (August 17, 1994) in FBIS-SOV (August 18, 19914): 18. [The Confederation of the Peoples of the Caucasus is the new name of the Assembly of the Mountain Peoples of the Caucasus.]

146. R. Jeffrey Smith, "U.S. Interests Seen Allied with Russia in Chechnya," *Washington Post* (December 25, 1994): A27; INTERFAX (August 7, 1994) in FBIS-SOV (August 8, 1994): 32.

147. Radio Moscow World Service (January 24, 1992): in FBIS-SOV (January 27, 1992): 50.

148. INTERFAX (March 13, 1992) in FBIS-SOV (March 16, 1992): 74–75.

149. *Rossiia* (December 16,1 1992): 4 in FBIS-SOV (December 22, 1992): 29–30.

150. INTERFAX (April 22, 1994) in FBIS-SOV (April 25, 1994): 48.

151. INTERFAX (March 13, 1992): in FBIS-SOV (March 16, 1992): 74.

152. *Nezavisimaia gazeta* (April 21, 1992): 3 in FBIS-SOV (April 22, 1992): 30.

153. *Za Vilnu Ukraiinu* [Lvov] (February 22, 1992): in FBIS-SOV (March 18, 1992): 46.

154. INTERFAX (October 16, 1992) in FBIS-SOV (October 20, 1992): 34–35.

155. INTERFAX (November 9, 1992) in FBIS-SOV (November 10, 1992): 51–52.

156. Radio Vilnius (December 20, 1994) in FBIS-SOV (December 21, 1994): 55; ITAR-TASS (December 4, 1994) in FBIS-SOV (December 5, 1994): 71.

157. Radio Vilnius (December 23, 1994) in FBIS-SOV (December 23, 1994): 39.

158. Tarmu Tammerk, "Baltics Concerned about Chechen Conflict," *Baltic Independent* (December 16–22, 1994): 1 and Tarmu Tammerk, "Chechen Crisis Prompts Baltic Support Statements," *Baltic Independent* (December 23, 1994–January 5, 1995): 3. OMRI Daily Digest (July 17, 1996) mentions an International Parliamentary Group on the Problem of Chechnya; INTERFAX (November 29, 1994) in FBIS-SOV (November 30, 1994): 71.

159. ITAR-TASS (December 28, 1994) in FBIS-SOV (December 29, 1994): 42.

160. INTERFAX (December 20, 1994) in FBIS-SOV (December 21, 1994): 42; *Holos Ukraiiny* (December 27, 1994): 5 in FBIS-SOV (December 29, 1994): 43–44.

161. See various articles under "Chechen President Comments on Attempted Coup," in FBIS-SOV (April 3, 1992): 43–45.

162. *Za Vilnu ukraiinu* [Lvov] (May 6, 1993): 2 in FBIS-SOV (May 13, 1993): 36–38.

163. INTERFAX (December 6, 1993) in FBIS-SOV (December 7, 1993): 35.

164. Radio Moscow World Service (February 6, 1993) in FBIS-SOV (February 9, 1993): 34.

165. Ostankino First Program (April 16, 1992) in FBIS-SOV (April 21, 1992): 29–30.

166. INTERFAX (February 10, 1994): in FBIS-SOV (February 10, 1994): 35.

167. INTERFAX (August 9, 1994) in FBIS-SOV (August 10, 1994): 20. Also Jamestown Monitor (February 4, 1997).

168. Elizabeth Teague, "Russia and Tatarstan Sign Power-Sharing Treaty," *RFE/RL Research Report* 3.14 (April 8, 1994): 21n. 16. Dunlop notes that Chechnya's economic decline actually began in the 1980s and was exacerbated by an ethnic division of labor: Russians dominated petroleum and other technical fields, while Chechens had rural or criminal occupations. Dunlop, *Russia Confronts Chechnya*, pp. 85–88.

169. *Komsomolskaia pravda* (June 4, 1992): 1 in FBIS-SOV (June 5, 1992): 66–67.

170. Shakhrai interview, ibid. Frederick C. Cuny, "Killing Chechnya," *New York Review of Books* (April 15, 1995): 15. Dunlop, *Russia Confronts Chechnya*, p. 127.

171. Russian Television Network (August 14, 1994) in FBIS-SOV (August 15, 1994): 24.

172. *Rossiiskaia gazeta* (May 28, 1993): 1 in FBIS-SOV (June 1, 1993): 61–62. Russian officials believed weapons, drugs, and contraband were being transported on—or hijacked from—railway lines crossing Chechnya. See Shakhrai interview with INTERFAX (June 6, 1994) in FBIS-SOV (June 7, 1994): 23–25. The region was also suspected of counterfeiting, which was undermining the Russian economy. ITAR-TASS (December 27, 1994) in FBIS-SOV (December 27, 1994): 26.

173. Radio Rossii (March 3, 1992) in FBIS-SOV (March 3, 1992): 59.

174. Lieven, pp. 337–338.

175. Alexander Zhilin and Philip Stepper, "Criminal Millions Killed Dudaev," *Moscow News* (May 30, 1996) via LEXIS-NEXIS.

176. Moscow Radio Rossii October 12, 1991, in FBIS-SOV (October 15, 1991): 54–55.

177. *Krasnaia zvezda* (April 21, 1993): 3 in FBIS-SOV (April 27, 1993): 46.

178. ITAR-TASS (May 26, 1993) in FBIS-SOV (May 26, 1993): 38.

179. ITAR-TASS (December 28, 1992) in FBIS-SOV (December 29, 1992): 36–37; Moscow Television (December 27, 1992): in FBIS-SOV (December 31, 1992): 36–37; *Rossiiskaia gazeta* (January 4, 1993): 1 in FBIS-SOV (January 5, 1993): 34–35; Payin and Popov, "Chechnya: From Past to Present."

180. INTERFAX (January 12, 1993): in FBIS-SOV (January 13, 1993): 38; *Rossiiskie vesti* (January 14, 1993): 2 in FBIS-SOV (January 15, 1993): 45.

181. See coverage of Shakhrai and Abdulatipov trip in FBIS-SOV (January 22, 1993): 52–55. *Izvestiia* (January 19, 1993) revealed the landing permission incident.

182. *Rossiiskaia gazeta* (February 16, 1993): 3 in FBIS-SOV (February 17, 1993): 45.

183. ITAR-TASS (February 14, 1993) in FBIS-SOV (February 17, 1993): 44; ITAR-TASS (March 28, 1993) in FBIS-SOV (March 29, 1993): 88.

184. *Rossiiskaia gazeta* (June 15, 1993): 1 in FBIS-SOV (June 16, 1993): 43.

185. See wire service reports in FBIS-SOV (April 19, 1993): 72–74 and (April 21, 1993): 44–45.

186. ITAR-TASS (May 21, 1993) in FBIS-SOV (May 24, 1993): 54.

187. *Nezavisimaia gazeta* (March 31, 1994): 1 in FBIS-SOV (March 31, 1994): 28–29. The Russian Duma's decree on settling the Chechen issue appeared in *Rossiiskaia gazeta* (March 29, 1994) FBIS-SOV (March 30, 1994): 31; ITAR-TASS (April 21, 1994) in FBIS-SOV (April 22, 1994): 46.

188. *Rossiiskaia gazeta* (April 24, 1992): 2 in FBIS-SOV (April 30, 1992): 41–44.

189. Sheehy, "Power Struggle," p. 24.

190. Dunlop, *Russia Confronts Chechnya*, pp. 134–139.

191. Jane Ormrod in Bremmer and Taras, p. 456, citing *Izvestiia* (November 27, 1991): 1. Also see *Rossiiskaia gazeta* (April 24, 1992): 2 in FBIS-SOV (April 30, 1992): 41–44.

192. Quoted in Dunlop, *Russia Confronts Chechnya*, p. 136.

193. *Svobodnaia gruziia* (February 20, 1993): 3 in FBIS-SOV (March 5, 1993): 34–35.

194. INTERFAX (April 18, 1994) in FBIS-SOV (April 19, 1994): 42.

195. NTV (July 22 1994) and ITAR-TASS (July 22, 1994) in FBIS-SOV (July 25, 1994): 29–30.

196. Maria Eismont, "The Chechen War: How It All Began," *Prism* 2.5 (March 8, 1996): Part 4. Also see *Rossiiskaia gazeta* (April 24, 1992): 2 in FBIS-SOV (April 30, 1992): 41–44 and Lieven, pp. 80–101 passim.

197. The Provisional Council's declaration was printed in *Rossiiskaia gazeta* (August 3, 1994) in FBIS-SOV (August 3, 1994): 26–27. A Maiak Radio Network interview interview with Avturkhanov appears in FBIS-SOV (August 3, 1994): 27–28; Payin and Popov, "Chechnya from Past to Present."

198. Eismont, op. cit.

199. ITAR-TASS (August 15, 1994) in FBIS-SOV (August 15, 1994): 28.

200. *Izvestiia* (March 5, 1994): 2 in FBIS-SOV (March 8, 1994): 19; *Izvestiia* (May 31, 1994): 4 in FBIS-SOV (June 3, 1994): 28–29.

201. Lee Hockstader, "Jubilant Chechens Ready to Celebrate," *Washington Post* (September 4, 1996): A17 and Lee Hockstader, "Kremlin, Russian Public Lend Tepid Support to Chechen Pact," *Washington Post* (September 1, 1996): A33.

202. Elizabeth Fuller and Scott Parrish, "Chechen Conflict Ends with Shaky Peace," *Transition* (February 7, 1997): 74–75.

203. *Segodnia* (February 22, 1994): 4–5 in FBIS-SPV (March 16, 1994): 19–26. Also see Maria Eismont, "Djohar Dudaev: Dead or Alive? Was He Killed Intentionally?" *Jamestown Monitor* (May 3, 1996).

204. *Rossiiskaia gazeta* (April 24, 1992): 2 in FBIS-SOV (April 30, 1992): 41–44.

205. *Pravda* (October 27, 1992): 1 in FBIS-SOV (November 3, 1992): 54–55.

206. See, for example, *Novaia ezhednevnaia gazeta* (August 9, 1994): 2 in FBIS-SOV (August 9, 1994): 25.

207. INTERFAX (February 24, 1 992) in FBIS-SOV (February 25, 1992): 55.

208. Quoted in Alan Cooperman, "Making Political Hay by the First of May," *U.S. News & World Report* (May 6, 1996): 51.

209. INTERFAX, October 16, 1991, in FBIS-SOV (October 17, 1991): 67; ITAR-TASS (June 1, 1994): in FBIS-SOV (June 3, 1994): 28.

210. *Smena* [Bratislava] December 10, 1991, in FBIS-SOV (December 17, 1991): 50–53.

211. Lieven, pp. 67, 69.

212. Reported in Elizabeth Fuller, "The Desperate Search for a Compromise in Chechnya," *Transition* (May 31, 1996): 24. Also Valerii Tishkov and A.S. Orlov,

eds., *Chechensky Krisis* (Moscow, 1995): 8, quoted in Lieven, p. 68 and Dunlop, *Russia Confronts Chechnya*, p. 216.

213. Lieven, p. 68.

214. Reuters (September 17, 1996); NPR Weekend Show, "Chechnya's King Arthur" (December 8, 1996), both available via LEXIS/NEXIS.

215. OMRI Daily Digest (August 2, 1996).

216. Lee Hockstader, "Jubilant Chechens Ready to Celebrate," *Washington Post* (September 4, 1996): A17; *Izvestiia* (March 5, 1994): 2 in FBIS-SOV (March 8, 1994): 19.

217. INTERFAX (March 26, 1994) in FBIS-SOV (March 29, 1994): 32; ITAR-TASS (May 23, 1994) in FBIS SOV (May 23, 1994): 6–7.

218. Cited in Teague, "Russia and Tatarstan," p. 20n. 6.

219. *Novaia ezhednevnaia gazeta* [Moscow] (August 4, 1994): 1 in FBIS-SOV (August 8, 1994): 21–23.

220. Jamestown Monitor (February 2, 1998).

221. *Izvestiia* (November 30, 1994): 2 in FBIS-SOV (November 30, 1994): 17.

222. Michael McFaul, "Eurasia Letter: Russian Politics after Chechnya," *Foreign Policy* 99 (summer 1995): 153.

223. Handwritten transcript of July 13, 1995, plenary session of the Constitutional Court of the Russian Federation, quoted in Payin and Popov, "Chechnya: From Past to Present."

224. Dunlop, *Russia Confronts Chechnya*, pp. 215, 218.

225. INTERFAX (March 29, 1994) in FBIS-SOV (March 30, 1994): 36; Pavel Felgengauer, "A War Moscow Cannot Afford to Lose," *Transition* (May 31, 1996): 28–31.

226. See coverage of Shakhrai's dismissal and reaction in FBIS-SOV (May 16, 1994): 18; (May 18, 1994): 20; and (May 23, 1994): 20–21.

227. ITAR-TASS (July 30, 1994): in FBIS-SOV (August 1, 1994): 22.

228. INTERFAX (May 6, 1994) in FBIS-SOV (May 6, 1994): 29–30.

229. For more on the manipulation of the meeting to prevent Baturin's attendance, see Jan Adams, "The Russian National Security Council," *Problems of Post-Communism* 43.1 (January/February 1996): 35–42.

230. Amy Knight, *Spies Without Cloaks* (Princeton: Princeton University Press, 1996): 177.

231. Peter Rutland, "Russia Sizes Up the 'Threat from the South': Unresolved Questions in Chechnya," OMRI Analytical Brief (October 15, 1996).

232. *Pravda* (June 2, 1993): 3 in FBIS-SOV (June 3, 1993): 44–45.

233. INTERFAX (August 22, 1994) in FBIS-SOV (August 23, 1994): 22. Also see *Sovietskaia rossiia* (August 23, 1994): 2 in FBIS-SOV (August 25, 1994): 18–19.

234. Russian Television (April 14, 1994): in FBIS-SOV (April 15, 1994): 34; INTERFAX (April 15, 1994) in FBIS-SOV (April 18, 1994):50. OMRI Daily Digest (June 6, 1996).

235. Richard Boudreau, "Dudayev's Death May Be Pivotal for Yeltsin," *Los Angeles Times* (April 26, 1996): A8.

236. INTERFAX (October 30, 1993) in FBIS-SOV (November 3, 1993): 55.

237. *Jamestown Monitor* (April 16, 1998).

238. *Jamestown Monitor* (July 16, 1998).

239. *Jamestown Monitor* (July 1, 1998).

240. *Jamestown Monitor* (July 9, 1998).

241. RFE/RL Tatar-Bashkir Report (November 20, 2000); RFE/RL Tatar-Bashkir Report (December 18, 2000).

242. Marcus Warren, "Tatarstan Writes Off Cyrillic Script," *Daily Telegraph* (September 1, 2000); RFE/RL Tatar-Bashkir Report (October 5, 2000); RFE/RL Tatar-Bashkir Report (November 6, 2000); RFE/RL Newsline (January 12, 2001).

243. INTERFAX (December 8, 2000).

244. For passport creation, see INTERFAX (August 9, 1994) in FBIS-SOV (August 10, 1994): 20. For foreign reaction, see Edward W. Walker, "No Peace, No War," p. 6n6.

245. Amy Knight, "The Enduring Legacy of the KGB in Russian Politics," *Problems of Post-Communism* 47, no. 4 (July/August 2000): 3–15.

246. Peter Ford, "Yeltsin Admits Aid Misses Chechnya," *Christian Science Monitor* (August 19, 1997): 6.

247. Giles Whittell, "Crime Funds Chechen War Effort," *Times* [London] (October 13, 1999).

248. Walker, "No Peace, No War," pp. 10–11.

249. *Jamestown Monitor* (February 5, 1998).

250. Lee Hockstader, "Chechens Vote for President Today," *Washington Post* (January 27, 1997): A14. Clara Germani, "Chechnya Stamps Independence with Its Presidential Balloting," *Baltimore Sun* (January 26, 1997) via LEXIS-NEXIS.

251. David Hoffman, "Moscow, Chechnya Sign Peace Treaty," *Washington Post* (May 13, 1997): A11; RFE/RL Tatar Bashkir Weekly Review (April 21–27, 2000).

252. Shaimiev interview with Moscow NTV (April 3, 1996) in FBIS-SOV (April 5, 1996): 28–30.

CHAPTER 6

THE KALININGRAD OBLAST—A TROUBLESOME EXCLAVE

Ingmar Oldberg

THE SPECIFICS OF THE REGION

All Russian regions are unique, but the *Kaliningradskaya oblast* is more unique than most. Besides being one of Russia's smallest regions (15,100 square km)—half the size of Belgium—it is also one of the newest. As part of German East Prussia (*Ostpreussen*), it was conquered from Nazi Germany in April 1945, ceded to the Soviet Union by the Western allies at the Potsdam Peace Conference in August 1945, and incorporated as an *oblast* into the Russian Socialist Federal Soviet Republic (RSFSR) in 1946. The main city changed its name from Königsberg to Kaliningrad in honor of the Soviet Head of State Mikhail Kalinin, who had just died. The larger southern part of East Prussia was given to Poland, and the northern Memel (Klaipeda) area of the Russian part was turned over to the Lithuanian Soviet Republic. Together with areas taken from Finland, Estonia and Latvia, the Kaliningrad region now is Russia's last remaining prize in Europe for its extremely costly victory in the Second World War.

Kaliningrad is also quite unique as a region because of the total change of populations. After 700 years of German settlement, all surviving Germans fled or were deported to the West after the war. The vacated lands were occupied mainly by Russians, but Ukrainians, Belarussians, and other Soviet nationals also moved in, merging into a typical Soviet Russian community. Now that over 50 years have elapsed, about two thirds of the present population are born in the region and are forming their own regional identity. The current population figure of 941,000 is still below the pre-war level, a fact probably unparalleled in Europe, and more than half the people live in Kaliningrad City (Swerew, 1996, p. 8 f; *Weekly News*, January 5–11, 1998 [ballad]).

Another characteristic, which Kaliningrad shares with Vladivostok in the Far East region, was the militarization of the region. The primary motive for Stalin's claim to the region in the first place obviously was strategic. In the postwar period the region developed into a military bastion in accordance with the offensive Soviet strategy directed against NATO forces in West Germany and the Baltic straits. The headquarters of the Soviet Baltic fleet was moved from Leningrad to the city of Kaliningrad, and the deep-sea port of Baltiisk (formerly Pillau) became a major naval base. The region was totally sealed off from Poland, no Western visitors were allowed, and even Soviet citizens had limited access. The armed forces and the military industry became the biggest employers in the region. The civilian structure was tailored to military needs, which greatly hampered and distorted Kaliningrad's economic development (Petersen & Petersen, 1992, p. 27 ff; Wellmann, 1998, p. 73 ff).

The withdrawal of Soviet (Russian) troops from first Central Europe and then the Baltic states via Kaliningrad in the early 1990s led to a temporary increase of troops and weapons there. This worried both Poland, which had no forces in the east, and the Baltic states, which were in the process of building defense forces from scratch. They therefore demanded the demilitarization of Kaliningrad. The perceived threat from Kaliningrad also contributed to their wish to join NATO.

Kaliningrad's geographic location is also unique. It is the westernmost region of the Russian Federation, close to economic hubs in Western and Northern Europe. Most importantly, it became an exclave separated from the rest of Russia, when Lithuania and Belarus regained/gained independence in 1991, and henceforth the only free connection to Russia was by the Baltic Sea. In this respect, Kaliningrad has been compared to such cases as Hong Kong (until 1997), Gibraltar, and Alaska, but the best analogy is the antecedent East Prussia, which in the inter-war period was separated from Germany by the resurrection of Poland.

Kaliningrad's exclave position automatically created transit problems. The most important railways and roads passed through Lithuania, and Russia wanted as free a passage as possible to Kaliningrad. To this end Russia used Lithuania's dependence on trade with Russia as a lever, several transit incidents occurred, and Russia tried (in vain) to play out Poland as an alternative route.

The United States, Germany, and other concerned states all supported the withdrawal of Russian forces from Central Europe and the Baltic states, and this encouraged Lithuania to allow the transit of troops home to Russia. However, Lithuania still perceived this as a threat even after the Russian occupation troops had left the country in August 1993, and imposed several restrictions on military transports. According to an agreement of 1993, which was later extended annually, Russia had to ask permission for every transport, submit to inspections, and pay fees. However, military transports soon tapered off or were transferred to the sea route. Civilian transport remained problematic as will be seen below.

The appearance of the Kaliningrad exclave on the ruins of the Soviet Union also gave rise to numerous territorial disputes. Nationalist groups in Germany, Poland, and Lithuania all claimed the region as theirs on various historic, legal, ethnic, and economic grounds. Others proposed the creation of a separate Russian Baltic state, a division of the region, a Russian-German-Polish condominium, or some kind of European overlordship. Such voices were especially strong in little Lithuania, which had the most reason to fear Russia. When he was President, Vytautas Landsbergis called not only for the demilitarization of the Kaliningrad oblast but also for its "decolonization"—whatever that means. In early 1994, when he became leader of the conservative opposition, he wanted the government to support the decoupling of Kaliningrad from Russia. All this naturally caused concern in Russia, which defended the inviolability of its borders.

However, the extreme nationalists in Poland, Lithuania, and Germany were few and not very influential, had a long-term perspective, and rejected violence. The governments in question officially recognized Russia's territorial integrity, because supporting territorial claims would destroy their relations not only with Russia but also with each other. Moreover, it would be incompatible with the principle of the inviolability of borders and be incompatible with NATO membership, a goal that both Poland and Lithuania aspire to. Besides, if the region after all was taken over, it would become an economic burden to any of these states, especially for Lithuania, and its Russian population would create great minority problems (Oldberg, 1998, pp. 16–24).

A new problem for Kaliningrad is the fact that Poland is scheduled to join NATO in April 1999, and Lithuania wants to follow suit. This means that this Russian region will border on a NATO state, and may later be surrounded by NATO states. Besides, Poland and Lithuania are seeking membership in the European Union (EU), which also is in a process of enlargement.

In sum, Kaliningrad has many specific features in comparison with other Russian regions and republics. To a large extent they determine Kaliningrad's relationship with the federal center in Moscow as will be seen in the following. The chapter first analyzes the positive signs of development toward free trade, political autonomy and demilitarization in Kaliningrad, and the support that was given to this in Moscow. Thereafter the factors *restraining* that development in Moscow, the effects they had on Kaliningrad as well as the internal economic problems in the region are scrutinized. Finally the different political reactions in Kaliningrad to the development are examined.

STEPS TOWARD A FREE ECONOMIC ZONE AND POLITICAL AUTONOMY

Ambitions in Kaliningrad and Foreign Support

The policy of democratization and transition to market economy, which was started by Gorbachev and continued by Yeltsin, opened the door to increased political and economic autonomy in the Russian Federation, including Kaliningrad. Western-inspired reform economists already in the late 1980s started to work out plans of a free economic zone, called "*Yantar*" (FEZ Amber) with the aim of restructuring and developing the economy of the region. The idea was exploit its favorable geographical position close to Western Europe with ice-free ports at the Baltic and railways with both European and Russian widths. Foreign investments were to be attracted by favorable taxation and customs rates, free profit export, a good industrial and social infrastructure, and a cheap and well-trained workforce. There were no ethnic conflicts in the area. It was pointed out that Kaliningrad had a well-developed ocean- going fishing fleet, in Soviet times third after those in Murmansk and Vladivostok, 70 percent or more of all amber assets in the world, and some oil reserves. Kaliningrad could become a center for economic cooperation in the Baltic region, a test case for market reforms in Russia, and a springboard for Western firms looking for the vast Russian market. Increased autonomy would enable the region to apply for support from European banks and institutions.

Yurii Matochkin (Kaliningrad's elected representative in the Russian Supreme Soviet), who became head of the region's administration in 1991, embraced the idea of a free economic zone. In 1993 Matochkin expressed the high hope that in 10 years Kaliningrad would become the Baltic Hong Kong. Local polls showed that the plans for a free economic zone were supported by 76 percent of the population in 1992, 64 percent in 1993, and especially by the youth (Dörrenbächer, 1984, p. 45 ff; SvD, June 12, 1993).

Profiting from the power struggle between President Yeltsin and the Supreme Soviet, Kaliningrad also wanted to increase its political power vis-à-vis Moscow. In 1993 both Governor Matochkin and the chairman of the regional Soviet, the communist Yury Semenov, even though supporting opposite sides in Moscow, agreed to propose a referendum on making the oblast a republic within the Russian Federation like the ethnic ones. This meant that the region should have its own constitution, laws and representation in federal bodies. The Kaliningrad administration already had its own department of foreign relations and planned to have a similar committee in the local Duma. However, the regional administration always emphasized that Kaliningrad was part of Russia and should remain so. Only small opposition groups in Kaliningrad, like the Baltic Republican Party, went further and proposed the creation of an independent Baltic, West Russian republic.[1]

In 1994 the Kaliningrad administration proposed new legislation to the Federal Assembly, according to which the regional "governor" would be a minister in the federal government. The region would have a separate line in the federal budget just like Moscow and St. Petersburg, and would be able to introduce customs, taxes, and quotas (*Segodnia*, May 28, November 26, 1994; NG, June 2, 1994). These ambitions were supported by Vladimir Shumeiko, the *oblast's* representative in the Federation Council and its speaker from 1993 to 1995. He also advocated autonomy for Kaliningrad in the form of a FEZ or "a special political entity" and hoped the region could become a center for international congresses and fairs and a territory for visa-free tourism (Shumeiko, 1995, p. 6 ff).

In the gubernatorial elections of 1996, Leonid Gorbenko, known as efficient director of the Kaliningrad fishing port and supported in the second round by the communists, narrowly defeated Matochkin but Gorbenko soon broke with them and fired the communist Vice-Governor. The regional Duma elected as Chairman Valerii Ustiugov, leader of a small reform-oriented party.

Gorbenko posed as a Yeltsin supporter at the same time as he endorsed the economic zone project and the goal of regional self-reliance. Interviewed by a Moscow newspaper, he pointed out that Kaliningrad was a kind of bridge between Russia and Europe and an avant-garde of Russian reforms, which should be granted wider powers by the center (*NG-Regiony*, April 7, 1998). He hired Yegor Gaidar, former Deputy Prime Minister and initiator of market reforms in Russia, as an economic adviser.[2] Gorbenko also pushed through a regional law on so-called local economic zones inside the region, offering extended rights and tax benefits in order to promote investments (NG, September 9, 1998).

Germany, Poland, and Lithuania for their own reasons supported the drive for economic liberalization and political autonomy in Kaliningrad and became its main trading partners.[3] The number of visiting Germans was especially great. A tourist industry developed in the early 1990s, hotels were built, and information material about the region was produced.

Lithuania and Poland opened consulates in Kaliningrad and signed agreements on visa-free travel and regional cooperation across the borders. Both states started to show real economic growth in the mid-1990s and aspired to become members of the EU. This could profit Kaliningrad in different ways, for example by providing a growing market for production with lower labor costs. In need of a Baltic port, Russia's closest ally Belarus also concluded agreements with the Kaliningrad region and opened offices there (*NG-Regiony*, November 27, 1997; Fairlie, 1998, pp. 182–187). Also the Nordic and other European states and organizations engaged in trade and aid projects to support Kaliningrad. Specifically, the EU launched some TACIS aid projects in the region.

Many people in Kaliningrad hoped for a breakthrough, when the South Korean car producer "Kia" in July 1996 signed an agreement with Russian partners on investing one billion dollars in a car assembly factory in Kaliningrad designed to put out 50,000–55,000 cars a year (*Segodnia*, July 31, 1966). In late 1997 the German Dresdner Bank signed an agreement with the region on a loan to small business, for the first time bypassing the federal center, as Gorbenko pointed out (Chronology, November 19, 1997 [Nupi]).

In order to show the success of the zone, it was pointed out that foreign trade increased fivefold between 1995 and 1997, and that Kaliningrad became one of the most attractive places in Russia with regard to the number of foreign companies. The region was allowed to keep a growing share of the taxes and payments it collected from 1992 to 1995, and tax collection improved in 1997. Real wages increased in 1996 faster than the Russian average, and immigration to the region remained higher than emigration (KP, August 29, 1996; NG, September 9, 1997; Fedorov & Zverev, 1995, p. 101).

Pointing to specific preconditions, the Kaliningrad authorities thus worked out ambitious plans for autonomy and free trade in the region, which also met support from abroad. They also achieved some positive results in economic terms. But the extent of support from the center was of course crucial for the idea of autonomy and free trade in Kaliningrad, and to this we will now turn.

The Center's Support

Gorbachev and later Yeltsin supported the ambitions of the Kaliningrad administration to the extent that these coincided with the general policy of economic reforms and free trade with the West. In July 1990 Kaliningrad became one of Russia's six Zones of Free Entrepreneurship. In June 1991 the region was granted customs and taxation exemptions; and in September 1991 the "Yantar" Free Economic Zone was officially established with the expressed aim of raising living standards and promoting foreign trade and investments. Matochkin was appointed head of regional administration by Yeltsin and thus seemed to enjoy his confidence. Moscow also issued several decrees promising agricultural and infrastructural investments. In December 1992, locally produced goods were exempted from export tariffs. Imported products were exempted from customs and turnover tax for ten years, unless they were sent forward to mainland Russia. The region was promised a say on land use, and to register and sign agreements with foreign firms (Dörrenbächer, 1994, pp. 32–42; Swerew, 1996, p. 13). Significantly, Kaliningrad was the only Russian region to switch over from the Moscow time zone to that of the Baltic states and Finland.

After years of deliberations in the Russian parliament, a federal law on Kaliningrad's status as a special economic zone (SEZ) and a power division agreement between the center and the region were finally signed in January 1996. According to both, the region received the right to conclude civil-law agreements with foreign investors. Products imported to the region from abroad, and products manufactured in the zone and then exported or sent to Russia were exempted from customs and other fees. Products were considered produced in the zone, if their value increased by 30 percent (15% for electronic products). The latter rules were intended to promote the processing of imported goods and foreign investment. Transit of goods through Kaliningrad to or from Russia was exempted from value-added tax. Investors could repatriate profits and capital without impediment. The regional administration was also allowed to introduce customs restrictions in order to protect local producers (RG, January 27, 31, 1996).

President Yeltsin's re-election in July 1996, his choice of reform-minded economists like Boris Nemtsov as Deputy Prime Minister in March 1997 and of Sergei Kirienko as new Prime Minister a year later—these factors also seemed to favor Kaliningrad's drive for autonomy. When Nemtsov visited Kaliningrad in July 1998, he praised the idea of a special economic zone, claiming that the region was more attractive geo-politically than St. Petersburg. He agreed with Governor Gorbenko on proposing an international tender for foreign managers at the regional administration board on the development of the region and its integration into the EU (*Weekly News*, August 3–9, 1998 [ballad].[4]

Some Russian politicians even favored more far-reaching alternatives for Kaliningrad. Vladimir Shumeiko, now ex-speaker of the Federation Council, claimed that the oblast was self-sufficient, more involved in the world economy than any other Russian region, and was one of the most developed subjects of the federation. He proposed further reforms and making Kaliningrad an autonomous Russian Baltic republic with the argument that the stronger Kaliningrad, the stronger is Russia (*Izvestiia*, July 17, 1998).

Vladimir Zhirinovskii suggested that the Kaliningrad region could be returned to Germany, if Germany concluded an alliance with Russia against the United States. His deputy chairman Aleksei Mitrofanov suggested less radical solutions such as a Russian-German zone of economic activity, common military maneuvers in Kaliningrad, and the creation of an autonomy for all Germans in Russia there (*Izvestiia*, April 7, 1997; Mitrofanov, 1997, pp. 190–193).

In tune with the trend toward democratization and liberalization that prevailed in the beginning of the 1990s, the federal authorities in Moscow thus generally supported the original plans in Kaliningrad concerning economic autonomy, and some politicians even advanced more ambitious ideas.

Demilitarization

Another factor promoting economic and political autonomy was the reduction of the military predominance in Kaliningrad, since the military sector is part and parcel of the federal state power. Even though the withdrawal of troops from Central Europe and the Baltics led to a temporary growth of forces and weapons in the region, President Boris Yeltsin's continuation of Gorbachev's policy of detente and disarmament in combination with a persistent economic crisis led to a decrease of troops in the Kaliningrad region from 1993, and the arsenal of weapons in the area remained far below the levels stipulated by the CFE agreements. When visiting Stockholm in December 1997,

Yeltsin promised that army groupings in northwestern Russia would be cut by 40 percent, and at the end of 1998 Russian diplomats reported that the promise had been fulfilled or over-fulfilled. According to the *Military Balance* published by the International Institute of Strategic Studies in London, the number of ground forces in the Kaliningrad region was 14,500 in 1998 compared with 103,000 in 1993. The naval forces were cut roughly by half with regard to manpower and by two thirds as for ships.[5] In 1994 the Baltic fleet started to participate in exercises with NATO in the Baltic Sea and to receive foreign naval ships in Baltiisk.

As elsewhere in Russia, military training and readiness were impaired as few exercises were held, maintenance and repair were neglected, salaries lagged behind if they were paid at all, and social conditions worsened among the officers, the best of whom left for the civilian sector. Many military industries were laid off or converted to civilian production, for example, the main military shipyard "Yantar" (Wellmann, 1998, pp. 75–86). In 1991 foreigners were allowed to visit the region, and border passages to Poland and Lithuania opened.

Numerous military garrisons and land areas were transferred to the civilian authorities. Even part of the naval port in Baltiisk was declared open to foreign trade, and the militarized Vistula spit across the sound was handed over to the municipal administration. The regional authorities became more confident vis-à-vis the military, sometimes even talking about "demilitarization." The military became increasingly dependent on support from the civil sector for housing and retraining officers.

This process of demilitarization in Kaliningrad also alleviated the fears in the neighboring states and increased their interest in supporting the economic zone. Thus, judging from the above, the free trade zone in Kaliningrad seemed to have good prospects and enjoy sufficient support from the federal center.

RESTRAINING FACTORS

Political and Economic Considerations in Moscow

However, the above evidence must be weighed against all the signs pointing in the opposite direction, and the underlying problems must be analyzed before a total assessment can be made. Despite the demilitarization of the region, military interests continued to play a role in different ways. After the Russian retreat from the neighboring states, Kaliningrad remained the only forward base for the Russian Baltic fleet, albeit a very vulnerable one. Calls for demilitarization in Kaliningrad from the neighboring states were constantly interpreted as designs on Russia's integrity, and demonstrative military exercises were regularly held in the region. During his 1996 re-election campaign, President Yeltsin made a point of visiting Kaliningrad and Baltiisk, stressing that the region belongs to Russia (KP, June 25, 1996).

NATO's eastern enlargement also spelled problems for Kaliningrad as noted above. Russian officials, especially military ones, thus declared that now Kaliningrad was threatened, not the Baltic states. They warned that if the Baltic states and Poland should join NATO, Russia would stop reducing and instead reinforce its military positions there, for example, by stationing tactical nuclear weapons in the region (*Gromov*, 1995, p. 12 f; Vardomskii, 1995, pp. 336–339).

Further, the military authorities in Kaliningrad still imposed restrictions on civilian activities and international trade, for instance in the Baltiisk straits. The military property and personnel that was turned over to the civilian authorities also became a burden on them. As the military units did not get money from Moscow, they soon became the main debtors to private companies for energy consumption, food, etc. and sometimes their supplies were cut short (*Weekly News*, March 30–April 5, 1998 [ballad]; NG, November 21, 1998).

Also, the economic and political development in Russia set definite limits for autonomy in Kaliningrad. The market economic reforms did not reverse the economic crisis, and nationalism became the dominant creed, which few politicians dared to resist. All this contributed to a political reaction against Yeltsin and his Western-oriented foreign and domestic policy. In the December 1993 Duma elections, Vladimir Zhirinovskii's chauvinist Liberal Democratic Party (LDPR) became the biggest party in Russia, and two years later the new Communist Party came out ahead of the LDPR, whereas the reform parties, which generally supported the government, remained weak (Vardomskii, 1995, p. 49; RG, January 6, 1996). This meant that the Duma was dominated by parties in opposition to Yeltsin.

When the Duma started to discuss a new federal law defining the status of the region, the Kaliningrad proposal "On Raising the Status of the Kaliningrad Oblast" was renamed "On Strengthening the Sovereignty of the Russian Federation on the Territory of the Kaliningrad Oblast" (NG, June 2, 1994; *Segodnia*, June 2, November 2, 1994).

In order to undermine Lithuania's drive to join NATO and to improve Russian transit through Lithuania, Russian nationalists and communists revived the claim on Klaipeda, which in their view had illegally been ceded to Lithuania. In October 1997 the Russian Duma therefore advised President Yeltsin not to sign a border delimitation treaty with Lithuania, since this would "freeze" the border question. Another aim was to improve the rules for transit across Lithuania, for which the Allied powers' access to West Berlin before 1990 was mentioned as a model (RG, October 4, 1997). Yeltsin signed the treaty, but it was not ratified by the Duma.

This political situation also influenced Yeltsin and his policy vis-à-vis Kaliningrad and other regions. In the new Russian Constitution, which was adopted in the December 1993 referendum, the personal powers of the President were enlarged, and the sovereignty of the ethnic republics was restricted. Regions (*oblasti*) like Kaliningrad were not granted the same status as them;

for instance, they were not allowed to have a constitution and a president. The federal government disavowed a trade agreement, which Kaliningrad had signed with Lithuania, and retained control over border and visa questions (Rapport, 1994, p. 5; *Izvestiia*, November 18, 1994). Different from Poland and Lithuania, Germany was not allowed to open a consulate in Kaliningrad.

In 1994, then Deputy Prime Minister Sergei Shakhrai—who had earlier headed a party defending regional interests—attacked "local separatism" and "creeping/Western/expansion" in Kaliningrad—specifically claiming that Germany was methodically fortifying its economic, cultural, and social positions there. (At the same time the figures he gave showed that Western investment was in fact very small.) He feared that economic advantages for Kaliningrad would turn out to be strategic losses for Russia. He thought that demilitarization would limit Russian sovereignty and recommended expanding the naval base. Shakhrai advocated "mechanisms of state regulation" in Kaliningrad and similar regions, more specifically a federal law, in which the state should take all responsibility for regional development. Free-trade zones should be confined to small areas like ports, which one could afford to improve, and strict customs control should be maintained, wrote Shakhrai (NG, July 26, October 26, 1994).

In March 1995 Yeltsin by decree suddenly abolished the customs exemptions of the economic zone that should have lasted for 10 years on the pretext that all regions of Russia should have equal terms. Russian regions in the Far North and Far East had complained that they too were isolated most of the year and needed special favors as well (Vardomskii, 1995, pp. 16 f, 48).

True, when the law on Kaliningrad at last was accepted by the Federal Assembly and signed by the President in January 1996, Kaliningrad got back its customs-free favors as noted above. However, according to the law, Kaliningrad no longer was a "free" zone—with all possible connotations—but a "Special" Economic Zone (SEZ). Federal oversight was emphasized, and only economic foreign relations were allowed. The federal government reserved control over licensing with regard to the military industry, mineral resources like amber, energy production, transport, and mass media. All transactions had to be made in rubles. A federal law could abolish the law if it collided with the vital interests of the federation.

According to the law, foreigners could not purchase land, only lease it; and the lease period was not defined, which was a problem for foreign investors (RG, January 31, 1996). The Russian Federation to date has no law allowing private ownership of land.

A crucial flaw was that the whole concept of a free-trade zone could be undermined by quota restrictions. The federal law allowed the Kaliningrad region to introduce quotas in order to protect local producers, but not to extend them. A motive for the federal government to place quotas on import from the West was the need to increase its revenues, as tax evasion became more and more alarming every year. Already in July 1996 quotas were placed on 22 import items, including food products, alcohol, cigarettes, petrol, construction material, and used cars ("Das Ende,"1996).

Moscow also retained its economic dominance in the region. As in other regions, the taxes were collected by Kaliningrad and sent to the federal center, which then redistributed them in the form of transfers. The problem was that Moscow could withhold the transfers, when the amount of collected taxes diminished. Thus, in 1997, Kaliningrad only received a third of the allotted budget transfers. The frequent promises to support the economic zone with federal investments were forgotten. The Kaliningrad budget depended on federal support for almost 30 percent, and the budget was often under-financed (by 40% in 1994) (KP, August 12, 1997, March 31, 1998). Further, almost all capital and all the major banks in Russia were concentrated in Moscow. The staff of federal agencies in Kaliningrad was bigger than that of the regional administration and absorbed half its budget (RG, January 27, 1996). Regional property made up only 12 percent, and even the regional administration building in Kaliningrad city was federal property (*Weekly News*, July 6–12, 1998 [ballad]).

Other problems existed with regard to cooperation with Western aid programs. The European Union TACIS program on improving the energy sector in the Kaliningrad region was frustrated by the monopoly position of "Gazprom," its preference for building big, inflexible power stations, and the low rentability of such projects due to the consumers' low morale in paying energy bills. The Russian side was also slow in reacting to the plans of forming an energy ring linking all the Baltic Sea states, which could offer Russia a market for electricity export (NG, July 31, 1997).

In 1998 the economic situation in Russia worsened. Russian export income decreased due to falling prices on the world raw material market, and Western investors lost confidence in Russia's financial system under the impression of the crisis in East Asia. Russia did not manage to curb tax evasion and could not pay its employees their wages, and therefore it desperately sought for ways to increase its income. In March the federal government introduced new quotas on customs-free import of several food products, spirits, cigarettes, petrol, building materials, used cars, and so on in Kaliningrad. Cars registered in Kaliningrad were forbidden to enter the rest of Russia, though they could go abroad, and ship transport rates from Kaliningrad to the rest of Russia were raised (*Weekly News*, March 16–22, 1998[ballad]; *Izvestiia*, July 17, 1998). In June 1998 the new liberal Kirienko government even proposed depriving Kaliningrad of the right to customs-free import to and export from Kaliningrad altogether and reforming all the economic zones in Russia as part of an anti-crisis program.

However, the State Duma, dominated as it was by the communists and their allies, rejected Kirienko's anti-crisis program and therefore did not even consider the proposal to abolish the zone. The federal government also seemed split on the issue. As previously noted Deputy Prime Minister Nemtsov defended the zone when visiting Kaliningrad in July, so did Yeltsin's special representative in Kaliningrad (*Weekly News*, June 26–July 5, August 3–9, 1998 [ballad]). Some liberal newspapers in Moscow also supported the special status of Kaliningrad even in the face of Western designs to take it over (*Izvestiia*, April 7, July 17; *NG Regiony*, April 7, 1998).

Most notably, the former speaker in the Federation Council Vladimir Shumeiko forcefully defended Kaliningrad's trade privileges by arguing that they only were in compensation for the region's geographical position. If they were taken away, the federation would have to pay more to sustain the region than it would receive in the form of customs revenues. Food prices would double, unemployment would rise sevenfold, imports be halved and exports fall by three times. Foreign investors would flee never to return, and a social disaster follow, favoring separatists who want to give Kaliningrad away to the neighbors or the Council of Europe. This was Shumeiko's reason for advocating a republican status as a lesser evil (*Izvestiia*, July 17, 1998; Chronology, July 20, 1998 [Nupi]).

In the end, the federal government decided to back down and let the zone be. Referring to the need to stop transshipment of goods to Russia without import fees, which cost the state several hundred million dollars a year, the government instead decided to issue an extended list of quotas valid until 2000 (*Weekly News*, June 29–July 5, July 13–19, 1998 [ballad]; Chronology, July 30, 1998 [Nupi]). Also Nemtsov saw fit to justify these quotas by claiming that they would help the center to support the region (*Weekly News*, August 3–9, 1998 [ballad]).

The economic collapse in Moscow in August 1998 worsened the situation still more. Foreign capital fled the country, the Russian ruble fell like a stone, the bank system broke down, and the government defaulted on its domestic and foreign debts. Because the government therefore could not win any more credits and loans, and no more privatization was under way, increasing state revenue by taxes and customs duties became all the more urgent. In effect changing the 1996 federal law, the State Tax Committee issued a "Temporary Ruling" according to which import goods to Kaliningrad, reprocessed or not, which were sent on to the rest of Russia were subjected to customs (RG, November 3, 1998). All this led to a scandal, when even humanitarian aid from Poland and Lithuania was subjected to excise and customs duties exceeding the value of the shipment (Yemelyanenko, 1998).

The financial collapse also resulted in a political crisis in Russia. Yeltsin dissolved the Kirienko government and when the Duma refused to accept Viktor Chernomyrdin as Prime Minister again, former Foreign Minister Yevgenii Primakov was finally appointed. A communist became deputy Prime Minister in charge of economy, and priority was given to stability ahead of market reforms. In his first speech as Prime Minister, Primakov emphasized state and central control as a way to avert an economic and political disaster. Observing that the whole state threatened to be split into regions, he announced that

Russia's integrity was to be a priority for the new government and that governors violating the Constitution could be dismissed (DN, September 12, 1998). As will be seen below this was a clear warning to Kaliningrad and some other regions. In the fall, several Moscow newspapers returned to the threat of separatism, which also Shumeiko's idea of an autonomous republic was said to promote, or of Germany taking over Kaliningrad (RG, September 15; NG, December 3, 1998).

In short, not only nationalists (possibly except LDPR), communists and the military establishment in Moscow were skeptical about autonomy in Kaliningrad. Also the federal authorities strove to restrict Kaliningrad's special economic zone privileges in customs-free import, as the economic crisis undermined the state finances. This was true even for Kirienko when he was Prime Minister, and only individual politicians and the liberal press pointed out the possible adverse consequences in Kaliningrad of more restrictions. The zone formally remained, still allowing free export of locally produced goods and favoring investments, but it was seriously crippled by quota restrictions on import, customs on re-export to Russia, and federal oversight over everything that smelled of foreign influence. Even though the ruble devaluation had made foreign import very expensive, the import quotas were kept.

Economic Problems in Kaliningrad

The military, political, and economic restrictions on Kaliningrad imposed by the federal center could not but disturb its development. There were also lots of problems inside the region that were partly all-Russian, partly specific. To start with, the heavy legacy of fifty years of planned economy and militarization was still strong in Kaliningrad and could not be wished away. The industrial products from there—like the rest of Russia—proved non-competitive on the international market. Its infrastructure was lopsided and worn down, and the environmental problems were enormous. All this required vast investments to be remedied. For example, the port of Kaliningrad had to be modernized in order to handle Western cargo, and the sea channel to Kaliningrad is only seven meters deep and so narrow that it generally only permits one-way traffic. Road and rail communications are slow. There are so far no regular ferry lines for cargo with Western states, and very few air connections with other states, none with the Baltic states. Civilian air traffic control is still dependent on support from Vilnius.

In the early 1990s, Kaliningrad's main industries, including ocean fishing and related industries, were already being hit very hard by the market-driven rises on oil prices. Catches went down dramatically; most of them were sold abroad, which angered foreign fishermen and deprived the home industry of fish, at the same time as imported fish products flooded the home market (Swerew, 1996, p. 10; Vardomskii, 1995, p. 11 ff).

Kaliningrad's exclave position was a liability in many respects. After being integrated in the Soviet economy, in 1991 the region found itself cut off both from its raw material base and its market in Russia. For example, 80 percent of its electricity came from the nuclear power station of Ignalina in Lithuania. Nowadays, most of its oil, natural gas and electricity comes from Russia at reduced prices, since the region still covers only 20 percent of its energy needs. It does not even have a refinery for its own oil, and the plans to build new electricity producing stations to substitute energy import have so far not been realized.

Nor could the region feed itself with respect to agricultural products. Transit and transport costs made food and industrial products from Russia 50 percent more expensive, and the tax and customs privileges allowing import were meant to compensate for this. Foreign products were thus often cheaper than Russian equivalents (NG, April 7, 1998). Consumers and traders favored import from abroad, whereas the few local producers wanted to restrict it. Thus a Lithuanian meat factory met great problems when establishing a conserve factory in the region (KP, January 31, 1998 [koenig]).

With regard to foreign trade and investment, the region itself offered only a small and poor market, and its attractiveness largely depended on free access to the rest of Russia. The above-mentioned problems with unstable and restrictive economic legislation with regard to Kaliningrad also served to scare away foreign business and investments. Therefore, even while Kaliningrad's foreign trade grew, its imports greatly exceeded exports in contrast to Russia in general, and they were increasing at a faster rate.[6] As for the trade structure, consumer products, mainly from Lithuania and Poland, and industrial products from the West dominated Kaliningrad's import and part of this was then sent on to Russia. It mainly exports half-processed goods or raw material, part of which originated in Russia.

Most joint ventures only existed on paper and were generally engaged in trade and services. The actual amount of foreign investment in the region was pitiful as compared with that in Poland, for example. Until 1996, the general volume was ten million dollars. Belarus in 1998 became the biggest investor in Kaliningrad, but only fictitiously, since the "investment" was made in order to overpass the non-convertibility of the Belarussian currency. Most of the money went into the gray economy (Fedorov, 1996, pp. 39–46; Samson & Lamande, 1998, pp. 9–12).

The center's introduction of customs fees and import quotas naturally disturbed foreign trade and investment. A major casualty was the South Korean "Kia" car assembly factory, on which so much hope was pinned. It had been established on the assumption that the import of components would be exempted from customs in accordance with the 1996 law, but later the authorities started to demand customs fees for them. The factory became unprofitable and switched production to Poland instead, and the tax police seized its property in Kaliningrad (News, January 12, 1998 [ballad]; *Weekly News*, April 27–May 3 [ballad]; NG, July 29, 1998). Another example was a chicken factory, the biggest in Russia, which also delivered heat to a suburb of Kaliningrad city. New tariffs on imported eggs in October 1998 brought it to the verge of bankruptcy (Chronology, October 22, 1998 [Nupi]).

Limitations and quotas also increased the temptation to engage in smuggling and corruption in the region. Further, since the quotas limits introduced in 1998 were very low and were quickly exhausted, and there were few local producers, the result was steep price rises for the consumers (*Weekly News*, March 23–29, 1998; *Izvestiya* July 29, 1998).

In view of these problems, Kaliningrad was superseded by the Baltic states and Poland, which became more attractive to foreign investors and international aid programs, since they provided more stable, favorable conditions and started to show real growth. Transit trade with the West, also Russian, went over from Kaliningrad to other Baltic ports, notably Klaipeda, which is a real free economic zone offering favorable rail rates through Lithuania.[7] Also St. Petersburg, much bigger than Kaliningrad with no transit problems, was a serious competitor in the Baltic Sea area. Indeed, Deputy Prime Minister Nemtsov in July 1998 had to admit that the economic zone law was only 10 percent effective in Kaliningrad, and advocated a new regional law to protect foreign investors.

Poland and Lithuania also found it easier to cooperate with each other than with Russia, and their integration with the EU in many ways tended to shut Kaliningrad out. In order to facilitate its entry into the EU, Poland as of January 1, 1998, introduced new rules for Russian citizens, who must have visas, invitations or prepaid hotel vouchers. Only after loud protests from Russia and concerned Polish businessmen were the rules softened with respect to Kaliningrad. In contrast, Poland concluded a free-trade agreement with Lithuania and imposed no visa requirement on its citizens.[8] Cross-border cooperation the Polish regions also lost momentum. Even Kaliningrad's cooperation with pro-Russian Belarus cooled off in 1997, when at Yeltsin's behest Gorbenko canceled a visit to Kaliningrad by President Alexandr Lukashenko in connection with the latter's arrest of Russian journalists (NG, September 9, 1997). Business with the major Western states was also hampered by the absence of consulates in Kaliningrad, so Kaliningraders had to get visas for those states at the embassies in Moscow.

The overall effect of the federal restrictions, the structural and specific problems in Kaliningrad, and lacking interest from abroad was that the economy of the region actually continued to deteriorate and industrial production to fall—more than the Russian average. For instance, in the first half of 1997 both industrial and agricultural production declined, including energy and bread production, as compared to the first half of 1996. Only the production of spirits grew by 110 percent, which is an unhealthy sign. Even the amber factory, which had a monopoly position on the market, went bankrupt (NG, September 9, 1997; *Weekly News*, October 12–18, 1998 [ballad]).

The potential of the industrial sector in 1997 was used only to 70 percent of the 1990 figure, in transport to a third, and the profits in the industry turned into losses in 1997. The amount of (total) investments fell by 20 percent as compared with the previous year, bringing Kaliningrad down from the 15th to the 32nd place among Russian regions, even though it is the biggest free-trade area.[9]

The economic crisis also led to social misery for the bulk of the population. Wages were lower and prices higher in Kaliningrad than in Russia proper. As in Russia, wages were often not paid, and in 1997 for the first time even pensions were delayed (NG, July 29, 1998). Unemployment grew, encompassing a fourth of the working population in the region and half of it in the countryside. About 60 percent of the population lived below the official poverty line in 1997.[10] As elsewhere in Russia, falling living standards especially befell state employees, pensioners, students, and so on. In 1998 even the number of militia men and tax inspectors was reduced. The regional administration staff was cut by half (*Weekly News*, August 31– September, 1998; *NG Regiony*, April 9, 1998).

The birth rate declined, mortality rose and health problems got worse. Kaliningrad became infamous in the whole world, when it was reported to have the highest incidence of AIDS in Russia and to be worst in Europe with regard to confiscated drugs (Krickus, 1999, p. 5). Many people survived only thanks to their private land plots or business in the gray sector of the economy, and a few became shamelessly rich. Some, including military officers and customs personnel, engaged in smuggling raw material, for example amber, abroad and importing Western goods like cigarettes and used cars, for further transport to mainland Russia (Fedorov & Sverev, 1995, pp. 100, 115; Krickus, 1999, p. 5). The imported cars had often been stolen in Western Europe, and many cars were reported stolen in Kaliningrad as well (*Weekly News*, March 1998, pp. 23–29 [ballad]).

The financial breakdown in Moscow in August 1998 with devaluation of the ruble and default on loans hit Kaliningrad exceptionally hard, because the city was by now dependent on food imports to about 90 percent. The imports all but stopped, the shop shelves were emptied and black market exchange reappeared. Consumer prices rose by three-four times, but wages remained the same (*Weekly News*, August 31–September 6, 1998 [ballad]; DN, September 14, 1998; Tracevkis, 1998).

Thus, for a variety of reasons the economic development in the special economic zone of Kaliningrad did not meet the high ambitions and expectations of its supporters and it came to be seen as a problem area as compared with the neighboring states. It tended to become a periphery both in relation to the rest of Russia and to the enlarging EU rather than a bridge between them.

Political Reactions in Kaliningrad

The fact that the economic crisis continued in Kaliningrad like in the rest of Russia soon led to growing skepticism in the population about the free economic zone. A 1993 poll showed waning support for the project and a 70 percent disapproval of foreign land ownership. Vladimir Nikitin, leader of a national patriotic society who was elected deputy chairman of the regional Duma in June 1993, argued that Russian, not foreign entrepreneurs should be favored. The worsening economic situation and the need of subsidies from the center spoke against any decoupling of the region from Russia. In fact, Nikitin claimed, Kaliningrad was the least suitable region to be a free zone (Dörrenbächer, 1994, p. 42 ff).

In, Kaliningrad, Russian nationalism and fear of Western influence were directed mainly against the many German visitors and businessmen as well as against Volga Germans who had recently moved to the region from other parts of the former Soviet Union. This hostility was probably most deeply rooted among elderly people who remembered the Second World War. As a consequence, street signs in German were forbidden by a regional Duma decision in 1994. The fear that rich Germans could buy up the whole region explained the reluctance to allow foreign ownership of land (see below). Digressing from his party leader's pro-German stance, a Liberal Democrat from Kaliningrad in the first federal Duma warned that a free economic zone could lead to a German take-over and make Kaliningrad a "small Alaska," which the Russians would be asked to leave (KP, April 5, 1994).

Following the general Russian trend, the Kaliningraders gave most votes to Zhirinovskii's ultra-nationalist party (30%) in the Duma elections of 1993, and two years later the communists became the main winners, whereas the reformers were split. The defeat of Yurii Matochkin, the main figure behind the free zone, in the gubernatorial elections in October 1996 can also be interpreted as a protest vote.

However, since then public opinion seemed to have shifted again. One poll in early 1998 showed that more than half the inhabitants favored closer ties with Poland and Germany. The Moscow press reported that people now felt abandoned by Moscow, so that if the federal capital could not help them, it should at least give them freedom to manage themselves. It was even claimed that the local people supported German territorial claims (*Izvestiia* and *NG Regiony*, April 7, 1998; Yemelyanenko, 1998).

The small Republican Party proposed a referendum on creating a sovereign Baltic Russian state, an idea that was assessed to enjoy backing from a third of the population. In order to earn money, they also offered NATO to rent deserted military posts in the region (NG, December 3, 1998; Yemelyanenko, 1998).

How then did the political decision-makers in Kaliningrad defend the region's special status vis-à-vis the center in this new situation? When the Kirienko government wanted to abolish several zone privileges, Governor Gorbenko, the oblast Duma and the business community in Kaliningrad were united in defending them. Gorbenko threatened to go to court, arguing that they were inscribed in the power division agreement between the federal center and

Kaliningrad and hence could not be changed unilaterally (*Weekly News*, June 29–July 5, 1998 [ballad]).

Regarding the controversial land question, Gorbenko's administration in 1997 proposed a law, which would allow the rent, sale, and mortgage of land in the Kaliningrad region similarly as had been approved in Saratov. They hoped that this would increase autonomy from Moscow. However, the regional Duma rejected the proposal, mainly due to the Communists' opposition (Chronology, December 18, 1997 [Nupi]; *Weekly News*, February 2–8, 1998 [ballad]). But later, when several more Russian regions had taken such laws, the Kaliningrad Duma was finally persuaded to adopt the land law in the first reading with a proviso that foreigners must not be allow into this trade. A Moscow paper saw this as the first step to losing Kaliningrad, but Gorbenko thought that also foreigners should be allowed to buy land (NG, November 28, 1998; Chronology, January 19, 1999 [Nupi]).

With regard to the important distribution of taxes, the Governor in April 1998 complained about the lacking transfers from the federal budget and asked whether it would not be better to let the region form its own budget. He wanted more powers but avoided the question of republican status (*NG Regiony*, April 7, 1998). Having lost hope of getting support for his stabilization program from Moscow, Gorbenko was even reported to have told the German journal *Der Spiegel* that "selling the region in order to pay the debts is fully permissible sooner or later"—a statement which caused alarm in Moscow (*Izvestiia* April 7, 1998).

The economic breakdown in August led to new initiatives from Gorbenko as well as governors of other regions. On September 8 he reportedly declared a "state of emergency" in Kaliningrad, assuming "full responsibility for political and economic decisions." The intention was to secure the supplies of food and fuel and stop "unwarranted" price hikes, not to limit the citizens' rights. Since the region had only received 30 percent of the promised transfers and money should not flow only in one direction, he raised the question of temporarily suspending payments to the federal budget (SWB BBC, September 9; NG, September 11, 1998).

But when Yeltsin's administration at once pointed out that announcing a state of emergency is the President's prerogative and Primakov threatened to dismiss Governors violating the Constitution, Gorbenko made clear that he had only declared a "situation of emergency." According to a second decree, the region should create a reserve of financial and material resources. The possibility of paying salaries out of unpaid transfers to the central budget and of to set up a system of state enterprises for trading foodstuffs was mentioned (SWB BBC, September 9–10; Chronology, September 17, 1998 [Nupi]).

As a member of the Federation Council, Gorbenko probably also contributed to the December 1998 agreement between the federal government and the regions, according to which the regions would receive 50.5 percent of all tax revenue collected locally, and the government would spend 14 percent of all taxes in the regions (RRR, January 14, 1999).

Gorbenko also intensified ties with foreign countries, which seem to go beyond economic relations. He strove for a program of economic cooperation with Belarus and suggested that Belarus could take care of federal debts to Kaliningrad (Chronology, September 17, 1998 [Nupi]). More important steps were taken to promote long-term cooperation with Lithuania. On a visit to Vilnius in October, Gorbenko called for investments in Kaliningrad, explaining that foreign companies could produce for the vast Russian market without taxes on production. He also called for more Lithuanian goods on a barter basis and supported plans of a new gas pipeline from Russia to Kaliningrad, which could give Lithuania a share of the profits (BT, August 27, October 16, November 5, 1998).

At the same time Gorbenko in other questions took views and decisions more in line with federal interests. He bowed to military concerns, when he in 1998 called for measures to prevent foreigners from entering and staying in the naval town Baltiisk without a permit. Concerning the effects of militarization in the region, he failed to understand how Kaliningrad was different from Gibraltar, which is both a naval base and a free economic zone (News, February 23, 1998 [ballad]; RG, September 15, 1998). On the other hand, he supported the implicit Russian claim to "Memel," and even after Yeltsin had signed the border treaty with Lithuania in 1997, he admonished the Duma not to ratify it (Chronology, April 30, 1997 [Nupi]; Chronology, November 27, 1997 [Nupi]). This must have pleased Russian nationalists but disturbed his relations with Yeltsin.

Concerning the important question of quotas, Gorbenko not only accepted federal laws about them, but also lobbied for them in Moscow. He wanted to protect local producers against cheap imports, and showed an understanding for "state interests" such as stopping the smuggling of Western cars and tobacco through Kaliningrad to the rest of Russia, noting that the United States also protects its market from Russian products (NG, April 7; Weekly News March 9–15, 23–29, 1998 [ballad]).

The reform-minded Duma chairman Ustiugov in March 1998 pointed out that the quotas were incompatible with free trade and led to price rises for the consumers rather than helping local producers, since the latter were still burdened by extreme taxes. He added that quotas on petrol and bananas could not possibly be justified with references to local producers (Whoiswho, March 23–29, 1998 [ballad]).

Gorbenko also justified the quotas by explaining that the region could earn money by selling quotas to businessmen. But others, including Yegor Gaidar, at one time Gorbenko's adviser, saw this as an invitation to corruption (*Weekly News*, March 16–22, 23–29, 1998 [ballad]). The Union of entrepreneurs thus criticized that when import quotas on grain and grain products were introduced in 1997, exception was made for one firm. Similarly, even if the Union liked the idea of local economic zones in the region in principle, the law on it was considered a "mafia law" inviting bribe taking, since a very small commission in the administration was to decide whom to give permission and whom not.

Gorbenko was further blamed for bad business deals with foreign firms, strong-hand politics and suppression of the opposition. Liberal newspapers in Moscow published this critique, whereas others defended the Governor (NG, September 9, 1997, July 29; RG, September 15, 1998).

Protests broke out when the Kaliningrad administration—unlike other Russian regions—first declined offers of humanitarian aid from Lithuania and Poland and instead turned to local businessmen for help in exchange of local tax privileges. But it soon changed its mind, and aid arrived for regional hospitals and the Baltic Fleet in Baltiisk, which had not received money in six months (*Weekly News*, September 14–20, 1998 [ballad]; RFE/RL Newsline, September 18, 1998).

All this developed into a serious conflict between Gorbenko and the regional Duma. Gorbenko refused to work with the Duma and reduced its funding, so that delegates received no salaries and could not even make telephone calls (*Weekly News*, July 26–August 2, 1998 [ballad]). In the fall of 1998 Kaliningrad elected a new mayor, who also opposed Gorbenko, which may explain why he wanted a greater share of the city's income taxes. The Duma tried to impeach Gorbenko, appealed to the President and Prime Minister for support, and in November a representative of Yeltsin arrived to mediate. Gorbenko promised to pay the Duma fairly in exchange for support for the land law (above), but the conflict was not solved (*Weekly News*, October 19–25, 26–31 1998 [ballad]; NG, November 21; RRR, November 5, 24, 1998).

Thus, the absence of support from the center to meet the economic hardship in the last few years seem to have made public opinion in Kaliningrad more critical of federal restrictions and more aware of the region's specific interests. The Governor wanted more decision-making powers and used the economic crisis to increase his own influence inside the region. But his support for import quotas in the alleged interest of local producers coincided with the federal interest in customs income and collided with consumer, free-trade interests represented in the regional Duma and the business community.

CONCLUSIONS

In line with the general policy of democratization, decentralization and the transition to a market economy, the federal government in 1991 approved of making Kaliningrad one of the free economic zones in Russia. Its location as the most western region of Russia close to European hubs facilitated foreign trade, which could make a real impact on this small region. The reduction of the military forces in the region and the opening of the borders reduced old fears among the neighboring states, which supported Kaliningrad's free zone ambitions by trade and aid. No neighbor raised serious territorial claims against this Russian region, and Poland's and Lithuania's economic progress and gradual integration into the European Union could under some conditions also favor Kaliningrad. A majority of the population in the region also shared these hopes at the time.

However, in 1993 Yeltsin started to counteract the decentralizing tendency in the federation by his new constitution. Russian nationalism, which found expression in the Duma elections, and lingering distrust in relation to the West, especially toward Germany, conspired to make the center suspect that a "free" zone and autonomy in Kaliningrad might jeopardize Russia's territorial integrity and security. In 1996, a federal law gave Kaliningrad special status, but it emphasized central political control. NATO's decision to include Poland as a member in 1999 and perhaps the Baltic states in the future fomented Russian fears of losing Kaliningrad as a Russian outpost.

Furthermore, the economic crisis in Russia continued. The federal center could not fulfill its promises of budget allocations to Kaliningrad and constantly looked for ways to increase its income by taxes and customs. The liberal Kirienko government in June 1998 even proposed to abolish Kaliningrad's customs-free import and export and reform the economic zones. Facing political opposition and legal problems, however, the government chose the less radical line of introducing import quotas and temporary rules for products from Kaliningrad to Russia. The financial collapse in August 1998 still more weakened the federal state and its ability to support the regions. Yet, the new government under Primakov tried to meet the problem by threatening to dismiss disobedient governors and put more emphasis on central administrative measures.

All this hindered the success of the economic zone in Kaliningrad, exposed its internal economic problems and undermined its relations with the neighbors. The lack of federal investment meant that the old infrastructure was not modernized. The small region had little internal resources, and its exclave position made it extremely dependent on preferential import tariffs, unless the center subsidized the region in other ways. With regard to foreign trade and investment, the region itself offered only a small and poor market, and its attractiveness largely depended on free access to the rest of Russia. The economic legislation was also especially unstable in Kaliningrad. All this in fact led to more economic problems, corruption and crime in Kaliningrad in comparison with many Russian regions and particularly the neighboring countries. It also scared away Western investors, who instead preferred Poland and the Baltic states, which offered better conditions. The internal problems seemed to isolate Kaliningrad from the enlarging European Union rather than to integrate it.

Like in the rest of Russia, these economic problems already about 1993 undermined support for the free economic zone and market economy in Kaliningrad. The increased Western presence in Kaliningrad also contributed to a nationalist reaction. However, the crisis continued and considerably worsened in August 1998, and Moscow did not fulfill its promises of support at the same time as it restricted Kaliningrad's special privileges. This made the public opinion disappointed and supportive of more autonomy so that the region could tend to its own interests and develop its ties with the neighboring states, which could and did give help.

Governor Gorbenko reacted to this by supporting the special economic zone concept, promoting privatization of land and demanding more transfers and decision-making power from the center. Like several other governors in Russia, he used the economic collapse in August 1998 to support his claim for more federal support and to increase his own economic control in the region, and also tried to improve ties with other states.

At the same time, Gorbenko had to be cautious, because if he went too far, his superiors in Moscow could dismiss him. He always defended Russian integrity and posed as a Russian patriot. He not only accepted federal laws undermining free trade by quotas, which served the state interest in customs revenues, but even promoted them in the alleged interest on protecting local producers. This, however, was unpopular among the local consumers and import firms, because it led to price rises and harmed business. A serious conflict developed with the regional Duma, which opposed the quotas and criticized him for corruption and anti-democratic leadership. Gorbenko's protectionist approach to autonomy in Kaliningrad, which reminds of Primakov's initial approach to meet the crisis on the federal level, thus stands against those who want free import even at the expense of federal interests. Considering the economic development, Gorbenko was not likely to be reelected in the gubernatorial elections in 2000.

Kaliningrad's position as an exclave thus forced Russia to grant it special privileges with regard to import, export and investment; otherwise the region had to be supported by subsidies and investments from the center. However, Russia's economic crisis made the latter impossible and moved the government to increase its income by imposing new customs rules on Kaliningrad. Russia's economic weakness and its inability to offer carrots instead of sticks thus tended to promote the tendencies toward real autonomy in Kaliningrad.

This also promoted the development of a special identity in the region, belonging to Russia but still special. A majority of the inhabitants are born in the region and have lived there all their lives. They see themselves as not only Russian but also as European and Central European with both old and new ties to Germany, Poland, and Lithuania. The development in the 1990s taught them that their interests are not identical with those of other Russians.

If the federal center would not allow Kaliningrad—formally or only *de facto*—to tend to its own interests, and take harsh measures against the region, the risk of separatism in the form of growing support for a separate Russian state on the Baltic would grow. The surrounding states are unlikely to support that; on the other hand they are not willing to take over the region either.

Still, all things considered, Kaliningrad seems to have a better position than many other impoverished Russian regions, since Western Europe would not like this region to become a threat to security in the Baltic region and is capable of helping it, if the internal conditions are favorable.

NOTES

1. In a poll, this idea was supported by eight percent, the autonomous republic by 18 percent in 1993 (Dörrenbächer, 1994, p. 45 f).

2. Gaidar spoke out against free-trade areas in general and saw sense in them only in Kaliningrad (KP, March 9–15, 1998 [ballad]).

3. The shares of Kaliningrad's foreign trade in 1997 were: Germany 20.6 percent, Poland 19 percent, Lithuania 10.5 percent (Samson & Lamande, 1998, pp. 3, 9).

4. A Moscow paper reported this as a tender for the whole region (RG, September 15, 1998).

5. The other services and the border troops are thus not included. The number of some important weapons changed in 1993–1998 as follows: Main battle tanks: 750 to 1,000 (increase), attack helicopters: 48 to 42, fighters: 35 to 28, submarines: 15 to 2, frigates: 24 to 4, patrol and coastal combatants: 140 to about 30. The naval forces were shared with the Kronshtadt base (*The Military Balance*, 1993–1994, 1998–1999, p. 111 ff; see also Moshes, 1998, pp. 13–14).

6. In three years, imports from Lithuania grew by 39 times (due to earlier blockade), Great Britain by 43 times (*Izvestiia*, April 7, 1998).

7. See Vardomskii (1995, p. 20 ff); NG (July 29, 1998); Samson and Lamande (1998, p. 2)

8. "Poland imposes restrictions," *RFE*/RL, 9 January 1998 (www.ballad.org/features/Action.la . . . news); "Polish visa for Kaliningraders," KP, 27 April–3 May 1998 (www.ballad.org/guests/pravda/week18).

9. See Aleksandr Ostakhov, "Komu nuzhen Zapad," NG, 31 July 1997, NG, 9 September 1997, 29 July 1998.

10. *Izvestiia*, April 7, 1998.

BIBLIOGRAPHY

Books, Chapters in Books, and Journal Articles

"Das Ende der Sonderwirtschaftszone?" *Königsberger Express*, 8 (1996): 3.

(Die) Zukunft des Gebiets Kaliningrad (Königsberg). Ergebnisse einer internationalen Studiengruppe. Sonderveröffentlichung, Köln: Bundesinstitut für ostwissenschaftliche und internationale Studien, 1993.

Dörrenbächer, Heike. *Die Sonderwirtschaftszone Jantar von Kaliningrad (Königsberg).* Arbeitspapiere zur internationalen Politik, 81 (1994). Bonn: Forschungsinstitut der Deutschen Gesellschaft für auswärtige Politik.

Fairlie, Lyndelle D. "Kaliningrad: Visions of the Future" in Joenniemi & Prawitz, 1998.

Fedorov, Gennadii M. & Zverev, Yurii M. *Kaliningradskie alternativy.* Kaliningrad: Kaliningradskii gosudarstvennyi universitet, 1995.

Gromov, Felix N. "Znachenie Kaliningradskogo osobogo raiona dlia oboronosposobnosti Rossiiskoi Federatsii." *Voennaia mysl*, 4 (1995): 9–13.
Grönick, Ritva et al. (eds.). *Vilnius/Kaliningrad: Ideas on Cooperative Security in the Baltic Sea Region*. Helsinki: Nordic Forum for Security, 1995.
Joenniemi, Pertti & Prawitz, Jan. *Kaliningrad: The European Amber Region*. Hampshire: Ashgate, 1998.
Krickus, Richard J. "The Plight of Kaliningrad: A Russian and International Problem." RRR, 21 January 1999.
The Military Balance 1993–1994, 1998–1999. London: International Institute of Strategic Studies (IISS) 1993, 1998.
Mitrofanov, Aleksei V. *Shagi novoi geopolitiki*. Moskva: Russkii Vestnik, 1997.
Moshes, Arkady. "Turn of the Century: Russia Looks at the Baltic Sea Region." Working Papers 12. Helsinki: Finnish Institute of International Affairs, 1998.
Müller-Hermann, Ernst (ed.). *Königsberg/Kaliningrad unter europäischen Perspektiven*. Bremen: Verlag H. M. Hauschild, 1995.
Oldberg, Ingmar. "Kaliningrad: Problems and prospects," in Joenniemi & Prawitz, 1998, 1–31.
Petersen, Phillip A. & Shane C. *The Security Implications of and Alternative Futures for the Kaliningrad Region*. Virginia: Potomac Foundation, 1992.
Rapport från CFF & FOA studieresa till Kaliningrad 5–8 April 1994. Stockholm: Centralförbundet Folk och försvar, 1994.
Samson, Ivan & Lamande, Vincent. "The European Union and the future of Kaliningrad," paper for the conference "Kaliningrad and European Integration." Kaliningrad, 8–9 September 1998.
Shumeiko, Vladimir. "Kaliningrad Region: A Russian Outpost." *International Affairs* 6 (1995): 3–7.
Swerew, Jurij M. *Russlands Gebiet Kaliningrad im neuen geopolitischen Koordinatenfeld*. Köln: Berichte des Bundesinstituts für ostwissenschaftliche und internationale Studien (BiOst) 6 (1996).
Tracevkis, Rokas M. "Kaliningrad Charms Vilnius." *Baltic Times*, 5–11 November 1998.
Vardomskii, Leonid, Vorobeva, Liudmila and Ershov, Aleksandr. *"Kaliningradskaja oblast Rossiiskoi* Federatsii: Problemy i perspektivy," in Kaliningradskaia oblast—Segodnia, zavtra, Moskva: Nauchnye doklady Moskovskogo tsentra Karnegi, 1995.
Wellmann, Christian. "Kaliningrad's Military Economy," in Joenniemi & Prawitz, 1998, 73–95.
Yemelyanenko, Vladimir. "Kaliningrad at an Impasse," *Moscow News*, no. 37, 24–30 September 1998.

Newspapers and Journals (Abbreviations)

Baltic Times (BT) (Riga).
Dagens Nyheter (DN) (Stockholm).
Izvestiia (Moscow).
Kaliningradskaia Pravda (KP).
Königsberger Express (KE).
International Affairs (IA) (Moscow).

Nezavisimaia Gazeta (NG) Moscow.
Nezavisimaia Gazeta-Regiony (NG-Regiony).
Rossiiskaia Gazeta (RG) (Moscow).
Segodnia (Moscow).
Svenska Dagbladet (SvD) (Stockholm).
Voennaia Mysl (Moscow).

News Bulletins and Internet Databases (Abbreviations)

Chronology of Events, Nupi Centre for Russian Studies, Norwegian Institute of International Affairs (at www.nupi.no/cgi-win/Russland/krono.exe), April, 12 Sept, 27 Nov, 18 Dec 1997, 12 March, 20, 27, 30 July, 8, 17 Sept, 3 Dec 1998, 19, 21 January 1999 (here called Chronology (nupi)).
Kaliningradskaia pravda, 31 January 1998 (at www.kp.su/koenig.su/maint) (here called KP (koenig)).
News, 9,12 Jan, 23 Febr (at www.ballad.org/features/Action.la . . . news%) (here called News ballad).
RFE/RL Newsline, Central & Eastern Europe, 18 Sept. 1998 (at www.rferl.org/newsline).
Russian Regional Report, Internet edition, EastWest Institute, New York (by e-mail subscription October 1998–February 1999) (here called RRR).
Summary of World Broadcasts, BBC Monitoring Service, SU/3327 B/15, SU/3328 B/19, 9, 10 September 1998 (here called SWB BBC).
Weekly news, *Kaliningradskaia pravda*, 8–14 Dec. 1997–23–29 Nov. 1998 (at www.ballad.org/guests/pravda/former) (here called Weekly news (ballad)).

CHAPTER 7

FEDERAL REFORM AND INTRAPERIPHERAL CONFLICT: THE CASE OF NENETS AUTONOMOUS OKRUG

Helge Blakkisrud

In the preceding chapters the process of restructuring Russia as a federation has been discussed within a center-periphery framework. The federalization of Russia has been portrayed as a process of delineating powers between the center and the periphery—an ad hoc process in search for some kind of equilibrium. This on-going process is not, however, limited to a redistribution of power between federal and regional levels; it also involves redefining the interrelationship between the *subekty*.

During the rigid centralism of the Soviet period horizontal relations between the regions were discouraged. In post-Soviet Russia the formerly irrelevant administrative borders suddenly became meaningful. This new situation brought about an abundance of intra-peripheral disputes; in the case of Ingushetia and North Ossetia the border question even led to armed conflict. One of the most intriguing problems that have arisen at the regional level concerns the status of a category of administrative units: the autonomous *okrugs*.

The autonomous *okrugs* represent a structural peculiarity inherited from the Soviet ethnofederal administrative design. The autonomous *okrugs* (or national *okrugs* as they were known until 1977) were established to provide territorial autonomy to the numerically small indigenous peoples of the Far North in the late 1920s and 1930s.[1] Like the republics these entities were ethnically defined, but while the autonomous republics were at the top of the administrative pyramid of the RSFSR, autonomous *okrugs* were placed at the bottom, being subordinated to *krai* or *oblasts*. Anyhow, as Soviet asymmetric ethnofederalism was covering up a reality of extreme centralism, the *okrugs* for a long time remained largely irrelevant as framework for interest aggregation and articulation.

A change set in with the onset of Gorbachev's reforms in the second half of the 1980s. Glasnost and perestroika unleashed a drive for enhanced sovereignty spearheaded by the Baltic republics, a process that grew into a tidal wave of demands for devolution of power and responsibilities dubbed the "Parade of Sovereignties." Eyeing a possibility for a more meaningful autonomy, until then slumbering *okrugs* jumped on the bandwagon, demanding to become autonomous republics or even union republics. As the Soviet Union passed into history and the new Russian leaders were to redesign center-periphery relations, they were forced to take these regional demands for autonomy into consideration. In spite of voices being raised in favor of rationalizing the federal structure through reducing the number of *subekty*, as well as streamlining it through the introduction of symmetric federalism (i.e., the introduction of *zemli* or *Länder*), the final outcome of the federal debate thus seemed guided by pragmatism.[2]

With the conclusion of a new Federal Treaty in March 1992, the federal leaders opted for a slightly modified version of the old Soviet structure, maintaining a distinction between ethnically and administrative-territorially defined units. As mentioned in Chapter 2, the *okrugs* signed a separate treaty.[3] This signified that the federal center recognized the *okrugs* as full *subekty*. What this implied for the *okrugs*' relationship with the *krais* or *oblasts*, however, remained unclear.

While the Federal Treaty in essence boiled down to an acceptance of status quo, the new Russian Constitution adopted in December 1993 has been interpreted as an attempt by the federal authorities to rein in some of the powers of the regions. With respect to the *okrugs*, the Constitution reiterated the Federal Treaty's recognition of them as full *subekty*. As pointed out in Chapter 2, Article 5.4 of the new Russian Constitution lays down that all *subekty* are equal (*ravnopravny*) as to their status vis-à-vis the federal center (*Konstitutsiia Rossiiskoi Federatsii*). Being recognized as equal to *krais* and *oblasts*, several autonomous *okrugs* demanded extensive autonomy or even full secession from the administrative-territorially defined units.

The *krais* and *oblasts* on the other hand could refer to Article 66.4 of the Constitution, which stipulates that the relations of autonomous *okrugs* forming part (*vkhodiashchie v sostav*) of a *krai* or *oblast* may be regulated by federal law and a treaty between the bodies of state power of the autonomous *okrug* and, respectively, the bodies of state power of the *krai* or *oblast* (*Konstitutsiia Rossiiskoi Federatsii*). This article implies that the *okrugs* are still administrative-territorially subordinate to the *krais* and *oblasts*. Consequently, according to the Constitution the *okrugs* turned out to be simultaneously equal and subordinate to the *krais* and *oblasts!*

Neither the Federal Treaty nor the Constitution did thus clarify the *okrugs*' position within the new federal structure. Instead, it was left to the *subekty* to fight out the battle for control over the *okrugs*. In several cases the federal authorities' reluctance to take a clear stance led to protracted conflicts between *okrug* and *oblast/krai* authorities. In this chapter we are going to look into one of these intraperipheral conflicts: the one between Nenets Atonomous *Okrug* and Arkhangelsk *Oblast.*

NENETS AUTONOMOUS OKRUG

Nenets Autonomous *Okrug* was one of the smallest autonomous entities within the former Soviet Union. With a population of a mere 55,000 scattered along the Arctic Coast of European Russia and an almost total dependence on the infrastructure of Arkhangelsk *Oblast*, which Nenets formed an administrative part of, one maybe should not expect a strong push for sovereignty or secession from the side of Nenets. Nevertheless, as the "Parade of Sovereignties" swept across the Soviet Union, demands for an upgrading of administrative status became increasingly frequent in the *okrug*. At the peak of the conflict, local leaders threatened to organize a referendum on the question of secession from Arkhangelsk. Before we turn to the specifics of the conflict and examine the motivation behind this mobilization, however, let us take a brief look at the history of the Nenets region.

Historical Background

The aboriginal population on the territory which today makes up Nenets Autonomous *Okrug* is the Nenets,[4] a North-Samoyedic group related to the Enets, the Nganasans and the Selkups (Khomich, 1966, p. 23). The Nenets, however, occupy a territory much larger than the present okrug. Historically they have inhabited an area that stretches from the eastern shores of the White Sea in the west to the Yenisei-delta in the east. The northern border is formed by the Arctic Ocean (although there have been Nenets settlements on the Kolguev and the Novaia Zemlia islands), while the southern border is less well defined.[5]

Up to the twentieth century, the Nenets lived in a subsistence economy based on nomadic hunting, fishing and reindeer herding. Taking into consideration the enormous distances and sparse population, the Nenets are surprisingly homogeneous in language and culture. Linguistically they are usually subdivided intoe two groups, the Tundra Nenets and the Forest Nenets, with the former making up more than 95 percent of the total population (Khomich, 1966, p. 20). Both groups have been organized in loose clan structures where pastures, rivers and hunting grounds were the collective property of the clan.

The current territory of Nenets Autonomous *Okrug* has traditionally belonged to the fringes of the Russian sphere of influence. The Russian expansion toward the north was headed by the Novgorodians. In Novgorodian chronicles it is told that the local population was paying taxes to Novgorod as early as at the end of the tenth century (Khomich, 1966, p. 42). After the fall of Novgorod in 1478, control over the European North was transferred to

Moscow. Although the supremacy of the Tsar over the inhospitable tundra east of the White Sea was contested neither by the local population,[6] nor by other states, the severe climate and the inaccessibility clearly limited Russia's ability to effectively rule the region.

The influx of Russian settlers in the pre-Soviet period was rather limited. Russian colonists had settled along the shores of the White Sea at an early stage, but it took a long time before they developed permanent settlements further east along the Pechora river.[7] Thus, in general Russian activity did not go beyond collecting fur tax (*yasak*) from the local population (Vitebsky, 1996, p. 94). The limited influence of Russian authorities is reflected in the fact that until the middle of the eighteenth century the Nenets were allowed to decide on the taxation level themselves (Eidlitz Kuoljok, 1993, p. 39).

Two important reforms in 1763 and 1822 were aimed at regulating and integrating the northern territories. The former reform meant an end to the earlier practice of self-imposed taxation. Thereafter the clan elders were to collect a fixed tax among the Nenets (Eidlitz Kuoljok, 1993, p. 41). The latter, so-called Speranskii reform[8] was an early attempt to protect the northern minorities. Among other things, it prohibited forced baptism of non-Russians. A special section, "*Ob inorodtsakh Arkhangelskoi gubernii, imenuemykh samoedami*" [On non-Russians in the Arkhangelsk Province called Samoyeds], dealt with the Nenets in European Russia, granting the Nenets internal self-government and the right to hold land. Most provisions set forth were, however, never enacted (Khomich, 1966, p. 46). The same year as the Speranskii reform was adopted, Russian missionaries launched a campaign to convert the Nenets. By 1830 almost all Nenets in the European North were baptized, while success was more limited beyond the Urals (Eidlitz Kuoljok, 1993, p. 41). Traditional shamanism, however, continued to play an important role alongside the official Christendom way into the twentieth century.

Soviet Nenets

Despite centuries of contact with Russian settlers, traditional ways of living prevailed among the Nenets until the October Revolution. Beginning from the 1920s, however, the northern territories gradually became drawn into the project of building a new Soviet state. In 1924, the People's Commissariat of Nationalities set up the Committee of the North,[9] which was to bear main responsibility for economic, administrative, legal and sanitary development among the northern peoples.

The Nenets in the European part of Russia took a more active part in the process of socialist construction than the other small nations of the Far North. As early as 1920, the year Soviet power was established in the Arkhangelsk region, a Nenets executive committee was formed in the Pechora district[10] (Eidlitz Kuoljok, 1985, p. 72). More importantly, an initiative taken by the 9th Nenets Soviet Congress in 1929 led the All-Russian Central Executive Committee (*VTsIK*) to establish a national *okrug* for the Nenets in European

Russia (p. 79). Nenets National *Okrug* set a precedent for the development of territorial autonomy among the small and less developed nations of the Russian Far North. On the basis of experiences drawn from Nenets National *Okrug*, eight additional national *okrugs* were established in the Far North the following year (Khomich, 1966, p. 235).

Originally, Nenets National *Okrug* formed a part of the Northern *Krai* (*Severnyi krai*), which included Arkhangelsk, Vologda, Niandoma and Severodvinsk *okrugs* and Komi Autonomous *Oblast* (*Vesti*, No. 1, 1994). In 1936 Komi was separated from the *krai*, and the following year the remaining territory was divided into two *oblasts*, Nenets becoming part of Arkhangelsk *Oblast*. For the rest of the Soviet period, Nenets National *Okrug* (from 1977 redefined as an autonomous *okrug*) remained a constituent part of Arkhangelsk *Oblast*.

In the economic sphere the onset of Soviet power brought an end to the tradition of Russian non-interference in the nomadic mode of production. Socialist construction meant the abolition of private property and forced collectivization of the reindeer herds. In many places the attempt to confiscate reindeer was met with bitter resistance, and herders killed off their animals rather than allow them to fall into the hands of the state (Vitebsky, 1996, p. 96).[11] However, the Nenets in European Russia seemed quicker to embrace the new socialist modes of production. By 1930 almost all of the Nenets in European Russia belonged to co-operatives (Khomich, 1966, p. 233). The process of collectivization of reindeer herds started in 1929. By the end of 1934 around 30 percent of the nomad households in Nenets were collectivized, compared to about 12 percent in neighboring Yamal (p. 238).

Although the herds were collectivized, nomadic life to a great extent remained more or less unchanged until the 1960s, when a campaign was launched to settle the Nenets and the other nomadic peoples of the North. A distinction was introduced between traditional nomadism (*bytovoe kochevanie*), which was branded as backward, and Soviet "production nomadism" (*proizvodstvennoe kochevanie*) (Vitebsky, 1996, p. 98). The latter encompassed only the male herders, whose movement with the herds was considered unavoidable, while women and children were to live a settled life in the villages. Concurrently, a system of exchange brigades, where the herders were to work on shifts on the tundra, was pioneered in the Nenets Autonomous *Okrug* (Eidlitz Kuoljok, 1985, p. 131). These developments finally eradicated the traditional life on the tundra.

In the cultural sphere, the legacy of the Soviet period is mixed. On the one hand Soviet minority policies encouraged a consolidation of Nenets identity. According to Lenin all ethnic groups were to go through three stages of development dubbed as "flourishing," "rapprochement" and "merger." Up to the revolution almost all members of the northern minorities were illiterate. The emphasis on the "flourishing" of the northern cultures led to the development of literary standards and an educational system (Eidlitz Kuoljok, 1985, p. 59) with the long-term goal of developing a new native socialist intelligentsia. The Soviet policy on minority languages in the 1920s and early 1930s undoubtedly contributed to the strengthening of some languages that otherwise undoubtedly would have disappeared. In addition, the establishment of Nenets National *Okrug* contributed to consolidating Nenets identity, although the fact that the Siberian Nenets were given two separate *okrugs* hampered the consolidation across administrative borders (Yamal-Nenets National *Okrug* was subordinated to Tiumen *Oblast* and Dolgan-Nenets National *Okrug* to Krasnoyarsk *Krai*).

On the other hand, Soviet policies also led to the eradication of the traditional cultural and political elite of the Nenets. With the swing away from the relative political liberalism of the early 1920s the key figures of the indigenous populations, the shamans and wealthy reindeer owners, were branded as enemies of the people and kulaks, persecuted, and killed.

There was also a shift in language policy. Gradually, the partly native-language education of the 1920s and 1930s was replaced by a strong tendency toward russification, with children being punished for speaking native languages at their boarding schools (Vitebsky, 1996, p. 97). The number of schools where Nenets was used as the language of instruction fell from 24 to two in the 1960s (Kaniukova, 1995). As a result, the proportion of Nenets speakers among the Nenets in Nenets Autonomous *Okrug* dropped from 64.0 percent to 44.8 percent during the last 30 years of Soviet rule (*Itogi vsesoiuznoi perepisi naseleniia 1959 goda. RSFSR; Natsionalnyi sostav naseleniia SSSR*).

The Soviet period was also marked by a huge influx of migrants into Nenets Autonomous *Okrug*. Integrating the Far North in Soviet society meant a demand for new skills. Various kinds of specialists and skilled laborers had to be sent to the Far North to conduct the industrialization and modernization programs. This development came to seriously shift the balance of population in the region. As a result of the immigrants' higher level of education and their specializations, they came to dominate the *okrug* politically, administratively, and economically. The Nenets, as well as the native, animal-based economy, were correspondingly marginalized.

Nenets and the Making of Russian Federalism

It took some time before the effects of *perestroika* reached the northern fringes of the Soviet Empire. In the late 1980s, however, the new political climate paved the way for a mobilization of the indigenous population and until then unprecedented level of criticism of Soviet policy on the development of the Far North. The official picture of the flourishing of the northern minorities was challenged and contrasted with the harsh reality of what was described as a severe economic, ecological and demographic crisis.

The industrialization and large-scale extraction of raw materials in the Far North had grave effects on the North's vulnerable environment. In Nenets

Autonomous *Okrug* the radiation of nuclear tests conducted on the nearby islands of Novaia Zemlia caused additional concern. This pollution, as well as that from the oil, gas, and other industries, threatened the very backbone of the indigenous economy: reindeer breeding, hunting, and fishing. As mentioned, the concept of flourishing of indigenous cultures was also covering up a reality of gradual russification. In general, the northern minorities experienced declining birth rates combined with high mortality and a life expectancy much lower than the Russian average (Vitebsky, 1996, p. 99).

Despite the grave situation depicted, the initial phase of native mobilization under *perestroika* was characterized by optimism. An Association of Peoples of the North was founded in Moscow in March 1990 with much publicity. The center's new concern for the problems of the Far North was illustrated by the fact that President Gorbachev and Prime Minister Ryzhkov both attended the inaugural meeting of the association. A long list of demands and objectives was produced, including demands for local control over the use of natural resources and the right to veto large-scale raw material extraction (Jensen & Magnusson, 1995, p. 166).

The new focus on the situation in the Far North coincided in time with the Baltic drive for sovereignty. This latter development gradually grew into a tidal wave of secessionism that swept across the Soviet Union in the late 1980s. Inspired by these developments regional leaders of the northern *okrugs* demanded an upgrading of the status of their units to that of autonomous republics. Chukchi Autonomous *Okrug* spearheaded this development by unilaterally declaring itself an autonomous republic in September 1990. Several other *okrugs* followed suit.

Nenets Autonomous *Okrug* was no exception to the rule. At the end of September 1990 the *Okrug Soviet* declared Nenets territory and its natural resources the property of the local population (*Nariana vynder*, September 29, 1990). On November 12, 1990, following the path of the other *okrugs*, the Nenets *Okrug Soviet* in an extraordinary session declared the *okrug* to be an autonomous republic within the RSFSR. The declaration, however, included a self-imposed moratorium. If the Congress of People's Deputies of the RSFSR would grant the *okrug* status of a *subekt*, the *okrug* would withdraw the demand for republican status (*Pravda severa*, November 15, 1990; *Nariana vynder*, November 15, 1990). The chairman of the *Okrug Soviet*, Leonid Sablin, explained the decision not in terms of secessionism, but in terms of establishing "normal business-like relations" (*Nariana vynder*, October 21, 1990), but the step was not well received in Arkhangelsk.

Gradually it became clear that the position of the center was that Nenets was to be treated as a *subekt* on par with Arkhangelsk. In late October 1991 President Yeltsin appointed Aleksandr Vyucheiskii as presidential representative to the *okrug* (*Nariana vynder*, November 2, 1991), and about a month later Yurii Komarovskii was named governor (*Nariana vynder*, December 10, 1991). Formal approval of the *okrug's* status as *subekt* came with the conclusion of the new Federal Treaty in March 1992. Nenets signed as an independent *subekt*, thus confirming its status as a constituent member of the Russian Federation.

The Federal Treaty contributed to clarifying the *okrug's* position vis-à-vis the federal center, but did not resolve the outstanding questions of Nenets's relationship with Arkhangelsk. In order to resolve this question the *okrug* authorities began drafting a law "On Nenets Autonomous *Okrug*." The draft ascertained that the *okrug* was still a part of Arkhangelsk *Oblast*, but included the right to secede "in a manner foreseen in the legislation of the Russian Federation" (*Zakon Rossiiskoi Federatsii "O Nenetskom avtonomnom okruge*," Chapter 2, Article 9). Pending the adoption of a new constitution, however, no such legislation existed at the moment.

The long-awaited new Russian Constitution was adopted in December 1993. As already mentioned, the Constitution did not clarify the question of distribution of power between the *okrugs*, the *subekty* they traditionally were subordinate to, and the federal center. Depending on which article of the Constitution one chose to use as a point of departure for interpreting the relationship between Nenets and Arkhangelsk, Nenets now seemed to be both equal and subordinate to Arkhangelsk *Oblast*. Not surprisingly, this ambiguity did nothing to reduce the friction between Nenets and Arkhangelsk.

In February 1994 the relationship between the two *subekty* reached its nadir. The previous year, the *okrug* administration had drafted a presidential decree "On Measures for State Support for Socio-Economical Development of Nenets Autonomous *Okrug*" (*Vesti*, No. 1, 1994). *The oblast* authorities in Arkhangelsk, however, kept blocking its adoption, protesting among other things against the opening of a branch of the Russian Central Bank in the *okrug* capital Narian Mar.

In response to this protraction, Governor Komarovskii threatened to turn to the people to strengthen the *okrug's* claim for independence through a popular mandate. On February 15, he issued a decree on holding a referendum on whether or not the *okrug* should form a direct part of the Russian Federation (*Vesti*, No. 1, 1994),[12] in other words, whether or not the *okrug* should continue to be geographically subordinated to Arkhangelsk.[13] The governor of Arkhangelsk, Pavel Balakshin, protested vehemently. As the *okrug* according to his view was situated on the territory of the *oblast*, the whole *oblast* should participate in a potential referendum. If, on the other hand, the referendum was to be held in the *okrug* on the basis of the *okrug* being the territory of a national minority, then, again according to Balakshin, only the minority should take part, and not the population as such (*Vesti*, No. 1, 1994).

Up till this point the federal center had been a more or less passive spectator to the brewing conflict. With Komarovskii pushing forward with a referendum that could have implications for the federal structure as a whole, federal authorities intervened. On March 11, President Yeltsin suspended Komorovskii's decree on the referendum as unconstitutional, violating Article 66 of the Russian Constitution (*Pravda severa*, March 12, 1994). At this point, however, the crisis had already peaked in Narian Mar. In an effort to prevent the referendum from being held, the administration in Arkhangelsk offered to sign a bilateral treaty with the *okrug*.[14] Referring to a preliminary agreement and the negotiations on a bilateral agreement, Komarovskii called off the referendum March 10 (*Nariana vynder*, March 12, 1994).

The subsequent negotiations were characterized as difficult. Nevertheless, after two weeks Balakshin and Komarovskii were ready to sign a bilateral agreement on mutual relations between state organs in Arkhangelsk *Oblast* and Nenets Autonomous *Okrug* (*Nariana vynder*, March 31, 1994). The first article of the bilateral agreement states that Arkhangelsk and Nenets are equal (*ravnopravnye*) *subekty* of the Russian Federation, whereas the latter with respect to territorial division forms a part of the former (*Dogovor o vzaimootnosheniiakh*). In order to improve the contact with the *oblast* authorities Nenets Autonomous *Okrug* committed itself to elect a deputy to the *oblast* legislature, the *Oblast Sobranie*, as well as to open a representation in Arkhangelsk (Article 3). The agreement was valid for a period of two years, but would be automatically renewed unless one of the parties wanted revisions (Article 5.3).

With the bilateral agreement in place, the tension wound down. The conclusion of the agreement did not, however, prevent the issue from resurfacing. In September 1995 Nenets adopted its *okrug* charter, the basic law of the *okrug*, a right granted the *okrugs* by the Russian constitution. Article 1 of the charter solemnly declares that the *okrug* is a full *subekt* of the federation and possesses all state authority that falls outside the exclusive authority of the federation or is a subject of joint jurisdiction between the center and the *okrug* (*Ustav Nenetskogo avtonomnogo okruga*). Article 2 ascertains that a division of the *okrug* or the *okrug's* merger with another *subekt* can take place only with the consent of a majority of the electorate of the *okrug* (Article 5.3). Not until Article 13 is Arkhangelsk *Oblast* mentioned. This article states that Nenets and Arkhangelsk exercise their authority as *subekty* on equal footing. At the same time, according to the Russian Constitution, Nenets forms a part of Arkhangelsk *Oblast*. Federal laws as well as the agreement between the organs of state power in the *oblast* and the *okrug* regulate the mutual relationship between the two (*Ustav Nenetskogo avtonomnogo okruga*, Article 13).[15]

When it was time to review the bilateral agreement between Nenets and Arkhangelsk in 1996, it was clear that the rather declaratory agreement of 1994 ought to be rewritten. Both units had adopted their own charters since 1994, a fact that should be reflected in the agreement. More important, some of the key figures from the 1994 conflict, both in the *okrug* and in the *oblast*, had since then been ousted from power, paving way for a more flexible approach.[16] The new agreement, concluded in June 1996, reiterated the predecessor's emphasis on the two units being equal and separate while united on a constitutional basis. The issue of co-operation and consultations in questions of common interest is however, much more pronounced than before (*Dogovor ob otnosheniiakh*).

In real terms, the relationship is still a bumpy one, as illustrated by the *okrug's* record on election participation: In 1994, in accordance with the bilateral agreement, the *okrug* participated in the elections to the *Oblast Sobranie* (*Pravda severa*, March 22, 1994). Two years later, however, the *okrug*, in spite of Yeltsin's recommendations, insisted on organizing gubernatorial elections separate from those of Arkhangelsk *Oblast* (*Nariana vynder*, September 3, 1996).[17] Although demands for full sovereignty have been abandoned and business on a day-to-day basis seems to run fairly smoothly, the contradictory notion of being equal and at the same time subordinate is still there. This contradiction threatens to reawaken the conflict.

Why Sovereignty? The Ethnic Argument

Why did Nenets Autonomous *Okrug* seek to become a sovereign *subekt*? The first argument that comes to mind is the ethnic one. After all, the rationale behind establishing the *okrug* in 1929 was the fact that an ethnic minority inhabited the area. With the new focus on the situation of the northern minorities and the "Parade of Sovereignties" sweeping across the country, it seems plausible at first sight that the ethnic argument would be central. A closer examination, however, refutes this.

Although a certain mobilization took place among the Nenets in the late 1980s, several factors hampered the creation of an effective Nenets lobby. One major problem was the combination of numerical weakness and geographical dispersion. The Nenets are the largest of the so-called northern minorities,[18] which together with the Komi and the Yakuts are the original inhabitants of the northern part of European Russia and Siberia. Even so, in 1989, the Nenets did not count more than some 34,000 individuals.[19] Moreover, the Nenets live scattered over a huge territory. Due to administrative arrangements of the Soviet period, the Nenets comprise the titular nation in no less than three different autonomous *okrugs*: Nenets (18.8% of the ethnic Nenets), Yamal-Nenets (61.2%), and Dolgan-Nenets (7.2%) (*Natsionalnyi sostav naseleniia SSSR*, 1991, pp. 44–48). In addition, there are also Nenets living in northern Komi and in Khanty-Mansi Autonomous *Okrug*. As a result of the Nenets internalizing the Soviet administrative division, the attention of Nenets activists has been more oriented towards the *okrug* capitals than toward the larger area settled by Nenets. This has prevented an institutionalized cooperation between Nenets organizations in Nenets, Yamal-Nenets, and Dolgan-Nenets.[20]

In addition to the Nenets being few, scattered, and split by administrative borders, the *okrugs* have not fully served their purpose of securing a national base for protection and promotion of Nenets culture. Gradually the Nenets were marginalized within all three *okrugs*. In the case of the Nenets autonomous okrug, the Nenets made up almost 40 percent of the population at the moment the *okrug* was established. In spite of considerable growth in real numbers,[21] however, their relative share of the population declined radically due to immigration from other parts of the Union. Already by the mid-1930s the Nenets' share of the population had fallen below 30 percent, and in 1959 it was further down to 11 percent (*Itogi vsesoiuznoi perepisi naseleniia*, 1963, p. 312). Since then, the situation seems to have stabilized. In the 1989 census 11.9 percent of a total population of 54,000 people were ethnic Nenets (*Natsionalnyi sostav naseleniia SSSR*, 1991, p. 44), hardly a viable basis for successful ethnic mobilization.

Moreover, even this modest figure gives an inflated picture of the strength of the Nenets population element, as a considerable proportion of the Nenets is linguistically and culturally assimilated. Although it is difficult to establish the number of acculturated Nenets, census material from the last years of Soviet power shows that the tendency to linguistic reidentification was particularly pronounced in Nenets Autonomous *Okrug*, where only 44.8 percent of the Nenets in 1989 declared Nenets as their mother tongue.[22] Linguistic assimilation has primarily been towards Russian. Among the Nenets in Nenets Autonomous *Okrug* 35.8 percent listed Russian as their first language.[23] A number of Nenets also declared Komi as their mother tongue.

As a result of substantial out-migration from the *okrug* since the breakup of the Soviet Union, the Nenets have probably increased their relative share of the population vis-à-vis Russians. It is estimated that the population has fallen almost 10 percent since 1989 (Makfol & Petrov, 1997, p. 1032), and it seems likely that the majority of the emigrants are ethnic Russians. Still, migration on its present scale is not sufficient to upset the ethnic balance, not to say create a basis for ethnically based Nenets separatism.

However, an attempt to form a Nenets interest organization was undertaken. In December 1989 the Association of the Nenets people—Yasavei was founded in Narian Mar. According to the organization's charter, it aspires to represent all Nenets in the *okrug* (*Ustav assotsiatsii*), and indeed Yasavei has been able to somewhat monopolize the representation of the Nenets. In the *okrug* charter, Yasavei has been recognized as a consultative organ in questions concerning the social and economic development of the Nenets (*Ustav Nenetskogo avtonomnogo okruga*, Chapter 4, Article 16). Although a proposal to introduce a quota for representation of the Nenets in the *Okrug Sobranie* was rejected by the Central Election Commission as unconstitutional (*Pravda severa*, February 18, 1994), representatives of Yasavei are invited to the meetings of the *Sobranie*.[24]

At first sight, it thus seems as if the interests of the Nenets are well taken care of. A closer examination of Yasavei reveals, however, that this is not necessarily the case. First of all the organizational structure of Yasavei is weak. The regional network is based on individuals rather than local branches, and the central level has suffered from a lack of organizational-administrative experience among the leadership (Khanzerova, 1995).[25] Yasavei's attempt to monopolize contact with the *okrug* administration as well as international contacts and the apparent lack of concrete results have led to increasing disillusion with the organization among the ethnic Nenets.[26] Already by the time of the second congress in April 1991 much of the initial national euphoria was gone (Korepanova, 1991). Gradually Yasavei became more of a hostage of the *okrug* authorities than an independent pressure group for minority interests.[27]

With scarce resources at hand the *okrug* administration has limited itself to paying lip service to the revival of Nenets culture. In the conflict between Narian Mar and Arkhangelsk references to the situation of the Nenets have therefore sooner been a pretext for other aims than an issue in its own right. Even Governor Komarovskii admitted in the wake of the clashes over the referendum that the national question was not an issue in the conflict between the two *subekty* (*Pravda severa*, March 16, 1994).

The Economic Argument

What then has been at stake? The answer is oil. At present the *okrug* belongs to the large group of *subekty* dependent on state subventions. Since 1994, the *okrug* has fallen into the category of "especially needy" (*osobo nuzhdaiushchiisia*) regions.[28] Still, the prospect of becoming a "Kuwait of the North" has probably been a main incentive for the *okrug* authorities in their attempt to secede from Arkhangelsk.

The fact that the northern tundra contains rich oil and gas deposits has been known for decades. Even so, due to inaccessibility and harsh climatic conditions, as well as Soviet oil and gas industries' focus on large production fields (Moe, 1994, p. 138), these resources remained largely untapped at the end of the Soviet period. Gradually, however, oil companies expanded their activities northwards through the neighboring Komi Republic, and in the mid-1990s plans were made for large-scale extraction of oil and gas in the Timan-Pechora region.

This region, which is situated partly in the Komi Republic, partly in Nenets, is considered the third most important oil reservoir in the Russian Federation.[29] While the local Komineft has developed the Komi part of Timan-Pechora, the still largely unexploited Nenets part has attracted the interest of several Western oil companies.[30] Due to several delays in the adoption of the legislation on production sharing agreements at the federal level, the output is still relatively modest. After the State Duma adopted the relevant legislation in December 1998 (*RFE/RL Newsline*, December 10, 1998), however, production is expected to soar over the next few years.

During the Soviet period it was largely irrelevant to regional authorities whether the oil extracted was found on the territory of Komi, Nenets, or Arkhangelsk, as exploitation policy as well as revenues from the sale were taken care of at the union level. The dissolution of the Soviet production system, however, led to an increased role for regional decision-makers. According to the law "On Subsoil Resources," adopted in February 1992, only 40 percent of the royalties were to go into the federal budget. The remaining 60 percent were to be split equally between the local budget and the budget of the *subekt* (*Zakon o nedrakh*, Article 42).[31] Moreover, if the oil was produced within an *okrug* forming a part of an *oblast/krai*, half of the amount allotted to the federal budget should be passed on to the *oblast/krai* (Article 42).

The new legislation further aggravated the conflict between the local authorities in Nenets and the *oblast* administration in Arkhangelsk. The oil fields in Arkhangelsk *Oblast* are located within the borders of the *okrug*. While the *okrug's* previous demands for increased sovereignty had been inspired primarily by "the Parade of Sovereignties" and the abstract principle of national self-determination, suddenly there were tangible economic benefits connected with a secession from Arkhangelsk. The prospect of collecting 60 percent of future royalties from oil and gas extraction in the *okrug*,[32] as well as controlling revenues from other oil and gas related activities, became a weighty argument for secession. If Nenets was allowed to keep this money without having to share with the rest of the *oblast*, the size of the *okrug* budget was likely to increase several times and the *okrug* to grow from "especially needy" to affluent in a few years.

In Narian Mar the authorities chose therefore to see the oil and gas resources as belonging to the *okrug* alone. Obviously, the oblast authorities did not share this position. Nenets Governor Komarovskii complained that the *oblast* administration was "clinging to the old ways and still consider our *okrug* part of the *oblast*" (*RFE/RL*, March 2, 1994). The *oblast* authorities in Arkhangelsk indeed claimed that the oil revenues should come to the *oblast* as a whole. In an interview with *Pravda severa* (March 16, 1994) Governor Balakshin explained this position by the fact that the *oblast* had had to carry the financial burden of developing Nenets infrastructure. However, when it was time to reap the harvest, the *okrug* wanted to keep it all.

In spite of the opposition from the *oblast* authorities, the *okrug* gradually gained the upper hand in the struggle over the distribution of oil revenues.[33] According to the law "On Subsoil Resources," royalties can be paid in cash as well as oil (*Zakon o nedrakh*, Article 42), and the Nenets authorities claimed the right to export 10 percent of the crude oil produced in the *okrug* (*RFE/RL*, March 2, 1994). Regardless of continued protests, the *oblast* administration saw just a small share of the export quota, while the Nenets authorities retained most of it (Moe, 1994, p. 139).

The optimal solution for the *oblast* would of course have been that the *okrug* budget remained part of the *oblast* budget. When this turned out to be impossible (due to the steadfast opposition of the *okrug* authorities as well as to federal legislation), the fall-back position of the *oblast* was to secure at least a minimum of formal unity with the *okrug*. The bilateral agreement between Nenets and Arkhagelsk concluded in March 1994 can thus be interpreted as an attempt from the side of the *oblast* to prevent ties being completely severed. The agreement implied acknowledging that the *okrug* was budget-wise independent from the *oblast* in return for the *okrug's* acceptance of remaining a part (*vkhodit v sostav*) of the oblast. This way the *oblast* authorities ensured that they at least received 20 percent of the royalties from the oil extraction in Nenets (i.e., half the amount transferred to the federal budget).

The Nenets authorities had little to lose from formally remaining a part of the *oblast.* In general, they had received what they sought. Although exploitation of the hydrocarbon resources has to be done in compliance with federal legislation, the *okrug* authorities were now able to run this process without interference from the oblast. Moreover, although the *okrug* for the foreseeable future will remain heavily dependent on the *oblast's* infrastructure, the bilateral agreement secured access to these services. The *okrug* authorities thus seemed to have it both ways.

Nenets Sovereignty

As we have seen, ethnic arguments were—and still are—put forward in the debate on Nenets sovereignty. Such references to the indigenous population's right to autonomy were to be expected, as the rationale behind establishing the *okrug* was to secure the interest of the ethnic Nenets. At least until the *okrug* was recognized as a separate *subekt* through the Federal Treaty and the Constitution, the *okrug* authorities could hardly justify secessionist demands without at least paying lip service to the principle of ethnic autonomy.

In general, however, the policy of the *okrug* authorities can hardly be interpreted as guided by the interests of the indigenous population. An economy based on reindeer herding is extremely vulnerable, as it requires immense tracts of clean land and water. The issue of survival of Nenets culture is therefore closely tied up with ecological and environmental issues. The *okrug* authorities' emphasis on developing oil and gas resources is thus bound to cause conflict with the maintenance of the traditional economy among the ethnic Nenets.

From the point of view of the *okrug* authorities sovereignty in a Nenets context is clearly first and foremost envisioned as economic sovereignty. The question of secession largely boiled down to the issue of control over future oil revenues. In the end, the case of the Nenets Autonomous *Okrug* thus turns out to be a typical example of how local authorities exploit the titular nation's right to self-determination and control over natural resources as a pretext for securing their own economic interests.

The Role of Federal Authorities

As we have seen, federal authorities only got directly involved in the dispute between Nenets and Arkhangelsk when the actions of *okrug* authorities threatened to have implications for the federal structure at large. Neither in the case of Nenets, nor with respect to other *okrug*-related intraperipheral conflicts has the federal government actively intervened to back one of the conflicting parties. Thus, in practice the triangular relationship between the federal center, the *krais/oblasts* and the autonomous *okrugs* has been reduced to a bilateral intraperipheral affair.

The federal authorities' lack of will to intervene in intraperipheral disputes can be illustrated by the problems of adopting a federal law regulating the relations between autonomous *okrugs* and the *krais* and *oblasts* (cf. Article 66.4 of the Constitution). Another example is the Constitutional Court's repeated refusals to solve the disputes through the judiciary. Although Chukchi Autonomous *Okrug* succeeded in a de jure recognition of its secession from Magadan *Oblast* in May 1993, the Constitutional Court has declined to rule on similar cases after the adoption of the new constitution. In 1996, the Constitutional Court dismissed the case of Khanty-Mansi and Yamal-Nenets v. Tiumen *Oblast* (*Rossiiskaia gazeta*, July 24, 1996). When the three *subekty* turned to the Constitutional Court the following year for an interpretation of Article 66.4, the Court referred to the lack of relevant federal legislation and, pending the adoption of such laws, encouraged the *subekty* to work out a solution among themselves (*Rossiiskaia gazeta*, July 22, 1997).[34] The Court's ruling thus did not make the relationship between the three *subekty* any clearer than it had been previously.

The federal authorities' reluctance to take a definite stand has led to the emergence of a variety of structural arrangements: full secession from the *oblast* (Chukchi Autonomous *Okrug*), trilateral agreements (e.g., between Komi-Permyak Autonomous *Okrug*, Perm *Oblast* and the federal center) and bilateral agreements (e.g., between Nenets Autonomous *Okrug* and Arkhangelsk *Oblast*). In the case of the more affluent *okrugs*, Khanty-Mansi and Yamal-Nenets, there now seems to be an attempt at securing sovereignty from within after the okrugs in 1997 took control over the *oblast* legislature (*IEWS Rossiiskii regionalnyi biulleten*, June 11, 1999). With respect to most of the poorer *okrugs* on the other hand, neither the *okrugs* themselves nor the regions they are subordinate to have made claims on each other.

The development of Russian federalism—in a center-periphery as well as in intraperiphery context—has so far been somewhat erratic, characterized by ad hoc solutions rather than a grand design. As a result of the federal authorities' inclination to accept idiosyncratic solutions, the federal structure is gradually growing ever more complex. For the *okrugs* this implies that the stronger takes what he wants while the weaker accepts what he is offered.

NOTES

Earlier drafts of this chapter have been presented at the conference "Perspectives on the Development of Russia as a Federation," Oslo, January 23, 1998, and the ASN Convention, New York, April 15–17, 1999. I would like to thank Statoil for financial assistance in connection with fieldwork in Nenets and Arkhangelsk in 1996.

1. There were ten autonomous *okrugs* in the Soviet Union, all located within the RSFSR: Agin Buriat AO, Chukchi AO, Dolgan-Nenets AO, Evenk AO, Khanty-

Mansi AO, Komi-Permiak AO, Koriak AO, Nenets AO, Ust-Ordyn Buriat AO, and Yamal-Nenets AO. With the exception of the two Buriat populated *okrugs*, they are all situated in the Far North.

2. For a discussion of the various positions in the debate over the Russian federal structure, see for instance Sakwa (1993, pp. 126–131).

3. At the signing ceremony March 31, 1992, the regions were presented three texts: one for the ethnically defined republics, one for the administrative-territorially defined units (*krais*, *oblasts*, and federal cities), and one for the ethnically defined units with a lesser degree of autonomy (autonomous *okrugs* and the auonomous *oblast*). The three texts specified the rights associated with each category of *subekty*. For the full text of the three treaties, see for instance Strashun (1996, pp. 191–216).

4. In Nenets language "nenets" means "man" (Eidlitz Kuoljok, 1993, p. 21). In prerevolutionary Russian sources, the Nenets were usually referred to as the Samoyeds.

5. Liudmila Khomich draws a line along the rivers Peza, Sula, Usa, along the watershed between Pur and Agan and along the lower part of Taz to Yenisei between Igarka and Dudinka, although she admits that in certain regions groups of Nenets moved far south of this line (Khomich, 1966, p. 16).

6. In spite of sporadic uprisings—the best known from 1825 to 1839, led by Vavlë Nenianga (see Khomich, 1966, p. 47)—Russia's control over the European North was never challenged.

7. Until the Muscovite principality took possession of Novgorod's colonies there were no Russians residing permanently in the Pechora region (Eidlitz Kuoljok, 1993, p. 21).

8. Named after Mikhail Speranskii (1772–1839), Aleksandr I's reform minister.

9. The Committee of the North was dissolved in 1935, as it was considered that the work of socialist construction had progressed so far as to obviate the need for a special state organization (Eilitz Kuoljok, 1985, p. 54). In 1962, however, a permanent working group for the peoples of the north was established under the Council of Ministers of the RSFSR (p. 54).

10. The Nizhepechorsk Samoyed *Volost* Executive Committee was established in the village of Telviska in June 1920.

11. As late as in 1990 it was claimed that the total number of reindeer had still not returned to the pre-collectivization level (Vitebsky, 1996, p. 96).

12. The question was formulated as: Soglasny li Vy s tem, chtoby Nenetskii avtonomnyi okrug v sushestvuiushchikh granitsakh vkhodil v sostav Rossiiskoi Federatsii neposredstvenno? [Do you agree that Nenets Autonomous *Okrug* within its present borders should be a direct member of the Russian Federation?] (*Vesti*, No. 1, 1994).

13. At this point, Chukchi Autonomous *Okrug* had already succeeded in a de jure recognition of its secession.

14. A draft treaty had already been prepared by the Arkhangelsk administration. According to the Russian constitution, relations between an *oblast/krai* and an autonomous *okrug* situated within the territory of the former may be regulated by federal law and an agreement between bodies of state power of the *oblast/krai* and, respectively, bodies of state power of the autonomous *okrug* (*Konstitutsiia Rossiiskoi Federatsii*, Article 66.4).

15. This provision corresponds with the aforementioned Article 66.4 of the Russian constitution.

16. Governor Komarovskii lost a vote of confidence in December 1995 (*Nariana vynder*, January 12, 1996) and was relieved of his duties by President Yeltsin on 22 February 1996 (*Nariana vynder*, February 27, 1996), while Governor Balakshin was forced to resign due to accusations of economic malpractice in February 1996. They were replaced by Vladimir Khabarov and Anotolii Yefremov respectively. There were also new legislatures in the two units.

17. In the end, gubernatorial elections were held December 1 in Nenets and December 8, 1996, in Arkhangelsk.

18. The northern minorities comprise 26 different ethnic groups. Most of these groups are relatively marginal, numbering from a couple of hundreds to a few thousand members (*Natsionalnyi sostav naseleniia SSSR*, 1991, p. 10).

19. The total number of Nenets in the RSFSR rose from 18,800 in 1926 (Simon, 1991, p. 374) to 34,200 in 1989 (*Natsionalnyi sostav naseleniia SSSR*, 1991, p. 10).

20. Interview with Prokopii Yavtysh, member of the board of Yasavei, Narian Mar (October 3, 1996).

21. In 1959 there were 4,957 Nenets living in the *okrug*. By 1989, the number had risen to 6,423 (*Natsionalnyi sostav naseleniia SSSR*, 1991, p. 44). The total number of Nenets in the Soviet Union went up from 16,400 in 1926 to 35,000 in 1989 (Eidlitz Kuoljok, 1993, p. 21).

22. The corresponding figures for Yamal-Nenets and Dolgan-Nenets were 94.2 percent and 81.4 percent (*Natsionalnyi sostav naseleniia SSSR*, 1991, pp. 44–48).

23. In 1989 65.8 percent of the total population of Nenets Autonomous *Okrug* were ethnic Russians. More than 80 percent of the population, however, stated Russian as their mother tongue.

24. Interview with Prokopii Yavtysh, member of the board of Yasavei, Narian Mar (October 3, 1996).

25. For instance, the first president of Yasavei, A. Adreeva, was forced to resign on charges of lack of financial control (*Nariana vynder*, November 19, 1991).

26. Various interviews in Narian Mar, October 1996.

27. An indication of the low support for Yasavei is the 1995 parliamentary elections, where the association's candidate, Olga Terletskaia, received only 2.7 percent of the votes in the Nenets single-madate constituency (Makfol & Petrov, 1997, p. 1037).

28. In 1995 more than 30 per cent of the *okrug* budget was covered by federal transfers (Makfol & Petrov, 1997, p. 1034).

29. In the Nenets part of Timan-Pechora alone there is an estimated oil reserve of 3,290 million tons as well as 458.9 billion m^3 of natural gas (Jumppanen & Hyttinen, 1995, p. 73).

30. An international consortium, the Timan-Pechora Company, was created in April 1994. It includes the U.S. firms Texaco (24%), Exxon (24%), and Amoco (16%) and Norway's Norsk Hydro (16%). In 1995, the Russian firms Rosneft and Arkhangelskgeoldobycha joined it, receiving a 20 percent stake in the project. Also other Western oil companies, notably French Total and Finnish Neste, have been involved in Nenets.

31. The increased influence of the *subekty* on exploitation of natural resources was later written into the Russian Constitution. According to the Constitution, the joint

jurisdiction of the Russian Federation and the *subekty* includes issues of the possession, use and management of the land, mineral resources, water and other natural resources (*Konstitusiia Rossiiskoy Federatsii*, Article 72, Paragraph 1c).

32. The Nenets Autonomous *Okrug* has, as the only *subekt*, no geographical-administrative subdivision.

33. It should be mentioned here that the distribution of potential oil wealth also has led to internal conflicts in Nenets. Especially under Governor Komarovskii the oil question caused conflicts between the executive and legislative powers (Makfol & Petrov, 1997, p. 1035).

34. As in the case of Nenets, the dispute between Tiumen and Khanty-Mansi and Yamal-Nenets is of economic rather than political or ethnic character. Over two-thirds of Russia's oil fields are located in Khanty-Mansi, while Yamal-Nenets houses 90 percent of the country's gas resources. The indigenous element in the two *okrugs* is even weaker than in Nenets, as the Khants and Mansi make up only 1.4 percent of the total population in Khanty-Mansi and the Nenets 4.2 percent in Yamal-Nenets.

BIBLIOGRAPHY

Dogovor o vzaimootnosheniiakh mezhdu organami gosudarstvennoi vlasti Arkhangelskoi oblasti i Nenetskogo avtonomnogo okruga. *Nariana vynder*, March 31, 1994.

Dogovor ob otnosheniiakh mezhdu Arkhangelskoi oblastiu i Nenetskim avtonomnym okrugom. *Nariana vynder*, July 9, 1996.

Eidlitz Kuoljok, Kerstin. *The Revolution in the North. Soviet Ethnography and Nationality Policy*. Uppsala: Studia Multiethnica Upsaliensa, 1985.

Eidlitz Kuoljok, Kerstin. *Nordsamojediska folk*. Uppsala: Finsk-ugriska institutionen, Uppsala Universitet, 1993.

Itogi vsesoiuznoi perepisi naseleniia 1959 goda. RSFSR. Moscow: Gosstatizdat, 1963.

Jensen, Jens-Jørgen & Märta-Lisa Magnusson. *Rusland—samling eller sammenbrud?* Esbjerg: Sydjysk Universitetsforlag, 1995.

Jumppanen, Pauli & Helena Hyttinen. *Economic Geography and Structure of the Russian Part of the Barents Region*. Helsinki: Ministry of Trade and Industry, 1995.

Kaniukova, R. Istoriia i budushchee natsionalnoi shkoly. *Nariana vynder*, May 24, 1995.

Khanzerova, V. Davno li 'Yasaveiu' zabliuditsia? ili Ot sezda k sezdu. *Nariana vynder*, March 22, 1995.

Khomich, Liudmila Vasilevna. *Nentsy: Istoriko-etnograficheskie ocherki*. Moscow: Nauka, 1996.

Konstitutsiia Rossiiskoi Federatsii. Moscow: Yuredicheskaia literatura, 1993.

Korepanova, L. Chto v upriazhk Yasaveia? *Nariana vynder*, May 7, 1991.

Makfol, Maikl & Nikolai Petrov (eds.). *Politicheskii almanakh Rossii 1997*. Moscow: Moskovskii Tsentr Karnegi, 1997.

Moe, Arild. Oil and Gas: Future Role of Barents Region. In Stokke, Olav Schram & Ola Tunander (eds.), *The Barents Region: Cooperation in Arctic Europe*. London: Sage Publications Ltd., 1994.

Natsionalnyi sostav naseleniia SSSR. Moscow: Goskomstat SSSR, Finansy i Statistika, 1991.

Sakwa, Richard. *Russian Politics and Society*. London: Routledge, 1993.

Simon, Gerhard. *Nationalism and Policy Toward the Nationalities in the Soviet Union: From Totalitarian Dictatorship to Post-Stalinist Society*. Boulder: Westview Press, 1991.

Strashun, Boris A. *Federalnoe konstitutsionnoe pravo Rossii: Osnovnye istochniki*. Moscow: Norma, 1996.

Ustav assotsiatsii nenetskogo naroda 'Yasavei' Nenetskogo avtonomnogo okruga Rossiiskoi Federatsii. Naryan Mar.

Ustav Nenetskogo avtonomnogo okruga. Naryan Mar.

Chapter 8

Assessing Russian Federalism

Daniel R. Kempton

There are many forms of center-periphery relations; from among these Russia has explicitly chosen federalism. Russian federalism was partly a conscious choice to address the acute problems faced by Russia at independence and partly an inherited legacy from the Soviet era. Soviet federalism was a charade; its federal structure was merely a way of organizing the Soviet Union's territorially based units. Real power remained with the Soviet Communist Party, based in Moscow. Many assumed that Russian federalism would be similarly fraudulent, but Russia had reasons for taking its federalism seriously. Is contemporary Russia a federal state? Because federalism is a flexible form of government, which is tailored to meet the needs of each state, each federal state is somewhat unique in both structure and function. Nonetheless, as argued in Chapter 2, there are certain conditions that are to some degree necessary for the survival of federalism, and other conditions that are beneficial. However, because Russia is an asymmetrical federation, the only way to accurately assess the progress of Russian federalism is to examine specific center-periphery relationships, as was done in the preceding chapters. This chapter will generalize from these conclusions, and more limited evidence from other cases, to provide an overall assessment of Russian federalism.

THE NECESSARY CONDITIONS OF FEDERALISM

Consensual Participation

The preceding chapters confirm that Russian center-periphery relations have undergone three institutional stages. The first institutional stage lasted from March 1990, when Yeltsin ascended to the chairmanship of the Russian Supreme Soviet, until December 1991 and the collapse of the Soviet Union. During this stage the conflict at the center between Yeltsin's Russian government and Gorbachev's Soviet government was sufficiently intense that all but the most radical unilateral declarations by the *subekty* went unchallenged by Moscow. In 1990 Komi declared its sovereignty from the Soviet Union and subsequently declared ownership of all its mineral resources. Also in 1990, with the blessing of both Yeltsin and Gorbachev, Kaliningrad became one of Russia's six Free Economic Zones. In June 1991 Kaliningrad was granted customs and taxation exemptions. Sakha unilaterally raised its status to that of a republic within Russia and claimed ownership of its vast natural resources. In July 1991 Ingushetia, which had broken away from Chechnya, also declared itself a republic. While some in Tatarstan sought independence, the government limited itself to declarations of sovereignty and increased political and economic autonomy.

Chechnya's November 1991 unilateral declaration of independence was seemingly the only challenge from the *subekty* rejected by Moscow. Even this did not meet with immediate response. The Chechen case suggests that Moscow's acceptance of *subekt* demands resulted more from an inability to respond than from real concurrence with the demands themselves. When Yeltsin was able to challenge Chechnya, he did so. Similarly, he later sought to reclaim powers from other *subekty*. While Stage 1 may have seemed to be a panacea for the *subekty*, because they were allowed to unilaterally claim powers, it had a serious drawback in that they often were not able to exercise the powers they claimed.

Stage 2, which began with the collapse of the Soviet Union in December 1991 and ended with the promulgation of a new Constitution, was more consensual in that the powers of the *subekty* were largely defined by negotiations. These negotiations took two forms. First, a number of *subekty* negotiated bilateral agreements, which gave them special powers and rights. Sakha, Tatarstan, and Ingushetia gained major tax relief including the ability to keep federal taxes within their respective republics. Komi and Sakha gained a greater share of the profits from their mineral resources. For Sakha this mostly entailed the clarification and implementation of previous promises. Sakha was promised new funds to help with its shortened transportation season. In Kaliningrad locally produced goods were exempted from export tariffs. Imported products were exempted from customs and turnover tax for 10 years unless they were sent forward to mainland Russia.

In these bilateral agreements, the republics generally fared better than the other *subekty*, which created asymmetries and resentment. To a large degree, however, the substantive chapters suggest that the gains of the individual *subekty* were also a function of the effectiveness of the individual *subekt* leaders and the strategies they pursued. More specifically, those leaders that were willing to trade their political support for Yeltsin for concessions to their own republic or oblast did quite well. This strategy was used successfully by Nikolayev in Sakha, Gorbenko in Kaliningrad, and Shaimiev in Tatarstan. This leads to the conclusion that leadership plays an unexpectedly important role in Russian center-periphery relations.

Collectively the *subekty* also developed a shared interest in collectively protecting the concessions they won from the center. This led to a second set of negotiations, which were multilateral and non-zero sum. Ultimately these collective negotiations resulted in the signing of the Federal Treaty in March 1993. Thereafter, whether the Federal Treaty would be incorporated into the new Constitution became a critical issue in center-periphery relations. Ultimately Yeltsin did not include the text of the Federal Treaty in his draft Constitution, but the Constitution explicitly recognized the treaty and accepted its terms when they did not contradict the Constitution itself.

Although Yeltsin took the sentiments of the *subekty* into account when finalizing the new Constitution, the volition of the *subekty* was constrained. In the end each *subekt* leader was given the limited choice of supporting or opposing the new Constitution. While the bilateral agreements and the Federal Treaty were negotiated through consensual processes, the Constitution was not. Yeltsin's advisors wrote it with no direct input from the *subekty*.

Could a Constitution imposed without consensus create a more consensual political system? Ironically, the answer appears to be yes. In the third institutional stage, the Constitution explicitly protected bilateral agreements and allowed for the consensual transfer of powers between the center and individual *subekty*. Thus, by 2000 most of the *subekty* had signed such agreements.

To say that the Russian system has become more consensual is not to imply that the *subekty* are more powerful or autonomous than in previous stages. In fact many *subekty* have lost significant powers since 1993 (see below). These losses were not entirely consensual. Sakha, Komi, and Kaliningrad have all resisted with only partial success. At the same time the *subekty*, both individually and collectively, have successfully resisted some unwanted changes. Gorbenko resisted Moscow's attempts to strip Kaliningrad of its tax-free status. Collectively, the *subekty* have resisted the attempts to re-divide Russia into fewer, more symmetrical units (see below.) They have also successfully resisted the federal government's efforts to develop legislation that would limit the breadth of bilateral agreements.

Written Constitution

As argued in Chapter 2, a federal system must have a relatively rigid contract, which specifies the rights and powers of the component governments. In the vast majority of cases this takes the form of a written Constitution. Clearly Russia did not have a valid constitution prior to December 1993. Both the 1977 Soviet Constitution and the 1978 Russian Constitution were largely irrelevant to Russian center-periphery relations.

The 1993 Constitution was the first to provide an explicit and meaningful discussion of Russian center-periphery relations. But does it provide a clear and binding division of powers between the federal government and the *subekty*? Many have claimed the Constitution is neither clear nor binding. The Constitution is frequently criticized for its ambiguity. Despite its extensive length, the Constitution does not fully spell out the role of each level of Russian government. Moreover, it creates an entire category of powers known as shared powers without spelling out the meaning of shared powers. Finally, it allows for powers to be transferred between levels. While this ambiguity can be frustrating for both political analysts and Russian politicians, it may serve to make the system more flexible and adaptive.[1] Those *subekty* that are capable of exercising greater autonomy and are more desirous of autonomy can be given more powers than those that are less desirous of autonomy or less well prepared to exercise it. Similarly, this ambiguity allows the federal government to distribute more or less autonomy to the *subekty* depending on the rapidly changing Russian economy.

A second criticism is that the Constitution is too frequently violated. According to Anatoly Chubais, then Presidential Chief of Staff, in 1996 the laws of about one-third of all the *subekty* violated the federal Constitution, including those of all but two of the republics.[2] In October the Central Electoral Commission found that the electoral laws of about 25 *subekty* violated the Constitution or the accompanying federal electoral law by illegally including residence and language requirements in their electoral laws[3] (Sakha is among these). Among the more serious charges, a Yabloko supporter in the Duma claimed that many of the *subekty* were run by "authoritarian regimes that violate human rights and the principle of separation of powers."[4]

Many Duma deputies argue that the center should have the power to punish *subekty* that pass legislation, charters, or constitutions that violate the Russian Constitution or federal legislation. After being reelected, Yeltsin signed a decree barring regional authorities from introducing taxes that were not specifically authorized by federal legislation.[5] However, he did not invalidate the many *subekt* taxes that already existed without federal authorization. He left the more vigorous attack to Chubais. In late October Chubais helped organize a conference on upgrading the federal government's oversight functions with regard to the observance of the federal Constitution and federal law.[6] The conference discussed various ways of rebuking *subekty* that had violated federal law. While Yeltsin took the soft approach, a commitment to meet with *subekty* leaders to discuss specific violations, Chubais advocated a harder line. He proposed the formation of a special body to monitor legislative activities in the *subekty*. According to a press analysis Chubais knew that "It is no secret that for a long time federation components have frankly not given a damn about the Russian Constitution and federal legislation," but he was afraid to take action. "All actions against federation components were thought to threaten the disintegration of Russia."[7] Nonetheless, the press report expressed doubt about who Yeltsin would back if Chubais took tangible steps to rein in the *subekty.*

In January 1997, Sergei Mitrokhin, a Duma Deputy from the Yabloko faction urged presidential action. He argued the president should be given:

> the authority to suspend or terminate regional laws that contradict federal legislation (in accordance with the court decisions), as well as the right to dissolve regional assemblies that pass such laws and to sack regional executives who disregard court rulings.[8]

Rephrasing Yeltsin's by then infamous quote, he called on the center to stop the *subekty* from taking as much sovereignty as they could swallow.

Three months later, Yeltsin went on the offensive again when he told *subekty* leaders in a national radio address, "Listen to my warning. You have to abide by the law whether you like it or not. I have the will power to make the whole country comply with the Russian Constitution."[9] He also attacked the *subekty* for widespread corruption. Alexksei Kudrin (Deputy Head of the Presidential Administration) subsequently explained that the administration was taking steps to tighten control over the *subekty.*[10] He warned that the president still had the power to remove *subekt* heads. Before 1996 no one questioned the president's power to remove the regional executives that he had appointed. Whether he ever possessed this power over the independently elected heads of the regions, or republic heads, was more questionable. By the end of 1997, the executive heads of all *subekty* were elected. Yeltsin had previously dismissed the governors of the Amur, Bryansk, and Vologda *oblasti.* Shortly thereafter, Yeltsin warned that no *subekt* leaders were immune to his anti-corruption drive. Corruption, he argued, was threatening the very existence of the state.[11] Mikhail Krasnov, Presidential Legal Advisor, contended Article 80 gave the president the power to remove *subekt* leaders when their laws or decrees contradicted federal law or the Constitution.

On April 25, 1997 the Duma passed a law declaring the Russian Constitution and federal legislation to be supreme[12] and empowering the federal government to force conformity of the laws and constitutions (or charters) of the *subekty* to federal standards. More significantly, if enacted the law would have invalidated the existing bilateral power-sharing treaties until such time as the Duma passed a separate law enacting each of the existing treaties,[13] and it would have circumscribed the breadth of all future agreements. The Federation Council, which wanted to preserve the powers of the *subekty*, rejected the law. Similarly Yeltsin, who wanted to force conformity to federal law without destroying his alliance with the *subekty*, also opposed it. Thus, as of 2000, the bilateral agreements remain central to Russian center-periphery relations.

Thus, although the 1993 Constitution is the first to provide an explicit and meaningful discussion of the division of powers in center-periphery relations, it remains subject to criticism both for its ambiguity and for the extent to which it continues to be violated.

Adjudication Between Levels

Before 1993 Russia did not have an independent mechanism for the unbiased adjudication of center-periphery disputes, the third necessary condition for federalism. Before the Soviet collapse, the Supreme Court, which was selected by the Supreme Soviet, was technically responsible for adjudicating center-periphery disputes. In reality, the members of the Supreme Court were chosen by the Communist Party and made the decision expected of it by the Party. With the Soviet collapse, the role of the Party ceased to be meaningful, but the court continued to owe its allegiance to the federal parliament. However, the autonomy and integrity of the court continued to be a source of considerable dispute. Moreover, the Supreme Court did not have a clear mandate to resolve center-periphery disputes, even if it had clear precedents and rules for doing so, which it did not.

Here too, the 1993 Constitution presents a watershed in Russian center-periphery relations. The new Constitution created both a Supreme Court and a Constitutional Court. According to the Constitution, the Constitutional Court is responsible for ensuring that the *subekty* comply with the Constitution (Article 125.2.b) and for resolving disputes "between state bodies of the Russian Federation and state bodies of the *subekty* of the Russian Federation" (Article 125.3.b) and between state bodies of the *subekty* (Article 125.3.c).

The Constitutional Court has far more legitimacy for adjudicating center-periphery disputes than any previous court. It consists of 19 judges, who are nominated by the President of the Russian Federation, but must be appointed by the Federation Council, which is composed of the representatives of the *subekty*. Among those who have the power to bring cases to the Constitutional Court are numerous federal organs (including the President, the State Duma, and the Supreme Court); but cases may also be brought to the Court by one-fifth of the members of the Federation Council. Moreover, the Federation Council or the parliament of any *subekt* can ask the Court for a binding interpretation of the Constitution.

The preceding chapters overwhelmingly demonstrate that the majority of center-periphery disputes are still resolved through bilateral negotiation. Yet this is also true in the United States and many other federal states. In most federal states center-periphery disputes are generally only brought to the court, or another adjudicator, when bilateral negotiations have failed. The preceding chapters demonstrate that the Russian executive has occasionally intervened to help settle disputes between *subekty*. For example, Yeltsin intervened in the dispute between the Nenets Autonomous Okrug and the Arkhangelsk Oblast to prevent them from taking unilateral and inflammatory actions. Similarly, when a dispute between Ingushetia and North Ossetia over the region of Prigorodny escalated to the brink of armed conflict, Yeltsin sent in federal peacekeepers. In both cases, while the federal government assisted the negotiation process, the case was ultimately settled by an agreement between the *subekty*. This practice thus seems to supplement rather than undermine the

Constitutional Court's role as the adjudicating body in Russian center-periphery relations—or periphery-periphery relations.

The real question is, can the Constitutional Court ajudicate center-periphery relations when needed? Although the Chechen war (Chapter 5) has undoubtedly been the most violent dispute in Russian center-periphery relations, the Primorskii Krai may provide a more important precedent.[14] Few if any *subekty* are as committed to independence as Chechnya. Conversely, many *subekt* leaders resemble Primorskii Krai Governor Evgenii Nazdratenko in both their corruption and their support for local autonomy as a means to protect their corrupt practices. The Constitutional Court has twice ruled on cases involving Primorskii Krai. First, when Nazdratenko removed the mayor of Vladivostok, ironically for alleged corruption, the court ruled his action illegal. Later, when the Krai's Duma sought to extend its term for an additional two years, the Constitutional Court ruled that this was a violation of the Russian Constitution. (As in other federal systems, the Russian Constitutional Court depends on the executive to enforce its decisions; and Yeltsin did not enforce this one.) In both cases the Constitutional Court—true to its chart— used a legitimate interpretation of the Russian Constitution to set useful demarcation in center-periphery relations.

Another relevant case took place in 1998 when the Ingush government tried to make its procuracy subordinate to the Ingush government, rather than to the Russian procuracy. However, the Constitutional Court ruled in favor of the Russian Procuracy's contention that the referendum to change the status of Ingush's procuracy was illegal. (This time the Court's decision was accepted and the referendum was cancelled.)

In sum, the Constitutional Court is not yet the undisputed adjudicator of Russian center-periphery relations. Its decisions are not always implemented. However, it has played a significant role adjudicating center-periphery conflicts and has far more legitimacy than any Russian institution that previously filled this role.

Federal Representation

Although there are many different mechanisms through which component governments may participate in federal politics, representation in the upper chamber of the federal parliament is by far the most typical. The brief summary of the evolution of Russian federalism in Chapter 2 found that the *subekty* had representatives in the Supreme Soviet of the Soviet Union, as well as the Russian Supreme Soviet. However, these representatives were nominated by the Party and elected by the people and thus had little or no loyalty to the emerging *subekt* governments. Moreover, in both cases a higher-level Congress of People's Deputies was elected by and from the Supreme Soviet. In this chamber, which served as the functional parliament, there was no guarantee of *subekt* representation.

Chapter 2 also discussed the battle over the method for selecting both the Duma and the Federation Council since the promulgation of the new Constitution. While the representatives to the Federation Council, senators, were initially elected, the executive and legislative heads of each *subekt* were eventually given seats. This is more direct representation than provided in most federal systems, including the U.S. Senate. The *subekty* have also increased the importance of their representation in the Duma, the lower house of the Federal Assembly. Since its inception in 1993, half of the Duma has been elected by district and half by party list. But a 1995 compromise marginally increased the *subekt* ties of those representatives elected by party list by limiting each party to 12 candidates on their list who did not have an announced regional affiliation.

It would seem then that the *subekty* now have significant representation in a meaningful body. Has this given them a meaningful role in federal politics? The preceding chapters provide at least anecdotal evidence to support an affirmative conclusion. Alexander provides evidence that the Komi used the Federation Council to protect its individual interests and to support the collective needs of the northern *subekty*. Although the Federation Council avoided any appearance of support for Governor Nazdratenko in Primorskii Krai, it simultaneously opposed Yeltsin's attempt to usurp his powers by increasing the role of his presidential representative. It thus backed the autonomy of the *subekty* without backing Nazdratenko. Similarly, Oldberg reports that Vladimir Shumeiko, the *oblast's* representative in the Federation Council and its speaker from 1993 to 1995, used the Federation Council to advocate and later defend Kaliningrad's status as a Free Economic Zone. Kempton and Robertson also note the prominent roles played in federal politics by Sakha's Nikolayev and Tatarstan's Shaimiev. Given the growing importance of *subekt* leaders in national politics, others may be tempted to follow Alexander Lebed's example and seek office at the regional level to provide a continuing base for their national aspirations.

While the Federation Council has not always defended every *subekt*, collectively the *subekty* have used it to hinder threats to their power. Thus the *subekty* now have a meaningful and institutionalized representation in federal politics.

A Division of Power Between the Levels of Government

As argued in Chapter 2, probably the most widely recognized necessary condition of federalism is a division of powers between at least two levels of government. The Constitution, along with the bilateral agreements, delineates Russia's current division of powers. While there is no clear measure of how much power must rest with the component governments, in a successful federation the division of powers cannot be unilaterally amended.

As detailed in Chapter 2, the Russian Constitution lists 18 powers that belong exclusively to the federal government (Article 71) and 14 issues that are placed under joint jurisdiction (Article 72.1), and the remaining powers are left to the *subekty*. Many *subekty* criticized the Constitution because it left relatively few meaningful powers for them. However, the Constitution allows the use of bilateral agreements to transfer specific powers to individual *subekty*. The main question then is whether the *subekty* have been able to use this system to acquire and maintain significant powers. James Alexander finds that many of the powers originally claimed unilaterally by Komi were later granted to Komi in its bilateral agreement of 1996. He concludes that this agreement gave the republic significant powers in foreign trade, attracting foreign investment and oil sales, and in controlling Komi's economic development. Daniel Kempton finds that Sakha actually claimed more powers in the first two institutional stages than it holds today. Nonetheless, Sakha has maintained considerable economic and political autonomy. It also receives a considerable proportion of its diamond profits. The special status it once had with regard to federal taxes is gone, but its powers are no less than those of most *subekty*. Oldberg's study of Kaliningrad seems to reach a similar conclusion. Although Kaliningrad lost some important economic powers, it now has considerably more economic autonomy than in the Soviet period. From Anne Robertson's chapter it is clear that Tatarstan has used this system to accrue more powers than possibly any other *subekt*, including economic autonomy and a significant share of its oil wealth.

In sum, it appears that there has been a significant ebb and flow of the powers granted to the *subekty*. Some *subekty*, like Sakha, Primorye, and Tatarstan, reached the zenith of their political and economic autonomy before the implementation of the new Constitution when they were freer to negotiate directly with the center. Others, like Kaliningrad and Komi, appear to have done better since the promulgation of the new Constitution. However, the net effect of this has been a gradual equalization and standardization of the powers granted to the *subekty*. Overall, the *subekty* clearly have far more powers than they did before the Soviet collapse.

The question then becomes whether these powers are sufficiently institutionalized that they cannot be unilaterally amended. To answer this question we must consider whether either the Constitution or the bilateral agreements can be unilaterally amended. The Constitution itself is extremely difficult to amend. Amendments to Chapter 3 of the Constitution, which contains the basic division of powers between the *subekty* and the center, can only "come into force following the approval by no less than two-thirds of the *subekty*" (Article 136). The *subekty* thus hold a collective veto over changes in their status.

The bilateral agreements are much easier to amend, since they require the consent of only two parties. But can either party amend them unilaterally? There is no evidence that unilateral declarations by the *subekty* are still possible under the new Constitution. To the contrary, some *subekty*, particularly those that gained the most in stages 1 and 2, have been pressured to yield some of the powers they had gained in previous agreements. Most notably, Sakha was forced to yield some control over the diamond industry and to pay its taxes like other *subekty*, rather than using its taxes first for federal programs within Sakha.

Because these republics had gained so much more than most other *subekty*, they were unable to rely on the other *subekty* to help them defend their gains. But when the federal government's actions seemed to entail new powers for the center, such as the attempt to remove Nazdratenko, the *subekt* leaders defended Nazdratenko despite their personal antipathy for him.

In sum, although some ambiguity remains, the division of powers among the levels of government provided by the Constitution and bilateral agreements is much clearer than any that Russia has previously known. Moreover, while the federal government has forced some concessions from specific *subekty*, it can no longer unilaterally change the overall division of powers. As Article 66.5 says, "The status of a *subekt* of the Russian Federation may be changed only with mutual consent of the Russian Federation and the *subekt* of the Russian Federation in accordance with federal constitutional law." Nor can it unilaterally change the status of any single *subekt*.

A Federal Political Culture

Most experts on federalism believe that federalism cannot survive long without a supportive political culture (see Chapter 2). Elements of a supportive political culture include: (a) the acceptance of multiple loyalties, (b) a tolerance for diversity, (c) a mutual forbearance and self-restraint in the pursuit of goals, (d) a commitment to negotiations as a method for resolving disputes, and (e) a willingness to change. While political culture is extremely difficult to assess, the general presumption is that Soviet political culture was inimical to federalism. Not only were multiple loyalties not welcome, loyalties that contradicted the goals of the Communist Party were traitorous. Not only was diversity not promoted, many forms of diversity (political, religious, or social) were publicly discouraged. The proselytization of religion was officially illegal. Not only was there no mutual forbearance in the pursuit of goals, but all means were legitimate in the pursuit of communism. Not only was there no commitment to political negotiations, but the Soviet leadership was supposed to be uncompromising in its pursuit of the correct path to communism. Finally, although there was a commitment to change, the direction of change was ideologically invariable.

On the surface there is not a lot of evidence that Russia is developing a more supportive political culture. Russians appear to be fed up with all levels of their government. Many ethnic and religious minorities still feel repressed and want greater autonomy. Conversely among Russians there is considerable resentment of ethnic minorities. There are also numerous ethnic disputes, some of which sporadically erupt in violence. However, before discounting Russian political culture, consider the findings from the substantive cases. Alexander notes the absence of popular experience with federalism and the lack of popular will for a federation per se. He also documents a tendency for people in Komi to see regional officials as mere bureaucrats responsible for local directives. Yet, he also finds that both conservative and reform-oriented opinion favor increased local control of the Komi's economic autonomy. This desire for economic autonomy, while rejecting political independence, could be seen as precisely the kind of multiple loyalty that federalism requires. Oldberg notes a similar shift in public opinion in Kaliningrad. He argues that the inability of the center to meet the krai's economic needs has led to growing awareness of the region's specific interests, and more demands for political autonomy. People feel abandoned by the central government, and believe they will prosper from growing economic ties to Germany and other Baltic states. Yet, this has not led to significant support for the formation of a separate Russian Baltic state. Thus, they too seem to support local economic autonomy within a politically united Russia. Potentially more importantly, Oldberg reports that people increasingly see themselves not only as Russians, but also as central Europeans. This is the sort of dual identity that can engender federalism.

Kempton's study of Sakha and Robertson's analysis of Tatarstan also both find support for the combination of local economic autonomy and federation with Russia. While many in Tatarstan appear to want more cultural autonomy, they have continued to support Shaimiev's evolutionary and moderate approach for establishing cultural autonomy. What is also interesting about these two cases is that non-Russian leaders led both *subekty*. Yet, in both cases the Russian population has supported the drive for economic autonomy, believing it also serves their interests. Unlike Dudaev in Chechnya, Shaimiev created more freedom for Muslims without wedding the government to Islam or persecuting other religions.

Some nascent support for federalism can also be found in Blakkisrud's study of the Nenets Autonomous Okrug. While Nenets's leaders see the economic benefits of controlling their own natural resources, they need the center to maintain a balance with the Arkhangelsk Krai. While only a few *subekty*, like Nenets, depend on the federal government to prevent territorial encroachment by other *subekty*, many share Nenets's dependence on the federal government for economic assistance. This is particularly true for resource producing *subekty* who need large amounts of capital investment to develop their resources. Thus, in most *subekty* local public opinion ascribes a potentially positive role to both the *subekt* government and the federal government as playing a positive role. The *subekt* government is expected to assert and protect local control over local resources, and the federal government is to assist in providing the means to develop local resources. This notion of the two levels of Russian government playing different, but positive roles may form the basis of future cultural support for federalism.

However, cases can also be found in the Russian Federation in which popular opinion turns decidedly against the federal government or alternatively the *subekt* government. In Primorskii Krai the government is perceived as so corrupt and unresponsive that much of the local population supports the federal government's efforts to remove Governor Evegenii Nazdratenko. Conversely, in Chechnya, the local population has largely supported the republican government's calls for independence and views the federal government as a force of Russian imperialism.

On the one hand, the case of Chechnya also demonstrates that the Russian Federation's toleration for diversity is limited. On the other hand, the lack of significant independence movements elsewhere, and the center's willingness to tolerate considerable economic and cultural autonomy are meaningful and hopeful developments.

In sum, Russia clearly does not have a political culture that engenders federalism to the same extent as the religious diversity of colonial America or the long history of regional autonomy in Switzerland. Conversely, when compared to the Soviet Union, there are significant and positive developments in Russian political culture.

THE BENEFICIAL CONDITIONS OF FEDERALISM

A Center-Periphery Balance

The argument that federations require an equal balance of power between the central government and the component governments was rejected in Chapter 2. In federal states the preservation of powers depends not so much on each level's ability to defend itself, but on a clear division of powers that is institutionalized in a legitimate Constitution and is supported by the political culture. However, if both levels of government have enough powers to protect themselves, this will benefit federalism.

In reviewing the cases it is clear that there is no easy way to know when a balance of power between the levels exists. Because the two levels commonly desire and hold different powers, assessing their relative powers is highly subjective. Their relative strengths can best be seen when one level is attempting to change the balance unilaterally and the other resists. In the first two institutional stages, the center offered little resistance to unilateral power grabs. The critical exception came in reaction to Chechnya's demand for independence. Although the conflict in Moscow initially prevented a firm response from the center, when the Russian response finally came it was a drastic one, invasions in 1994 and 1999. The central government and the *subekty* have both likely learned important lessons from the events in Chechnya. The *subekty* clearly learned that there are limits to the center's tolerance for unilateral action by individual *subekty.* Moscow learned that the cost of maintaining Russia's territorial integrity by force can be extremely high. Ultimately, a permanent solution to the Chechen problem will likely require some compromise.

During the third institutional stage, attempts to change the balance of power unilaterally became rare. However, it is worth considering two cases in which the center tried to unilaterally alter the balance of power. First, in 1996 Yeltsin tried to increase the power of his appointed representatives to the *subekty*, which according to the Chairman of the Constitutional Court was the most effective way of checking the *subekty*.[15] In January Chubais warned governors that the government was considering reinforcing the powers of presidential representatives.[16] According to some sources the decree had been prepared back in the fall of 1996, but Yeltsin was hesitant to sign the decree because doing so risked endangering his alliance with the *subekty* before the presidential elections.[17] Belatedly, on July 9, Yeltsin signed the much-discussed decree.[18] The decree took three steps to dramatically increase the power of the presidential representatives. First, the representatives will supervise the personnel of all 90 federal agencies that have branches in each of the *subekty*. Second, the representatives will coordinate the activities of the regional branches of those agencies. Finally, they will monitor the use of federal funds in the *subekty*. Informally, they would serve as the eyes and ears of the president in their respective *subekty*. For the first time presidential representatives would be sent to all the *subekty*, including the republics.

Subekt leaders were unimpressed with the center's claims that the decree would merely reduce "the burden" on them. The governor of the Saratov Oblast threatened to liquidate the position on the grounds that it was unconstitutional, if Yeltsin continued to increase the power of his representatives.[19] (Many governors have historically undermined the independence of the presidential representative by developing close ties to their respective presidential representatives, and in some cases even hiring them onto their staffs.[20]) Meanwhile the Federation Council is challenging the constitutionality of the decree in court.

Primorskii Krai Governor Evegenii Nazdratenko, whom Yeltsin repeatedly accused of incompetence and outright corruption, has launched a second unilateral challenge. In May 1997 Yeltsin replaced his presidential representative to the krai, who had become too friendly with Nazdratenko, with a Yeltsin loyalist.[21] Then in July he issued a decree stripping Nazdratenko of his powers and replacing him with his newly appointed presidential representative. This initially appeared to be an ideal test case for Yeltsin. Nazdratenko was an arrogant and blatantly corrupt figure, unpopular domestically and among many of the *subekt* leaders. As expected, the leaders of the other *subekty* said little to defend Nazdratenko, but they vigorously argued against Yeltsin's right to remove Nazdratenko.[22] Ultimately, the Federation Council as a whole approved a letter to Yeltsin condemning his actions. In a spirit of compromise, they proposed a law that would allow the president to remove *subekt* leaders, but only with the support of the Federation Council and only when a violation of civil rights had occurred. Thus far, no compromise has been reached and Nazdratenko continues to defy Yeltsin and his decrees.

What these cases would seem to indicate is that the distribution of power is sufficiently balanced to make it difficult for the center or the *subekty* to unilaterally change the balance.

Symmetry among the Components

Potentially as problematic as a power imbalance between the center and the components is an asymmetry among the components themselves. As Elazar argued, federal systems in which "one entity is clearly dominant" are likely to fail.[23] Although Russia does not have this problem, there is considerable asymmetry among its components, both in terms of the distribution of resources among Russia's *subekty* (political asymmetry) and in terms of the legal powers they have been granted (constitutional asymmetry). Not surprisingly, therefore, analysts of Russian federalism have warned that the asymmetry among Russia's components is destructive to federalism and "may destroy constitutional norms."[24]

The evidence suggests that after 1965 there was a gradual convergence of Russia's regions and republics.[25] They were becoming more and more alike in terms of indicators like infant mortality, economic productivity, standard of living and crime. At the start of *perestroika* the trend toward convergence was quickly reversed. Since Russian independence the gap between the poorest and the richest *subekty* has grown rapidly. In the last three years, the richest nine *subekty* have gone from a per capita income 3.19 times that of the poorest 10 *subekty* to having per capita income 3.66 times that of the poorest *subekty*.[26] Since greater wealth is often translated into greater political power, this can be seen as a net increase in political asymmetry.

At the same time, the preceding chapters and the above discussion of the division of powers suggest that constitutional asymmetry, the balance of legal powers, has fluctuated. In the first two institutional stages constitutional asymmetry increased as the resource rich *subekty*, generally the republics, demanded and received new powers and rights. However, the promulgation of the new Constitution has introduced two new trends. First, those *subekty* that signed some of the earliest bilateral agreements and gained the most extensive powers, such as Sakha and Tatarstan, have lost powers. Second, many of the *subekty* that had not signed bilateral agreements have now done so.

The political and constitutional asymmetry in Russian federalism has created at least three different problems. First, the donor *subekty* feel that they have been unjustly required to subsidize their less well-endowed neighbors. As Robertson reported, the imbalance between what Tatarstan contributes to the center and what it receives from the center has been a source of frustration and engendered demands for autonomy. Similarly, in October 1996 Moscow Mayor Luzhkov complained that a mere 10 donor *subekty*, primarily regions, were subsidizing the rest of Russia.[27] He suggested that the donor regions, including Moscow, should be allowed to keep 60–65 percent of their taxes; and the other *subekty* should be told to "look after yourself." (Luzhkov subsequently convened meetings among these so-called donors, in order to form a common front.[28]) The argument over the number of donor regions, and their burden, provoked considerable controversy. Analysts typically placed the number of donor *subekty* at between nine and 15. Aleksandr Lavrov, adviser to the territorial department of the President, concluded that there were actually 32 donor regions. However, he complained that dividing the *subekty* between donors and recipients was "an infantile disorder of Russian federalism."[29]

Echoing Luzhkov, the chairman of the Federation Council Committee on Constitutional Legislation and Legal issues said the inequality of the *subekty* was one of the most pressing issues facing Russia.[30] In his view, the asymmetry was in direct contradiction to the promise of equal treatment contained in the Constitution. Yeltsin himself argued in his radio address that the unevenness of economic development among the *subekty* was the most acute problem Russia faced.[31]

A second problem attributable to asymmetry is that the poorer *subekty* contend that the greater wealth of their neighbors results not from their greater natural resources, but from the political concessions they have won from the center. Federal leaders too sometimes blame the inequality on the bilateral agreements. While railing against the "double standards" among the treatment of Russia's *subekty*, Federation Council Chairman Yegor Stroev criticized the highly favorable terms received by a select group of *subekty*.[32] (Sakha was singled out for special mention.) Similarly, Valerii Zubov, the Governor of Krasnoyarsk, said that the leaders of the 17 member Siberian Accord opposed the special privileges granted to some *subekty*, again Sakha was used as an example.[33] Luzhkov himself once joked that maybe Moscow should join Tatarstan or Sakha, in order to take advantage of their deal.

Sergei Sharkrai, the Chairman of the Commission for Preparing Treaties, contended that the treaties have kept the peace and are helping to build order from the ground up. Increasingly, however, such a positive assessment of the treaties is rare. On the other extreme, a conference on Russian federalism recommended reducing the total number of *subekty* to 10 or 12.[34] Reportedly, such diverse leaders as Mayor Luzhkov and Deputy Prime Minister Chubais both ultimately support just such a change. The Duma sought a general law delimiting the division of power between the federal government and *subekty*. However, the law they passed in April 1997 would have voided all existing bilateral agreements.[35] Thus it was not acceptable to either the Federation Council or the government. Instead, the government's policy, spearheaded by Chubais, was to gradually curb the most obvious excesses on a case-by-case basis (see the Division of Power, above).

A third form of asymmetry is created by the nested nature of some inter-*subekt* relationships. In addition to the 21 republics, 49 oblasty (regions), and 6 krai (territories), the Russian Federation contains one autonomous oblast, 10 okruga (autonomous areas) and two federal cities (Moscow and St. Petersburg). The latter 12 *subekty* are all contained inside of other *subekty*. For example, the Nenets Autonomous Okrug is contained inside of the Arkhangelsk Oblast. Historically, government of Nenets was largely subservient to that of Arkhangelsk. As Helge Blakkisrud points out, Article 66.4 states that "the relations of autonomous okruga forming part (*vkhodyashchie v sostav)* of a krai or oblast may be regulated by federal law and a treaty between the bodies of state powers of the autonomous okrug and, respectively, by the bodies of state power of the krai or oblast." This implies that the autonomous okruga are subordinate to the *subekty* in which they are situated. Conversely the Constitution twice states that "All *subekty* of the Russian Federation shall be equal (*ravnopravny*) among themselves" (Articles 5.1 and 5.4). Therefore, the Constitution at points implies subordination and at others insists on equality.

In practice this makes for a difficult relationship. Ultimately, after considerable acrimony and some pressure from Moscow, Nenets and Arkhangelsk reached a bilateral agreement, in which profits from Nenets's resources were shared. Nonetheless the relationship continues to be a bumpy one. Although the specific disputes vary for each of these nested relationships, their nature is essentially the same.

In sum, the asymmetry among Russia's *subekty* is considerable and remains a source of problems between specific *subekty*, between groups of *subekty*, and between the *subekty* and the center. Nonetheless, peaceful solutions are being found to many of these problems, and the center has consciously reduced the political asymmetry since the promulgation of the new Constitution.

Federal Political Parties

The development of federal political parties is one of the beneficial conditions of federalism in which Russia would appear to be the most deficient. Non-centralized parties are helpful to federalism because national parties need to keep their regional affiliates happy in order to win national power. Therefore, some of the tough bargaining in center-periphery relations occurs within the party structures, rather than being left for the government to resolve.

From the perspective of building federalism, the main problem with Russia's parties is not that they are overly centralized; it is that they are overly personalistic. Thus, instead of serving as forums for negotiating national consensus, they are simply a reflection of the views of their leaders. When leaders lose power, their parties collapse. For example, when Chernomyrdin was Prime Minister and in the eyes of many, Yeltsin's heir apparent, his "Our Home Russia" was a leading political party. However, after Yeltsin removed Chernomyrdin as Prime Minister, Our Home Russia rapidly declined in importance. When Vladimir Putin became Prime Minister, his associated "Unity Party" rose from nowhere in two months to finish a remarkable second in the 1999 parliamentary elections. Similarly, all of the preceding chapters highlighted the importance of *subekt* leaders in *subekt* politics. In the case of Sakha, Kempton contended Nikolayev's relationship with Yeltsin was a key to Sakha's early success in gaining concessions from Moscow. Robertson pointed to differences between Shaimiev and Dudaev and their choice of strategies to explain the very divergent paths taken by Tatarstan and Chechnya.

James Alexander also notes the underdevelopment of parties in Komi. He concludes that Komi's non-professional legislature and its law requiring the republic's head to sever his ties to all political parties inhibits the development of parties in the republic. This practice is widespread among the *subekty*. Moreover, the Constitution similarly bans the Russian President from maintaining ties to a political party. Even more importantly, Alexander notes the importance of varied election schedules. The need for cooperation between local and national parties is dramatically reduced by the fact that *subekt* and federal elections are not held on the same schedule, which minimizes the benefits of cooperation between *subekt* and federal parties.

A positive development in 1999 was the effort by Shaimiev and a number of other *subekt* executives to form a bloc of regional movements to back candidates in the December 1999 Duma elections and the 2000 presidential race.[36] If this effort succeeds, it could form the basis of a truly federal political party and be of considerable benefit to the evolution of federal political bargaining. As of winter 1999, however, Russia's party system remains underdeveloped from a federal perspective. Today, the reformulated Communist Party is the only truly national party.

A Non-centralized Bureaucracy

A highly centralized bureaucracy is inimical to federalism, since it provides an easy tool for the center to control the policies of the component government. Component governments also depend on the center to implement their policies. The Soviet Union maintained the archetypal centralized bureaucracy. All roads led to Moscow, and all bureaucratic decisions passed through Moscow. If an auto plant in Tatarstan needed fuel from a refinery in Bashkortostan, the decision—and possibly even the oil—had to go through Moscow.

When the Soviet Union collapsed, control of the huge Soviet bureaucracy in the *subekty* was up for grabs. The practical effect of the *subektys'* grabs for sovereignty in the first two institutional stages was that many *subekty* took control and responsibility for many bureaucracies based on their territories. Sakha and Tatarstan were the most extreme examples. Both received the right to control the expenditure of federal taxes spent by federal agencies on their territories. Ultimately, however, we saw that many of these extreme concessions were taken back. Discussed above was also Yeltsin's decree that increased the powers of the presidential representative and extended that system to republics. The center is also acting more decisively to maintain control of the bureaucracy under its control. In 1998, for example, it intervened to stop a referendum, which—if passed—would have transferred control of the procuracy in the Ingush Republic to the republican government.

Clearly, control of the Russian bureaucracy is still an area of considerable political conflict. However, it is equally clear that the Russian bureaucracy today is considerably less centralized than it was a decade ago.

Democracy

As argued in Chapter 2, democracy is not a necessary condition for federalism. Many ancient federal systems, and some modern ones as well (e.g., the United Arab Emirates), were not democracies. Nonetheless, democracy can be of considerable benefit to federal systems. Democracy typically empowers minority groups by giving them the vote and by creating systems that are not winner takes all. Federalism also allows many minority groups to sustain themselves by making them the majority within a specific component of the larger state. Thus in democratic states with significant minorities, minority groups frequently become a solid basis of support for maintaining federalism.

On one hand, Russia has clearly made dramatic strides since the last decade. Russia has had a democratic, internationally monitored presidential election (two if the 1991 election is included). It held parliamentary elections in 1993, 1995, 1997, and 1999. In all of the parliamentary elections (for the Duma) an opposition party won the most seats. On the other hand, there has been evidence of significant fraud and corruption in Russia's federal elections. Moreover, serious questions can be raised about Yeltsin's attack on the old Supreme Soviet, which some have likened to an internal coup. There have also been criticisms of the fairness of the Constitutional plebiscite. Overall, while Russian democracy may be overly personalistic and suffers from occasional corruption, Russia is far more democratic today than at any time at since 1918.

The preceding chapters reached some remarkably similar conclusions on the state of democracy in the individual *subekty*. First, while all of the *subekty* analyzed have held reasonably democratic elections, they all seem to have experienced some fraud and irregularities. Second, in most of the *subekty* discussed, the central leader has played a very powerful role. As result, *subekt* elections seem to focus more on personalities than on issues or parties. A more positive interpretation can be put on the October 1996 gubernatorial elections in Kaliningrad, in that an incumbent leader was defeated at the ballot box. Third, when you combine the personalistic nature of democracy in the *subekty* with the lack of federal oversight, noted by Alexander, it tends to breed corruption. While the level of corruption certainly varies, and no explicit comparisons were made, corruption appears to present a serious problem for all the *subekty*. Finally, a few *subekty* have suffered from potential serious breaches of the democratic process. In Sakha, Nikolayev considered extending his term without benefit of an election. While Nikolayev backed down, the parliament of Primorskii Krai succeeded in extending its term. Although Spiridonov in Komi acted strictly within the parameters of the Komi Constitution and the Komi Law on Executive Authority, he manipulated the selection of Komi's State Council to ensure a supportive and dependent legislature. Nonetheless, the conclusion drawn above for Russian democracy also holds for the *subekty*. While the practice of democracy in the *subekty* is significantly flawed, it is far more democratic than ever before.

Economic Conditions

Although there are no economic conditions that are common to all federal systems both past and present, economic factors have been critical to the survival of some federal systems and to the destruction of others. In Nigeria most of the oil wealth is concentrated among the people of the south, while the largest population group, the Hausa-Fulani, lives in the north. This incongruity between the concentrations of wealth and populations has generated numerous problems in Nigerian politics and was a major distal cause of the Biafran Civil War. Conversely, many Canadians believe that a split with Quebec would leave both English-speaking and French-speaking Canada vulnerable to economic domination by the United States. Similarly, the anticipated economic benefits to be derived from a common market have generated an evolution toward federalism in the EU.

At first glance, one might assume that the Soviet legacy would overwhelmingly favor continued federation among the remaining components of Russia. The Soviet Union built one of the world's most autarkic economies. Its economic dependence on foreign trade was minimal. At the same time, because of the Soviet predilection for huge industrial factories Soviet production of any given manufactured good was often concentrated in a single gargantuan factory. The relevant result was that the economies of what became Russia's *subekty* were once highly integrated and were extremely dependent on trade with one another.

When the Soviet Union collapsed, imports were opened up and Russian consumers were given a choice between low-quality Russian goods, and inexpensive yet higher-quality imports; Russians have overwhelmingly chosen the latter. As a result Russia's industrial production has rapidly collapsed. In turn, inter-*subekty* trade has declined precipitously. Because of its location, among our cases Kaliningrad's realignment of trade has been most dramatic. As Oldberg notes, Kaliningrad's foreign trade increased five-fold between 1995 and 1997. Foreign trade rapidly replaced goods previously purchased from the former Soviet Union. As a result, nearly all the *subekty* are becoming more economically isolated and less integrated.[37]

Even more important than trade for the success of a federal system is the economic cooperation between the federal government and the component governments. In Russia, the federal government depends on the *subekty* governments to collect many of the taxes that provide its income. At the same time, the *subekty* depend on the federal government and its greater concentration of fiscal resources to build and maintain their transportation infrastructure, to spur development, and to create the economic conditions that will attract new investment. If either or both sides fail to meet their financial obligations, economic conditions could quickly become a detriment to Russian federalism. Once again, such issues are best answered by reference to the specific cases.

In Komi, Alexander reports that both sides are failing in their obligations. As he artfully reports, Komi pretends to collect taxes and Moscow pretends to pay the republic. As a result conditions are worsening for both sides. Without the promised federal transfers, Komi has been unable to pay the coal miners, an industry that is the backbone of Komi's economy.

Similarly, Kempton reports that Sakha has repeatedly not received enough funding to import the goods it needs during the few summer months when the Lena River is still unfrozen. To protest, in 1994 Sakha's parliament declared an economic emergency and threatened to withhold the shipment of diamonds and other resources. While Yeltsin repeated his promises for aid and interest-free credit, then Finance Minister Panskov alleged that funds for the North had been diverted illegally to private accounts.[38] In subsequent years the credit available for transportation continued to be insufficient, and both sides blamed the other.[39] Other areas experienced similar problems. In 1997 the federal government budgeted $919 billion rubles to support federal programs in the north, but by September it had spent only $24 billion.[40] The Children of the North Fund had received only 23 percent of its allotted funding. But according to the Chairman of the Duma's Committee on the Problems of the North, it is the 1998 budget which could "create economic catastrophe in the North." Reportedly, with the strategic food supply nearly depleted, the new budget was bereft of funds to subsidize food for the North.

Overall, Moscow has reduced subsidies to the *subekty*. The 1997 budget left the *subekty* responsible for financing 80 percent of all education; 88 percent of healthcare costs; 80 percent of social spending, and 70 percent of all major projects.[41] The 1998 budget proposed by Yeltsin was to make even more dramatic cuts in the level of subsidies, from 66.0 trillion rubles to 38.5 trillion rubles.[42] After the Russian economy collapsed in 1998, much of what was budgeted for the *subekty* was never sent.

Kaliningrad's initial complaint was that the restrictions the center placed on Kaliningrad's Free Economic Zone (FEZ) status led to social misery in Kaliningrad. Later, however, residents of the oblast soured on the whole FEZ concept, as it failed to deliver results. Oldberg concludes that instead of becoming an economic bridge to Europe, as Kaliningrad's leaders anticipated, the oblast was becoming a Russian economic periphery. In October 1996 elections the main proponents of FEZ status were voted out of office. Less than two years later the Russian economy went into a monumental meltdown. Federal support for the *subekty* plummeted even further. *Subekty*, like Kaliningrad, that were in a position to increase their ties to other states did so. Conversely, Kaliningrad's ties to neighboring Lithuania and Germany increased markedly.

While most *subekty* tried to maximize both their economic autonomy and the benefits they received from the center, Chechnya's President Dudaev voluntarily severed Chechnya's economic links to the center. He believed that Chechnya's oil resources, and its location along the natural transportation route for the rich Caspian oil fields would turn Chechnya into "the Kuwait of the Caucuses." He was wrong. Without Russian investment Chechnya's oil production dwindled, and without Russian cooperation it could not transport its own oil, let alone that from the Caspian. The economy collapsed and corruption proliferated. The economic repercussions of Chechnya's bid for independence and the subsequent Russian invasions likely made other *subekt* leaders hesitant to push their autonomy too far.

As Robertson points out, Shaimiev in Tatarstan took a very different tact. He negotiated as much economic autonomy as Moscow would allow. In 1994 he signed one of the earliest and most extensive bilateral agreements with Moscow. While Tatarstan has experienced some loss of autonomy since 1994, it has not been nearly as extensive as that experienced by other republics.

Although Tatarstan is often the model that other *subekty* seek to emulate, it too is disappointed with Moscow. Tatarstan is one of Russia's few donor regions (see the section on asymmetry), and Tatarstan's leaders argue there is a considerable imbalance between what Tatarstan contributes to Russia in taxes and the subsidies it receives in return. Thus, despite their considerable autonomy and economic success, Tatarstan's leaders believe the federal government has failed to live up to its promises. Tatarstan is not alone in this sentiment. The most radical reaction thus far was that of then Governor Yuri Nozhikov of Irkustk.[43] In March 1997 Nozhikov claimed that in 1996 Irkutsk had contributed over 4 trillion rubles (approximately $700 million) to the federal budget, but received nothing in return. By his estimate, the federal government owed the region some 2 trillion rubles ($357 million) in back wages, pensions, and benefits. Nozhikov thus announced that he was suspending all tax transfers to Moscow. While Nozhikov received the rhetorical support of many *subekt* leaders, he received no tangible assistance.[44] The federal government responded with both threats to dismiss Nozhikov and a promise from Chernomyrdin to transfer additional funds to the region. The revolt was settled quickly and Nozhikov resigned shortly thereafter.

Although the federal relationship with Russia may have lost some of its gloss from the Tatar perspective, Robertson believes that Shaimiev is not likely to follow Chechnya's example. Shaimiev recognizes that Tatarstan's oil is largely worthless without Russia's refineries and pipelines. This is why he initially rejected total independence, and it is why he will likely continue to support a federal arrangement.

At the same time, the federal government reports that the *subekty* have not lived up to their financial obligations. While no other *subekt* leader followed Nozhikov's brash challenge, Irkutsk was not the only *subekt* not paying all its bills. In July 1997 Aleksei Kudrin claimed that while the federal government owed some 7.7 trillion rubles in back wages to government employees, the *subekt* governments collectively owed 25.6 trillion rubles.[45] Kudrin said that the federal government would contribute 2.2 trillion rubles to help the *subekty* pay their arrears, but the *subekty* would have to pay the rest. His solution for the *subekty* was a familiar refrain, privatization. The government believed such sales would simultaneously raise revenues for governments at multiple levels and move forward its objective of privatizing the economy. Back in February 1996 Yeltsin issued a presidential decree (no. 292) legalizing the transfer of federal equity stakes in private companies as a way for the federal government to repay its debts to the *subekty*. In September 1996, the federal government said that the *subekt* governments could keep up to 90 percent of the revenues from such sales.[46] Kudrin suggested that such sales could raise up to 5 trillion rubles. During a spring 1997 trip to Sakha, Chubais criticized the *subekty* in general, but implicitly Sakha in particular, for demanding ever more subsidies, without even trying to raise capital through privatization.[47] Shortly thereafter, Sakha's government announced its intent to sell of 49 percent of its stock in *Sakhazoloto* (Sakha Gold).

The federal government has shown similar angst over the *subekty*'s failure to make their payments to the center, particularly to the federal pension fund.[48] By March 1997, the *subekty*'s debt to the federal budget was in excess of 35 trillion rubles. According to one government spokesman, delays in payments from the *subekty* were leading to delays in pension payments nationwide. Allegedly, some *subekty*, including Sakha, had unilaterally reduced their payments by as much as 40–50 percent. Sakha was also singled out for particular scorn for its failure to transfer tax dollars to the federal budget. According to Deputy Finance Minister Vladimir Petrov, by May 1997 Sakha, Tatarstan and Bashkortostan—all of which had signed special bilateral treaties with the federal government to keep a greater portion of their taxes at home—owed the federal budget a combined 1 trillion rubles in back taxes in the first quarter of 1997.[49] Analysts speculated that the divisions within the federal government, that Sakha had once exploited, no longer existed. Thus Sakha would now have to meet its debts.[50] The message apparently struck home in Sakha and elsewhere. By the end of June the chairman of the federal pension plan reported that 90 percent of the *subekty* had now paid their debts to pension earners.[51] Similarly, to force a Tatar oil company to pay its taxes, Moscow cut its export quota by one-third.

In sum, the integrated economy that existed prior to the breakup of the Soviet Union has rapidly deteriorated. Cheaper, higher-quality imported goods have rapidly replaced internal trade in consumer goods. At the same time, raw materials producers increasingly find more reliable markets and higher prices for their goods when exported abroad. Even more detrimental to federalism has been the failure of both the *subekty* and the federal government to live up to their financial obligations to one another. If not reversed, Russian economic trends could become a serious impediment to federalism.

CONCLUSIONS

It is now clear that Russia does not fully possess all of the necessary conditions for the success of federalism. However, after reviewing the six necessary conditions, there have been numerous and notable advances since 1993.

1. Before 1993 Russian center-periphery relations were far from consensual. Instead, individual *subekty* unilaterally claimed varied powers from the center. After 1993 negotiated bilateral agreements became the standard means for specifying center-periphery relations.
2. Despite the many criticisms of the 1993 Constitution, it has provided the first meaningful and legal binding demarcation of the powers in Russian center-periphery relations.
3. Although its decisions are not always honored or implemented by the Russian executive, the Constitutional Court has played an increasingly significant role in adjudicating center-periphery conflict, and has far more legitimacy than any other Russian institution that previously filled this role.
4. Although numerous disputes remain over the directness of *subekt* representation, particularly in the Duma, the Federation Council has given the *subekty* a meaningful and regular role in federal politics.
5. The 1993 Constitution provides a division of powers between the levels of government that, despite its ambiguity, is the clearest Russia has ever had. More important, either the federal government or the *subekty* cannot unilaterally alter the existing division of powers.
6. While Russian political culture is not particularly supportive of federalism, there are far more positive signs than were apparent in Soviet political culture, which was largely inimical to federalism.

Our assessment of the beneficial conditions was probably even more pessimistic, yet the same trend was apparent. With one critical exception, Russia has made considerable progress in creating the conditions beneficial to federalism.

1. It would be hard to argue that there is a "balance" between the powers of the federal governments and the *subekt* governments. However, there is certainly more of a balance than during the Soviet period. Moreover, both levels appear to be sufficiently powerful to prevent unilateral grabs for power by the other level.
2. The political asymmetry remains considerable and may be continuing to grow. In short, some *subekty* are simply wealthier and more powerful than others. However, there is no single *subekt* , or group of *subekty*, which can dominate Russian politics. Moreover, the federal government has reduced the constitutional asymmetry (the inequity in the powers given to various *subekty*) since 1993.
3. Although Russian political parties remain undeveloped, there is an increasing potential for center-periphery bargaining within party structures. Because Russian politics remain highly personalistic, center-periphery relations have frequently hinged on personal relations.
4. The Russian bureaucracy has undergone a fairly dramatic decentralization, which should be of benefit to the success of federalism.
5. While the practice of democracy is flawed, Russia is far more democratic than at any time in the recent past.

One potentially beneficial condition for the growth of federalism that is clearly worsening in Russia is the economy. The once integrated and autarkic

Soviet economy has collapsed, and inter-Russian trade has been rapidly been replaced with foreign trade. Even more important, both the *subekty* and the federal government believe that the other is not living up to its financial obligations. This has led to growing conflict, instead of to the economic interdependence so beneficial to federal systems.

Whatever conclusions we draw about the success of federalism in Russia must be tentative since Russia remains in a state of considerable flux. The most obvious conclusion is that the Russian Federation, as the name implies, is a functioning federal system. As argued in Chapter 2, the most basic definition of a federal system is *self rule plus shared rule.*[52] Russia today possesses at least two levels of government, each of which has meaningful autonomy on certain issues. This is in itself an important and remarkable change from a decade ago. At the same time, as specified in the Constitution and as seen in the preceding chapters, there are many issues over which Russia's component governments and federal government share power. However, the shared governance inherent in federalism has given Russia highly conflictual center-periphery relations. This is neither surprising, nor decisive. As argued in Chapter 2, federalism is a system designed not to eliminate center-periphery conflict, but to channel it. With the notable exception of Chechnya, federalism has helped channel Russian center-periphery relations into the spheres of political struggle and negotiation.

Will Russia be a successful federal system? While answering this question is presently beyond the means of academics, the preceding chapters provide considerable evidence that Russia has created or acquired many of the attributes that could make Russia a successful federal system. However, these attributes remain extremely underdeveloped relative to other federal systems. Whether Russia's progress is sufficient is yet to be determined.

NOTES

1. Edward W. Walker, "Designing Center-Region Relations in the New Russia," *East European Constitutional Review*, 4, 1 (Winter 1995): 54–60.
2. RIA Novosti, 27 December 1996; and OMRI, *Russian Regional Report*, 2(13), (17 April 1997).
3. OMRI, *Daily Digest*, 24 October 1996.
4. OMRI, *Russian Regional Report*, 2(3), 22 January 1997.
5. *OMRI Russian Regional Report*, 18 September 1996.
6. Segodnya, 30 October 1996.
7. *Kommersant-Daily*, 30 October 1996.
8. OMRI, *Russian Regional Report*, 2(3), 22 January 1997.
9. Quoted in Michael Specter, "Russia's Regions Continue to Defy Yeltsin," *New York Times*, 25 March 1997.
10. OMRI, *Russian Regional Report*, 2(11), 20 March 1997.
11. Reuters, Moscow, 6 June 1997; and RIA, *Novosti*, 8 June 1997.
12. RFE/RL, *Newsline*, 1(21), 29 April 1997.

13. IEWS, *Russian Regional Report*, 2(15), 30 April 1997.

14. Jason Bitter, "The Primorye Energy Crisis," a paper presented at the 29th Annual National Convention of the American Association for the Advancement of Slavic Studies, 12–15 November 1997, Seattle, Washington.

15. *Segodnya*, 30 October 1996.

16. *St. Petersburg Times*, 20–22 January 1997.

17. IEWS, *Russian Regional Report*, 2(13), 17 April 1997; and IEWS, *Russian Regional Report,* 2(125), 10 July 1997.

18. IEWS, *Russian Regional Report*, 2(13), 17 April 1997; IEWS, *Russian Regional Report,* 2(26), 17 July 1997; and RFE/RL, *Newsline*, 1(73), 15 July 1997.

19. RFE/RL, *Newsline*, 1(104), 27 August 1997.

20. IEWS, *Russian Regional Report*, 2(20), 17 July 1997.

21. For a thoughtful study of Nazdratenko's challenge, see Jason Bitter "The Federal, Regional & Local Struggle over the Primorye Energy Crisis," a paper presented at the 29th Annual National Convention of the American Association for the Advancement of Slavic Studies, 12–15 November 1997, Seattle, Washington.

22. IEWS, *Russian Regional Report*, 2(22), 19 June 1997; IEWS, *Russian Regional Report,* 2(25), 10 July 1997; and *The Globe and Mail* (Canada), 10 July 1997.

23. Elazar, 1987, p. 244.

24. IEWS, *Russia Regional Report*, Special Supplement, v. 3, n. 16, 23 April 1998.

25. *Rossiyskiye gazeta*, 20 May 1997.

26. RIA, Novosti, *Ekonomika i zhizn*, 18, 1997.

27. OMRI, *Daily Digest*, 207, 24 October 1996.

28. IEWS, *Russian Regional Report*, 15 January 1997.

29. *Rossiiskiye vesti*, 6 August 1997.

30. OMRI, *Daily Digest*, 17 January 1997.

31. RIA, *Novosti*, 8 June 1997.

32. IEWS, *Russian Regional Report*, 2(31), 18 September 1997.

33. RFE/RL, *Newsline*, 1(29), 13 May 1997.

34. IEWS, *Russian Regional Report*, 2(13), 17 April 1997.

35. *Kommersant-Daily*, 26 April 1997.

36. Judith Matloff, "Power Splinters in Russia," *Christian Science Monitor*, 10 June 16, 1999.

37. RIA, Novosti, *Ekonomika i zhizn*, 18, 1997.

38. *Izvestiya* (1 July 1994):1; *Nezavisimaya gazeta* (20 October 1994): 5; OMRI, *Daily Digest* 102, Part I (26 May 1995); *Segodnya* (5 July 1994): 2, in *FBIS-SOV*-94–129 (6 July 1994): 33.

39. *INTERFAX* (20 October 1994), in *FBIS-SOV*-94–204 (21 October 1994): 37; IEWS. *Russian Regional Report,* 2(4), (29 January 1997); OMRI, *Daily Digest,* no. 184, Part I (23 September 1996); and IEWS, *Russian Regional Report,* 2(4), (29 January 1997).

40. IEWS, *Russian Regional Report*, 2(31), 18 September 1997.

41. OMRI, *Daily Digest*, 24 October 1996.

42. Irina Demchenko, Reuters, 20 August 1997.

43. OMRI, *Daily Digest*, 47, (7 March 1997); and RFE/RL, *Newsline*, 5 March 1997.

44. IEWS, *Russian Regional Report*, 2(10), 13 March 1997.

45. IEWS, *Russian Regional Report*, 2(20), 17 July 1997.

46. OMRI, *Daily Digest*, 14 November 1996.

47. IEWS, *Russian Regional Report*, 2(22), 19 June 1997.

48. IEWS, *Russian Regional Report*, 2(9), 6 March 1997; and IEWS, *Russian Regional Report,* 2(10), 13 March 1997.

49. RFE/RL, *Newsline*, 55, 21 May 1997.

50. IEWS, *Russian Regional Report*, 2(18), 22 May 1997.

51. RIA, *Novosti*, 28 June 1997.

52. Elazar, 1987, p. 12 (italics in the original).

PART II

Center-Periphery Relations in the Former Soviet Union: Diverse Solutions

CHAPTER 9

STUDYING LOCAL POLITICS IN THE FORMER SOVIET UNION

Terry D. Clark

What is local politics? If politics is, in Harold Lasswell's definition, the process by which humans collectively decide who gets what, when, and how, local politics is the occurrence of these distributive functions at the level closest to the individual: generally the city, town, or village. Local politics is distinguished from central (or national) government, which occurs at the nation-state level. The central government is the set of institutions that comprise the state and lie at the heart of national politics. The synonymous set of institutions at the local level is the local government. In all federal systems and most unitary political systems, there are intermediate levels of government between the national (center) and local (periphery). In Russia, a federation, the intermediate level of government comprises the 89 regions and republics of the federation; in Lithuania, a unitary state, the intermediate level of government consists of the 10 *apskritis* whose governors are appointed by the central government and which act as extensions of the central government.

Scholars of local politics have chosen to study their subject in either of two ways: in isolation or as a constituent part of the total political system. Those adopting the former approach largely ignore national and intermediate levels of governance, focusing on local or urban politics. Their analyses generally assume some non-trivial degree of autonomy at this level, autonomy understood as freedom from central government restraints. In contrast, scholars taking the systemic approach focus on the total system of center-periphery relations and place the question of local autonomy at the very center of their research.

Both approaches to the study of local politics are driven by a normative bias that local government is necessary and good for democracy.[1] Democratically elected office holders at the local level are closer and more responsive to their constituents than are politicians in the central government. The greater saliency in the lives of the average citizen of the issues with which local government deals generates greater public participation, enhances pluralism in the democratic process, and holds local politicians more accountable. Further, local governments contribute to the legitimacy of the modern democratic state by improving the efficiency with which it is able to deliver services and collect taxes, both of which are accomplished at the local level.[2] While the claim is not uncontested,[3] it is frequently argued that the decreased load on the center together with supposed greater innovation and initiative at the local level results in cost savings as well. Finally, stronger local government has been recommended as a means for resolving the threat of fragmentation of the state stemming from ethnic divisiveness.

STUDYING THE "LOCAL" IN ISOLATION

The central question for scholars studying local politics in isolation from the rest of the political system is who benefits from the distribution of political services at the local level. Two distinct traditions have been employed in answering the question: institutionalism and behavioralism. Institutionalists have looked for the answer in the design of political rules that constrain distributional outcomes in such a way as to benefit one or more specific group against others.[4] The unequal impact of non-partisan elections, at-large versus district elections, and mayoral versus city manager systems has been most frequently subjected to analysis. The general consensus is that non-partisan elections and at-large elections reduce participation in favor of more affluent voters and result in underrepresentation for the poor and minorities.

In contrast, behavioralists find the cause of unequal distribution of political goods in the political resources available to different social groups. Beginning with Floyd Hunter, elite theorists have long argued that a privileged class dominates all politics. By virtue of their ownership of economic, social, cultural, and informational resources members of this class are able to control questions of extraction, allocation, and distribution of resources at the local level.[5] Logan and Molotch have offered a more sophisticated version of elite theory. They argue that local politics is dominated by a coalition, the core of which comprises those who own commercial property. Possessing a non-mobile asset, these renters must increase local land values in order to increase their potential profits. If land values increase, they are able to charge more for the use of their assets. Closely allied with them are other groups which will profit from increasing land values as well: bankers, construction companies, real estate firms, newspapers, universities, and politicians who benefit from higher tax revenues. Together they comprise a "growth machine." To increase land values, the "growth machine" diverts local resources to entice businesses to locate in the locality, creating a demand for commercial property. While politicians representing the poor, minorities, and other groups disadvantaged by these policies may be elected to office, they are likely to be dissuaded from redirecting the flow of local resources away from economic development programs by the realization that such efforts could reduce the tax revenues available to them and their constituencies. Should they nonetheless attempt to do so, the "growth machine" is able to muster the economic, political, social, and informational resources necessary to it to throw the offending party out of office in subsequent elections.[6]

While elite theorists have tended to focus largely on economic resources as the basis for political dominance by a privileged group at the local level, principal-agent analysis has argued that the focus should be on the control of political resources exercised by professional civil servants in the city administration. While politicians working with any number of citizen groups may enact policies and programs, they are dependent on the trained local professionals to execute them. Possessing the technical expertise to do so and having at its command more information about the policy arena, the professional class in essence is able to exercise a significant degree of discretion in distributing goods and services. Public choice theorists take the argument a step further, contending that the trained local professionals will exercise this discretion in the interests of themselves and their constituencies.[7]

Many scholars contend that elite theory and public choice theory are overly class based. More importantly, they are essentially non-democratic, denying voice to women, minorities, and the poor. They argue instead that citizen groups, not a privileged few, exercise ultimate control over local political questions surrounding distribution of goods and services. In essence, they focus their analysis on the existence of a vibrant civil society at the local level.

Among the earliest of these approaches was pluralism, first expounded by Robert Dahl. Dahl argued that local policy decisions are the result of competition between coalitions of citizen groups. Such citizen groups are comprised of overlapping membership and have access to a relatively evenly distributed set of political resources. The victorious coalition on any issue is that which can muster the largest number of citizen groups with the greatest resources. Because membership is overlapping and coalitions change from issue to issue, all citizens are assured of victory on at least some of their political positions.[8]

In the 1970s and 1980s, scholars noted a qualitatively new form of citizen political activity at the local level. The global economic crisis of the era resulted in privatization of public services and a general retreat from a commitment to the welfare state. Organizing at the grassroots level in response, citizens challenged control of public goods and services being transferred into private hands by these policies. The organizations spawned by such community mobilization became known as urban social movements. Scholars studying the phenomenon contended that urban social movements constituted a citizen effort to halt erosion in democratic control over community decisions.[9] Among the most noted of these scholars, Manuel Castells argued that political change at the local level emerges from the clash between urban social movements and vested interests intent on maintaining government policies which create an uneven distribution of power and resources. Absent such community mobilization, non-majoritarian rule by elites would be the norm.[10]

Scholars of urban social movements agree that they are movements uniting citizens across classes on any number of dimensions. Some are formed to fight declining public services and the gradual disinvestment of neighborhoods. Their targets have ranged from schools and garbage collection to bank loan policies and discrimination in the insurance industry.[11] Other urban social movements are defined by a common struggle for culture and social identity. Many of these groups are based on gender relationships, ethnic and national identities, and sexuality. The politics of culture and the identity politics in which they engage is generally focused on challenging the prevailing status quo.[12] It would be a mistake, however, to conclude that all urban social movements are leftist in their politics. Indeed, many right-wing groups, to include those of the religious right, have engaged in political activity at the grassroots level as well. What distinguishes them is that they tend to support the deconstruction of the welfare state. These efforts threaten to delegitimize the state, the target of most left-wing community mobilization.[13]

The Systemic View

The problem with approaches focusing solely on local government is that they ignore the very real effect that other levels of governance as well as the "system" itself have on local politics. Indeed, given the constraints placed on local governments by these "exogenous" variables, some question whether local governments are in any meaningful way autonomous. Gurr and King have identified two types of constraints on local government. The first are those imposed by *local* economic and social factors such as the tax base or the structure of the business community. More recently scholarship has moved away from a focus on *local* economic constraints and recognized the growing reality of the global market. The second comprise constitutional and legal limitations imposed by the central government.[14]

Much of the system-level literature maintains that local politicians are highly constrained by the global economy. Marxists of course have long contended that such is the case. Because governments are dependent on capitalists for taxes, business occupies a privileged position. From this position they are able to control the politics of the central government. Local government is only an extension of capitalist control at the center or at best an arena for lesser social groups and classes to have some share in the wealth being generated. In essence, democratic politics is the handmaiden of capitalist accumulation. More recently, regulation theorists have argued that capitalism has managed to survive by creating a system assuring capital accumulation and uniting the global economy, the state, and local politics.

The trend toward privatization and "shrinking" government budgets in response to the international economic crises of the 1970s and 1980s has led many non-Marxist scholars to conclude that the global economy severely constrains local government as well.[15] In what remains one of the most succinct explications of the problem, Paul Peterson[16] argues that capital is largely mobile in the global economy. As a consequence, local governments must place their highest priority on economic development, which means in essence diverting resources to infrastructure development and reducing taxes on businesses. Cities which fail to engage in the "bidding war" to entice business will lose jobs and tax revenues. This single-minded pursuit of economic development undermines democratic accountability and responsiveness at the local level. Further, it constitutes an assault on the majoritarian principle. Despite citizen demands, resources available for quality of life and welfare policies are greatly limited by the need to divert them to goods and services demanded by the business minority.

Others, however, argue that local politics is not as marginal as Peterson's dictum of a single local interest in economic development would indicate. They note the existence of a dual base of power at the local level. While economic power is in the hands of private business interests, elected officials hold political power. Distinct from each other, neither is independent of the other. Business is subject to local policy, but policy may result in the relocation of jobs. Hence, the two are joined in a symbiotic relationship.[17] Further, business communities comprise competing interests. This competition permits political officer holders to engage in bargaining that gives them greater room to meet the demands of their constituencies than might otherwise be expected. Hence, urban political office holders have a far broader range of choices than Peterson allowed.[18]

The term "urban regime" has been coined to describe these broad coalitions uniting business and political interests. Political office seekers are drawn to the coalition by the need to maintain political power and the desire to generate economic growth. Business interests are attracted by the need to have access to those who make public policy and the desire to generate profits. United informally at best and divided on a great number of issues, the interests of each are counterbalanced by the demands of coalition building.[19]

If the literature on global economic constraints focuses on challenges to local autonomy created by systemic characteristics, the literature on the restrictions imposed by central governments (Gurr and King's second category of constraints) most clearly draws our attention to the relations between the national government and local government, or center-periphery links. Such constraints may be constitutional or legislative restrictions, or they may result from the acts of the government in interpreting and implementing policy. Among the more important concepts here is the distinction between decentralization and deconcentration. Decentralization occurs when local governments have both resources and the authority to use those resources.

Deconcentration indicates that resources are devolved to the localities from the center but their use is still under central direction.[20] The normative preference in the literature is for decentralization.

Decentralization is not synonymous with federalism, nor do local governments in federal systems necessarily have greater autonomy than those in unitary systems. It is frequently noted that U.S. cities possess a very limited degree of autonomy. In fact, the differences between federal and unitary government are not so great as commonly thought. As B.C. Smith notes, the only major difference relating to national-local links is that in federalism the structure of these relations cannot be changed without adhering to a constitutional procedure involving the local governments in the decision. In unitary systems, changes can be made by a simple legislative act or government policy.[21]

Local governments possess varying degrees of autonomy. A challenge for scholars has been how to measure these differences cross-nationally. It is clearly not enough to simply look at formally delegated functions. While this might give us some idea of the range of services performed at the local level, it tells us nothing about the ability of local government to decide how those services are delivered. To correct for this problem, Page and Goldsmith suggest that we consider two additional factors: discretion and access. They understand discretion as the "ability to influence the way in which functions are carried out" (how to deliver services) and access as "the nature and level of contact between the center and local government actors" (can local government influence central actors).[22] However, discretion and access collectively fail to capture still another aspect of autonomy: the ability to initiate new programs and services. Gordon L. Clark identifies initiative as one of two factors necessary for comparing local government autonomy. His second factor, immunity, "functional freedom from oversight of higher levels," effectively captures Page and Goldsmith's criteria of discretion and access.[23]

What Works?

Besides measuring local government autonomy, scholars have also been interested in determining the necessary conditions for increasing local government autonomy. This is all the more important given the numerous cases in which decentralization has notably failed.[24] What conditions permit local government to obtain a non-trivial degree of autonomy? Finances are most often cited in the literature. In particular, it is thought to be critical that local governments possess an independent power to collect revenues. Lacking such a financial base, local governments are virtually prohibited from exercising any discretion in initiating or shaping local programs and policies. An independent revenue source is all the more critical if central bureaucrats are opposed to decentralization. Such is likely to be the case given that their own power will be diluted by the introduction of local administration with the authority to act independently of the center.[25] Central bureaucrats can use the dependence of local governments on central government grants to shape local programs.

Indeed, they can go so far as to dictate how monies allocated in the central grants are to be used, thereby leaving local governments with little to no room for discretion.

More recent scholarship has recognized however that local government dependence on central grants is not enough to assure central control. Simply stated, an independent revenue source is not in and of itself sufficient to deny autonomy to local government. No matter how much financial control the center has, it is nonetheless dependent on the local level. The very fact that local politicians and administrators are the ones who execute central programs gives them an informal grant of discretion. There is simply no means available to the central government to guard against the infusion of local priorities into these programs. This is all the more the case the further removed the locality is from the center geographically and the degree to which the local government exercises control over the actual expenditure of funds. Just as important is the fact that the central government is dependent on local government for information. Control over the information that the center must act on gives local officials extraordinary power to shape policies and programs at their level.[26]

If the power to independently collect revenues is not sufficient by itself to establish local autonomy, what other factors are necessary? The literature points to two other elements: a trained professional administration at the local level and a viable local political process. In the absence of a trained professional administration, local governments will lack the technical expertise to plan and execute policy initiatives. Further, a competent professional core of administrators can assist locally elected politicians in lobbying and exerting pressure on central ministries to support local initiatives. Given their expertise, direct familiarity with local conditions, and control of information, they are able to frame the terms of debate in ways that are beyond the capacity of central administrators.[27] There is a risk in this, however. A trained professional administration may also become part of a national association that creates a unified, professional interest. Working at all levels of governance they can undermine policies and programs legislated or decreed by democratically elected officials and supported by a majority of citizens.[28]

Just as important for securing the autonomy of local government and assuring the success of decentralization is the existence of a local political process. Wunsch understands this as essentially the existence of a local politics. By this he means the presence of political actors with local policy choices that they are able to convey to citizens and the existence of an active civil society capable of mobilizing the public and holding elected officials accountable.[29] Local politicians with active policy agendas are crucial to the existence of a local politics. Equally important are local political parties strong enough to help them to convey political information to citizens. If these parties have ties with national parties they will further assist in giving local politicians access to those at the center. However, there is a risk that too-strong ties could develop between national and local party organizations that would subordinate local party organizations to national policy goals.[30]

An active civil society at the local level also greatly assists in the attainment and maintenance of local autonomy from the central government. Organizations uniting citizens at the grassroots level are able to support and sustain local initiatives against the opposition of the central government. Further, by holding politicians accountable, they serve as a buttress against the attempts of the center to co-opt local politicians and administrators.

Approaches focusing on the local level of government are concerned primarily with the equitable distribution of goods and services. The systemic approaches ask whether local government is even relevant in the determination of such outcomes. The economistic theories largely argue that it is not. Global economic realities severely constrain choices available to local government, forcing them to engage in a single-minded drive for economic development. Students of state-imposed limits on local government leave room for a substantial measure of local autonomy in determining distributional outcomes. However, the degree to which local governments can act independently of the center is dependent on any number of factors, to include the existence of a vibrant local political process, a trained professional administration, and control of budgetary resources. The remaining chapters in this part of the book will consider these and other issues in the non-Russian successor states of the Soviet Union.

NOTES

1. For the argument in favor of stronger local government in post-Communist Europe, see Robert J. Bennett, ed., *Local Government and Market Decentralization: Experiences in Industrialized, Developing, and Former Eastern Bloc Countries* (New York: United Nations University Press, 1994). For the same argument in the developing world, see James S. Wunsch and Dele Olowu, *The Failure of the Centralized State: Institutions and Self-Government in Africa* (San Francisco: Institute for Contemporary Studies, 1995).

2. B.C. Smith, *Decentralization: The Territorial Dimension of the State* (London: George Allen and Unwin Ltd., 1985).

3. For the argument that the introduction of strong local governments increases overall public expenditures, see Hal Wolman and Sharon McCormick, "The Effect of Decentralization on Local Governments," in Robert J. Bennett, ed., *Local Government and Market Decentralization: Experiences in Industrialized, Developing, and Former Eastern Bloc Countries* (New York: United Nations University Press, 1994).

4. For reviews of the literature on the impact of institutions see S. Welch and T. Bledsoe, *Urban Reform and Its Consequences* (Chicago: University of Chicago Press, 1988); J. Svara, *Official Leadership in the City* (Oxford: Oxford University Press, 1990).

5. Floyd Hunter, *Community Power Structure: A Study of Decision Makers* (Chapel Hill: University of North Carolina Press, 1953).

6. John R. Logan and Harvey L. Molotch, *Urban Fortunes: The Political Economy of Place* (Berkeley: University of California Press, 1987).

7. W.A. Niskanen, *Bureaucracy and Representative Government* (Chicago: Aldine Atherton, 1971).

8. Robert Dahl, *Who Governs? Democracy and Power in an American City* (New Haven: Yale University Press, 1961).

9. Harry C. Boyte, *The Backyard Revolution: Understanding the New Citizen Movement* (Philadelphia: Temple University Press, 1980).

10. Manuel Castells, *The City and the Grassroots: A Cross-Cultural Theory of Urban Social Movements* (Berkeley: University of California Press, 1983); Manuel Castells, *The Urban Question* (London: Edward Arnold Ltd., 1977).

11. Gregory D. Squires, ed., *From Redlining to Reinvestment: Community Responses to Urban Disinvestment* (Philadelphia: Temple University Press, 1992).

12. Marcy Darnovsky, Barbara Epstein, and Richard Flacks, eds., *Cultural Politics and Social Movements* (Philadelphia: Temple University Press, 1995).

13. Robert Fisher and Joseph Kling, eds., *Mobilizing the Community: Local Politics in the Era of the Global City,* Urban Affairs Annual Review 41 (London: Sage, 1993).

14. T. Gurr and T. King, *The State and the City* (Chicago: University of Chicago Press, 1987).

15. Chris Pickvance and Edmond Preteceille, *State Restructuring and Local Power* (London: Pinter Publishers Ltd., 1991).

16. Paul Peterson, *City Limits* (Chicago: University of Chicago Press, 1981).

17. S. L. Elkins, "State and Market in City Politics: Or, the Real Dallas," in Clarence Stone and H.T. Sanders, eds., *The Politics of Urban Development* (Lawrence, Kansas: University of Kansas Press, 1987); Todd Swanstron, *The Crisis of Growth Politics: Cleveland, Kucinich, and the Challenge of Urban Politics* (Philadelphia: Temple University Press, 1985).

18. Clarence Stone, *Regime Politics: Governing Atlanta, 1946–1988* (Lawrence: University of Kansas Press, 1989).

19. Ibid.

20. James Fesler, *Area and Administration* (Birmingham: University of Alabama Press, 1949).

21. B.C. Smith, *Decentralization: The Territorial Dimension of the State* (London: George Allen and Unwin Ltd., 1985).

22. Edward C. Page and Michael J. Goldsmith, "Centre and Locality Functions, Access and Discretion," in Edward C. Page and Michael J. Goldsmith, eds., *Central and Local Government Relations: A Comparative Analysis of West European Unitary States,* pp. 1–11 (London: Sage Publications Ltd., 1987).

23. Gordon L. Clark, "A Theory of Local Autonomy," *Annals of the Association of American Geographers* 74, no. 2 (1984): 195–208.

24. See for example Joseph R.A. Ayee, "The Measurement of Decentralization: The Ghanaian Experience, 1988–1992," *African Affairs* 95 (1996): 31–50; James S. Wunsch and Dele Olowu, *The Failure of the Centralized State: Institutions and Self-Government in Africa* (San Francisco: Institute for Contemporary Studies, 1995); Richard C. Crook, "Four Years of the Ghana District Assemblies in Operation: Decentralization, Democratization and Administrative Performance," *Public Administration and Development* 14 (1994): 339–364.

25. Joseph R.A. Ayee, "The Adjustment of Central Bodies to Decentralization: The Case of the Ghanaian Bureaucracy," *African Studies Review* 40 (September 1997): 37–57.

26. R.A.W. Rhodes, *Control and Power in Central-Local Government Relations* (Westmead, England: Gower Publishing Company Ltd., 1981); J.D. Stewart, "Grant Characteristics and Central-Local Relations," in George Jones, ed., *New Approaches to the Study of Central-Local Government Relationships*, pp. 10–17 (Westmead, England: Gower Publishing Company Ltd., 1980).

27. Ibid.

28. Rhodes, *Control and Power in Central-Local Government Relations.*

29. James S. Wunsch, "Decentralization, Local Governance and the Democratic Transition in Southern Africa: A Comparative Analysis," paper presented at the African Studies Association annual meeting in San Francisco, California, 23 November 1997 (revised 22 November 1997).

30. John Gyford, "Political Parties and Central-Local Relations," in George Jones, ed., *New Approaches to the Study of Central-Local Government Relationships*, pp. 28–39 (Westmead, England: Gower Publishing Company Ltd, 1980).

Chapter 10

Regionalism in Post-Soviet Ukraine

Paul Kubicek

In addition to constructing democratic institutions, implementing economic reforms, and securing their state's independence, Ukrainians in the post-Soviet period have faced yet another challenge: creating a civic, unified nation out of a country with a very uneven and incoherent identity (Kuzio, 1998a, p. 165). Ukraine, as a new state, has few myths, symbols, and traditions upon which to draw, and within its current borders exist diverse peoples with different cultural, historical, and ethnic backgrounds with differing expectations and priorities. Given the state of development of Ukrainian society, particularly the acute and seemingly never-ending economic crisis, drawing all these strands together will be a very difficult task. While there certainly is Ukrainian nationalism, it remains a "minority faith" (Wilson, 1997), and it is highly uncertain if there is a Ukrainian national identity or idea that is generally embraced as the primary focus of loyalty or political orientation. Instead, many continue to identify with the Soviet Union or *sovetskii narod* and/or identify themselves based on the region in which they live (Miller et al., 1998; Pirie, 1996; Democratic Initiatives, 1995). Looking at the barriers to national integration in Ukraine, one finds that region, ethnicity, and language (related but far from identical factors) play an important role in creating fundamental divisions in the country (Solchanyk, 1994; Arel, 1995; Holdar, 1995; Subtelny, 1995; Khmelko & Arel, 1996; Pirie, 1996; Barrington, 1997; Hesli et al., 1998; Kuzio, 1998a, 1998b; Khmelko & Wilson, 1998; Liber, 1998; Riabchouk, 1998).

This chapter will focus on regionalism and center-regional relations in Ukraine. It will examine how region manifests itself as a political cleavage in terms of party development, voting behavior, and public opinion. It will highlight those issues on which region matters most, as opposed to others where there is a cross-regional consensus. It will also highlight the most serious center-regional dispute, which was over the status of Crimea. In conclusion, it will suggest that while regionalism is a very important in Ukrainian politics, it need not mean that Ukraine is doomed to witness centrifugal forces that have torn apart other post-communist countries.

REGIONS IN UKRAINE

While some divide Ukraine in two along the Dniepr River into western and eastern regions, Ukrainians frequently claim that there are three, four, or five "Ukraines." Borrowing from Agnew, who defined region as a construction created by differing cultural norms, inter-ethnic competition, history and collective memories, and economic development patterns, one could identify five distinct regions of Ukraine: west, central, east, south, and Crimea. These are highlighted in Figure 10.1 and data about each of these areas, along with select *oblasti* (provinces), are presented in Table 10.1.[1]

Table 10.1
Regional Differences in Ukraine

Region/ *Oblastr*	% total pop., 1996	% urban, 1996	% ethnic Russians, 1989	% agri. total output, 1989	% total industrial output, 1989	Index of industrial production, 1996 (1990=100)	Real GDP per capita, in $, 1995
West	22.1	49.8	5	22.0	16.5	41	2,087
Lrvivsrka	5.4	60.9	7	3.9	5.1	31	1,856
Ternopilsrka	2.3	43.7	2	3.3	1.5	48	2,135
Ivano-Frankivsrka	2.9	43.3	4	2.1	2.2	49	2,177
Central	26.7	64.4	10	34.1	23.9	49	2,730
East	35.7	82.7	34	26.4	48.2	45	3,157
Donetsrka	10.1	90.3	44	4.9	13.7	46	3,659
Luhansrka	5.4	86.4	45	3.3	7.4	34	2,829
South	10.1	65.2	24	12.8	8.3	63	2,426
Crimea	5.1	70.5	67	4.7	3.1	46	1,950
Total	100.0	67.8	22	100.0	100.0	50	2,620

Sources: Ukraine in Figures, 1996 (1997); Harris, 1993; Dolishnii, 1992; United Nations 1997.

Figure 10.1
Ukraine and Its Regions

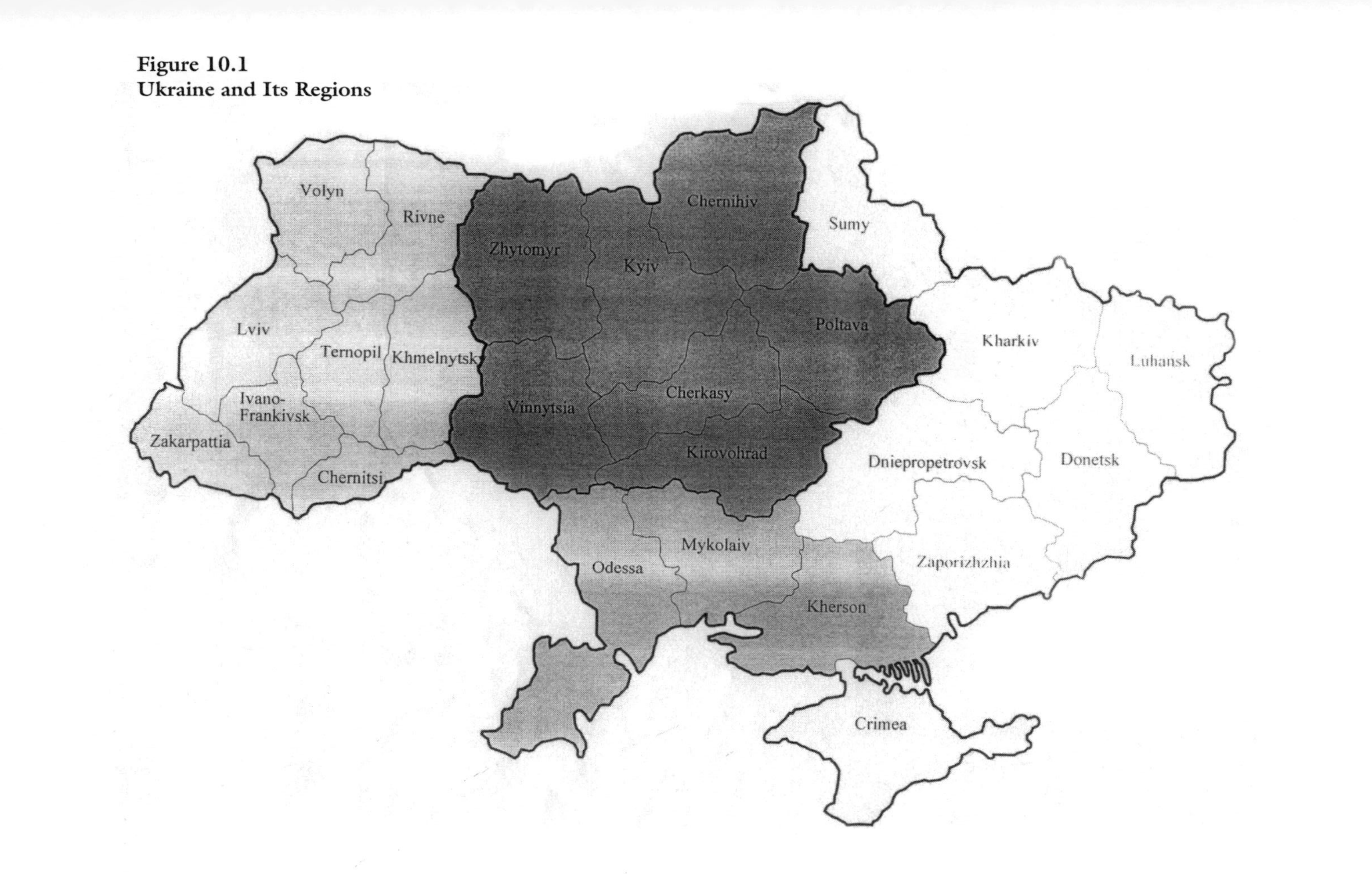

The eastern region is the most heavily industrialized and urbanized area of the country. Next to Crimea, it also has the highest percentage of ethnic Russians, particularly in the *oblasti* of Donetsk and Luhansk (the Donbas), and Russian is the primary language spoken in large cities. This region was integrated into the Russian Empire centuries ago, and Russian immigrants flocked here during its industrialization in the late Tsarist/early Soviet period. It maintains extensive cross-border links with Russia, and maintaining ties with Russia as well as protecting the rights of Russians and Russian speakers have been top priorities of people here. Its historical experience and economic structure differ markedly with that further to the west. These *oblasti* also have a number of large, aging, smokestack industries and mining operations, enterprises which account for the region's higher than average GDP/capita but are not likely to be profitable without maintenance of state subsidies. From the table above one sees that it has been hit harder than average by drop-off in industrial production. For this reason, eastern Ukrainians are typically more cautious on movement to the market and favor preserving much of the Soviet-era support system.

The Western area of the country has a completely different history, ethnic composition, and economic structure. Most of this region of Ukraine was incorporated into the USSR only in 1939, meaning it escaped the worst of Stalinist repression. Previously, it had been part of the Austro-Hungarian Empire and then divided between Poland, Romania, Hungary, and Czechoslovakia. Many of its residents harbor memories of pre-Soviet rule and affiliate with the Uniate (Greek Catholic) Church, and some fought against Soviet occupation into the early 1950s. Anti-Russian feelings run deep here, Sovietization was relatively mild, and few Russians live in the region. Ukrainian nationalist feelings are very strong, especially in the *oblasti* of Galicia, Lviv, Ivano-Frankivsk, and Ternopil. This region is often dubbed the "Piedmont" of Ukraine, and many of the leading figures in the Ukrainian nationalist movement come from this area. Economically, agriculture and light industry predominate, as the region largely escaped Soviet-style industrialization. Due to geographic proximity and historical ties, many here see their region as part of Central Europe and view Western countries, not Russia, as the most likely and promising economic partner.

The large central area is overwhelmingly ethnically Ukrainian and largely Ukrainian-speaking, although in the city of Kyiv Russian is the more frequently heard language. In general it lacks traditions of Ukrainian nationalism as found in the west, due in large part to the repression under the Tsars and Stalin which crushed any incipient formation of Ukrainian national identity. Since independence, it has followed a relatively moderate political course, receptive to some of Westerners' call for national rebirth but also to the leftist reaction emanating from the east. Its economy is mixed between industry (largely in Kyiv) and agriculture, and it has generally fared better than the eastern region since 1990.

The southern region falls in-between the central and eastern regions in terms of ethnic composition and economic structure. There is a sizeable Russian minority, again particularly in the cities. There was for a time a "Novorossiya" pseudo-separatist movement centered in Odessa, but it failed to attract public support. Ukrainian-national consciousness has been low in this region, and because of its port cities it has more of a cosmopolitan flare than other regions of the country. The region is also more urbanized than average and contains some large enterprises like those in the east, although the overall presence of industry is less. Issues of economic autonomy have been high on regional elites' agendas, although in general the area is the most politically quiescent in the country. Overall, one finds the region a bit less "extreme" than the east in pushing for special political status and ties with Russia.

Crimea deserves a category all to itself. Unlike all other regions of Ukraine, it has an ethnic Russian majority, most of who moved to the region after 1945. Moreover, given the fact that it was transferred to the Ukrainian Soviet Socialist Republic from formally Russian jurisdiction only in 1954 by a whim of Khrushchev to celebrate three centuries of Russian-Ukrainian friendship, it is hardly surprising that residents of Crimea continue to identify strongly with Russia or the Soviet Union.[2] Broken economic ties with other post-Soviet states have hurt the economy, which had a specialized agricultural industry and a sizeable tourist industry with an all-Union constituency. From the perspective of Kyiv, there have been numerous problems in this region: a separatist movement emerged; Russian politicians have claimed Crimea as a part of Russia; local politicians have pushed hard for more autonomy and/or union with Russia; and controversy has arisen over the relocation of exiled Crimean Tatars. These developments have made Crimea the most restive of all the regions and will be examined more fully.

Due to the variety of historical, cultural, and economic differences mentioned above, there is a distinct regional factor in Ukrainian politics, even when other variables, such as ethnicity, are controlled. West and east, as one might expect, are the most polarized, and many in Crimea have their own distinct set of concerns. The remainder of this chapter will examine some manifestations of regionalism in Ukrainian political life.

REGIONAL VARIANCE IN PUBLIC OPINION

Given the cultural, historical, and economic differences across regions in Ukraine, one would expect substantial variance in public opinion and/or broader questions of political culture. Indeed, this is the case, but it bears emphasis that there is more consensus on some basic issues than on others. Survey evidence suggests that there is little cross-regional variation on the value of political and civil rights, beliefs that the Mafia or big business have the real authority in the country, or the fact that people are not pleased with the state of the economy and have seen their living standards plummet (Hesli et al., 1998).

Residents of Donetsk and Lviv, commonly juxtaposed as the extremes in Ukraine, place relatively the same priority on the need to provide material well-being to the population, build effective legislative, executive, and judicial authority, defend civic peace and order, and guarantee a multi-party system and freedom of speech (Nebozhenko, 1997).

The main issues that separate citizens in various regions are foreign policy concerns, issues of language and culture, economic prescriptions, and relative satisfaction with democratic performance and the overall direction of the country, the last of which what might be dubbed a "satisfaction/alienation" score. Data from a May 1994 survey of 1807 Ukrainians conducted by the Democratic Initiatives Center in Kyiv that cover some of these dimensions are presented in Table 10.2 (Golovakha & Panina, 1995).[3] They reveal quite clearly a sharp division of the "West versus the rest" on foreign policy, and less acute but still discernible divisions on economic preferences. Not surprisingly, given the salience of these two cleavages in Ukrainian politics, one also sees great differences in political party preferences across regions. Data on language/cultural issues are not included in this survey, but others report, for example, that those in Lviv *oblast* are far more likely (31%) than residents of Donetsk (7.4%) or nation-wide (17.1%) to put priority on the renaissance of the Ukrainian nation (Nebozhenko, 1997).

One fundamental question is whether regionalism in Ukraine is a constant or is growing more or less acute over time. Certainly, one could argue either that living in the same polity should produce some convergence in public opinion, or that the severe socio-economic crisis or actions of political entrepreneurs who play upon regional differences could widen existing divisions. In

Table 10.2
Public Opinion, by Region, on Various Questions, 1994

Question	Kyiv	West	Central	East	South	Crimea	Total
% preferring broader ties with CIS and/or Russia	44.5	28.6	64.0	67.4	62.3	72.3	58.2
% preferring broader ties with Western countries	16.7	29.0	11.8	8.8	10.1	2.2	13.4
% believing complete transition to a market economy is necessary	43.3	30.9	25.7	25.3	35.2	22.7	29.7
% approving of development of private business	52.2	55.4	36.2	38.5	54.7	55.5	44.0
% supporting advocates of capitalism	24.4	1.8	6.5	12.3	10.8	5.6	12.7
% supporting socialists	11.1	7.8	21.1	31.6	21.0	18.9	22.1

Source: Democratic Initiatives Center, 1995. N = 1807.

order to address changes in public opinion over time, we need to use surveys that have been replicated several times. Perhaps the best source would be the Eastern Eurobarometer surveys, conducted annually under the aegis of the European Commission. These surveys ask four questions in their standard battery that are of interest to us: foreign policy orientation (with which country/countries do you see the future of your state tied?), satisfaction with democracy and the overall direction of the country, and support for a free market system. Data from the 1992–1996 surveys, broken down by region, are presented in Table 10.3.

From Table 10.3 one sees that regionalism is most acute on foreign policy orientation, that there is some variance (sometimes marked) for the evaluative questions, and that there is much less difference on free market orientation. This underlies the fact that the strongest aspect of regionalism (due to geographic, ethnic, and economic factors) is orientation to Russia. However, from a Ukrainian state or nation-builders perspective, it is disturbing that the most dissatisfied or perhaps even "alienated" citizens are in eastern and southern regions. Voters in these regions are more likely to vote for the anti-system communists, in addition to expressing little pride or association with symbols of the Ukrainian state (Miller et al., 1998). Consistent with these findings, the Donetsk-Lviv comparative survey reveals that residents of Donetsk are far more likely to believe that people cannot influence authorities, that it makes no sense to participate in politics, and that most politicians only think about their own interests (Nebozhenko, 1997). While these areas (Crimea possibly excepted) are unlikely to support a Russian "fifth column" in Ukraine, these findings belie hopes that over time those in the east and south would begin to identify and support Ukrainian institutions. The change over time in Crimea is perhaps even more dramatic and disheartening. In 1992 Crimeans were even more satisfied than those in the west with the general direction of the country and were even modestly pro-Western in foreign policy orientation. However, by 1996 one finds that their level of dissatisfaction has increased, they are less pro-market, and they are decidedly more pro-Russia. This evidence refutes claims that the Crimean problem (discussed in more detail below) has been "solved." Of note as well is the fact that the marginal differences in free market orientation also help confirm that the main cleavages in Ukraine center around foreign policy/cultural issues and that regional and ethno-cultural identities, as opposed to class or occupational identities, are primary (Miller et al., 1998).

Do these results show that region, when other factors are controlled, does in fact matter? Table 10.4 presents results from a logistical regression analysis of the Eastern Eurobarometers from the "bookend" years of 1992 and 1996. Factors found to be important in other analyses of surveys—age, education, ethnicity, gender, and assessment of changes in income—have been included. The results are not that surprising. Region remains the primary factor explaining foreign policy orientation, even when ethnicity of respondent is controlled. With the exception of the southern regions, region is not very significant in

Table 10.3
Dynamics of Public Opinion 1992–1996

Region		Satisfied with direction of country (-2, 2 = dissat)	Satisfaction with democracy (4 = max dissat)	In favor of free market (1 to 2, 1 = for)	Future most tied up with U.S. or EU (by %)	Future most tied up with Russia (by %)
Mean	1992	1.64	3.09	1.53	32.4	37.4
	1993	1.86	3.31	1.62	33.6	45.0
	1994	1.82	3.26	1.61	21.5	49.2
	1995	1.82	3.31	1.70	25.5	59.1
	1996	1.77	3.17	1.68	28.3	51.5
West	1992	–.01	–.14**	.00	+14.8	–21.5
	1993	–.16**	–.24**	–.15**	+14.8	–29.8
	1994	–.07**	–.07	+.01	+4.3	–13.6
	1995	–.16	–.16**	–.05	+12.5	–31.6
	1996	–.14***	–.18**	–.03	+17.8	–30.0
Central	1992	–.01	–.05	–.03	+0.2	+1.8
	1993	+.01	+.08	+.03	+5.1	–5.6
	1994	+.05*	+.10*	–.02	–1.0	+2.0
	1995	–.03	+.04	–.04	+5.8	+5.3
	1996	–.06**	–.12**	–.08**	+4.1	–15.3
South	1992	–.06	+.30**	+.15**	–13.5	+4.5
	1993	.00	–.06	+.04	–2.5	+1.2
	1994	+.04	–.13	–.14*	–1.5	–1.2
	1995	+.08*	+.19*	+.09*	+1.2	+1.7
	1996	+.04	–.02	+.08	–10.8	+6.0
East	1992	+.05**	+.10**	.00	–9.4	+14.6
	1993	+.10**	+.13**	+.08**	–13.7	+22.2
	1994	.00	–.07	+.01	–7.9	+12.3
	1995	+.04**	+.03	+.03	–11.2	+13.2
	1996	+.10**	+.16**	+.01	–9.0	+14.9
Crimea	1992	–.21**	+.09	–.06	+2.9	–3.6
	1993	–.07	–.20	–.05	+4.4	+1.0
	1994	+.06	–.11	+.17*	–5.2	+20.2
	1995	+.16**	–.03	–.02	+3.8	+16.5
	1996	+.09	+.21*	+.20**	–12.2	+30.6

*significant at .05 level
**significant at .01 level

Table 10.4

Logistical Regression Estimates from Survey Years 1992 and 1996

Variable	GENDER		SATISDEMO		FREEMARK		PROWEST		PRORUSS	
	1992	1996	1992	1996	1992	1996	1992	1996	1992	1996
West	–.019***	.143	.206*	.179	–.055	–.152	.263***	.279**	–.572***	–.610***
East	–.133	–.472***	–.403***	–.334***	–.036	–.079	–.215**	–.306*	.273***	.344***
South	.161	–.154	–1.140***	–.110	–.423**	–.219	–.408*	–.328*	.065	.164
Crimea	.485***	–.318	–.201	–.093	.038	–.706***	.034	–.262	–.096	.639***
Household Finances	.480***	.598***	.397***	.491***	.438***	.388***	.123*	.156*	–.058	–.171**
Age	–.002	–.004	.000	–.015***	–.03***	–.017***	–.024***	–.017***	.012**	.017***
Education	.199*	.327**	.025	.012	.283**	.146	–.014	.146	.096	.137
Income	.001**	–.025	.001**	.001*	.005	.003	.000	.003	.000	.001
Urban	–.011	.114	–.164	.011	.184*	.170*	–.055	.076	.138*	–.174*
Male	.116	.198*	.116	.013	.154*	.089	.036	.049	.034	.079
Russian	–.259**	–.032	–.013	–.121	–.031	–.038	–.074	–.380***	.026	.381***
N	1400	1200	1400	1200	1400	1200	1400	1200	1400	1200
% Correctly Estimated	67.58	79.00	79.74	79.84	67.77	69.87	68.58	66.89	64.35	66.89

*p<.05
**p<.01
***p<.001

terms of free market orientation. It does, however, have a more pronounced effect on evaluative questions, and here one sees the dichotomy between the west and east more clearly than on free market orientation. However, as one might guess, the far most important explanatory factor for these questions is change in household income, which is also more negative on balance ($p < .05$) in the east than in the west. Also of note is that ethnicity does not have nearly as pronounced an effect as region.

This analysis suggests that region be taken seriously as one of the most important factors underlying many basic issues in Ukrainian politics. Wide divides on foreign policy/cultural issues are those that are most notable, but those in the east, south, and Crimea also have much more negative assessments of the performance of the Ukrainian state and economy. Evidence indicates that they feel less connected to the state and less supportive of state institutions (Barrington, 1997; Miller et al., 1998). This is clearly a problem in terms of building a unified national community among all Ukrainians. To the extent that regional divisions manifest themselves in politics, one might worry about the viability of the Ukrainian state.

Regional Voting Patterns

The clearest evidence of regional splits in Ukrainian political life comes from electoral data. The overall pattern has been relatively consistent: the eastern and southern *oblasti*, along with Crimea, are bastions of support for communist and other leftist parties, whereas national-democrats and radical nationalists draw almost all of their votes from the West and the city of Kyiv. No single tendency dominates in the central regions. Over time, neither the communists nor the nationalists have been able to make a dent in the other's constituency. This shows a rather hard polarization among voters in these regions, especially given the disparity in the two sides' positions.

Notably, there was a moment of relative consensus in December 1991, when Ukrainians voted in a referendum on national independence and chose the country's first president. Independence was supported in all regions of the country: over 98 percent in Galicia, over 90 percent in most of central Ukraine, over 80 percent in Russified *oblasti* such as Donetsk and Luhansk, and even by 54 percent in Crimea. This boded well, although arguably voters in different regions voted for independence for different reasons: those in the west for cultural/national rights and those in the east and south for potential economic benefits. In addition, among six candidates for the presidency, Leonid Kravchuk, the former head of the Ukrainian Communist Party's Ideology Department and speaker of the republican Supreme Soviet, received a majority of the vote in 21 of the 25 *oblasti* (the three of Galicia and Chernitsi being the exceptions). He promised stability and a moderately nationalist course that would promote a civic identity binding all to the state, which was more attractive to voters than the nationalist platforms of his leading rivals from the Rukh movement. And, to his credit, as president he tried to enact policies to balance the demands and interests of various regional constituencies.

However, few were satisfied in the first years of independence. The nationalists on the right felt that Ukraine should do more to safeguard its independence and to move faster with the "Ukrainization" of the state. Those on the left believed that the state should do more to protect declining living standards and develop close ties with Russia. Predictably, each was centered on a regional core: Galicia and the Donbas, respectively. Leftists directed their anger at the president, who began to wrap himself in the Ukrainian flag and made efforts to centralize executive power. Nationalists attacked the still communist-dominated parliament, which had been elected under Soviet law in 1990, and rallied behind the president (Kubicek, 1996). Rukh organized a signature campaign for the dissolution of parliament, which failed. Striking miners in the east, however, managed to secure concessions from Kravchuk in the fall of 1993, which led to new parliamentary and presidential elections in the spring of 1994.

As one might have predicted, these elections had a strong regional flavor. Due to complications with the electoral law,[4] in particular the implicit encouragement of "independent" candidates to the detriment of party-nominated candidates, calculating a precise party vote or party affiliation of victorious candidates for these elections is difficult. As one sees in Table 10.5, independent candidates won a majority of votes in all regions. Moreover, due to the fact that minimum turnout requirements of 50 percent were not met in several districts, repeat elections were held from 1994–1997, and some three dozen seats remained unfilled throughout the legislative session. The results[5] in Table 10.5, however, nonetheless reveal distinct regional patterns, with the east and west, in particular Galicia and the Donbas, at the two extremes. While some (Kuzio, 1998b) downplayed the role of region itself as a factor in the elections, there is little doubt that cleavages along cultural, economic, state-building, and foreign policy questions coalesced to produce marked regional variance.

In June and July of 1994, presidential elections were held. Seven candidates ran, but the contest boiled down to a showdown between Kravchuk and Leonid Kuchma, a former plant director who had served as prime minister from 1992–1993, was co-founder of the Inter-Regional Bloc of Reforms (based in eastern Ukraine), and was president of the leading industrial lobby. Kravchuk presented himself as a defender of Ukrainian statehood, but was largely silent on issues of economic reform. Kuchma, while clearly the favorite of the state sector, discussed the need for economic re-structuring as well as improving relations with Russia. Given the salience of the Russian question as well as Kuchma's connections to the industrial establishment of the east, it is not surprising that the results were defined by region. Kravchuk won in all but one "Right Bank" (of the Dniepr) *oblast*, garnering 95 percent of the vote in Galicia, and Kuchma won in the eastern and southern *oblasti*, winning almost 90 percent of the vote in Crimea and Luhansk. The results are displayed in Figure 10.2, and show clear movement away from Kravchuk and toward

Table 10.5
Results of 1994–1995 Parliamentary Votes by Region

Region/ *Oblast*	% vote for Com- munist/ Socialist parties	% vote for na- tional- demo- cratic parties	% vote for centrist parties	% vote for others	MPS from Com- munist bloc	MPS from na- tional- demo- cratic bloc	MPS from centrist bloc	Unaffil- iated MPS
West	7.3	23.8	1.5	67.4	8	62	9	14
Lrvivsrka	2.9	27.3	2,4	67.4	0	18	0	4
Ternopilsrka	1.0	43.4	0.1	55.5	0	6	0	7
Ivano-Frankivsrka	1.2	16.7	0.1	82.1	0	11	1	0
Central	19.6	11.3	2.9	66.2	26	33	16	25
East	34.0	4.2	4.7	57.2	80	9	55	14
Donetsrka	39.9	2.6	4.5	53.0	29	1	13	4
Luhansrka	43.4	1.7	3.6	51.3	18	1	5	1
South	26.5	5.7	4.3	63.5	23	5	4	8
Crimea	19.3	5.5	1.5	73.8	7	1	6	3
Total	22.3	11.2	3.3	63.2	143	110	90	64

Source: Central Election Commission Data.

Kuchma as one moves from west to east. These differences, it bears emphasis, are not an artifact of ethnic variance. Even assuming all Russians in Donetsk, Luhansk, and Crimea voted for Kuchma, a majority of ethnic Ukrainians voted the same way.

What explains these voting patterns? Three answers—language, foreign policy, and economics—seem relevant. The first is language policy. Kuchma, who took Ukrainian lessons in 1994, promised to protect the rights of Russian language speakers, which several analysts believe constitutes a near majority of all Ukrainians and an overwhelming majority of urban residents (Arel, 1995; Khmelko & Arel, 1996; Riabchouk, 1998). Kravchuk, more due to his support from the nationalist camp than due to his actual statements, was associated with an "Ukrainization" policy that many perceived as radical and threatening. Evidence suggests that language use of voters was a primary explanatory factor of the results, with Russian speakers voting for Kuchma, who himself needed tutoring in Ukrainian during the campaign (Khmelko & Wilson, 1998). Second, foreign policy divided both the candidates and the electorate. Policies of strengthening state sovereignty and movement away from Russia were popular in Western Ukraine, where those in the east, south, and Crimea blamed the loss of ties to Russia for the economic crisis and believed

Figure 10.2
Results of 1994 Presidential Elections

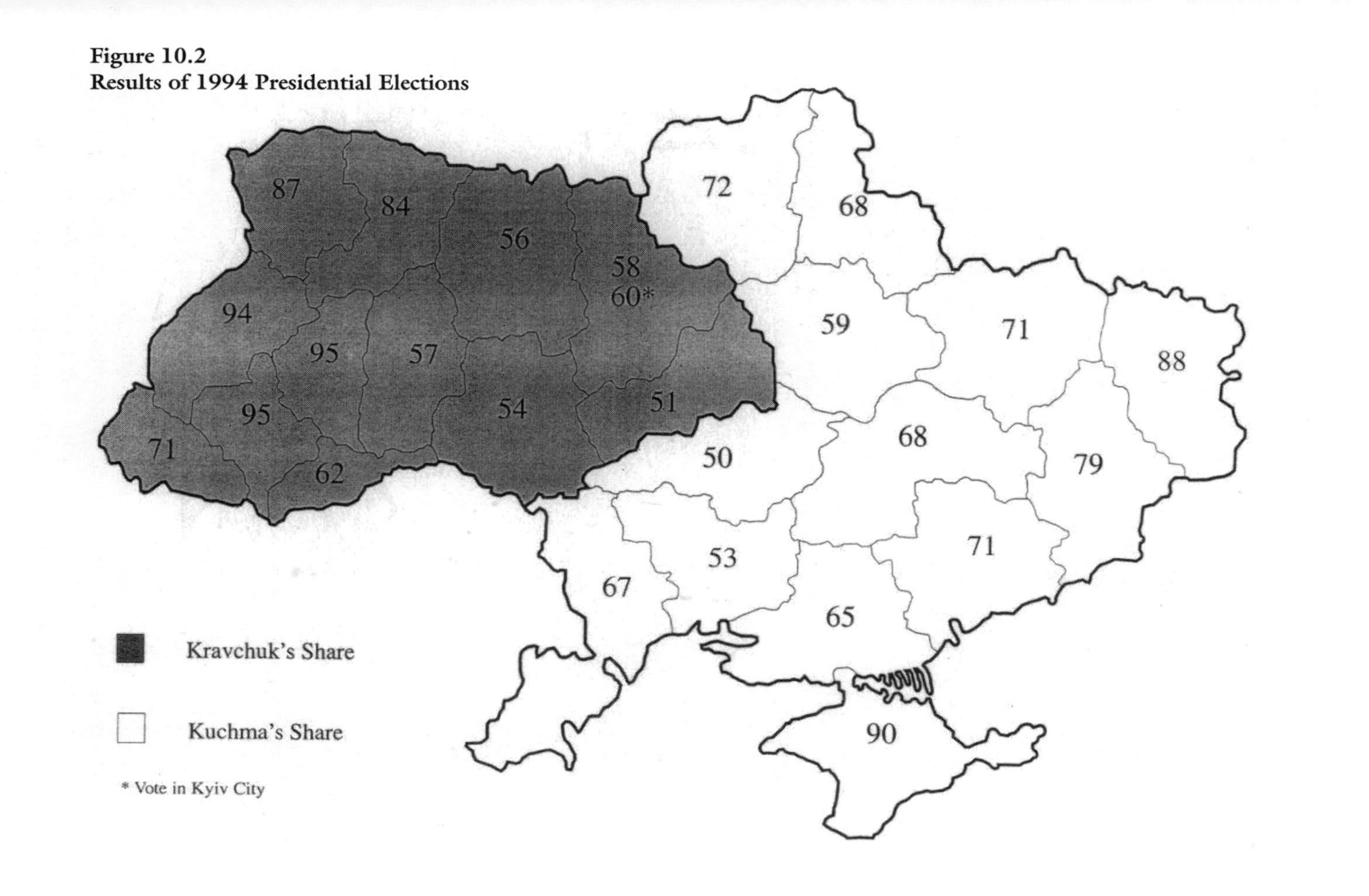

that sovereignty should not be pursued at the cost of losing potentially profitable ties to Russia and the CIS. The two main slogans of the candidates, "*derzhavnist*" (statehood) for Kravchuk and "Fewer Walls, More Bridges (to Russia)" for Kuchma summed up their positions. Finally, economics was paramount in the minds of most voters—surveys regularly reported that rising prices, losses in economic security, and declining living standards were their primary concerns. This, arguably, proved to be the downfall of Kravchuk, as he never was able to articulate and develop a clear economic program[6] and had to accept responsibility for the deep economic crisis in the country.[7] Kuchma, although he served an undistinguished year as Prime Minister in the midst of the crisis, could still claim, due his background as a factory director, to be a man who knew how to get things done. While there was perhaps less regional polarization on economic issues, Kuchma nonetheless crafted his populist appeals to business and labor in the more industrialized east and south together with some assertions that he would push through with economic reform. Kravchuk, whose silence on basic economic issues was deafening, could credibly promise little more than more of the same.

Kuchma, however, bucked the expectations of both his supporters and opponents. Rather than falling into Russia's lap and forgoing economic reform, he made efforts to mend fences with the west and announced a series of "radical" reform programs that would qualify Ukraine for IMF assistance. His programs, however, became watered down over time due to the necessity to make compromises with a "centrist" bloc dominated by state directors that held the balance of power in parliament (Kubicek, 2000). Moreover, politics in Ukraine became dominated by disputes between Kuchma and the *Verkhovna Rada* (parliament) on a new constitution and presidential powers as well as battles between Kuchma and his appointees as Prime Minister over executive power. These debates brought the work of the government to a standstill and furthered polarization in the country, as Kuchma (now supported by national-democrats) found backing in the west and his largely leftist opponents were based in the east and south. Eventually, Kuchma did prevail against his foes, winning approval of a largely presidential system in the constitution and sacking his Prime Ministers, but little was done to further development of a civic discourse or adopt policies that would improve living standards and give people confidence in the future.

Amid continuing crisis and growing public frustration with politics, new parliamentary elections were held in March 1998 under a new mixed majoritarian/party list law that mirrored Russia's in most respects except that the threshold for winning seats by party list is 4 percent, not 5 percent. One of the motivations behind this change was to encourage parties to think and act nationally so they could garner as many votes (and representatives) as possible. New "centrist" parties were formed by prominent politicians, including former Prime Minister (1996–1997) Pavlo Lazarenko (*Hromada*) and former Prime Minister (1995–1996) Evhen Marchuk and Kravchuk (United Social

Democrats), and Kuchma himself encouraged the formation of the Popular Democratic Party, nominally headed by then-Prime Minister Valery Pustovoytenko. In total, 26 parties registered for elections. In short, institutionally one would have expected region to exert a weaker role than in the elections four years earlier. Moreover, given Kuchma's flip-flop from 1994–1998 and the resolution of various disputes with Russia (Kubicek, 1999/2000), one might have expected less regional polarization. However, during the campaign the divide between east and west was still abundantly clear, and many parties concentrated their efforts on specific regions in lieu of spreading resources across the country.[8]

The results show quite clearly that regionalism has not waned in Ukraine. Table 10.6[9] provides results of party vote by region and select *oblasti*. National-democrats, led by Rukh, won most of their votes in the western regions and in the city of Kyiv. Communist and their allies dominated in all other areas, winning a plurality in all but one *oblast*. A few centrist parties fared well in various areas (*Hromada* captured 35.3 percent of the vote in Dnieprpetrovsk, the United Social Democrats got 31.1 percent in Zakarpattia), but none managed to establish itself as a truly national party.

Making systematic comparisons with the 1994 elections is problematic, given the changes in the electoral law and the (dis)appearance of a number of parties. In terms of overall results, one could say that the 1998 elections produced a parliament more leftist in orientation than the previous one, although

Table 10.6
1998 Parliamentary Election Results by Region

Region/*Oblastr*	% vote for Communist/ Socialist parties	% vote for national-democratic parties	% vote for pro-Kuchma centrist parties	% vote for other centrist parties
West	15.5	31.4	15.5	12.8
Lrvivsrka	6.4	48.4	14.8	8.4
Ternopilsrka	5.5	35.3	10.0	12.9
Ivano-Frankivsrka	5.5	35.0	9.5	13.5
Central	43.0	14.6	10.7	12.6
East	41.5	6.6	8.4	27.9
Donetsrka	41.5	6.6	8.4	27.9
Luhansrka	55.6	4.3	10.5	14.3
South	43.4	10.3	13.9	15.0
Crimea	45.7	7.8	10.4	10.6
Total	37.2	15.6	14.2	14.9

Source: Central Election Commission Data.

again the communists and their allies do not possess an absolute majority. The left slightly gained (36.8% of seats to 35.1% previously) and the national-democrats were the biggest losers (13.5% from 27%). The total ratio of communist to national-democratic votes grew from 2.0 to 2.5. The swing votes in parliament, as before, belong to a still-nebulous center (28.7% of seats), whose parties are divided by personal rivalries more than any specific program, and independents (17.6%), who are generally owners/directors of large enterprises and collective farms.[10] Clearly, however, the parliament is deeply divided and decision-making will be difficult. For example, the first session of the new parliament was dominated by debate over who should be the speaker. It took over twenty votes to finally produce a winner. Such a fiasco does not bode well.

Regional divisions are still very apparent in the election results, although rather than portray them as west vs. east one can see signs that it is more like the west versus the rest. National-democratic, as well as far right nationalist parties, cannot break out of their niches in the west, whereas the leftist parties did make some clear gains, especially in the central region. Overall, leftist parties won overwhelming pluralities (if not majorities) in all but one non-western *oblast*. Western *oblasti*, primarily the three of Galicia, are the only ones in which these parties did not get over ten percent of the vote and in which national-democrats won overwhelming pluralities. While a rigorous comparison of results remains problematic, one does find a high degree of correlation ($p<.01$) for communist/socialist votes (.831) and national-democratic votes (.834) between 1994 and 1998 that holds across all regions. In other words, there was no marked voter shift. Regional differences remain rather constant and significant.

As a conclusion to this section, it would be appropriate to consider what is reflected by the strong correlation between region and political orientation of voters. It cannot be simply explained primarily by orientation toward the market or reforms. As seen in the review of public opinion data, there are no substantial regional differences on these dimensions. True, the communists and the national democrats do present differing economic programs. However, given the fact that majorities of westerners in the surveys above do not claim to support a primarily free market economy, it would be hard to argue that vote for the national democrats is based on socio-economic interests or preferences. Instead, one would have to consider the importance of politics of symbols, culture, identity, and affection, as the communists clearly represent a pro-Russia orientation and strive to appeal to those frustrated with the current state of post-Soviet Ukraine. Those who have a rosier assessment of current conditions and have greater hopes for the future of Ukraine are more likely to be persuaded by the appeals of the national-democrats. Thus, support for parties in Ukraine runs along the ethnic/territorial/cultural cleavages that are less negotiable and more "primordial." Arguably, the existence of these types of cleavages makes national consolidation and the functioning of democracy more difficult, as it becomes very difficult to find a consensus on basic issues or to make necessary compromises. While the state has not collapsed, it has been embroiled in several controversies with regional overtones. Two of these are examined below.

Center-Regional Struggle: Conflict in Crimea

Despite some evidence of its potential to do so, regionalism has not precipitated full-fledged political or ethnic conflict in Ukraine. There has yet to be a "Ukrainian" Abkhazia, Chechnya, Osh, or Trans-Dniestr. True, there have been small-scale movements in the Donbas, southern *oblasti* (the Novorossiya movement), and in Zakarpattia demanding economic and/or political autonomy (Solchanyk), but these never amounted to much. Polls revealed that in almost all areas of Ukraine there was widespread acceptance of Ukraine's borders, and most Ukrainians (79%) link their personal fates with the fate of the current territory (Kuzio, 1998b, pp. 79–80). The most visible exception has been in Crimea, which presented Kyiv with both a domestic and foreign policy challenge.

As mentioned above, Crimea is a unique region in Ukraine. It is the only one with an ethnic Russian majority, it was transferred from Russia to Ukraine only in 1954, and its tourism industry and its specialized agricultural production were extensively tied to the all-Union economy. Many there identify with the USSR or their region; few identify with Ukraine. In addition, the city of Sevastopol is the headquarters of the Black Sea Fleet, claimed by both Moscow and Kyiv. Moreover, the Crimean Tatars, exiled by Stalin in 1944, call the peninsula their homeland and have returned *en masse*, creating greater ethnic, political, and economic problems. Finally, due to Crimea's ethnic composition, history, and strategic significance, it has been a major source of friction in relations between Russia and Ukraine.

Since 1991, there have been a series of crises relating to Crimea's status within Ukraine, the rights of people living there, and ownership of the Black Sea Fleet and jurisdiction over Sevastopol. In 1989–1990, many ethnic Russians in Crimea began to get nervous over Ukrainian nationalism, and in a January 1991 referendum Crimean voters overwhelmingly supported regional autonomy, which was granted to the peninsula by the Ukrainian parliament the next month. This restored Crimea as an autonomous republic, a status that was stripped from it by Stalin in 1946. Tensions, however, increased after Ukraine declared independence on August 24, 1991. Russians in Crimea found themselves citizens in a new country, in which they were a minority, and Russians in Russia found the loss of Crimea hard to accept. Yeltsin announced that Russia reserved the right to review borders, and politicians across the Russian political spectrum rejected Ukraine's claim on Crimea. In September of that year, the Crimean parliament even declared sovereignty for the region.

Kyiv was alarmed by these developments and tried to forge a compromise with Crimean leaders. Russian leaders encouraged would-be Crimean separatists and pushed their own claims as well, maintaining that the 1954 transfer was not valid. Most vociferous, perhaps, was then Russian vice-president Aleksandr Rutskoi, who, on a visit to Sevastopol, claimed:

> If one looks at history, then again history is not on the side of those who are trying to appropriate this land. If, in 1954, perhaps under the influence of a hangover or sunstroke, the appropriate documents were signed according to which Crimea was transferred to Ukrainian jurisdiction, I am sorry, such a document does not cancel out the history of Crimea. (Solchanyk, 1994, p. 54)

Anatolii Sobchak, mayor of St. Petersburg, echoed this sentiment, asserting, "Crimea has never belonged to Ukraine, and there is no legal or moral grounds for Ukraine to lay claim to Crimea" (Solchanyk, 1994, p. 54). Crimean leaders, who were overwhelmingly ethnically Russian and feared possible Ukrainization from the center, threatened to hold a referendum on Crimea's status and in May 1992 adopted a new constitution and declared independence. Kravchuk reacted quickly, warning that Ukraine would not permit secession and declared Crimea's independence unconstitutional. Although tensions were quite high, cooler heads prevailed: Crimea revoked its declaration of independence, and a new law was adopted that gave Crimean authorities jurisdiction over local matters (education, culture, language, etc.).

This proved to be only a temporary solution. In 1993, Russian politicians again intervened in Crimean affairs, most notably on July 9 when the Duma claimed Sevastopol as a Russian city. Some Ukrainian politicians interpreted this as tantamount to a declaration of war against Ukraine. Meanwhile as the Crimean economy deteriorated, especially relative to the Russian one, the spirit of compromise began to erode (Dawson, 1997). Demonstrations by separatists and Russian nationalists increased, and the Crimean parliament created a Crimean presidency, a move that many believed would allow Crimeans to push their claims more forcefully against Kyiv. In the presidential vote in January 1994, Yurii Meshkov from the Republican Party of Crimea (a Russian nationalist party) won, and the Russian bloc swept parliamentary elections in the spring, shutting out pro-Ukrainian candidates.

The stage was set for renewed confrontation, which began in May 1994 when Crimean authorities restored their 1992 constitution, thereby establishing a right to secede. Kravchuk and the authorities in Kyiv, meanwhile, warned the Crimeans about adopting any laws that would violate Ukrainian law. Notably, polls revealed that a majority of Ukrainians in all regions in the country, as well as a majority of ethnic Russians, thought Crimea should remain a part of Ukraine (Kuzio, 1998b, pp. 115–116). Military intervention from Kyiv was debated as a possible solution. In the end, however, the pro-separatist Crimean leadership again backed down. Perhaps, they reasoned they would lose in any military confrontation and could not count on Russian support. More likely, according to one source (Dawson, 1997), they were a disparate group, with various ideological and ethnic/cultural preferences and could not maintain a united front, as the Russia bloc collapsed and Meshkov found himself embroiled in a battle for power with parliament. In March 1995, the Ukrainian parliament annulled Crimea's constitution and abolished the post of the presidency. There was no public outburst in Crimea in support of Meshkov and his allies, the government fell, and again accommodation was sought with Kyiv.

Since then, much has gone Kyiv's way. Crimea remains an autonomous region but it is clear that Kyiv, not Simferopol, has ultimate authority. In November 1995, a new Crimean constitution that was in accordance with Ukrainian law was adopted. Kyiv later approved it. Pro-Russian forces remain in disarray and have lost public support to the main-line Communist Party, arguably because the public is tired of conflict and wants leaders that would focus on economic issues instead of courting confrontation (Dawson, 1997). In May 1997 Kyiv and Moscow finally signed a long-awaited treaty on cooperation that recognized borders and divided up the Black Sea Fleet. And, most recently, in October 1998 Crimea adopted still another constitution, one that provides for no separate citizenship or legal system and even recognizes Ukrainian as the sole state language in the region. According to one report, the new document is "a complete victory for Kyiv" (*Kommersant*, 1998).

From Kyiv's point of view, the worst appears to be over, but problems remain. Many Russians, including a majority in the Duma and Moscow's Mayor Yurii Luzhkov, insist that Sevastopol is a Russian city. Public alienation, as we saw above, has grown in Crimea, and identity is centered on entities other than Ukraine. Now, however, conflict in the peninsula itself centers on the Crimean Tatars. Over a quarter of a million Tatars have returned to Crimea (they are now just over 10% of the total population), and they are demanding economic concessions (i.e., housing) and political rights. Money, however, is short, and many are still not citizens of Ukraine, meaning that they cannot vote. This led to clashes with police in the run-up to the 1998 parliamentary elections, and the leading Tatar faction, led by Mustafa Dzhemilev, has allied with Rukh, as the Tatars fear Russian nationalists. Because their quotas were stripped, Tatars have no representatives in Crimea's parliament, and there is a good deal of animosity between the Tatar leadership and Kyiv. Finding a just solution to the competing claims of various groups in Crimea will continue to be a challenge.

CONCLUSION: HOW STRONG IS REGIONALISM IN UKRAINE?

Regional divisions in post-Soviet Ukraine have been marked and show little sign of abating. Region has been a defining characteristic of presidential and parliamentary elections, it has been a factor in constitutional debates, and there is widespread evidence of cleavages in public opinion on a variety of issues by region. In general, the pattern has been that those in western Ukraine favor a western orientation for the country, policies to promote Ukrainian language and culture, and a stronger state and presidency. They vote for nationalist candidates and parties and show more satisfaction with the current state of affairs than those living in the more Russified eastern and southern areas. In the latter regions, communist and other leftist parties dominate, as their platforms stress a pro-Russian orientation, more local autonomy, and maintenance of state subsidies. Looked at from this perspective, the division is black and white, and there is little room for a gray zone in which compromises might be made. The two extreme sides, with diametrically opposed policies and values, could tear the country apart.

Clearly, however, this has yet to occur. When necessary, compromises have been made (i.e., on Crimea, on Ukrainization policies), although some might suggest that the country was harmed because decisive action, especially on economic matters, was not taken for fears of exacerbating inter-regional tensions. Both Kravchuk and Kuchma have been very sensitive to regional problems, and interestingly both started as darlings of voters in the east but gradually shifted toward policies favored by those in the west without inducing a major backlash. True, there have been crises, but the extremists on both sides do not have the power and arguably the public support to push their case to the limits. Notably, Rukh and other national-democratic parties have eschewed alliances with militant nationalists on the far right, such as the Ukrainian National Assembly, which have been politically marginalized. There has also been some development of a "patriotic left," which accepts the need to safeguard Ukrainian sovereignty. Is there then any hope that the nation-building process in Ukraine might be able to overcome existing regional and ethnic barriers?

Some would suggest so. Riabchouk (1998), for example, points to survey evidence revealing that Ukrainophone Ukrainians account for a minority (roughly 40%) of the population, primarily in rural areas. Roughly a third of the population is Russophone Ukrainian, which constitutes a moderate center between the Ukrainian-speaking Ukrainians and the ethnic Russians. Ukrainization, therefore, has only a limited constituency that can be politically mobilized. Instead, Riabchouk suggests, what is emerging in Ukraine is a bicultural community, one that is complicated by its diversity but because of demographic factors is "doomed to mutual toleration and the search for compromise" (p. 83). The weakness of Ukrainian nationalism makes ethnic mobilization difficult and therefore favors the development of nation building on a civic basis. Paradoxically, he argues, "national emancipation in Ukraine may succeed only to the extent to which civic integration will be achieved" (p. 91).

One hopes this will come about, and there are some signs this is occurring. The constitution has been adopted, relations with Russia have been normalized, and slow Ukrainization of state institutions is proceeding without great public outcry. The economy is still a problem, and the 1999 presidential elections, in which Kuchma will likely be challenged by forces on the left, are likely to focus more on fixing the economy because this is the primary concern of the all-important political center. Region and ethno/cultural issues, of course, will still be important and will have to be addressed, but they need not doom Ukraine to perpetual instability and prohibit gradual movement toward national consolidation.

NOTES

1. Some might dispute the placement of some *oblasts* in particular regional categories, particularly Khmelnytsky into the west and Sumy into the east. This is done in large part to allow us to construct regional categories for public opinion data from the Eastern Eurobarometer surveys, which grouped regions in a similar manner and from which data are presented below.

2. One opinion poll from early 1996 found 32 percent of Crimeans identified with the USSR, 28 percent with Crimea (as a separate entity), 16 percent with Russia, and only 11 percent with Ukraine. See Kuzio (1998b, p. 88).

3. Regional categories are consistent with what was presented in Figure 1, with the one exception that Khmelnytsky is placed in the central region.

4. The elections were held under a majoritarian, single-member district electoral law, and work collectives and constituencies of voters, as well as parties, were allowed to nominate candidates. Parties nominated only 13 percent of all candidates, and over half of those elected were independents, usually directors of enterprises or collective farms or local politicians with name recognition.

5. Percentage of vote here is from all districts' first round of voting in March 1994. Categories are as follows: Communist/Socialist Parties include both those parties and Peasant Party; national-democratic parties include Rukh, the Republican Party, the Democratic Party, and the Christian Democratic Party, centrist parties include those in "New Ukraine," the Inter-Regional Bloc of Reforms, and the Liberal Party. Blocs are defined by fractions in parliament. The Communist bloc includes the Communists, Socialists, and Agrarians; the national-democrats include Rukh, "Statehood," Reforms, and Agrarians for Reforms (formed in 1995); and the centrists include "Unity," "Center," and Inter-Regional Reform Group.

6. Indicative of the drift in his economic policy, when asked if he had any plans to include Ukrainian Gaidars or Fedorovs in his self-described "reform team," Kravchuk asked, "Do you know any?" (*Post-Postup* [Lviv], September 29, 1993). The Kyiv newspaper *Nezavisimost* offered $150 for anyone who could demonstrate that Kravchuk had a serious electoral program. See Kuzio, p. 39.

7. According to the World Bank, inflation in Ukraine in 1992–1993 was 1,210 and 4,735 percent and the decline in GDP was 12.5 and 7.2 percent. See World Bank, pp. 173–174. Studies also showed wages did not keep pace with inflation and overwhelming numbers (over 85%) of Ukrainians in all surveys reported drops in the their standard of living.

8. Only two parties, Hromada and the Communists, ran candidates in every district.

9. Party blocs are defined as follows: the left include the Communist Party, the Progressive Socialist Party, and the Socialist-Agrarian bloc; the national-democrats include Rukh, Reforms and Order, the bloc "Forward Ukraine!" and the Christian-Democratic Party; the pro-Kuchma center is made up of the Popular Democratic Party, the Agrarians, the bloc of democratic parties NEP, the Labor-Liberal Bloc, and the bloc "Labor Ukraine"; the other centrists are *Hromada*, the United Social Demo-

crats and the Greens. This represents 15 of the 16 parties that received over one percent of the vote. Together they received 82 percent of the vote.

10. Making regional comparisons for seats in parliament by bloc cannot be done because half the seats were chosen by national party list.

BIBLIOGRAPHY

Agnew, John A. *Places and Politics: The Geographical Mediation of State and Society.* Boston: Allen and Unwin, 1987.

Arel, Dominique. "Ukraine: The Temptation of a Nationalizing State." *Political Culture and Civil Society in Russia and the New States of Eurasia.* Ed. Vladimir Tismaneanu. London: M.E. Sharpe, 1995.

Barrington, Lowell. "The Geographic Component of Mass Attitudes in Ukraine." *Post-Soviet Geography* 38, no. 10 (1997): 601–614.

Dawson, Jane. "Ethnicity, Ideology and Geopolitics in Crimea." *Communist and Post-Communist Studies* 30, no. 4 (December 1997): 427–444.

Democratic Initiatives. "Ukrainian Society 1994–1995." Kyiv: Democratic Initiatives, 1995.

Dolishnii, Mariian. "Regional Aspects of Ukraine's Economic Development." *The Ukrainian Economy.* Ed. I.S. Korpeckyj. Cambridge: Harvard University Press, 1992.

F-4 Laboratory of Perspective Developments. *Ukrainskyi parlament, 13–ho sklikannia.* Kyiv: F-4 Laboratory, 1995–1996. (data also on website www. online. com.ua/vrada/default).

Golovakha, Evhen, and Natalya Panina. "Public Opinion in the Regions of Ukraine: The Results of a National Poll." Kyiv: Democratic Initiatives Center, 1995.

Harris, Chauncy. "The New Russian Minorities: A Statistical Overview." *Post-Soviet Geography* 34, no. 1 (1993): 1–28.

Hesli, Vicki, Reisinger, William, and Miller, Arthur. "Political Party Development in Divided Societies: the Case of Ukraine." *Electoral Studies* 17, no. 2 (June 1998): 235–256.

Holdar, Sven. "Torn Between East and West: The Regional Factor in Ukrainian Politics." *Post-Soviet Geography* 36, no. 2 (1995): 112–132.

Khmelko, Valeri, and Dominique Arel. "The Russian Factor and Territorial Polarization in Ukraine." *The Harriman Review* 9, no. 1–2 (Spring 1996): 81–91.

Khmelko, Valeri, and Andrew Wilson. "Regionalism and Ethnic and Linguistic Cleavages in Ukraine." *Contemporary Ukraine: Dynamics of Post-Soviet Transformation.* Ed. Taras Kuzio. London: M.E. Sharpe, 1998, pp. 60–80.

Kommersant (Moscow). October 23, 1998.

Kubicek, Paul. "Dynamics of Contemporary Ukrainian Nationalism: Empire-Breaking to State Building." *Canadian Review of Studies in Nationalism* 23, no. 1–2 (1996): 39–50.

Kubicek, Paul. "Russian Foreign Policy and the West," *Political Science Quarterly* 114, no. 4 (1999–2000): 547–568.

Kubicek, Paul. *Unbroken Ties: The State, Interest Associations, and Corporatism in Post-Soviet Ukraine.* Ann Arbor: University of Michigan Press, 2000.

Kuzio, Taras. "Ukraine: A Four-Pronged Transition." *Contemporary Ukraine: Dynamics of Post-Soviet Transformation.* Ed. Taras Kuzio. London: M.E. Sharpe, 1998a, 165–180.

Kuzio, Taras. *Ukraine: State and Nation Building.* London: Routledge, 1998b.

Liber, George. "Imagining Ukraine: Regional Differences and the Emergence of an Integrated State Identity, 1926–1994." *Nations and Nationalism* 4, no. 2 (April 1998): 187–206.

Miller, Arthur, Klobucar, Thomas, Reisinger, William, and Hesli, Vicki. "Social Identities in Russia, Ukraine, and Lithuania." *Post-Soviet Affairs* 14, no. 3 (July–September 1998): 248–286.

Nebozhenko, Viktor. "Politychna elita i politychny protses u dzerkali hromads?koyi dumky zakhodnoyi Ukrainy," *Stavropihion* (Lviv) (1997): 65–81.

Pirie, Paul. "National Identity and Politics in Southern and Eastern Ukraine." *Europe-Asia Studies* 48, no. 7 (November 1996): 1079–1104.

Riabchouk, Mykola. "Civil Society and Nation Building in Ukraine." *Contemporary Ukraine: Dynamics of Post-Soviet Transformation.* Ed. By Taras Kuzio. London: M.E. Sharpe, 1998, 81–98.

Solchanyk, Roman. "The Politics of State Building: Centre-Periphery Relations in Post-Soviet Ukraine." *Europe-Asia Studies* 46, no. 1 (January 1994): 47–68.

Subtelny, Orest. "Russocentrism, Regionalism, and the Political Culture of Ukraine." *Political Culture and Civil Society in Russia and the New States of Eurasia.* Ed. Vladimir Tismaneanu. London: M.E. Sharpe, 1995.

Ukraine in Figures 1996. Kyiv: Naukova Dumka, 1997.

United Nations. *Human Development Report 1997.* New York: United Nations, 1997.

Wilson, Andrew. *Ukrainian Nationalism in the 1990s.* Cambridge: Cambridge University Press, 1997.

World Bank. *World Bank Development Report 1996.* New York: Oxford University Press, 1996.

CHAPTER 11

NATIONAL-LOCAL LINKS IN LITHUANIA

Terry D. Clark

While there have been comparatively few studies of decentralization in Lithuania, those which have considered the issue have been uniformly pessimistic, concluding that the trend has been towards re-centralization and concentration of authority in the hands of the central government.[1] The conclusion rests largely on an institutional analysis. While the design of institutions linking the central government with local government in Lithuania clearly indicates an effort by the central government to re-centralize political authority, an institutional analysis alone is overly static, ignoring the interaction between national and local political forces.

The process of decentralization and institution building is a dynamic one. It begins with the decision to elect local officials accountable for the execution of responsibilities recently devolved from the central government to the local level. Whether or not it is the intent of the central authorities that the newly elected officials be "co-equals" with a significant degree of autonomy (the product of decentralization) or mere extensions of the center implementing national policies under the supervision of central ministries,[2] rational self-interest in most cases will dictate that these local politicians pursue efforts to achieve local autonomy. That they possess a separate popular mandate from nationally elected officials gives them a valuable resource in launching what amounts to a protracted bargaining process with central authorities over the contours of national-local relations.

I will argue that when viewed in this light the prospects for achieving a more balanced partnership between the center and the localities in Lithuania is quite a bit more optimistic. Indeed, despite the persistent attempts by the center to subordinate institutions of local government, the latter continue to exercise a significant degree of autonomy. In making the case, I will begin by briefly describing the evolution of institutions linking the center with local administrations. I will then argue that the process has resulted in a struggle over the division of responsibilities between the center and the local governments. This is most evident in the emergence of a "local" politics, which has made it possible for decentralization to occur. I will conclude by considering the dimensions on which the process of decentralization will be played out: the division of resources between Vilnius and the localities, the effort to develop a professional administration, and a developing civil society.

The chapter's argument rejects the view that the demands of the global economy preclude local governments from engaging in any significant degree of initiative apart from pursuing the sole interest of economic development.[3] While local government may be somewhat limited by the realities of the global market, it nonetheless exercises a non-trivial degree of initiative in local matters. Business interests and local politicians at the local level are locked in a symbiotic relationship in which neither holds the upper hand. Local politicians need business investment to assure a vibrant economy and a healthy tax base while business interests need access to local officials to assure policies favorable to them. The relationship of mutual dependency permits for bargaining between the two, which permits greater room to meet the demands of non-business constituencies than might otherwise be expected.[4]

I consciously adopt the view instead that the major constraints on local government are those imposed by central governments. Local autonomy is circumscribed by a combination of political institutions and budget limitations established by legislative act, government action, or constitutional mandate.[5] These legal and institutional limitations are the arenas in which the bargaining process between national and local political elites takes place.

THE CONTOUR OF NATIONAL-LOCAL LINKS

The laws enacted by the Supreme Council following the restoration of Lithuanian independence reflect an expectation of consensual and relatively harmonious interaction between the center and local governments. Where disagreement might occur, it was *assumed* that the center would make the final decision. Such a relationship between Vilnius[6] and the localities was not only thought advisable, but likely given three factors: the size of the country which suggested that autonomous local governments would be a considerably inefficient means for ruling the country, the economic crisis being endured by the entire country which demanded a unified response focusing on the nation's needs (not those of one locale pitted against those of another), and the Soviet experience of central control of local authorities. Indeed, the purpose of local governments appears to have been envisioned as assisting the central ministries in Vilnius in managing the economy more efficiently rather than as a means to decentralize political authority in order to extend democratic governance to the local level.[7]

The expectation of consensual relations between Vilnius and the localities and the assumption of the center's supremacy are reflected in unclear delineation of responsibilities between the two. For instance, the 1990 Law on the Fundamentals of Local Government established a confusing system of 426 rural communes, 22 rural districts, 81 towns, 44 regions, and 11 cities. All 584 of these local units were given the same responsibilities for assuring the economic well-being of their region.

The Constitution passed in the national referendum of October 25, 1992 was equally vague and ambiguous concerning the relationship between the center and local governments. Article 120 declares that local governments are sovereign; however, Article 123 establishes that they will be subjected to monitoring by a government representative to assure their compliance with the Constitution, the laws of the national legislature, and the decisions of the central ministries. Further, while Article 122 gives them the right to determine their own budget, the center's control over tax collection and distribution have never permitted them to do so. Finally, Article 47 stipulates that only the central state or private citizens may own property. Hence, local governments are virtually without resources.

It quickly became apparent that both the expectation of consensual relations between the center and the localities as well as the assumption of the supremacy of the central government was not shared by local elites. Despite their relatively weak Constitutional position, local governments began to challenge the ministries of the central government. The first challenge came from the eastern regions. Dominated by the Polish ethnic minority, the local governments surrounding Vilnius declared themselves autonomous in what they at least overtly claimed was necessary in order to defend the Polish language and culture.[8] Subsequent challenges emerged from local governments in the country's two largest cities, Vilnius and Kaunas, as well as in several regions.

The central government's response to these challenges has been to reduce the ambiguities in national-local relations by redesigning the institutional structures in such a way as to establish the supremacy of the center. This has occurred in a step-by-step, evolutionary manner. As early as 1992, the government secured a legislative act giving it the right to remove mayors and/or dissolve local self-governments and impose direct rule by the center.[9] In 1993, an enabling law permitted Vilnius to establish the representatives in the localities envisioned by the Constitution to supervise and control the decisions and acts of local governments. These government representatives were vested with the power to declare any local acts null and void. Legislation in 1994 further reorganized local government. In place of the previous system with its 584 units of local self-government, a system of 44 regions and 12 cities was created. Additionally, the country was divided into ten districts (*apskritis*). Many of the functions that had previously been managed by the regions and cities were transferred to these districts whose Governors were appointed by Vilnius and which functioned as administrative arms of the central ministries coordinating and monitoring local governments.[10] In essence, the central government had two institutions attempting to control the localities, the government representatives and the District Governors. The system was rationalized following the 1996 elections to the national legislature when a new law placed the government representatives under the district governors.[11]

The central government's efforts to re-centralize political authority would appear to argue that a discussion of center-periphery relations in Lithuania is a closed one. Such is not the case, however. While the position of local governments has certainly been weakened by legislative acts, local elites continue to use institutions of local self-government to engage in bargaining with Vilnius over resources as well as development strategy. Indeed, the evolution of national-local relations in the Lithuanian case is far from over. The remainder of this essay will consider the key dimensions on which this struggle is taking place.

The Elite Struggle for Control

Seen by themselves, the central government's efforts to re-centralize power suggest a one-sided imbalance in the relationship between the center and local governments in Lithuania. However, a more fully nuanced analysis which considers both levels of governance more appropriately suggests continued bargaining over the form that relationship will take. The division of political authority and responsibilities lies at the heart of the dispute.

That a dispute exists is reflected in the government's efforts to re-centralize as discussed previously. Were there no effort by local officials to contest central government control of local decisions, there would be no such government reaction. The absence of such a conflict would be problematic. Besides signaling the unwillingness of local elites to represent local interests, the result would be that the central ministries would simply dictate policy that the localities would administer. This would constitute a situation in which local governments were mere administrative arms of the center. As a consequence, local concerns would be largely ignored by the political system.

The contest between national and local elites was made possible by the introduction of elections at the local level, in essence creating competing popular mandates between the two levels of governance. National-local conflict has been particularly notable when the party in control of the central government is faced with a majority of local governments controlled by the opposition. Such has often been the case. Elections at both the national and local level are dominated by five political parties—the Homeland Union (Conservatives of Lithuania) and the Christian Democratic Party on the political right, the Lithuanian Democratic Labor Party (LDLP) and the Lithuanian Social-Democratic Party (LSDP) on the left, and the Center Union (CU) in the center. In the period immediately following the re-establishment of independence, the

Sajudis government (the precursor to the Homeland Union) of Gediminas Vagnorius had to contend with LDLP local governments. The LDLP governments (of which there were three from 1992 to 1996) that succeeded the Vagnorius government were faced with the Conservatives wresting control of most local governments following the 1995 local elections. The current Conservative government of Gediminas Vagnorius has not been without local opposition as well. Of the 56 local governments contested in the 1997 local elections, the Homeland Union (party of Vagnorius) won only 25 mayoral seats,[12] less than a majority.

Even when the same party wins at the national and local level, national-level elites are not able to dictate political outcomes at the local level. In the 1997 local elections, the Homeland Union (Conservatives) should have obtained the mayoral seat in 44 localities based on the party having obtained a plurality of seats.[13] However, it was not able to muster the support of members of political parties in the national-level ruling coalition in a number of localities (the coalition includes the Homeland Union, the Christian Democratic Party, and the Center Union). Among these were the city of Klaipeda and six regions (Birzai, Jonava, Jurbarkas, Kupiskis, Sirvintai, and Trakai). In Klaipeda the Homeland Union candidate for mayor was defeated when six of his own party members spoiled their ballots rather than vote for him.

Differing electoral outcomes at the national and local level together with the inability of national-level elites to control local politics through their party organizations strongly suggest the existence of a local politics representing diverse interests from those at the national level. Further, they constitute clear evidence that local politics matter. This is further demonstrated in the fact that local politicians have frequently challenged the center. In many instances local issues have come to overshadow national-level issues in importance. Such has been the case in the city of Siauliai.

The fourth largest city in Lithuania, the city is home to one of the largest air bases in the former Soviet Union. City leaders have seized on the idea of converting the airport and the area immediately surrounding it into a free economic zone with the aim of revitalizing the city's economy. Given that Siauliai sits astride the major rail link in the country, the potential is quite large. Indeed, Philips Corporation has taken a keen interest in the project to the point of breaking ground to build a factory and distribution center in the zone. Siauliai's plans have drawn concerns from economic interests in Vilnius and Kaunas, the country's two largest cities. At one point in spring and summer 1996 the issue dominated the legislative session of the national legislature as deputies, notwithstanding party affiliation, staked out positions based on their region's interests. In the city of Siauliai itself the Homeland Union split over the issue after the national party demanded a revision to the free economic zone which threatened to exclude the airport from any tax incentives.[14]

In the 1997 local elections, the Homeland Union won a narrow plurality in Siauliai. While its candidate for Mayor, Alfredas Lankauskas, ultimately won the position, he did so only with the votes of left of center and centrist parties generally in opposition to the Conservatives. These deputies voted for Lankauskas because he steadfastly supported the free economic zone against his own party's position throughout 1996. Indeed, many in his own party would prefer another candidate for mayor. In the days leading up to the local elections, Lankauskas was placed fifth on the local party list. Further, it was decided by the local party organization that Lankauskas would not be nominated for Mayor following the elections. When Lankauskas succeeded in wresting control of the party list, a number of Homeland Union members resigned in protest.

Local politicians reflect local politics, and these politics are not always agreeable to the central government. Again, the case of Siauliai illustrates the point. Despite having been elected on the list of the Homeland Union, Lankauskas remains a thorn in the side of the Conservative government. Like many local mayors, Lankauskas uses his mandate at the local level to defend local interests against the central government. While the District Governors review every decision taken by the cities and regions, they cannot by themselves force a change. They are restricted to pointing out problems they see with such acts in writing to the respective Mayor. Should the Mayor elect not to make the requested changes, the Governor's only remaining recourse is to refer the matter to the courts.

The Siauliai District Governor has already referred several decisions of Siauliai City to the courts. One of them deals with alleged improprieties concerning public bidding over the public transportation system. The Governor claims that the City gave preferential treatment to the bid of the city bus park over a private company seeking to take commercial ownership of some of the more profitable routes. Despite a limited budget, the City monetarily supports the bus park's operations. Should the bus park's profits be further reduced by the loss of these routes, the City's budget would be further taxed to make up for the lost revenue. Relations between the Governor and Mayor are also stretched by the free economic zone project. Reflecting the view of many in the central government, the Governor is concerned that the firm that won control of the project has yet to make public its development plan. Equally troubling to the Governor is that the firm depends at present on funds from the state budget.[15]

There are indeed so many points of contention between the Governor and Mayor Lankauskas that the former openly states that he considers the Mayor the representative of an opposition party despite his having run on the Homeland Union ticket.[16] The situation, similar to those in other cities and regions of the country, demonstrates that there is an on-going contest between elites in the central government and elites in the localities. In the absence of such conflict, the center would rule unimpeded. While the struggle concerns whether local issues ultimately will be decided by the central ministries or popularly elected local organs of self-government, the ultimate end will be a clearer division of responsibilities and authority between the central government and local governments. The central government has surely evidenced its determination in the contest by attempting to re-centralize authority. This is particularly evident in the establishment of the District Governors. However, this has in no way resolved the situation. Given the evidence there is every right to believe that the contours of the national-local relationship are yet being worked out. While the final outcome is not likely to be an all-powerful center, the degree of autonomy which local governments will enjoy will depend on what occurs in three critical arenas: the division of resources between Vilnius and the localities, the development of a professional administration, and the emergence of a civil society at the local level.

The Division of Resources

Lithuanian local governments are hampered by a lack of control over resources. As a consequence, they experience difficulties in pursuing local initiatives. Two aspects of this problem are most crucial: the division of state property and local budgets. All property was owned by the state during the Soviet-era. While privatization has led to economic decentralization, the central government has been reticent to permit local governments to manage what public property remains. This has been a major issue of contention between Vilnius and the localities, particularly in regards to property that has been transferred from city management to the Districts, to include secondary schools and secondary health care facilities. Further, local governments are severely restricted in the uses to which they can put public property. Permits for use of public property—municipal or state—requires the approval of the District, and licensing and inspection for construction on private and public lands is under the purview of the District.

Local government responsibilities and initiatives are even further restricted by the budget. While localities are permitted to collect fees and revenues, the sources are limited. Typically, municipalities and regions obtain revenues locally from market fees, transportation and parking fees, rent of public property under their control, and licenses for businesses. These revenues constitute only about one to two percent of the local budget.[17] The remainder is provided by the national budget with most of it being earmarked for such functions as the operation of schools, public health care, roads, and municipal operations. Consequently, local governments have very little money available for discretionary spending and local initiatives.

Despite resource limitations, many local governments have nonetheless managed to pursue a great number of local initiatives. Indeed, there are a number of options for increasing resources available to the localities. Among them are lobbying the national legislature and central government for direct investments in local projects, securing loans using what limited municipal property is available as collateral, and raising rents and utility rates. Some mayors have used a combination of these methods to finance such projects as environmental cleanup, upgrade of city transportation systems, and improvements to social welfare services. Perhaps the most innovative solution to budget constraints, however, is lobbying for private investment funds. Siauliai's Mayor Lankauskas succeeded in gaining funds from Philips Corporation and other potential investors in the free economic zone for a number of projects to include a new children's home and a sports club.

A Professional Administration

Despite central government control over most property and budget resources, a well-trained professional administration can be a valuable resource in helping local governments to achieve a non-trivial degree of independence from central governments. This is particularly the case given the fact that local governments are charged with delivering goods and services at the local level. This fact alone gives them a significant degree of discretion in the actual distribution of those goods and services. Further, the central government's dependence upon information provided by local governments gives the latter significant influence in shaping central government policy and budget priorities at the local level.

However, in the Lithuanian local case there is a dearth of trained professional administrators. Public administration in Lithuania is largely inherited from the Soviet era. Soviet civil servants were trained to execute central directives. At the local level there was little room for initiative. Further, there was little to no horizontal coordination between field elements of central ministries. All decision-making authority and responsibility for coordination rested with the center. Even republic-level ministries in Vilnius were left with little authority as a great number of decisions were deferred to Moscow. Hence, public administrators at every level throughout the country are poorly trained for the new political environment in which they find themselves.

Re-training the country's civil servants has not been an easy process. While laws have been passed requiring such programs be established, the general lack of funding in government budgets has made it difficult at best to execute the intent of these laws. The lack of a national structure for training in public administration, the lack of in-service training possibilities, inadequate curricula and training materials, and a dearth of competent instructors compound the funding problem.[18]

The persistence of Soviet-era attitudes on the part of public administrators provides a strong impetus toward centralization. This tendency is exacerbated by the distrust that most politicians, particularly those on the political right, have for the bureaucracy at all levels. As a consequence, at the local level public administrators are permitted virtually no discretionary authority by elected officials. The committee system established by the City Council closely supervises the activities of the city administration. In practice virtually every act of the city administration requires the prior approval of a committee or the Executive Board that comprises the heads of committees, the mayor, and the deputy mayor. This includes such routine matters as licensing a kiosk for operation, issuing a building permit, authorizing the occupation of a city managed dormitory room, and placing children in the custody of relatives.[19] As a result local politicians are overly involved in administrative matters. With correspondingly less time available for local political issues, the threat is that they could possibly gravitate toward fulfilling the role of senior administrators of central government directives and policies.

However, the impetus to centralization is balanced by the fact that elected officials in the central government experience the same difficulties with public servants in the ministries. Thus the time that they can devote to trying to control local affairs is equally limited. Given this situation, the comparative pace of development of the professional administration at the center and in the localities is critical. Whichever develops the most rapidly will provide political elites at the corresponding level with an advantage in the process of negotiating national-local relations. Since training programs and budgets are likely to be controlled at the national level, the central government would appear to have the edge in the race. Using these resources the central bureaucracy may well be able to co-opt local administrators. In such a case, local administrators would work in tandem with their colleagues in the central government against local autonomy. However, given the lesser complexity of administration at the local level and the smaller number of public servants required, it is far more likely that the pace of developing a professional administration will be faster in the localities. Such is particularly true for the larger cities and towns. Indeed, some of the larger localities have already begun to establish training programs for their own administrators.

A Local Civil Society

Aside from the presence of dynamic local elite, the most critical factor may well be the emergence of a vibrant civil society at the local level. A civil society is comprised of a dense web of interest groups in which citizens hold multiple and overlapping membership. Local politicians can use these organizations as allies to mobilize citizens in support of local initiatives. In a democracy, such support is crucial to sustaining local elites against opposition from the central government.

While there is clear evidence of an emerging civil society at the local level in Lithuania, it is hardly the case that citizens have yet developed a dense or overlapping web of interest groups. During the Soviet era, citizens had been organized in a wide range of state-controlled associations, to include labor and professional unions, organizations for the disabled, and women's groups. Upon independence, these groups found themselves in a radically new situation. If in Soviet times such groups had served largely as "transmission belts" relaying information from the political authorities to the citizenry, they were now expected to press for the interests of their membership with state and local authorities. Making the situation even more difficult was that these same organizations lost their formal ties with the state. In such an unaccustomed position, the leadership and members of most of these groups were simply unable to adapt. Lacking the most rudimentary understanding of collective bargaining and the political power of numbers, leaders were reduced to pleading for state and local subsidies from state organizations while their members in a style reminiscent of Soviet practice petitioned city hall individually.

However, such has not been the fate for all of Lithuanian society. If Soviet-era organizations and the social groups that they supported have receded, many newer groups have emerged. Indeed, citizen activity has been quite strong among certain social groups, in particular pensioners and the new business class. Highly motivated by their low pensions, pensioners of Lithuanian nationality have taken the lead in organizing behind the political right, particularly the Homeland Union (Conservatives of Lithuania). While turnout for local elections has been generally low, turnout among this group of voters has been high and accounted for the right-wing parties' margin of victory in the 1997 local elections. Despite limited local resources, pensioners have managed to gain assistance in the form of cash subsidies for public transportation, reductions in utility rates, and tax relief owing to their political and organizational skills in most localities. Local governments also frequently respond to their demands for symbolic gestures supporting Lithuanian nationalism or denigrating the Soviet era "occupation." Such acts include the renaming of streets, the relocation of Soviet gravesites, and the establishment of patriotic monuments.

Business interests have organized at the local level as well. Many cities and towns have an association of small businesses while virtually every region now has a chamber of commerce and the country's larger enterprises have united in an Association of Industrialists. The Association was instrumental in the success of the Homeland Union in the 1996 national elections, and one of its members is member of the cabinet in the current government.

While other citizen groups have been less successful, they have nonetheless managed to gain the ear of local governments when they mount an extraordinary effort. On one such occasion, a group of citizens concerned about the adequacy of a proposed run-off ditch near Siauliai's airport was able to get the city to divert funds to ensure that the ditch would provide sufficient drainage so as not to endanger their property. Despite such successes, however, Lithuanian civil society presently lacks a dense web of private associations at the local level. Further, there is a virtual lack of overlap in membership between organized groups. This is most clearly the case for the Russian-speaking community in most locales. Virtually isolated from the remainder of local interest groups that refuse to join with them in any coalition activities, the Russian community in most locales is extraordinarily limited in its ability to defend its interests.

CONCLUSIONS

The evidence presented in this chapter demonstrates that decentralization in Lithuania is not proceeding without difficulties, the most pressing of which is the relative lack of financial resources at the local level. City budgets are tight and most major decisions concerning property are still controlled by the central government through the agency of the District Governors and their staffs. This creates the threat that ultimately local elites may decide to seek patronage from the center having concluded that local resources are too paltry to squabble over.

Nonetheless, the contours of national-local relations in Lithuania are still to be decided. Despite limited control over budgetary resources, local governments manage to continue to challenge the central government on such issues as Siauliai's free economic zone and other local initiatives in Klaipeda, Kaunas, and Vilnius. Starting with their popular mandate, politicians at the local level have used their political skills and personal connections to mobilize citizens and gain funding support from any number of sources for their initiatives. The result has been a protracted bargaining over the form that national-local relations will assume.

While local elites will continue to battle the center for control over budget resources and property, whether local governments ultimately exercise a non-trivial degree of autonomy will depend far more on the outcome of processes in two other arenas, the development of a professional administration and the emergence of a civil society. Indeed, the results of the struggle in these arenas will probably directly determine the outcome of the struggle for budgetary control. It is imperative that local governments shape the training of administrators at their level in order to assure that the central government is not able to assert control over local politics by creating a unified administrative system that essentially relegates local administrative elements to the role of field elements of central ministries. At the same time, local politicians need to work with local organizations and groups to strengthen their role in the political process. Such groups will be able to provide elected officials with a means to inform the public on local issues as well as valuable political capital in conflicts with the center.

NOTES

Research for this chapter was supported in part by a grant from the International Research and Exchanges Board (IREX), by funds provided by the National Endowment for the Humanities, the United States Information Agency, and the U.S. Department of State, which administers the Russian, Eurasian, and East European Research Program (Title VIII).

1. Artashes Gazaryan, "Local Government in Lithuania in the Transition Period," in *Local Government in Eastern Europe: Establishing Democracy at the Grassroots,* Andrew Coulson, ed. (Aldershot, England: Edward Elgar Publishing Company,

1995), 133–144; Artashes Gazaryan and Max Jeleniewsk, "Political and Economic Issues in the Re-creation of Lithuanian Local Government," in *Transformation from Below: Local Power and the Political Economy of Post-Communist Transitions*, John Gibson and Philip Hanson, eds. (Cheltenham, UK: Edward Elgar Publishing Limited, 1996), 57–72.

2. R. Rhodes, *Control and Power in Central-Local Government Relations* (Westmead, U.K: Gower, 1981); Michael Goldsmith, ed., *New Research in Central-Local Relations* (Aldershot, UK: Gower, 1986).

3. See Paul Peterson, *City Limits* (Chicago: University of Chicago Press, 1981); and Chris Pickvance and Edmond Preteceille, *State Restructuring and Local Power* (London: Pinter Publishers Ltd., 1991).

4. Clarence Stone, *Regime Politics: Governing Atlanta, 1946–1988* (Lawrence: University of Kansas Press, 1989).

5. David Judge, Gerry Stoker, and Harold Wolman, eds., *Theories of Urban Politics* (Thousand Oaks, CA: Sage Publications, 1995).

6. Used in this context, Vilnius refers to the central government. Vilnius occupies a distinct position in Lithuanian politics. As the capital, it is home to the central government. At this same time, it like other Lithuanian cities has an elected local government. Both are discussed in this chapter.

7. Gazaryan, 1995.

8. The central government responded to the challenge by imposing direct rule in 1991 declaring that the regions had supported the putschists in Moscow in the August coup of that year.

9. While the government was not successful in obtaining the necessary legislative concurrence to any effort to execute this power, the mere fact that it could do so served to intimidate local authorities.

10. In an interview with Paulius Skardzius, Head of the Local Affairs Section, Ministry of Public Administration Reforms and Local Authorities, on 20 June 1997, he stated that while the intent was to subordinate all previously existing local activities and field agencies of the central ministries under the District Governors, opposition to the plan from some of the ministries has not permitted this goal to be fully realized as of yet.

11. While the decision was partially motivated by the new legislative majority's desire to replace these representatives, most of whom had been appointees of the previous government (now in opposition), the move made for more efficient control being exercised by the center by consolidating the two positions charged with essentially the same functions under one head.

12. Local elections are decided on the basis of a proportional electoral system. In essence, voters select from among parties in local elections. Each party achieving a threshold of 5 percent of the votes cast obtain a share of seats in the City Council roughly proportional to the election results. (Given that a certain percentage of the electorate casts votes for parties not achieving the threshold, in most cases parties will receive a greater proportion of the seats than the percentage of the vote that they manage to capture in the election.) Mayors, who head the city administration, are then elected by City Councils. In those cases in which no one party holds a majority of the City Council seats, coalitions must be formed.

13. Citizens in local elections in Lithuania vote for parties as opposed to individual candidates. Seats in the City Council are distributed to the political parties achiev-

ing a 5 percent threshold in proportion to the vote they receive. Following the elections, the City Council elects a Mayor. In the absence of a single party controlling a majority of seats, a coalition of parties is necessary in order to elect a Mayor.

14. For a full description of these events see Terry D. Clark, "Free Trade Zone Project Brings Out Regional Rivalries," *Transition* 2, no. 16 (9 August 1996): 52–55.

15. Interview with Vincas Girnius, Siauliai District Governor, 26 June 1997.

16. Ibid.

17. Interview with Paulius Skardzius.

18. "Country Profiles of Civil Service Training Systems," SIGMA Papers: No. 12, Paris: Organisation for Economic Co-operation and Development, 1997, pp. 121–138.

19. Terry D. Clark, "Who Rules Siauliai? A Case Study of an Emerging Urban Regime," *Slavic Review* 56, no. 1 (Spring 1997): 101–122.

CHAPTER 12

CENTRAL POWER AND REGIONAL AND LOCAL GOVERNMENT IN UZBEKISTAN

Lawrence R. Robertson and Roger D. Kangas

This chapter reviews the evolution of central government relations with regional and local governments in Uzbekistan. While legally, there is a clear division of authority, the central government retains significant political and economic control of the regions. The chapter concludes with an examination of public opinion data on popular attitudes towards these three levels of government in the country from a representative nationwide survey conducted at the end of 1996 and beginning of 1997.

INTRODUCTION

Uzbekistan provides an alternative model of center-periphery relations in a new state to the disorganization and de facto decentralization evident in some of the other former Soviet republics like Russia. Uzbekistan has a strong executive branch, built on the executive committees (*ispolkoms*) of the Soviet period as well as purported Uzbek historical traditions of appointed governors (*Hokim*) who oversee the activities of local administrations (*Hokimiat*). These appointed officials, as well as representatives from the Presidential apparatus, provide direct links between the central government in Toshkent and the 12 regions and one autonomous republic of the country—as well as to lower-level cities and districts within the regions.

Constitutionally, there are distinct responsibilities assigned to each of these levels and, at least on paper, there is the semblance of a multi-layered (albeit non-federal) state structure. The reality, though, is that the lower levels still abide by policy dictated from above. Accountability of higher offices to lower constituencies simply does not exist. This is not to say that regional officials are incapable of acting independently or introducing policy measures on their own. However, such cases are contrary to the norm. Regional bosses run the risk of being sacked at any time, as legally, they are in office completely at the behest of the president. Acting counter to the overall wishes of the president will most likely have an adverse effect on one's position. Perhaps more intriguing are the *mahalla*, or neighborhood, structures which de facto address matters on their own. A traditional aspect of Central Asian society, the *mahalla* is being recreated in independent Uzbekistan. When it comes to addressing the day-to-day problems of Uzbek citizens, the *mahalla* has become a vehicle through which such matters are addressed—at the local level.

In this chapter, we will examine the political system looking from the top down: by looking at the Karimov presidency, then the political system in general, and then the dynamics of relations between the center and periphery. At this point, we will turn to economic and social issues. Finally, we will examine how the population perceives these relations and evaluate possible impacts of popular attitudes on the future success of the political system in Uzbekistan. Ultimately, power remains centralized in Uzbekistan and this poses a problem for any initiatives originating from the periphery.

Uzbekistan and the Karimov Presidency

Islom Karimov, the former first secretary of the Uzbek Communist Party, dominates Uzbekistan. On December 29, 1991, Uzbekistan held its first post-Soviet election. Karimov easily won, receiving 86 percent of the vote—in an election where the opposition candidate, Mukhammad Solih, was restricted in his campaigning and dissemination of information. In spite of these limitations on Solih, regional results of the presidential vote reflected some dissatisfaction. Solih, who is the leader of the now-outlawed "Erk Demokratik Partiiasi," won 58.5 percent of the vote in the *Khorezm Wiloyat* (formerly known as *Oblast*). While this was Solih's home region, the opposition candidate fared well in the other outlying *wiloyatlar* as well. Even in Qashqadaryo, where Karimov was once the Obkom secretary in the Soviet period, Solih won 19.3 percent of the vote.[1] "Unofficial" tallies suggest Solih's vote was higher, but these have never been substantiated.

Since the election, Karimov has been able to deftly establish control over the political, economic, and social life of the country through a centralized state and the manipulation of an "authoritarian political culture."[2] Perhaps the most obvious form of the latter was the 1996 "660th Jubilee" of Tamerlane—a recently established political icon of Uzbekistan and hero of President Karimov himself. In one of his books, Karimov stressed that, "our duty is to replenish our national spiritual treasury with new names and works by our great ancestors—philosophers, scholars, and creators of beauty." By presenting himself as a caretaker and cultivator of a new, national history,

Karimov is able to attain a wider support base among the population of the country.[3] By making Uzbeks proud of their past, Karimov is establishing himself as an essential figure in modern Uzbekistan.

If one were to assess the possible "future leaders of Uzbekistan" during the Soviet period, Islom Karimov would probably not have been high on anyone's list. Biographies written in recent years now say otherwise, and note his drive, honesty, and integrity—character traits that would "naturally" lead him to his current position.[4] However, the truth is perhaps a bit less dramatic. Islam Karimov worked his way into the Soviet system the "old-fashioned way," he earned his party card while moving up a technocratic career path. In 1960, at the age of 22, he became an engineer for the Toshkent Aviation Factory, where he worked for the next six years. During this time, he specialized in accounting and finance and in 1966 moved over to the Uzbek SSR office of the State Planning Agency, *Gosplan*. He remained with *Gosplan* for 17 years, becoming a key leader of the agency's Uzbek republic branch in the early 1980s.

A crisis in the political nomenklatura of Uzbekistan presented Karimov with a unique opportunity. The "Uzbek Affair," or the "Great Cotton Scandal" was just breaking open and scores of key officials in Uzbekistan were being accused, arrested, and (in the case of two) executed for embezzling funds associated with the cotton shipments out of the republic. Among those investigated was First Secretary of the Uzbek SSR, Sharaf Rashidov. Rashidov's sudden death in October 1983 obligated the government to select a new leader—and one that would, according to General Secretary Yurii Andropov, be a clean person. Imanjon Usmankhojaev was selected almost immediately as not politically connected to Rashidov because Usmankhojaev was from the Ferghona region and Rashidov was from Jizzakh. However, within three years, Usmankhojaev was ousted from office due to "ineffective leadership" and replaced by Rafiq Nishanov.

During these changes in office, Islom Karimov was able to move up to a position of political importance. In 1983, he was named Minister of Finance and in early 1986 was appointed head of Uzbekistan's branch of *Gosplan* and Deputy Head of State. It seemed that he had won the favor of Usmankhojaev. However, when the latter was removed from office, Karimov's fortunes changed. Nishanov did not favor Karimov and sent him to be the *Oblast* Secretary of Qashqadaryo. According to Karimov, his "dismissal" was the result of a falling out with the Uzbek party administration over a report he had written entitled "On the Problems and Prospects for Economic Development in Uzbekistan," which offered a critical assessment of the republic's current situation.[5] As an obkom secretary of a relatively poor region of Uzbekistan, Karimov was definitely outside of the "mainstream" of republic-level politics: which was his good fortune. In his own words, he was able to hone his administrative skills at a local level, remaining distant from the purges and counter-purges that were taking place at the national level.

In the late 1980s, other pressures emerged in Uzbekistan. Mikhail Gorbachev's *perestroika* campaign was in full swing and nationalist movements in the Soviet Union had begun to openly question and challenge the Communist Party authority. While the nationalist movement might not have been as strong in Uzbekistan, the newly formed organization "Birlik" held demonstrations calling for greater Uzbek language rights. Ethnic differences also became the cause of violence in Uzbekistan, especially in the Ferghona Valley. A series of such crises prompted the removal of Rafiq Nishanov in 1989 and, once again, required that the national CPSU look for a viable party leader in Uzbekistan. On July 23, 1989, the Central Committee of the Communist Party of Uzbekistan elected Islom Karimov First Secretary.

Karimov's ability to maintain power at this stage was nothing short of remarkable. The riots that caused the removal of Nishanov did not disappear. Indeed, in 1990 and 1991, ethnic riots in the Ferghona Valley, particularly in the Kyrgyz SSR's Osh *Oblast*, threatened stability in the region. However, Karimov was able to use these events to affect political changes at the *oblast* level and direct the blame accordingly. In addition, because the central government in Moscow was pre-occupied with its own political drama, the likelihood of Gorbachev paying much attention to events in Uzbekistan was low.

Following the lead of other First Secretaries in the Soviet Union, Islom Karimov assumed the office of the Union Republic President in 1990. By the time he ran for President of the Republic of Uzbekistan in 1991, as noted earlier, Islom Karimov had already established his power base in the country. This is not to say that there would be challenges to his authority. In October 1991, over 200 members of the *Oliy Majlis* (Supreme Soviet) signed a petition demanding Karimov's resignation—on the basis that he was the "former Soviet leader" of Uzbekistan. The movement did not gain enough support and Karimov was able to maintain power. Not surprisingly, the individuals who signed the petition were eased out of office—especially when the *Majlis* was reduced from 500 to 250 members in 1994.

In his tenure as President of the Republic of Uzbekistan, Islom Karimov has been able to craft an institutional structure that is multi-layered and yet responsible to the center—with the presidential apparatus as the core of government. According to official data, in March 1995, 99.96 percent of the electorate voted in a referendum on extending Karimov's term of office until 2000—a measure that 99.3 percent of voters approved. In January 2000, Karimov won the support of over 95 percent of the electorate in a two-person presidential contest. Emphasizing his overwhelming support was the fact that his opponent, Abdulhafiz Jalalov, openly admitted that he voted for Karimov, as well. Add to this the ability to remove opposition figures before they become too powerful, it is easy to see how Karimov has become the key figure in Uzbek politics.

The Uzbek leadership justifies its authoritarian policies by invoking the threat of Islamic fundamentalism and its spread to Uzbekistan via civil wars in

Tajikistan and Afghanistan, both of which are home to many ethnic Uzbeks. At the same time, President Karimov has tried to present himself as a merciful leader and has issued amnesties to prisoners on a periodic basis. For instance, prior to his June 1996 visit to the United States, he released over 80 prisoners, including two political prisoners. The image of the "benevolent leader" is key to Karimov's self-established role in Uzbekistan. By presenting himself as a guarantor of stability in the country, Karimov has apparently remained popular with the majority of Uzbek citizens who appear supportive of his authority.

What makes this authority even more profound is that the president has been able to ensure that the constitution and legal structure of the state afford him such power. It is to these institutional levers of power—particularly as they relate to regional and local government—that we will now turn.

The Structure of Central, Regional, and Local Government

At least on paper, political power is distributed among a number of levels in Uzbekistan. Constitutionally, the president is afforded a wide range of responsibilities, including the right to initiate and approve of legislation and government policy and appoint (and dismiss) top national and regional officials. The appointed Prime Minister, Utkir Sultanov, heads the Cabinet, which is the highest executive council. However, he must answer to the President and he, too, can be dismissed by him at any time. Karimov has been more than willing to exercise such power and has successfully created an environment wherein the cabinet is constantly reshuffled and potential rivals or successors are rotated out of high office before they become too popular. This was most likely the case of First Deputy Prime Minister Ismail Jurabekov, who was also seen as an influential person until his ouster from power in 1998.[6] Indeed, in an average year, he removes five to six *Hokims* (out of 14), in addition to numerous cabinet members.

The *Oliy Majlis* (Supreme Council or Soviet) is a direct carry-over from the Soviet period, with some changes. According to the constitution, the *Oliy Majlis* is the highest political body in Uzbekistan. It is charged with initiating and passing legislation, as well as executing policies through committee work. It meets on a regular basis—two times a year plus any special sessions—and has both public and closed sessions. To date, however, it takes the lead from the president and spends most of its two sessions per year discussing and passing presidential proposals and decrees. Clearly, this suggests that it is not the rule-making body of Uzbekistan. Since independence the *Oliy Majlis* has only voted against President Karimov once—and that was to consider the extension of his presidential term part of his first rather than second term against his "objections" (which allows him to run for reelection in the year 2000). Karimov, in a series of speeches in 1996 and 1997, criticized the *Oliy Majlis* for this "lack of initiative" and called upon it to be more forceful in legislation. To date, the

Speaker of the *Oliy Majlis*, Erkin Khalilov, remains a loyal Karimov supporter and has not taken up this challenge with any major initiatives.

Originally comprised of 500 members, the *Oliy Majlis* was reduced to 250 seats with the December 25, 1994 elections.[7] According to law, the seats are based on single-member districts with 50 percent plus one of the votes required to win. If no candidate receives this mandate, a run-off election is held between the top two, with a simple majority required for victory. Following the December 5, 1999 election, the current breakdown of seats in the *Oliy Majlis* by party is as follows: People's Democratic Party (HDP)—48; Social Democratic Party (Adolat)—11; Progress of the Fatherland Party—20; Fidoqlar— 24; unaffiliated—147. The latter groups represent deputies from local councils and associations who are technically non-party candidates, including 16 that are from registered "initiative groups." That almost all are card-carrying HDP members means that the HDP effectively holds nearly 200 of the 250 seats in the legislature. In addition, in 2000, the Progress of the Fatherland Party opted to dissolve and merge with the Fidoqlar party, thus consolidating the seat-allocation of the respective parties. It remains unclear how the legislators view their own role—as representatives of specific districts and localities or as policy-makers responsible to the central government. Because Uzbekistan's system is centralized, the latter obligation most likely dominates. Simply put, the legislature is too new, and too weak, to become a forum for regional and local considerations and constituencies.

A similar situation exists for the judiciary system. The judicial branch is hierarchical with regional bodies and a Supreme Court in place. According to the constitution, the Supreme Court oversees challenges to existing laws and ensures adherence to the constitution on the part of the president and the legislature. However, no such challenges have taken place and the court remains passive in its activity. The justices are all appointed by the president and can be removed by the president as well. While officially the *Oliy Majlis* confirms the president's appointees, to date all have been unanimously confirmed.

These three levels of government are paralleled at the local levels—*wiloyats* (regions), districts, and *mahallas* (neighborhoods). Uzbekistan is divided into 12 *wiloyats* (provinces), the Autonomous Republic of Karakalpakistan, and Toshkent city (*Shahri*). These 14 administrative units then are divided into a total of 164 districts, which in turn are divided into cities of provincial subordination, rural councils, and urban settlements. And each of these rural councils is composed of a number of villages. Each one of these units has both an appointed *hokim* as well as a directly elected council (*majlis*). The president selects the former and the latter are elected in regional races. The terms of office tend to be 4 years, although the *Hokims*, as already noted, are dismissed at will by higher-level executives. Powers for regional officers tend to be limited, since their revenues are basically restricted to what is provided by the central government. The power to appoint and remove officials as well as set goals for regional production and financing are strong indicators that the central government still maintains a firm control over the regional governments. And party affiliation is not seen as a factor at this level of administration.

There is also a local level of government called the *mahalla*, or "neighborhood." As will be discussed in a subsequent section, the *mahallas* predate the Soviet era as political and social entities. In practice, the *mahallas* were a means through which issues of local concern (water rights, property disputes, and even social order) were addressed before Sovietization. Not surprisingly, given the cultural importance of age and status in Uzbek society, these regional organizations are often selected among more traditional leaders (village elders, or "aksakals"). In recent years, Karimov has put greater emphasis on this level of government to address issues of "immediate social need." Public opinion polls also suggest that the *mahalla* is fast becoming an important organ of government, ranking second behind the presidency as the most influential or respected level of government in the country. In theory, these community associations also play the role of bridging local government and civil society.

All of these levels of local government are theoretically in charge of the economic, social, and cultural development of their regions. Each component develops and implements its own budget, may have the right to impose local fees and taxes, and provides the local legal system and police protection. Laws guide the executive and government administration "on state authority in the regions" and "on bodies of citizens' self-management" (September 2, 1993). In practice, however, most executive authorities operate as an extension of the central government—as transmission belts to implement central policies. The April 14, 1999, revision of the second law is not expected to change the top-down practice of local government in the country.

In the end, the structure of center-periphery relations in Uzbekistan only underscores the president's authority. While other political bodies have specific rights and responsibilities, there is sufficient latitude given to the president to override these other forces. Indeed, as there have been no real challenges to Karimov by the regional officials, he has acquired both de facto and de jure control of the political system. It is to the area of actual politics—and the informal relationships that exist between the center and periphery—that we will now turn.

THE POLITICS OF CENTRAL GOVERNMENT RELATIONS WITH REGIONAL AND LOCAL GOVERNMENTS

In principle, politics in Uzbekistan begins with the electoral system. For both presidential and parliamentary elections, a winner-take-all system is utilized, with a 50 percent plus one vote needed to win. If no one receives the required percentage, a run-off between the top two takes place within a month. Electoral laws of December 1993 (for national elections) and May 1994 (for regional and local elections) clarify the procedural rules. Voter turnout is generally reported to be between 93.6 percent (the 1994 legislative election) and 99.9 percent (the 1995 presidential referendum), although independent observers have put the actual percentages much lower in the past elections. These Soviet era–like numbers are mostly for international consumption and to help legitimize the president's image in the country. Other studies suggest actual turnout was lower: only 81 percent of those surveyed in a 1996 International Foundation for Election Systems (IFES) poll said they voted in the 1994 legislative election and 78 percent said that they participated in the 1995 referendum to extend Karimov's mandate.[8]

Technically, Uzbekistan is a multi-party system and people are legally free to form political parties as long as they are properly registered. At present, the Halq Demokratik Partiiasi (People's Democratic Party) is the only significant political party in the country. The pro-government party in the country, the HDP is the successor to the Communist Party of Uzbekistan (CPUz), which was renamed in August 1991. Following the failed anti-Gorbachev putsch of that month, Islom Karimov, while still President of the Uzbek SSR, resigned from the Communist Party and helped found the HDP. Conveniently, it was able to occupy the office space, publications, and organizational and financial network of the CPUz, making it easy to maintain a prominent position in the country.

In addition to the HDP, there is the "Progress of the Fatherland Party" (Watan Tarakiati Partiiasi, WTP), the "National Revival Democratic Party" (Milli Tiklanish Demokratik Partiiasi, MTDP), the *Adolat* ("Justice") Social Democratic Party of Uzbekistan and the "Self-Sacrificers Party" (Fidoqlar). The WTP was founded in 1993 and declares itself a "loyal opposition" to the HDP. The MTDP and *Adolat* were founded in 1995 and likewise consider themselves to be constructive, or loyal, opposition parties. Finally, "Fidoqlar" ("Self-Sacrificers") formed in early 1999 as a party for youth. As noted above, the Progress of the Fatherland Party officially merged with Fidoqlar in 2000. With the exception of the HDP, though, these parties are weak in the regions and tend to be Toshkent-based. To an extent, the limitations are self-imposed. For example, the chairman of Fidoqlar stresses that they must first work on attracting the young people of Uzbekistan to their party before they can consider looking at other constituencies. In addition, representatives of these opposition parties all note that "confrontational opposition" is not constructive and that it's important during a time of transition to work toward a common goal. One common goal is supporting the presidency of Islom Karimov.

Because of this dynamic, as well as the restrictions on parties that oppose the presidency, it is difficult to consider Uzbekistan a true multi-party state. In the past, opponents to President Karimov formed political parties to organize their followers. These efforts resulted in the short-lived parties Birlik, Erk, and the Islamic Renaissance Party (IRP). Birlik ("Unity") was founded in 1988 as a social movement advocating greater Uzbek cultural and linguistic rights. With independence in 1991, it attempted to become a political force against

Karimov's HDP. Because of irregularities with candidate registration, its leader Abdurahim Polat was unable to participate in the 1991 presidential election. After a series of crackdowns, the organization was not allowed to re-register in 1993.

Other opposition groups have faced similar problems. Members of Birlik who split over ideological and tactical differences with Polat formed Erk ("Will") in April 1990. Its leader, Mohammed Solih, was allowed to participate in the 1991 presidential election and received 14 percent of the vote. Conflicts over its right to hold rallies and distribute newspapers and other publications led the government to deny the party's re-registration effort in 1993. Like Birlik, its leaders went into exile. The Islamic Renaissance Party (IRP) has never been allowed to register. Its leader, Abdulla Utaev disappeared in December 1992 and has not been heard from since. The September 19, 1996 law on political parties explicitly prohibits the formation of political parties based on religious grounds, thus sealing the legal fate of the IRP. Efforts to unite the opposition in the past five or six years have fallen short of their goals, largely because of the difficult conditions for the opposition and personality differences among the leaders. One recent effort—the fledgling "People's Unity Movement" (Halq Birligi, or HB) which hoped to register for the 1999 legislative elections, but did not.

From the above discussion, it is not surprising that "electoral politics," such as it is, tends to be marginal in Uzbekistan. While political parties must provide evidence that they have at least 3,000 members in at least eight regions of the country for registration, the provision was included to proscribe regional parties rather than facilitate the development of national ones. At the local level, political party affiliation appears to be embryonic, at best. Local councils (*majilis*) and executives (*hokims*) are often "independent" when it comes to party membership. At the *mahalla* level (neighborhood), family loyalty, if anything, is more important. Such lack of identification has hampered the opposition parties' efforts to develop effective support bases. In 1992, for example, the Erk leadership in Toshkent had difficulty in gaining the support of the Bukharan branch. Beyond the regional offices in Khorezm, most Erk branches were small operations, which were easily monitored and neutralized by the government. The situation is no different today. Indeed, officials of the legalized opposition parties recognize that, while they have representation in the regions—generally only at the wiloyat level—their Toshkent offices remained paramount to their organizations. In short, local party organizations—outside of regional offices for the HDP—are almost nonexistent.

This should not be a surprise, because political power is concentrated in the hands of the president. With legislative politics weak in the country, party affiliation is not deemed important and efforts to strengthen party apparatuses in the region are not vigorous. In lieu of party politics where policy initiatives are openly proposed, debated, and resolved, the actual political process in Uzbekistan remains relatively closed. Although draft laws and presidential decrees are readily published and announced in the media, the political process in which they are developed takes place outside of the public arena. And when government decisions are made, explanations are usually not forthcoming. The reality of presidential rule is that—even in legislation pertaining to the regions—the central government makes decisions first. It is up to the regions to act upon the decrees, as they consider appropriate.

At least according to a number of these decrees, the regions do have some nominal power. The December 1992 constitution outlines the role of local government, as does, in more detail, the 1994 Law on Elections to *wiloyat*, Regional, and City Councils of People's Deputies. Legal reforms have also made it possible for search warrants to be authorized and issued by local (*mahalla* and district) militia, and as yet there have been no successful challenges to the legality of such warrants. Regional leaders in Bukhoro and Samarqand admit, though, that budgetary shortfalls and the need to rely on the center for funding limit their ability to effectively govern their *wiloyats*. Recent discussions in the *Oliy Majlis* on regional and local taxation measures have so far not resulted in a clear policy on tax collection and revenue sharing—beyond the current central allocation of national tax revenues.

Anecdotal evidence of innovative *Hokims* and municipal leaders suggests that this is changing, and that there are some individuals willing to take the initiative on reform. In addition, since 1995, President Karimov has spoken on the issue of local-level reform and the need for new personnel. To this end, he has replaced a majority of the *wiloyat* and *raion Hokims*, often filling the posts with individuals who have backgrounds in finance or public administration. That said, continued complaints about local leaders operating in a corrupt or inefficient manner (especially during harvest season, for the rural regions) only underscores the belief that problems remain. As the system is a unitary one, ultimately all such employees work for the central government. More importantly, as noted above, local officials continue the practice of waiting for presidential decrees or actions before they decide how to act, thus dulling the possibility of initiatives being taken at the lower levels of government.

Regional diversity is crucial to understanding the complexity of center-periphery relations in Uzbekistan. The physical geography of the country cannot be undervalued in this assessment. Uzbekistan's topography ranges from empty desert in the west to the densely populated, fertile Ferghona valley in the east. The country, and especially the Republic of Karakalpakistan, suffers from the shrinking of the Aral Sea, as well as desertification and the overuse of fertilizers, pesticides, and irrigation water in agriculture along the Amu Darya, Sirdaryo, and Zarafshon rivers. Uzbekistan borders Kazakhstan, Turkmenistan, Afghanistan, Tajikistan, and Kyrgyzstan. And some parts of the country are difficult to get to from other regions. The Ferghona valley is divided between Uzbekistan and Kyrgyzstan in an especially complicated arrangement. Uzbekistan remains dominated by agricultural production, especially cotton and wheat. Import-substitution industrialization since independence has led to the development of some new industries behind tariff protection and central subsidization through directed credits. The government has also developed oil and natural gas resources to the point where Uzbekistan is self-sufficient in oil and exports gas to some of its neighbors.

The size, composition of the population, and economic structure of these regions vary. In particular, the capital city has a more diverse population and hosts the strongest academic institutions in the country. The result is that people in the rest of the country see Toshkent, and the surrounding *wiloyat*, as alien regions associated with Russian rule. At minimum, while it remains "the center" of national politics, Toshkent does not seem to fully understand regional issues. Aggregate levels of economic production differ widely in the country. Because agriculture is under-rewarded at the expense of industry, regions that are less agrarian have a higher regional per capita domestic product. And the variation in incomes is substantial, with people in the capital on average earning 50 percent more than the national average while inhabitants of the poorest regions of Karakalpakistan, Namangan, Samarqand, and Surkhondaryo earn an average of less than 70 percent of that of the country as a whole.

In one of the more insightful studies of regionalism in Uzbekistan, Don Carlisle notes that Uzbekistan should really be looked at as a collection of regions.[9]

Table 12.1
The Population of Uzbekistan at the Start of 1998

	Population	Percent
Uzbekistan		100.0
Karakalpakistan	1,447,100	6.1
Andijon	2,098,100	8.9
Bukhoro	1,369.200	5.8
Jizzakh	914,400	3.9
Qashqadaryo	2,051,000	8.7
Nawoiy	762,600	3.2
Namangan	1,841,700	7.8
Samarqand	2,561,200	10.9
Surkhondaryo	1,644,100	7.0
Sirdaryo	643.500	2.7
Toshkent Shahri	2,117,800	9.0
Toshkent	2,288,100	9.7
Farghona	2,561,200	10.9
Khorzam	1,263,000	5.4

Source: State Department of Statistics, Chislennost' naseleniya Respubliki Uzbekistan na 1 Yanvarya 1998 (Toshkent: State Department of Statistics, 1998), p. 13.

Table 12.2
The Population of Uzbekistan at the Start of 1998

	1996 (PPP$)	Percent of National Average
Uzbekistan	2,469	100.0
Karakalpakistan	1,686	68.3
Andijon	1,983	73.3
Bukhoro	2,562	103.8
Jizzakh	1,999	81.0
Qashqadaryo	2,359	95.6
Nawoiy	3,609	146.2
Namangan	1,697	68.8
Samarqand	1,725	69.9
Surkhondaryo	1,690	68.5
Sirdaryo	3,179	128.8
Toshkent Shahri	2,590	104.9
Toshkent	2,590	104.9
Farghona	3,300	133.7
Khorzam	3,114	126.2

Source: State Department of Statistics, Chislennost' naseleniya Respubliki Uzbekistan na 1 Yanvarya 1998 (Toshkent: State Department of Statistics, 1998), p. 13.

From the Ferghona Valley and Toshkent in the north and east, to the ancient cites of Samarqand and Bukhoro in the physical center of the county, and the south and far west (the latter including Karakalpakistan), Uzbekistan is regionally situated. Elites in each region tend to forge their own alliances, and it is not uncommon for the top elite of each region to be in competition with the leaders of other regions for scarce resources and political power. Thus, for example, when observers note that leaders from the Samarqand region of the country dominate the Karimov administration, it is also a statement noting that Karimov's own region of Samarqand is ascendant. The importance regional competition plays in the national political game is difficult to understand. This kind of opaque regional politics has continued since the formation of the Soviet Union and the early attempts by the Bukhoro elite to dominate politics. The rise to power of Islom Karimov, noted earlier in this chapter, was also a product of regional rivalries. For outsiders, such dynamics at the regional and local level are almost impossible to decipher.

Policies of central leaders in Soviet and then independent Uzbekistan towards regional and local governments have varied from concern for the forms and practices of regional authority to heavy-handed central control over the regions. Regional appointments in Uzbekistan are of great political significance, if anything as such sinecures can be either rewards or punishments for those close to the president. Recalling Karimov's own "exile" to Qashqadaryo in the mid-1980s, he has done the same to others. For example, in early 1992, Karimov made an almost clean sweep of the regional offices, putting his more trusted allies in the key Ferghona districts and in Bukhoro and Samarqand. The general trend is that as Karimov increased his power and authority, the central state has become more assertive in its relations with the regions. At the same time, in 1999, President Karimov has at least nominally pushed to have the regions initiate more programs and legislation.

As an example of the first tendency, recognizing regional autonomy when the position of the central authorities is relatively weak, the March 1990 legislation that established the presidency in Uzbekistan took great care to recognize that this new institution would not infringe on the rights of then Karakalpak Autonomous Soviet Socialist Republic.[10] However, as old institutions were solidified and new institutions were created by the strengthening regime, the nominally autonomous republic was instead brought under the direct supervision of the government and the existing leaders of Karakalpakistan were forced to resign. By July 1997, when President Karimov made an inspection tour of the Karakalpak Autonomous Republic to force the retirement of these new incumbents whom he blamed for poor cotton harvests, the republic was treated the same as any other *wiloyat*. Karimov imposed the standard central response to political and economic problems in Nukus—a purge of the leading cadres.

Another example of this stock response is Karimov's treatment of the leaders of Farghona. The region had long been a problem for Karimov: in November 1996, the President made an inspection tour of the region to take local officials to task for corruption and tolerating high levels of crime. This was followed by the replacement of the *Hokim* (administrative head) of *Ferghon*a *Wiloyat* in February 1997 following Karimov's criticism of the 1996 economic production from the region. There is also scattered evidence of civil unrest in this region since December 1997. The government has blamed attacks on the police in Namangan in Farghona on unofficial Islamic groups and arrested and imprisoned members of purported Wahhabi sects in response to these attacks. And Karimov's replacements in the region have not lasted. In November 1998, the *Hokim* of Samarqand—Alisher Mardieyev—was removed after less than two years in office and replaced with a trusted Presidential ally from the center, Erkin Ruziev—whose job it is now to clean up that *wiloyat*.[11] The regional change was accompanied at the center by the firing of Jurabekov, Karimov's First Deputy Prime Minister in charge of monitoring regional bosses, who was sacked as too powerful for Karimov's comfort.[12] Again, it should be noted that personal relations are difficult to verify in these situations. Nevertheless, given the traditional role of such ties in Uzbekistan, it is to be expected that they play a role in the political process of that country.[13]

Within each *wiloyat*, there are pressures to perform, fulfill quotas to the center, encourage foreign investment, and address the problem of land reform in a way that is not problematic. This is particularly true in the "tourist" *wiloyats* of Bukhara and Samarqand where Ministry of Foreign Affairs offices have been established to monitor foreign groups passing through these regions.[14]

Key obstacles for regional governments are the initiation of policy, budgetary funding, and the efficient provision of service. In order to carry out their ever-scrutinized tasks, fulfill plans, and improve social and economic conditions in their regions, it is essential that these issues be resolved. The lack of specific information from the regions makes it difficult to assess the magnitude of the overall problem of regional governance. Regional bosses and their spokesmen are unwilling to criticize the Karimov government and independent newspapers, such as they are, do not levy charges against the center. On the contrary, if there are complaints, they are almost always directed against the regional *hokim* or council—usually just prior to their sacking by the central government. The main products of regional and local governments—their economic and social policies—are the subjects of the next two sections.

The Economics of Central Government Relations with Regional and Local Governments

Budgetary controls remain a significant factor in center-periphery relations in Uzbekistan. It is estimated that over 80 percent of the *wiloyat* budgets are actually dictated from the center. This is not just the out-sourcing of moneys, but also includes directives on how to spend funds. However, while local governments receive most of their support from the central budget, certain cities and regions (Toshkent and Samarqand for example) do have local taxes on businesses that support some local government activities. Data on such revenues, unfortunately, is unavailable. In general, municipal governments must comply with the national budget plans but do not always receive sufficient funds from the center. This is clear from the common criticism of *wiloyat*, district, and city officials (and sometimes removal from office) by the president or one of his subordinates for not adequately meeting the demand for basic services, which includes worker's salaries, pension payments, equipment and road upkeep, and so on.

At the center, authoritarian control is also evident in the economic reform program of successive Uzbek Prime Ministers and their governments. After initially delaying economic reform and retaining to the extent possible the institutions of the command economy, the authorities introduced a comprehensive stabilization and economic reform program similar to those adopted by other CIS states, albeit with a more gradual timetable for implementation. Reform was announced in conjunction with the introduction of the new national currency, the sum, in July 1994. The character of the reform plan and these policies are consistent with the governments declared emphasis on maintaining social stability by avoiding rapid restructuring with sharp costs to the population. The combination of the absence of reform, this program, and inherited structural attributes of the Uzbek economy resulted in a cumulative decline in the real GDP of the country far less than most other post-Soviet states. According to International Monetary Fund (IMF) staff estimates, economic output fell "only" 11 percent from 1992 to 1997, including a return to growth in 1996.[15]

While only between a third and a quarter of GDP comes directly from agriculture, periodic poor harvests have had a disproportionate impact on macroeconomic results.[16] Much of the industrial sector focuses on cotton processing as well. And this impact again appears in part related to government policies imposed due to social stability concerns. The government reacted to a poor 1996 grain and cotton harvest by increasing lending and credits to the agricultural sector—increasing the fiscal deficit and driving up inflation. Larger grain imports also worsened the external balance of the country and created additional pressure on the currency. The poor harvest led Uzbekistan to temporarily change government economic policies towards reform to reach an agreement with the IMF on a systemic transformation facility. However, other government responses to the crisis soon led to a suspension of this agreement by the IMF as the government missed its targets for deficits, inflation, and other indicators. The poor cotton harvests in the last years of the 1990s prompted Uzbek officials to discuss financing options with the IMF.[17] However, relationships between the government and this international financial institution remain strained.

Government policies aim for food self-sufficiency through a switch to grain production, but simultaneously the state depends on cotton, the main crop in the country, for revenues and exports. And state policies that emphasize strengthening the state and social stability over growth and reform in agricultural production inhibit rural development. A system of state orders has been maintained for both grain and cotton. And the government mandates the sale of cotton through a state monopoly. Prices are also set artificially low for both crops, with the state gaining in arbitrage the difference between low domestic prices and higher world market prices through cotton exports. The former state and collective farms dominate agriculture as nominally "private" cooperative (*shirkat*) farms. This allows the regime to characterize 98 percent of all agricultural production as produced in the non-state sector.[18] The contribution of private (*dekhkan*) farms to production remains small. On the other hand, the household plots of the rural population, as in the Soviet period, provide most of the vegetables and fruits and almost all of the meat produced in Uzbekistan. These products are then marketed directly to consumers for cash rather than through retail trade outlets.

Land tenure remains controversial, with state ownership retained and private sales banned even in the new June 1998 land law. Housing and small enterprises have also been largely privatized, with the government turning them over to residents and employee cooperatives, while large and medium-sized industry has faced little actual privatization. While the regime characterizes many as non-state, privatization has been nominal, with large shares still held by the state and other shares transferred to other state organizations.

In other ways, these policies that are allegedly to maximize stability instead suggest an unstable future. The population, especially in rural areas, continues to grow at a rapid rate while economic output has declined or grown at a slower rate: official figures claim a plausible 1.6 percent real GDP growth in 1996 but implausible 5.2 percent growth in 1997 and 4.4 percent in 1998.[19] Growth in 1999 and 2000 were more in the area of 3 to 3.5 percent. With this development path, the excesses connected to Soviet-era cotton monoculture have basically continued despite strong criticism of the social and environmental costs of these policies in the perestroika period. The heavy use of fertilizers and pesticides with inefficient irrigation continues to degrade the soil, cause health problems in rural areas, and shrink the Aral Sea. And conditions for much of the population have apparently stagnated or declined. Despite these economic efforts to maximize stability, the real monthly minimum wage appears to have declined dramatically from 1991. Wages in the state sector are also tied to minimum wage levels. And most social transfers are pegged to the minimum wage and so have also declined in real terms. These other transfers, developed to replace subsidies for food and other items that were dismantled at the end of 1994, go to needy families and to support children. Average wages have done better and apparently remained above 1991 levels in real terms for almost continuously since 1993.[20]

But policies that attempt to maximize short-term stability may in the long term prove destabilizing. Authoritarian rule appears to have a thin base, with grave uncertainties about who will succeed Karimov.[21] Repression of dissent, which has waxed and waned somewhat erratically against secular groups, has remained fierce against Islamic groups. The rejection of secular opposition may make political Islam a more powerful force: without an alternative, more dissent may turn towards Islam. And the rapidly growing population will be in search of employment in the future.

Other perils to stability, which are emphasized by the regime, are from weak neighboring states of the region, in particular Tajikistan and Afghanistan. Uzbek support and limited intervention on the size of ethnic Uzbek and secular forces in both countries has failed, with the Taliban increasing its control of Afghanistan and the United Tajik Opposition brought into the government in Tajikistan. While official pronouncements emphasize the external threat to the stability of the country and opposition to foreign meddling in Uzbek domestic politics and society, the possibility of contagion through disaffected Uzbeks within the country seems far more possible than direct foreign intervention in Uzbekistan.

Social Policies

Social protection is central to the approach of the government to gradual reform. While some aspects of the Soviet-era system remain essentially intact, such as the pension system, other areas have been decentralized. Most significantly, since 1998 the program providing financial assistance to low-income families has been shifted to *mahallas.* While the central government budget provides the funding, the *mahallas* select and monitor beneficiaries. *Mahallas* appear to have wide discretion to decide the benefits to be received by each applicant family, with no quantitative criteria set out for the provision of benefits. Because such regulations were enacted so recently, it is too early to determine how effectively they will address social needs.

One issue that has been left largely in the hands of the central government is minority education and opportunity. Uzbekistan is relatively homogeneous, compared to other Soviet successor states, with over 75 percent of the population identifying themselves as ethnic Uzbeks in the 1989 census. The percentage breakdown of the minority population is as follows: 6 percent Russian, 5 percent Tajik, and 4 percent Kazakh, and almost 10 percent other groups, including the Karakalpaks, who have their own autonomous region. While the Russian minority does not pose a direct threat to the regime, their very presence means that Russia will continue to feel that it must play a role in the region. Indeed, Russian-Uzbek relations center on the status of the Russian minority and the freedom of the Orthodox Church in the country. Russia could step up pressure on Uzbekistan if far-right politicians in Russia insist that the minority is unfairly persecuted.

A more immediate concern is the Tajik minority, which is centered in the Bukhoro-Samarqand region, the "historic center" of Uzbekistan. Tajiks have long claimed these cities to be culturally Tajik, and organizations like "Samarqand" emerged shortly after independence to promote the rights of this minority. Deemed a threat to state stability by the Karimov administration, this organization was denied the right to register and its leaders were briefly imprisoned. Further complicating the situation is the fact that ethnic Uzbeks living in northern Tajikistan are frustrated with that country's policies, leading to irredentist sentiments in both directions across the same border. According to residents in the Bukhoro-Samarqand region, added to this is the fact that ethnic Tajiks are are more prevalent than the official government counts. Estimates of 15 percent or higher have been given, although there is no documented proof. The government ostensibly plans to conduct a nation-wide census by 2001, which could clarify the ethnodemography of the country.

Regardless of ethnic background are the family relations that dominate local life in Uzbekistan. Unfortunately, the research conducted on this issue has not really advanced our understanding of the situation in the past 20 years. Articles written in the 1970s and 1980s, which outlined regional differences and family relations still merit study today, however few new explanations have been forthcoming. In large part, this is not a result of the quality of scholarship; on the contrary, there are excellent works being written on Central Asia today. Rather, it is that the inner workings of family and clan relations are simply not going to be grasped by short research trips to the region. These "private" relations will remain outside the purview of public discourse for some time to come. As noted in the discussion above on the political dynamics in Uzbekistan, regional differences do matter, and it is often the case that particular "clans" dominate specific areas. To manage this web of relationships and potential rivalries required political acumen reminiscent of pre-Soviet Emirs. Ironically, the rivalries that exist today, if one looks at the geographic distribution of political elite, parallel those of the nineteenth century. This was a problem noted by the Soviet leadership when it took over Central Asia in the 1920s, and remained an issue throughout the Soviet era.

This discussion of regional differences draw one back to the institution mentioned at the beginning of this section: the *mahalla*. In his effort to centralize authority, President Karimov has actually increased the powers of the local, sub-national governments in Uzbekistan. The *mahalla*, or "local community," has become an important part of the president's restructuring plan. Traditionally, in pre-Russian Central Asia, the *mahallas* were means by which local disputes were settled and forms in which the central government could collect taxes and levy militaries, if needed. Dispute resolution would require that the village or rural elders, the aqsaqals, preside over specific cases and pass judgment. Often, these entailed issues such as water rights, property inheritance, and access to agricultural or grazing lands. Familial matter, such as marriage disputes, also included the participation of the village elder women. Indeed, this "parallel system" was meant to keep things in order and to have conflicts not escalate to bloodshed.

The Sovietization of the region was particularly harsh on these practices, as the notion of non-elected village elders interpreting social customs was simply unacceptable. Economic matters, such as water rights, were to be subsumed under the control of planning agencies and economic ministries. Social and legal matters, likewise, were taken over by more centralized institutions. It was often the case that the village elders, the aqsaqals, were forced to publicly perform demeaning tasks, such as building latrine trenches, in an effort to destroy this social institution. In the late 1930s, such figures were often considered "enemies of the state" and simply purged.

As is being discovered, though, the practices of the *mahalla* did not disappear during the Soviet period. They simply adapted to their new, harsher surroundings. Thus, when President Karimov opted to revive such institutions, they took root very quickly. The IFES survey found that popular attitudes towards the *mahallas* are still relatively positive.

From the perspective of President Karimov, this can generally be seen as a positive development for three reasons: First of all, he can present himself as a defender of "traditional values" and a leader who wants to return to the people what is rightfully theirs. Second, the *mahallas* serve an important practical function; by resolving many local issues at the local level, the political system should, in theory, become more efficient. Third, by preventing local issues and disputes from rising up to the national level, problems do not land on his doorstep quite as much and he can concentrate on other matters. The failure of a *mahalla* to resolve a question does not reflect poorly on the president.

VIEWS OF CENTRAL, REGIONAL, AND LOCAL GOVERNMENT

With political power vested in the central government of an authoritarian regime, popular opinion in the regions may seem superfluous. After all, decisions are made in Toshkent—more specifically in the presidential apparatus—and the regions have little room to maneuver beyond the parameters set for them. At the same time, with Karimov's emphasis on the *mahallas* in the past few years, the lower level are clearly seen as important outlet for mass participation in a limited set of issues. Thus, how the center and regions cooperate in these areas is important. More incumbent for the central leadership is to know when things aren't working well in the regions. A lack of understanding in this area could prove fatal to the region. Particularly in authoritarian regimes, an inability to read potential crises before they escalate is essential to the longevity of the central government.

Anecdotal evidence suggests that the politically active people in the region consider Toshkent to be unresponsive to their needs. They stress that the central government does not understand their situations and is incapable of solving the problems in their particular region. In many ways, the Soviet-era perception that the regions held of Moscow (considered to have the power but not cognizant of region-specific crises) has transferred to a post-Soviet *wiloyat* perception of the Uzbek capital. This is particularly true with budgetary allotments, as noted earlier, and with legal recourse. Government officials working in the Ferghona Valley, Bukhoro and Samarqand complain that they are given quotas, but often not the means to achieve them. Thus, when they fail to meet these targets, as they inevitably will, political casualties may result. This has appeared to be a more acute problem in recent years, as opposed to the early-1990s, most likely in light of the fact that the central government has altered the financial distribution process in the country. The Soviet-era "safety net" system has disappeared, with the exception of some basic staples and services.

Mass opinions may be studied by surveying a subset of the population and generalizing from the sample to the whole population. While the authoritarian regime in Uzbekistan makes public opinion a difficult topic to study, a few independent opinion surveys have been done in the country.[22] While the authorities are not supportive of independent research on society and are reticent, to say the least, about public opinion polls, surveys have included questions that investigate popular attitudes towards regional and local government as well as the central administration.

The data examined below are from an IFES survey sponsored by the United States Agency for International Development.[23] IFES conducted a nationwide, almost representative survey in Uzbekistan at end of 1996 and start of 1997 which asked a battery of open and closed questions and frequently categorized the large number of unanticipated answers volunteered by numerous respondents.[24] The poll examined the views of 1,830 adults who were surveyed over three weeks in December 1996 and January 1997.

Each of the sections below briefly considers the nationwide situation and then examines the views of across the 14 *wiloyat*-level divisions of Uzbekistan. While the number of citizens polled across the country provides statistical confidence that these attitudes are representative of the population as a whole, much less confidence is possible about popular opinion in the 14 provincial-level divisions since the number of respondents from even Ferghona, the most populous region of the country where 206 people were interviewed, is so small.[25]

The first two questions asked individuals about their level of satisfaction with their own quality of life as well as their view of the general situation in the country. In Uzbekistan, 70 percent of the population claimed that they were fairly well off individually while 57 percent asserted that they were fairly satisfied with the situation in country.[26] Between 79 and 55 percent of the population asserted that the situation was fairly good in all 14 *wiloyat*-level administrative divisions. Only in Nawoiy and the city of Toshkent, the two most urban *wiloyats* and the most prosperous regions in terms of per capita GDP, did the percentage that asserted their personal quality of life was fairly bad nudge above a quarter of those surveyed. Regional trends in popular assessments of the situation in the country as a whole have a similar pattern: the majority of respondents in all but the city of Toshkent were satisfied or very satisfied, with over a third fairly dissatisfied in only the city of Toshkent and the surrounding *wiloyat*. Finally, the percentage of respondents that asserted they were very dissatisfied rose above 10 percent in only Karakalpakistan and the city of Toshkent—the most opposite regions of the country in almost all respects.

Respondents were asked which state structures currently had the greatest influence on their lives. In the country as a whole, 53.1 percent of those surveyed asserted that the Presidency had the most influence while only 2 .4 and 7.8 percent thought their *wiloyat Hokimiat* or rayon/city *Hokimiat* had the greatest effects on their lives respectively. On the other hand, 19 percent of respondents noted that the actions of their *mahalla* have the most effect on their lives. In all *wiloyat*-level divisions, a plurality of respondents asserted that the President was more influential than any other institution. In all but Bukhoro and Qashqadaryo an absolute majority of respondents agreed. Only significant numbers of residents of Bukhoro (9%) and Andijon (5%) felt their *wiloyat Hokimiat* was most influential organ, while rayon or city *Hokimiats* were seen as most powerful by high numbers of respondents in Andijon (17%), Bukhoro (18%), Jizzakh (10%), and Toshkent city (10%). Assessments that *mahalla* influence was the most substantial was above 30 percent of respondents in Qashqadaryo and Nawoiy, above 20 percent in Bukhoro, Samarqand, Surkhondaryo, and Sirdaryo, and above 10 percent in all but Andijon and Namangan.

Levels of faith in the potential of state institutions, rather than their actual performance as discussed in the previous section, are higher across the board and have a structure similar to their views on current influence. While 69.2 percent or those polled in Uzbekistan felt that the President "can do the most to solve the problems our society faces," only 2.1 and 5.1 percent asserted the same thing about their *wiloyat* or rayon/city *Hokimiat*, and 9.9 percent had the highest opinion of the future of their *mahalla*. Views that the president had the greatest potential approached less than an absolute majority in only Farghona and support for the potential of *wiloyat Hokimiats* never exceeded five percent of those polled in any region. Only Andijon had over 10 percent of respondents with the most faith in rayon/city *Hokimiats* and respondents looked at the potential of their *mahalla* as the strongest at rates approaching a quarter of those polled in only Karakalpakistan, Nawoiy, Ferghona, and Khorezm.

When asked whether the local organs of power have more or less real power compared to the pre-independence period, 60.4 percent of respondents in the country as a whole asserted that the local authorities have greater authority now, 20.7 percent claimed less power, and 18.9 percent did not respond or did not know. The sample of residents of Bukhoro and Sirdaryo were particularly prone to see stronger local officials in the current period; over 80 percent asserted their officials had more power since independence. Absolute majorities claimed their local officials were more powerful that before in all but four of the five *wiloyats* noted below. On the other hand, a majority of respondents in Jizzakh claimed their local government had less power, as did almost 40 percent of those queried in Samarqand and Khorezm. Respondents lacked knowledge or refused to respond to this question in Andijon and Ferghona, where around 40 percent of those polled did not know or refused to answer the question.

Despite the government's stress on the social safety net, the population in Uzbekistan reports receiving few substantial social benefits from their local governments. At the national level, 72.2 percent of those surveyed responded negatively when asked whether they or anyone in their immediate family had received any kind of subsidy in the past year that they needed to support their standard of living through the local authorities. On the other hand, only 25.9 percent reported receiving these kind of benefits. The regional distribution of these reported benefits varies. Over a third of the population reported being subsidized in Namangan, Surkhondaryo, Ferghona, and Khorezm and less than 20 percent of the population claimed they received support in Karakalpakistan, Qashqadaryo, and Toshkent. Regional levels of poverty seem to have little to do with the provision of aid. For example, Karakalpakistan, the poorest region, has less of the population receiving aid than relatively prosperous regions like Ferghona (see Table 12.2).

The population was also asked whether the composition of local government had changed with independence or whether "the people who run things in your *mahalla* and local organs of power today are pretty much the same people who were running things even before independence?" Popular opinions about the degree of change of personnel were sharply divided. At the national level, 39.2 percent of respondents asserted that different personnel were running their local governments while 26.6 percent viewed these cadres as unchanged in composition. And 26.7 percent of respondents volunteered the not very informative opinion that some government personnel were new and some were the old leaders. This response makes the analysis of this question difficult for Andijon, Bukhoro, and Namangan, where 61, 47, and 43 percent of respondents respectively gave this vague reply. At the regional level, a plurality of respondents asserted that their local officials were predominantly the same people as under Soviet rule in only Surkhondaryo (46%). Around a third of the populations of Karakalpakistan, Qashqadaryo, Samarqand, Toshkent City, Khorezm, and Toshkent felt that the same people were in charge. However, over half of those polled noted the dominance of new people in Jizzakh, Nawoiy, Samarqand, and Sirdaryo (where 82% had this opinion) and almost half asserted the same in the city of Toshkent and *Ferghona wiloyat.*

As noted earlier, if there is to be an increase in power at the local or regional level, it will most likely take place with the *mahalla*. The survey asked respondents to characterize the level of activity of their *mahalla*. Nationwide, almost 60 percent of those asked asserted that their *mahalla* was very or fairly active, while a third claimed their *mahalla* was not very active or inactive. The percentage of respondents that reported their *mahalla* was very active ranged from a low of 2.8 in Karakalpakistan and 2.9 in Nawoiy to 31 percent in Namangan—with responses nearing 20 percent in Andijon, Surkhondaryo, and Ferghona. A majority or plurality of respondents asserted their *mahalla* was fairly active in all but Karakalpakistan, Jizzakh, and Sirdaryo, where inactive (31%) or not very active (47 and 52%) were the most common sentiments respectively. Assessments were particularly split in a number of regions; in Jizzakh and Qashqadaryo the population split almost down the middle on this question, with about half noting high levels of activity and half asserting their *mahalla* was passive.

When asked whether their *mahalla* had been reorganized, at the end of 1996 only 16.3 percent of the population of Uzbekistan asserted that such change had occurred. Two-thirds of respondents noted that no reorganization had taken place (19% of those polled did not know or chose not to respond to this question). None of the 14 regions had a plurality of respondents affirm reorganization. Around a third of those surveyed noted reform in only Namangan, Surkhondaryo, and Khorezm. The population knew little in Andijon and Toshkent, where a plurality of respondents chose don't know or did not respond. And the lack of reform was the opinion of an absolute majority of those questioned in all the rest of the regions. In Sirdaryo, remarkably, all

54 people surveyed said reform had not yet taken place. Over 80 percent claimed no reform in Jizzakh, Qashqadaryo, and Nawoiy.

Mahalla participation appeals to the organization for help, and perceptions about whether this form of local government was actually helpful also vary across regions (and across ethnic groups in the country). When asked whether they participate in the activities of their community organization, 64.7 percent of those polled in Uzbekistan as a whole responded affirmatively, a third negatively, and only one percent did not know. The populations of some regions were far less likely to report participation. Only around a quarter of the population of Karakalpakistan and Toshkent, just over half those in the city of Toshkent, and under 60 percent in Andijon claimed to have participated in their *mahalla*. The highest levels of participation were reported in Ferghona, where almost 85 percent of those surveyed claimed to play a part in their *mahalla*. Nationwide, only 13.3 percent of the survey claimed to often turn to their *mahalla* for help, while 43.4 percent said they rarely looked to their community organization and 42.5 percent claimed to never turn to their *mahalla*. An absolute majority of respondents in Karakalpakistan, Andijon, Qashqadaryo, and Toshkent claimed to never go to their community association for aid. In addition, never was the most popular response in Namangan, Samarqand, Bukhoro (in the latter, rarely was equally popular as a response). On the other hand, 23 percent of those surveyed in Nawoiy and 26 percent in Ferghona claimed to often turn to their *mahallas*. Single-digit responses to this option were only reported in Karakalpakistan, Andijon, Bukhoro, and Toshkent. Ethnicity appears influential in this regard. Two-thirds of the 147 ethnic Russians and 42 Karakalpaks in the all Uzbekistan poll claimed to never turn to their *mahalla* while only 38.1 percent of ethnic Uzbeks gave this response. An ethnic Uzbeks claimed to often turn to their community organizations at the highest rate of the seven groups enumerated in the survey (15.4%). Of those nationwide that had turned to their community organization for help, only five percent found that the *mahalla* usually did not help them. However, respondents across Uzbekistan split relatively evenly on whether *mahallas* were usually or sometimes helpful with each response chosen by around a quarter of the total survey.[27] Appealing to their *mahalla* was found usually to be helpful by about half of the respondents in most *wiloyats* that sought assistance and sometimes helpful by the rest. Dissatisfaction, a response that their *mahalla* usually didn't help them, was only asserted only as often as a third of the time in Karakalpakistan. High proportions of satisfied members were found in Andijon, where almost three-quarters of members that made appeals found their *mahalla* usually helpful. The proportion of the membership that made appeals and were somewhat satisfied, as compared to usually satisfied, was fairly close in most regions, with the exception of Bukhoro, Nawoiy, and Jizzakh, where few claimed to usually find some satisfaction.

The often bipolar patterns in the popular attitudes of the population towards the institutions examined above reflect both the centralized state and domination by the President as well as show scattered support and use of lower-level organs, especially the *mahalla*. And some regional differentiation is evident, although higher levels of support for *hokims* might be transient and change rapidly with pension and wage payments and arrears or other local policies.

CONCLUSIONS

Authoritarian rule and the blending of Uzbek and Soviet institutions characterize the relations between the center, regional authorities, and local governments. On the one hand, President Karimov has been able to call on pre-Soviet institutions such as the *mahalla* and the *Hokimiat* to establish the kind of local government and sort of center-periphery relationship that existed throughout much of Central Asian history. On the other hand, the mechanics of the centralized system still reflect the Soviet era in both politics and economics. Central planning and authority—especially through budgetary control—remains dominant. Thus, any effort on the part of local or regional political figures to act autonomously is clipped by constraints from the center.

A centralized national political system with a fragmented local power system only increases the likelihood of a "disconnect" between the regions and the center, and widens the gap between those who are in power and those who are not. Indeed, as national policies become perceived as "irrelevant" to the regions, the likelihood that actions taken at the local level may run counter to the ideals of the national government increases. And as Uzbekistan enters the twenty-first century, this, above all else, may present the most significant challenge to the central leadership.

NOTES

1. Pravda vostoka, 1 January 1992, p. 1.
2. William Fierman, "Political development in Uzbekistan: democratization?" in *Conflict, Cleavage, and Change in Central Asia and the Caucasus*, ed. Karen Dawisha and Bruce Parrott (New York: Cambridge University Press, 1997), 360.
3. Karimov, 1997.
4. Levitan, 1995.
5. Ibid., p. 7.
6. Karimov brought Jurabekov back into the government in April 1999 as head of the State Committee for the Supervision of Water Resources, an important post in since the agricultural sector is almost completely dependent on irrigation.
7. Candidates ran for the 250 seats in what was billed as the first multi-party election in the country. Run-off elections were held for 45 seats in January and February of 1995.
8. Steven Wagner, "Public Opinion in Uzbekistan 1996" (Washington, D.C.: International Foundation for Election Systems, 1997).
9. Carlisle, 1986.

10. Gregory Gleason, "Uzbekistan: from statehood to nationhood?" in *Nations and Politics in the Soviet Successor States*, ed. Ian Bremmer and Ray Taras (New York: Cambridge University Press, 1993), 331.

11. Interview with Ruziev, May 1999.

12. Economist Intelligence Unit, *Country Report Uzbekistan*, 4th Quarter 1998, p. 13.

13. Gregory Gleason, "Fealty and Loyalty: Informal Authority Structures in Soviet Asia," *Soviet Studies* 43 (1991): 613–628.

14. Interview, May 1999.

15. International Monetary Fund, *Republic of Uzbekistan: Recent Economic Developments* (Washington, D.C.: IMF, 1998), 8.

16. Ibid., p. 27.

17. Economist Intelligence Unit, *Country Report Uzbekistan*, 2nd Quarter 1999.

18. *Pravda Vostoka*, January 21, 1998, p. 1.

19. Economist Intelligence Unit, *Country Report Uzbekistan*, 2nd Quarter 1999, p. 6.

20. International Monetary Fund, *Republic of Uzbekistan: Recent Economic Developments* (Washington, D.C.: IMF, 1998).

21. The person that they had demanded replace Karimov—then Vice-President Shukhrullo Mirsaidov—was also removed from office: first designated "State Secretary" (when the office of Vice President was abolished), and then out of office completely. Since 1992, Mirsaidov has been charged with various economic crimes and abuse of office charges, and his family has faced repeated persecution.

22. See Graham Smith et al., *Nation-building in the Post-Soviet Borderlands: The Politics of National Identities* (New York: Cambridge University Press, 1998) and Nancy Lubin, "Islam and Ethnic Identity in Central Asia: A View from Below," in *Muslim Eurasia: Conflicting Legacies*, ed. Yaacov Ro'i (London: Frank Cass, 1995).

23. We would like to thank Anthony Boyer and Rakesh Sharma at IFES and Steve Wagner at QEV Analytics for sharing the data and information about the methodologies used by their Uzbek contractor. USAID, IFES, and QEV Analytics are not responsible for the analysis and conclusions of this chapter.

24. The survey is almost representative. Representativeness is difficult to determine since there is no good data to provide an accurate baseline of the characteristics of the population. I make the most simple assumption for statistical purposes—that the sample is a random one, which leaves the probability of sampling error driven by number of people sampled and the distribution of responses to questions. The statistical margin of error, the confidence interval around each estimate, is determined for the hardest hypothetical case—when answers to a question are split 50–50. The margin of error calculated in this manner is plus or minus 2 percent. A few particular problems made the survey less than representative. The sampling frame left out 3.7 percent of the population (around 800,000 people) that were residents of geographically inaccessible regions or ones under martial law. The city of Termez, on the border with Afghanistan, and one district in Nawoiy are the only the only two regions that were excluded where a significant percentage of the population of their respective *wiloyats* were not included in the sampling frame.

25. To avoid imputing a false sense of accuracy to the polling data, we have not used decimal places in the discussion of regional results and rounded the data to the

nearest percentage point. Under a hundred respondents were surveyed in the least populous *wiloyats*: 54 in Sirdaryo, 70 in Nawoiy, 79 in Jizzakh, and 95 in Khorazm.

26. These results are paradoxical. Responses to a later question find that 71 percent of Uzbekistanis strongly or somewhat agree that "their family constantly doesn't have enough money to buy basic foods" which is difficult to square with high levels of satisfaction. This contrast suggests the difficulties of conducting "honest" surveys in an authoritarian state where the population appears reluctant to criticize their government. Responses to the first few questions may be less valid than those later in the questionnaire that are answered after the interviewer has built up at least some rapport with respondents.

27. Less confidence should be placed in the representativeness of even these nationwide results since almost 45 percent of those surveyed, 793 people, were not asked whether their *mahalla* was helpful since they had already said they never turn to their community organization for help.

CHAPTER 13

IDENTITY/DIFFERENCE IN CENTRAL ASIA: TRIBES, CLANS, AND *MAHALLA*

Anthony Bichel

This chapter explores the construction of identity/difference in Central Asia by examining some of its most prominent social institutions, tribes, clans and *mahalla*[1] and their roles within the frameworks of governance of the Central Asian states. By situating the discussion within a critical framework the chapter seeks to focus on the interpretive elements of political analysis in respect to the depiction and ordering of Central Asian civil society.

INTRODUCTION

Our assumptions about the constitution and behavior of the world greatly influence our interpretations of it. The world is an interpreted space, filtered through ideological, rhetorical, philosophical, mathematical, scientific, linguistic, gendered, racial, cultural, religious, and political theories. Nothing escapes this filtering process. Difference[2] is one of the primary themes of critical theory, which is as much a method of inquiry as it is an explanatory and conceptual framework. Expressed through a variety of paradoxical pairings, such as identity/difference and inside/outside, difference facilitates the critical theorist's perspective by providing a solid means to identify and distinguish subjects/objects that have been hermetically sealed off from debate through the use of exclusionary discourse.

Difference is fundamental to the interpretation of identity and fact. This is especially true within science where objective knowledge is produced through a process of exclusion by which negative elimination stands in place of positive affirmation; objects are defined by what they are not as opposed to what they are. A common example of this phenomenon is the nation state, which is defined principally by its negative (exclusive as opposed to inclusive) characteristics, such as territorial sovereignty. By employing difference in this fashion it becomes possible to extend the application of critical theory to Central Asia by problematizing the nature and role of indigenous institutions such as tribes, clans and *mahalla* within the matrix of state/local relations.

Meta Theories

Usually reserved for templates such as modernity and postmodernity, meta theories serve to shape and inform debate by establishing guidelines for inclusion and exclusion. In Central Asia, the discourses on identity and ethnicity have developed to the point where they are inseparable from the study of the region and therefore serve a gate-keeping function that makes clear and rigid distinctions between the initiated and the uninitiated. These discourses have assumed great importance in the legitimization of Central Asian scholarship, and as such they have become sacred texts that are often beyond reproach. By subverting this disciplinary process of exclusion, we can decouple these interpretive practices from their totalizing frameworks.

Identity

Deconstructing, describing, defining, discovering, and disciplining identity is one of the leading academic fads of the day, attracting scholars from across disciplines. Philip Gleason credits Eric Erickson with popularizing the term *identity* in the late 1950s, further noting that its subsequent exponential rise in usage led Robert Coles to describe it as the "purest of cliches" (Gleason, 1983).

Leaders worldwide use the language of identity, claiming an interest in protecting and enhancing national identities. This global discourse on identity is a recent one, and a testimony not to the universality of identity concerns but, rather, to the "rapid spread of hegemonic ideas about modernity and ethnicity" (Handler, 1994). Richard Handler cautions academics that the first step in analyzing these public discourses on identity is for scholars to distance themselves from the "ideologies of identity." Handler recognizes that leaders manipulate Western sympathies to the concept of identity as a tool for international recognition because identity "is a language the empowered understand" (1994).[3] Handler, in strident postmodern style, describes the western concept of identity in the last two centuries "as an object bounded in time and space, as something with clear beginnings and endings, with its own territoriality" (1994). Postmodernists such as Handler lament the spread and commodification of a realist perception of identity throughout the world and its attendant discourse, "identity politics."

Similar concerns have also been addressed by Harrison White, who takes the position that identity is not "the common sense notion of self, nor does it mean presupposing consciousness and integration or presupposing personality" (1992). White, a sociologist, prefers to define identity as "any source of action not explicable from biophysical regularities, and to which observers can attribute meaning" (1992). Identities, he continues, are "perceived by others as having an unproblematic continuity . . . persons develop only under special social circumstances" (1992). Accordingly, identities are derivative forms of interpretation to be extracted from basic principles of social action and not, as some claim, something to be atomistically imagined as pre-existing entities outside of the social imaginarie. The thrust of his argument centers around the aspects of contingency and control as they relate to the formation of individuals and their melding to society via social networks of interaction. Borrowing from Harold Garfinkel (1967), White uses the example of a playground[4] to demonstrate how children are products of compound social identities and their meaning as persons is anchored in the various networks of the site. White also argues that social organization is but a by-product of the assembly of this process (1992). What we call identity, and perceive as social structure, is the result of contending counteractions locked in a dynamic equilibrium.

Central Asians have long suffered from an identity crisis. One identity sprang from a loose affiliation of nomadic tribes and clans, who wandered the steppes in seasonal patterns following their herds in search of fresh grasses. The other was the product of an urban-centered aristocracy and merchant class who lived in the great and prosperous trading cities that defined the Silk Road. Each group had its own particular character, customs and habits that differentiated it from the other. Intertribal warfare, interceding invaders such as the Persians, Romans, and Chinese, and the geographically disparate nature of Central Asians' lifestyles prevented ethno-homogenization and instead laid the groundwork for cultural harmonization, the subordination, not assimilation, of one group or idea to some higher order. Societal allegiance was based on one's genealogical and geographical relationship (kinship) with the *khan* (king) and not on any sense of meta-personality, such as ethno-nationalities, that is, Uzbeks, that are understood today.

Ethnicity

Ethnicity and identity are probably the two most popular topics of discussion within the field of Central Asian studies. Together they represent a system of intelligibility, the proscribed *raison d'etre* of the Central Asian states. Ethnicity and its handmaiden identity sit poised above the discussion of tribes, clans and *mahalla*, legitimizing their particularistic interpretive discourses while simultaneously benefiting from the structural support created by the ethnically-derived regional and blood allegiances of the tribe, clan and *mahalla*. This reflexive sentiment posits ethnicity/identity as social constructs rather than physical manifestations—making all arguments on the subject subservient to the interaction characteristics of these social phenomena that most scholars take for granted as fixed and tradable commodities.

W. Lloyd Warner in 1941 (Sollors, 1986) coined the term *ethnicity.* It is a derivative of the Greek *ethnikos*, which originally meant "heathen" or "cultural strangers." In conjunction with this usage, others, such as Albert Robillard (1997) and Deane Neubauer (1998), have argued that ethnicity is a global phenomenon created by the imperial expansion of Europe and the United States with the ethnic *Other* placed in contradistinction to the globalizing European self.[5] Ever since ethnicity has been understood as a concrete social fact, used in everyday conversation, scientific discourse, writing and politics.

Contemporary explanations of ethnicity are wanting in a number of regards. First, most explanations focus too strongly on the definitional characteristics of ethnicity rather than on its socially negotiated achievement. When I speak of ethnicity as a socially negotiated achievement, I am referring to the interaction practices involved in the recognition and production of ethnicity, practices such as the ritualistic cleaning of tea cups at a neighborhood chai house, patterns and styles of dress, measures, ingredients and preparatory elements of food dishes, and so on. Considering that ethnic representation often carries with it specific practices and that those practices are frequently learned not only by their practitioners but also by practitioners of differing habits, there is a definite culture of reflexive recognition of both other and self embedded within the framework of ethnic identification. Second, by operationalizing the characteristics of ethnicity, scholars have reduced an open-ended (unfinished) enterprise to a finite and quantifiable commodity ripe for exploitation on the open market. Third, in an attempt to situate ourselves within the ethnic framework that we have constructed, scholars tend to be overly sympathetic to the cultures in question in our efforts to see them as more like ourselves. Fourth, because scholars have failed to balance these incongruities we have excused ourselves from answering the questions surrounding shared cultural achievements and biologically manifest attributes of place. To the extent that many of the cultural practices that go into the manifestation of ethnicity are geographically specific, we must recognize the environmental components as unique rather than as mere circumstance. A "common homeland" is not sufficient in and of itself; the composition of that homeland matters if only to the extent that said practices have been adapted to account for changes in its condition.

Accordingly, all facets of ethnicity can be construed as, and reduced to, a series of interpersonal practices that are subject to continuous interpretation and revision, not only by the participants but also by non-participating observers. The signification of certain practices, such as outdoor cooking, entails much more than the simple recognition and cognitive processing of "I see someone cooking on a grill." Mentally we extrapolate to fill in the blanks of our always incomplete perceptions, as Garfinkel[6] has noted. In this same fashion we can cumulatively add up the sum total of our perceptions of others in ways that work to create (reproduce) ethnicity as an overlying veil of interpretation and meaning as a response to our perception of several otherwise independently intelligible events. Thus the Uzbek tea-house (*chai hana*) and its attendant customs becomes recognizable not as a series of individual accomplishments, but rather as a complete event that bespeaks one's ethnic preferences.

Despite its contentiousness, ethnicity is perhaps most often discussed in terms of its political ramifications; hence "ethnic group" is a term often confused with culture. By identifying themselves ethnically, a group escapes classification by others. Furthermore, institutions such as tribes, clans and *mahalla* lend support to these constructions by providing a recognizable facade that legitimates the group's identification. Because the West privileges ethnic identities, groups are wise to describe themselves in these terms.

If we look at ethnicity and identity as social achievements, then we must rethink some of our assumptions about the situation in Central Asia today. Much of the literature on the region is premised on the assumption that ethnicity is something tangible, and that as a result of its efficacy it is the most formidable of all forces in Central Asia.[7]

Given the history of the region, with its long lines of conquerors, one could make the argument that the various expressions of ethnicity, vis-à-vis the demarcation of the titular ethnic groups, have at least as much to do with self-expression and self-assertion as they do with historical evidence, precedent or cultural revival.[8] The latter, often associated with the concept of achieved identity, is frequently linked to the power struggles among various elites[9] within the society, or as Roosen states, "cultural revivals are never truly a return to the past. The past is usually reconstructed to serve the group as they try to go forward" (Fitzgerald, 1993).[10] Roosen also argues that ethnic assertiveness is related to the defense of social or economic interests and that people change their ethnic identities only if they can profit by it. He writes: "[E]thnicity has to do with material goods, whether in a positive or negative way. . . . The longing for material goods does not by itself procure ethnic identity and ethnicity. Ethnicity, however, is directly concerned with group formation, and thus with power relations" (Roosen, 1989).

Commodification, whether of culture or ethnicity, is just another manifestation of power. The ability to control the production, reproduction and dissemination of one's culture, particularly when that culture is tied politically to an ethnic history, is essential to the survival of the ethnic identity. It goes to the heart of the interpretive practices that formulate ethnicity. Trading on the particular manifestations of tribe, clan and *mahalla* serves only to reinforce the overarching assumptions of identity/ethnicity, ultimately leading to the destruction of the former in favor of the consecration of the latter. This leads to the reflexive collapse of all of these institutions.

Indigenous Institutions: Tribes (Plemia)

Winthrop's *Dictionary of Concepts in Cultural Anthropology* provides generally accepted definitions of terms that are widely used and abused among Central Asian scholars. Winthrop defines a tribe as a "culturally homogeneous, non-stratified society possessing a common territory, without centralized political or legal institutions, whose members are linked by extended kinship ties, ritual obligations, and mutual responsibility for the resolution of disputes" (1991). Winthrop further notes that there is an ethnic or cultural identity associated with tribes, an idea supported by John Honigmann, who conceived of tribes possessing three common attributes: a common territory, a common language, and a common culture (1964).

There is a great deal of latitude in the ways that Central Asian scholars use terms such as tribe and clan. This is due in part to the different affinities and experiences that scholars from such diverse fields as linguistics, psychology, anthropology, political science, sociology, religious studies, and the humanities bring to their work. Central Asia is less an organized discipline than a ready case study, and it is precisely because of this "inclusiveness" that the terminology of the region has yet to be resolved. In addition to the academic turf battles, there are legitimate reasons for the semantic confusion. While the peoples of Central Asia are commonly referred to as a homogeneous collective, in fact there are notable distinctions between the tribes of this region that predate Russian and Soviet interference. Martha Brill Olcott delineates these distinctions into two general categories: (1) the historical economic distinction between nomadic and sedentary cultures and (2) the Turkic or Persian origins of the languages of the people (Olcott, 1994).

To discuss these distinctions is itself a problematic endeavor representative of the identity crises created by conflicting and overlapping identity labels given to the Central Asian peoples. The sedentary/nomadic culture and Turkic/Persian language distinctions are widely understood as predating Russian influence, while the nationalistic labels Uzbek, Tajik, Turkmen, Kyrgyz, and Kazak are a product of the Soviet period. So when these terms are used in collusion to simplify explanations of Central Asian culture and identity, historically and culturally inappropriate interpretations result, adding yet another chapter to the mythological fiction that has come to be called the history of Central Asia.

The nomadic/sedentary distinction has led to distinctive uses of the terms *clan* and *tribe*, terms used to refer as much to a people's way of life as to their relationships. The nomadic cultures were those of the peoples today labeled as Kazaks and Kyrgyz, while the Uzbeks and Tajiks had a sedentary culture. Olcott notes that the people who came to be separated into Kazaks and Kyrgyz were frequently closely related families distinguished principally by their migration patterns. Tajiks and Uzbeks used similar farming methods, but spoke Persian and Turkic dialects, respectively (Olcott, 1994). There are dozens of "identifiable" tribes in Uzbekistan. The most commonly cited number in pre-Soviet times was 92, discounting the Sarts (Schoeberlein-Engel, 1997). The majority of the population belonged to just a few dozen tribes: Oghuz, Qarluq, Kipchak, Jalair, Barlas, Qungrat, Manghit, Laqay, and Yuz. Today there is much less emphasis on tribes than existed in the past. Most observers find that Uzbeks themselves find little use or value in perpetuating their tribal lineage (Makarova, 1997), choosing instead to privilege other institutions.

Shahram Akbarzadeh writes more cautiously of tribalism in Turkmenistan, noting that "tribal affiliations could seriously jeopardize the unity of Turkmens as a political unit" (Akbarzadeh, 1999). What distinguishes the Turkmenistan case from other Central Asian states is the role of *Turkmenbashi*[11] played by President Saparmurat Niyazov. There are serious paradoxes at work in Turkmenistan. Even though the existence of tribes is officially denied, the *Turkmenbashi* has referred to them as a divisive force in Turkmen society. Yet, like President Karimov, the *Turkmenbashi* has used the institution to his political advantage—incorporating five carpet designs belonging to the Akhal Teke, Yumut, Salar, Ersari, and Kerki tribes into the national flag in order to legitimize his own rule and co-opt the allegiance of other tribe members, many of which still retain their influence from the Communist era. The leading tribe in Turkmenistan is the Teke. President Niyazov is a member of the Akhal Teke tribe. Despite the official denials, Turkmenistan has managed to successfully incorporate the most abstract of the indigenous Central Asian institutions into its civil life.

Clans (Rods)

In the eyes of many scholars, clans are seen as the basic political units of organization in Uzbekistan and the whole of Central Asia (Bohr, 1998). Despite the popularity of this claim, it remains largely undocumented and highly contentious, particularly in the eyes of government officials and bureaucrats intent on building secular nation states. Conversely, there are almost as many interpretations of the clans, their role in society, their origins, their institutions, their customs and their geographic distribution as there are people willing to expound on the issue itself. Some scholars treat the subject as the keystone to understanding and explaining Central Asian society and politics.[12]

Rakhat Achylova has written that since Kyrgyzstan gained its independence, tribal communities (with their associated clan structures) "once again became the fundamental institutions necessary for the survival of individuals and families," testifying to the institution's long-lasting viability and continued relevance (Achylova, 1995). Others have suggested that the entire enterprise be disregarded altogether, noting that the lack of professional agreement stems from the lack of evidence and knowledge. Still other scholars dismiss the words tribe and clan and the ideas they represent as "Western constructs" which have no meaning whatsoever in Uzbek society. About the only thing that can be said with certainty is that the enterprise of indigenous institutions is likely to remain a highly contentious issue as the various factions of this debate, the traditionalists, modernists and postmodernists continue to struggle for the supremacy of their cause.

To further complicate matters, the term *clan* is employed differently across Central Asia. In Kazakstan, Kyrgyzstan, and Turkmenistan the clans are based on lines of descent, emanating originally from the Kazak greater, lesser and golden hordes. Their respective political and social structures are based on kinship, which was traced patriarchally. Their territories are named after the inhabiting groups (Turkomen = Turkmenistan, Kazaks = Kazakhstan, Kirghiz = Kyrgyzstan, and Kara Kalpaks = Karakalpakistan[13]), rather than the more pervasive reverse pattern. This nomadic model of clan identification contrasts with the sedentary model of clan organization and identification in Uzbekistan and Tajikistan. In these two countries clans are based on regional networks of patron-client relations, themselves based on the political and administrative institutions of their respective states; consequently, clan names are a derivative of their geographic locale, most often an oasis city, rather than blood lines. Uzbek examples include the Samarqand, Bukhoro, Toshkent, and Kharazm and Fergana clans. Examples from Tajikistan include the Khujandi, Kulabi, and Qurghonteppa clans.

While membership in both nomadic and sedentary clans is based on interpersonal relationships, and as such is limited and fixed, interaction between clans is very fluid, particularly in economic terms. Politically there is less fluidity.[14] I believe this is due in part to the very personal nature of the region's politics, where the level of offense is often attached locally, at home, to one's self, wife, or mother, but I also believe that the early partitioning of the region based on assumed ethnic identities and loyalties, and the subsequent commodification of these identities, plays a major role as well.

Accordingly, most of us are consociationally[15] blinded to other realities because our gaze is restricted to a limited spectrum of social understanding based largely on personal experience. Journalism has suffered from these phenomena since its inception, mistaking eyewitness accounts for truth and objective reporting for understanding. The only thing objectionable in this sense is the positioning of the reporter's subject vis-à-vis the reporter himself. The distance between the two is not physical but rather socio-cultural. The simple designation of something as curious or of interest as an object of study transforms it into a subjective article, ripe for manipulation.[16]

Hence the notion of "clans" arises in order to explain and relate the local institutions of kinship and family to the greater societal surrounds. Evidence for these analyses abound in the daily lives of the Uzbeks as familiar patterns, obligations and daily chores is conducted in the open. Perhaps it is the malleability of the term that lends itself to such broad assumptions about power and influence, or maybe it is the subconscious validation of our own experiences as we strive to relate the comparatively independent western worlds of home and work and our own familiar relationships within these contexts. In a fashion reminiscent of our own imagined pasts, we project not only our experiences onto others but also our fantasies as well. In this fashion we romanticize the notion of family, treating it as if there is something unusual about people helping their familiars to the mutual exclusion of others in order to better their own circumstances.[17]

Clans are most commonly described as the institutions that exercise localized control of politics and economics. Generally they are perpetuated through family bloodlines, geography, and past allegiances. Regional power groupings maintain local bases of support while national offices preserve regional and local connections. Members of President Karimov's clan (Samarqand-Jizzakh) hold most high offices in Uzbekistan's government. The main competitors are the rival Toshkent and Fergana-Namangan-Andijon alliances (Bohr, 1998). Nepotism[18] is generally accepted if not expected, and members of a single clan often dominate government ministries. Contrary to the apparent reality of the influence of clans in Uzbekistan, President Karimov states:

> It seems quite natural for people to provide mutual aid to each other when they are related to some extent by kinship. But when, through groups based on kinship, regional or ethnic principles are developed (mostly informal) in governmental or other structures, prompted by their narrow interests, and these groups promote their interests over the interests of the state to the detriment of the common cause and nationwide interests; when in order to achieve their goals such groups plan to move up their members into the existing state power or other sorts of hierarchy, then it becomes dangerous. (Karimov, 1998)

Dangerous to whom? Obviously, Karimov has benefited greatly from his clan affiliation, the very exercise of which serves to legitimate the enterprise within the state structures of Uzbekistan, but he would deny the same avenue to others under the guise that such exercises of unmitigated kinsmanship would somehow harm the country.[19] Karimov also writes about clans in terms of their threat to the stability and security of society—this after first laying down the premises in the above quote that there are understandable and legitimate reasons for the development and exercise of clans. Karimov grounds these security concerns in the ethnic-based self-consciousness that clans represent, which when paired with the "ultimate goal" of clans to elevate their members into the highest reaches of government encourages a set of priorities that competes with the state for loyalty and influence, and ultimately retards the development of a national consciousness in favor of local articulations (Karimov, 1998).

Loyalty to one's own clan and to the "constitutional" framework that the clans represent often supersedes loyalty to either ethnicity or the state, but by no means can it be said that these familiar relationships are universally recognized or accepted. What is most frequently forgotten in this debate is that there are millions of Uzbeks and other Central Asians who identify very strongly with the state of their birth, Soviet created or otherwise. To these people, most of who live in the major cities, talk of clans, tribes, and blood allegiances is tantamount to folklore. These people constitute the engineers, doctors, technicians, and other professionals of their countries, their governments' best hope for manufacturing a unified national identity.

The definitive glue that holds these familiar arrangements together is the ancestral lineage from which each of the clans takes its identity. Lawrence

Krader has written perhaps the most telling expose on Central Asian genealogical structures and heritage. In his book *Peoples of Central Asia* Krader writes:

> The entire social system of the Central Asian peoples is oriented to the past. The genealogies which the peoples maintain are at once constitutive and symbolic of this orientation. . . . [A] Central Asian descent line is founded upon a genealogy which is known and shared by all its members. It is a unilineal descent group; descent is traced in one line only: the male line. Relationship through the mother and through the female kin is not counted for purposes of clan membership; the genealogy is actually the roll call of the clan. [These] genealogies may be likened to the charter of incorporation, a roll call of the membership, a passport for the establishment of identity, an insignia to show relative rank, and a claim on hospitality and cooperation. The genealogical kin-group, whether village, lineage, clan, clan-confederation, or tribe, was like a corporation in some respects, like a state or nation, and like a trade or labor association. (1963)

Krader's insights into the functional elements of the clan resonate as clearly as his understanding of its origins, complexities and functions. Krader illuminates a subject that is difficult for those living in contractually oriented (Western) societies where familiar relationships are repressed in favor of the efficient delivery of consumer goods and services.[20] To the extent that clans provide for the needs of the people they remain vibrant institutions; however, as the mechanisms of the state are slowly substituted in place of familiar arrangements, then clans too begin to lose their sense of purpose, followed in quick succession by their means of action. As they stand today the clans of Central Asia are too diffuse and ambiguous to perform effectively in the current political environments, but they remain important symbols of power, order, and prosperity.

Mahalla (Neighborhood)

Mahalla (*Mahallah*) translates from its Arabic roots as encampment, neighborhood or community (Britannica, 1999). The term *guzar* is often used in place of *mahalla* among the Tajiks living in Uzbekistan.[21] There are many other variants in existence throughout the Muslim world. Familiar institutions are not uncommon internationally, but they tend to flourish more in societies that de-emphasize contractual social relations. As such they are more common in eastern societies (Haas, 1997).[22]

Although too little has been written about *mahalla*, there is a small body of literature from which to draw. Donald Carlisle, the most prolific scholar on this subject, describes the *mahalla* as being "based in familial networks and cemented by genealogical principles, the *mahalla* constituted the neighborhood where a Muslim was born, reared and ordinarily lived for his or her entire life" (Carlisle, 1991). Ekaterina Makarova takes a similar view, noting that "the *mahalla* determines the whole range of social relations of an individual in daily life" (1997). The *mahalla* provides goods and services to its constituent members, such as tables, utensils, and other practical items (Koroteyeva and Makarova, 1996).[22] Accordingly a *mahalla* can also be considered a small economy of sorts due to the interactive nature of its activities. Events such as weddings, funerals, birthdays, and so on are times where gifts are exchanged among participants. Whether the gift is in the form of goods, such as food, or services, such as entertainment or religious functions, there is a constant flow of material between members. This exchange of goods and services helps reinforce the members' loyalty to their community by adding a dimension of economic necessity to the familiar basis.

Sergei Poliakov helps puts the *mahalla* into perspective historically by noting that the *mahalla* "is a transformation of the traditional Central Asian society of neighbors, adopted for modern social and economic conditions" (1992). He and others have noted that the *mahalla* first gained outside recognition when the Soviets took charge of the region. The Soviets tried to eradicate the *mahalla* as a center of public life because it provided a contrary focus of civil duty and social responsibility that conflicted with the "new Soviet man." Failing to accomplish that task, the Soviets looked for ways to incorporate, and thereby control, the *mahalla*. They established local electoral commissions and party associations within each *mahalla*. The *mahalla* lost its economic function because the state was in control of the means of production, but otherwise the institution was not only preserved, but also guaranteed to spread throughout the cities and countryside.

Today the entire population of Uzbekistan belongs to one of the more than 10,000 *mahalla* (Bohr, 1998). Unlike tribes and clans, *mahalla* are widely recognized and accepted by the people of Uzbekistan as a legitimate institution of traditional origins with modern applications. For example, since 1992 *mahalla* in Uzbekistan have enjoyed official recognition and sanction vis-à-vis their inclusion in the state Constitution as "organs of self-government" (Bohr, 1998).[24] No other institution in Uzbekistan has as much influence as the *mahalla*, and as such it is the definitive social, economic and political institution of Uzbekistan. It is the alpha and omega of Uzbek identity, the central component of Uzbekness. Presently the government of Uzbekistan employs the *mahalla* as part of its means of maintaining power. The *mahalla* is the primary site and source of state welfare assistance, with the local leader[25] having total control over who receives what and how much (Karimov, 1998).[26]

In short, *mahalla* are the center of Uzbek daily and economic life. They are largely based on kinship, but that is not as strict a designation as it once was. They represent the basic administrative division of the country and the primary vehicle for the exercise of its power. The *mahalla* serve as a means of surveillance and as vehicles for the construction of national identity. *Mahalla* and their members are required to participate in all national festivals and cultural celebrations. The rural *mahalla* have a greater degree of control over their economic fate than their urban counterparts, but given the poor crop yields the past few years, that freedom remains an open question.

It is ironic that while western democratizers have foresworn the *mahalla* in favor of alien institutions and customs, the Central Asian Mafia has capitalized on the practical value of these cultural institutions as a means of expanding their drug trade. Accordingly:

> [T]he mafia gangs have set up their "businesses" in the heart of the *mahallas* with complete impunity, especially as it is easy to buy respectability and popularity by financing construction of a mosque or a chaikhana (tea-house). As one good turn deserves another, the *mahallas* guarantee watertight protection and nobody says aloud what everybody knows; that the chaikhanas serve tea to the neighborhood elders while they chat the day away, and at night play host to prostitutes and card-players—and serve as reception centers for drugs brought in by petty couriers. (OGD, 1998)

The resilience of social institutions is always best demonstrated by their continued ability to meet human needs. Thus the *mahallas* survived Soviet rule, local governance and western indifference. Regardless of any individual government's design the *mahalla* will persist because of the role it serves in the survival of the Central Asian populace. Democratically speaking, the *mahalla* are one of the most promising indigenous institutions in the region. Their locality makes them invaluable conduits of information and communication between the government and the people; their tradition lends itself to the legitimization of the government, and their organization secures and encourages the development of civic individuals. As a potential avenue for increased popular participation in government, the *mahalla* remains unparalleled among competing indigenous institutions.

SUMMATION

The future relationship between the central governments of the Central Asian states and their respective indigenous institutions and the impact that these relationships will have on the continuing democratization of the region is a topic worthy of further research. Each state will have to be studied individually in order to account for and appreciate the subtle differences in the tribal, clan and community structures. Many Central Asians remain skeptical of Western institutions such a political parties; yet they are reticent to explore the boundaries of their own indigenous institutions. Trapped within social, cultural and political systems that depend on their indigenous (local) characters to legitimate the ruling political regimes, the Central Asians find themselves and their collective heritage inadvertently supporting the logic of repression that prohibits their full fruition. In public the institution of the *mahalla* is evoked constantly as proof of the continuation of indigenous traditions and democratization, but in private the most democratic elements of the tradition are quietly repressed in the interest of national security. Practically speaking it is highly unlikely that any political successor or challenger could arise outside of these institutions and it is for that reason that these institutions will not soon disappear regardless of official doctrines to the contrary.

In conclusion what can be said about the relationship between the centralized state governments and the various forms of tribalism, clannism, and community in Central Asia? As we have seen tribes, clans and *mahalla* are seemingly trapped between two competing epochs of history—posterity and modernity. As relics these institutions serve to remind the Central Asians of their collective triumphs, defeats, and cultural tenacity. As modern organs of Central Asian states they portend an opportunity for the Central Asians to overcome the Western conceits and prejudices frequently associated with democracy. Whether the Central Asian states will develop participatory styles of government that capitalize on their rich indigenous institutional structures or not depends as much on Western agendas as it does Central Asian sensibilities, and in the end that stipulation may make all the difference.

NOTES

1. *Mahalla* are vernacular expressions of community within Central Asia, ranging in form from extended families and rural collectives to urban/suburban neighborhoods/subdivisions. The term *mahalla* is of Arab origin and has been adopted to greater and lesser degrees across the region; however, the term is most frequently associated with communities in Uzbekistan.

2. I define difference as the embedded forms of alienation within each socially constituted achievement.

3. The reader should consider Handler's cautions when analyzing Uzbekistan's President Islam Karimov's attempts to lay claim to the Central Asian "Great Man" tradition. The reader should also note David Lowenthal's words on identity and heritage, as Karimov seemingly already has: "Heritage has always obsessed those fortunate enough to have it. It explicitly endowed its possessors with sovereignty over others' lands and lives, and lent permanence to power and privilege. Heritage was not only what rulers were entitled to; it defined them and assured their rule. And its loss spelled impotence. Echos of these older modes of heritage [and identity concepts] can yet be heard [in Uzbekistan]" (Lowenthal, 1994).

4. Garfinkel uses a playground full of children to accentuate his point about interpretive practices and communication by calling attention to the act of playing by deconstructing each of the interactive elements involved in watching children play.

5. Ethnicity undoubtedly existed before this expansion wherever people of different languages and cultures encountered each other, but this consciousness served to localize identities, rather than to socially validate ethnicity as a universal fact.

6. Harold Garfinkel (1967) is responsible for popularizing Karl Mannheim's "documentary method of interpretation" by way of his own work in ethnomethodology. Garfinkel is most interested in the "underlying patterns" that Mannheim's (1969) work suggests and how these patterns, which Garfinkel refers to as practices, are socially constructed and construed. In effect, Garfinkel is interested in how people communicate with one another given that people never actually say what they mean, whether intended or not, and that since social discourse somehow continues unabated, despite its shortfalls, there must be a shared universe of meaning that is simultaneously related to and estranged from actual conversants.

7. It is almost impossible to read any work on Central Asia without stumbling over the issue of ethnicity (Dannreuther, 1994; Kangas, 1994; Malik, 1994; Rashid, 1994; Starr, 1994; Smolansky, 1994; Saivetz, 1994; Szporluk, 1994; Naumkin, 1994; Paksoy, 1994; Mandelbaum, 1994; Dawisha and Parrott, 1994; White et al., 1993; Clark, 1994: Rubin, 1994, Duran, 1992; Becker, 1994; Blank, 1994; Batalden & Batalden, 1993; Fuller, 1991, 1992, 1993, 1994a, 1994b, 1994c; Makhamov, 1994; Atkin, 1994a, 1994b, 1997a, 1997b; Nissman, 1995, 1997; Ochs, 1997; Ghorban, 1993; Karasik, 1993; Karpat, 1995; Manafi, 1993; Ramazani, 1992; Munro, 1994; Black, 1991; Karimov, 1992, 1993; Bremmer, 1997; Fierman, 1991, 1997; Goodman, 1994; Haghayeghi, 1995; Hiro, 1995; Spolnikov, 1994; Hauner, 1990; Ohmae, 1993; Olcott, 1994a, 1994b, 1994c, 1996, 1997a, 1997b; Katz, 1995; Huskey, 1997a, 1997b; Rupert, 1992; Gankovsky, 1994; Allworth, 1965, 1990, 1994; Hunter, 1996; Holmes, 1997; Kaiser, 1994; Critchlow, 1991, 1994a 1994b; Pipes, 1994; Mesbahi, 1995; Cullen, 1994; Islam, 1994; Lubin, 1994; Rumer, 1994; Hale, 1994; Konarovsky, 1994; Amin, 1994; Sajjadpour, 1994; Sayari, 1994; Payin, 1996; Asankanov, 1996; Kremenyuk, 1996; Porkhomovsky, 1994; Fridman, 1994; Panarin, 1994; Malashenko, 1994; Zviagelskaya, 1994; Ferdinand, 1994; Akiner, 1994, 1995; Bondarevsky & Ferdinand, 1994; Robins, 1994; Saleh, 1995; Hyman, 1994; Gleason, 1993, 1996, 1997a, 1997b).

8. Sovietologist John Paxton concurs that the creation of the five Central Asian republics, carved as they were from the various *khanates*, is the root cause of the ethnic strife that plagues the region today, since the decision about which republic to join and, consequently, which ethnic label to adopt depended primarily on the region in which an individual's village was located or the language spoken at home, rather than a preconceived idea of ethnicity (Paxton, 1988).

9. This notion of "achieved identity" presents an interesting paradox, whereby the most vocal champions of cultural revivals are almost always the educated elites among the ethnic group in question. This is paradoxical because the slogans of ethnogenesis are formulated by the very people farthest removed from the traditional culture that they are seeking to reestablish.

10. The Hawaiian renaissance of the late 1970s is another good example of this point.

11. The interpretations of this title include "first citizen" of Turkmenistan, "tribal chief" and "unifying core for all Turkmen tribes."

12. Gregory Gleason employs the term "clanocracy" to describe the interrelationship between clans and politics, noting that in Central Asia "clanocracy is the foundation of the national consensus" (Gleason, 1997). Gleason remains isolated in the Central Asian literature in his criticism of Western democratic institution-building efforts in relation to the indigenous structures.

13. Karakalpakistan is actually an autonomous *Vilayet* (administrative district) in Uzbekistan. Located at the northwestern end of the country, Karakalpakistan was officially part of Kazakstan until 1932 when the Soviets transferred it to Uzbekistan. The Karakalpaks, who are ethnically related to the Kazaks, were traditionally a nomadic people.

14. Instances of ethnic violence have been almost endemic. To the extent that one's job, housing, socio-economic status and political influence can be tied in one way or another to one's ethnicity, there is little room for "socially constructed" enterprises. Feelings of animosity run deep among the peoples of the Central Asian repub-

lics, encouraged by the Soviets, Russians and other invaders. Evidence of this hatred abounds: the riots in Alma-Ata during December 1986, Fergana in June 1989, Dushanbe in February 1990, and the Osh province of Kyrgyzstan in June 1990 (Zainutdinov, 1990). Paradoxically, apart from the riots in 1986, 1989, and 1990, relations between Central Asia's many ethnic groups have been marked by a striking absence of violence. The lack of violent ethnic conflict in Central Asia since independence is especially noteworthy, given the sharp decline which each of the states has suffered in its economy, severe dislocations in the workforce, reductions in patterns of national wealth and in standards of living. Central Asia has suffered virtually every social ill, hyperinflation, rising unemployment, rising death rates, falling birth rates, deteriorating health care, government corruption and crumbling infrastructure, which could be expected to increase social tension and so make inter-ethnic violence more likely, yet Central Asia has recorded no large-scale ethnic-based disturbances since 1991.

15. I am using this term in the absence of any other suitable phrase. By it I mean to describe the social and cultural constructs that enable one to recognize what they see as an event, such as a wedding party, a funeral, or a demonstration.

16. A good example of this phenomenon in Western society would be a home decorated with angel-topped trees, garland, blinking lights, and mistletoe in July. The same Christmas narrative that so wonderfully explains the decorations in December fails to (re)produce itself convincingly when it is distanced from its "proper" time and place. Other cultural miscues also abound. For example, Western reporters have on occasion seen fit to mockingly note the voracious shopping habits of Central Asian dignitaries while on business trips to the West, contrasting their seemingly lavish spending sprees with the sad state of their national economies. Like the Christmas decorations which remain meaningful only within a specific context, the cultural texts of gift giving—where the traveler is expected to purchase gifts for all of his family, friends and co-workers—the shopping sprees are contextual, and thus easily misread by observers reared in a consumer culture.

17. We in America have fallen in love with the notion of community and are seeking to vindicate those feelings by elucidating instances of our dreams that are manifest elsewhere in the world. Call it a clan, global village, ohana, *mahalla*, community, barrio, ghetto, or hood, all bespeak the same desire for human connectedness. Because we in the west do not organize our lives around our families as do the Central Asians, we fail to recognize the similarities in our own daily lives, similarities that seem strange to us by comparison but not by reason.

18. Patricia Carley has noted the depths to which political nepotism is ingrained throughout Central Asian society, adding that during the period of Soviet rule, Soviet ideology helped to reinforce the more corrupt elements of these institutions by delegitimizing the more traditional moral and social restraints originally imposed by the tribal/clan divisions (Carley, 1995).

19. President Karimov is not alone in his concerns about the development of indigenous institutions, albeit for decidedly different (personal) reasons. Rakhat Achylova also expresses concern about the "paradox" of tribalism in that "it is difficult to develop a true democracy if the boundary between political roles based on individual merit and political roles based on tribal affiliation becomes blurred. Political participation and entitlement based on particularistic tribal affiliation present the first step toward exclusionary politics" (Achylova, 1995).

20. What I am trying to say here is that an individual's personal consumption habits often supercede duties and obligations to family—the exchange of goods and services between family members has come to replace much of the qualitative aspects of home life, so much so in fact that we find it necessary to differentiate "quality time" from that of our normal routines.

21. According to Sergei Poliakov, the Tajik name for *mahalla* is *avlod*, which is another Uzbek word for clan. He also notes that the institutional history of the *mahalla* originated with and parallels that of the Tajik extended family, but that over time, and under Soviet supervision, the *avlod* lost its economic and social functions to the *mahalla*, thus becoming strictly a kinship group similar to the Uzbek clan (1992). Poliakov's use of *avlod* in favor of *guzar* is not problematic, but his point of origination is. No other source collaborates his rendering of the institution's history, which raises nationalistic and ethnic questions that are common among scholars of Central Asian history.

22. The Hawaiian *ohana* provides an example of an institution that parallels the Uzbek *mahalla*. Both institutions are predicated on mutual cooperation and an exacting loyalty to the group. Participation in communal activities, like street cleaning, policing, weddings, rites of passage, and other festivals, is expected, unlike the traditional "volunteerism" of western, particularly American, culture. Each person is expected to give to the community those services they are capable of providing, or to put it into more recognizable terms "to each according to his needs and from each according to his ability." In Uzbekistan, as in Hawaii, being excluded from the community means facing the difficulties of life alone, and it is for that reason that the greatest fear facing anyone living under such conditions is to be an outcast from the community.

23. Recently, in conjunction with the USAID sponsored "Red Apple" project (which distributes contraceptives and contraceptive technology to women in Uzbekistan) a number of *mahalla* in the Tashkent area have been enlisted in the delivery of health/educational information to the local residents (Red Apple Contraception Program http://www.tfgi.com/projects/hl_5_97.htm). The focus on women's issues is due in part to a 1995 decree that declared that a woman would serve as the second in command of every *mahalla*, and that the same women would further connect the *mahalla* to the state organs by simultaneously serving as the *ex officio* head of the local Women's Committee (Bohr, 1998).

24. Unlike the Soviets who only begrudgingly granted legitimacy to the *mahalla*, the government of Uzbekistan moved swiftly to appropriate their socio-cultural value as a measure of the authenticity of the government's "Uzbekness." By encouraging the (re)creation of such a well-worn tradition the Karimov government sought to solidify its credentials as the protector of the people, guardian of the collective memory and keeper of the faith.

25. The terms *hokim* (leader or boss) and *aksakals* (chairman) are both used to describe the leadership of the *mahalla*.

26. In 1997 a series of arrests occurred in a number of *mahalla* across the country. The Foreign Broadcast Information Service reported on March 27, 1997 that the chairmen of several *mahalla* were either under arrest or investigation for corruption and mismanagement of the following *mahalla*: Forty Years of Victory, Kyzyk Askar, Erkin, Pakhtaobod, Bog Kucha, Akkurgan, Safar-Ata, Chorvador, Malik, Sh. Rashidov, and Oltin Vodiy. A number of financial institutions were convinced to make inappropriate loans to certain family members, and that the Chairmen were over-compensat-

ing their own families and relatives with state funds. These patterns are not unique to Uzbekistan as mafia-style organizations are all too common throughout the FSU and the west.

BIBLIOGRAPHY

Achylova, Rakhat. "Political Culture and Foreign Policy in Kyrgyzstan." In Vladimir Tismaneanu, ed., *Political Culture and Civil Society in Russia and the New States of Eurasia.* Armonk, NY: M.E. Sharpe, 1995.

Akbarzadeh, Shahram. "National Identity and Political Legitimacy in Turkmenistan." *Nationalities Papers* 27, no. 2 (1999): 271–290.

Akiner, Shirin. "Post-Soviet Central Asia: Past Is Prologue." In *The New States of Central Asia and Their Neighbors,* ed. Peter Ferdinand. New York: Council on Foreign Relations Press, 1994.

Akiner, Shirin. *The Formation of Kazakh Identity: From Tribe to Nation-State.* London: The Royal Institute of International Affairs, 1995.

Allworth, Edward. *Central Asian Publishing and the Rise of Nationalism.* New York: The New York Public Library, 1965.

Allworth, Edward. *The Modern Uzbeks: From the Fourteenth Century to the Present; A Cultural History.* Stanford: Hoover Institution Press, Stanford University, 1990.

Allworth, Edward, ed. *Central Asia, 130 Years of Russian Dominance, A Historical Overview.* Durham, NC: Duke University Press, 1994.

Amin, Tahir. "Pakistan, Afghanistan and the Central Asian States." In *The New Geopolitics of Central Asia,* eds. Ali Banuazizi and Myron Weiner. Bloomington: Indiana University Press, 1994.

Asankanov, Abilabek. "Ethnic Conflict in the Osh Region in Summer 1990: Reasons and Lessons." In *Ethnicity and Power in the Contemporary World,* ed. Kumar Rupesinghe and Valery A. Tishkov. Tokyo: United Nations University Press, 1996.

Atkin, Muriel. "The Politics of Polarization in Tajikistan." In *Central Asia: Its Strategic Importance and Future Prospects,* ed. Hafeez Malik. New York: St. Martin's Press, 1994a.

Atkin, Muriel. "Tajikistan's Relations with Iran and Afghanistan." In *The New Geopolitics of Central Asia,* ed. Ali Banuazizi and Myron Weiner. Bloomington: Indiana University Press, 1994b.

Atkin, Muriel. "Tajikistan: Reform, Reaction, and Civil War." In *New States, New Politics: Building the Post-Soviet Nations,* ed. Ian Bremmer and Ray Taras. Cambridge: Cambridge University Press, 1997a.

Atkin, Muriel. "Thwarted Democratization in Tajikistan." In *Conflict, Cleavage, and Change in Central Asia and the Caucasus,* ed. Karen Dawisha and Bruce Parrott. Cambridge: Cambridge University Press, 1997b.

Batalden, Stephen K. and Sandra L. Batalden. *The Newly Independent States of Eurasia: Handbook of Former Soviet Republics.* Phoenix, AZ: ORYX, 1993.

Becker, Seymour."The Russian Conquest of Central Asia and Kazakhstan: Motives, Methods, Consequences." In *Central Asia: Its Strategic Importance and Future Prospects,* ed. Hafeez Malik. New York: St. Martin's Press, 1994.

Black, Cyril E., ed. *The Modernization of Inner Asia.* Armonk, NY: M.E. Sharpe, 1991.

Blank, Stephen. "Soviet Reconquest of Central Asia." In *Central Asia: Its Strategic Importance and Future Prospects*, ed. Hafeez Malik. New York: St. Martin's Press, 1994.

Bohr, Annette. *Uzbekistan Politics and Foreign Policy.* Washington, DC: The Royal Institute of International Affairs, 1998.

Bondarevsky, Grigory and Peter Ferdinand. "Russian Foreign Policy and Central Asia." In *The New States of Central Asia and Their Neighbors*, ed. Peter Ferdinand. New York: Council on Foreign Relations Press, 1994.

Bremmer, Ian. "Post-Soviet Nationalities Theory: Past, Present, and Future." In *New States, New Politics: Building the Post-Soviet Nations*, ed. Ian Bremmer and Ray Taras. Cambridge: Cambridge University Press, 1997.

Carley, Patricia M. "The Legacy of the Soviet Political System and the Prospects for Developing Civil Society in Central Asia." In *Political Culture and Civil Society in Russia and the New States of Eurasia*, ed. Vladimir Tismaneanu. Armonk, NY: M.E. Sharpe, 1995.

Carlisle, Donald S. "Uzbekistan and the Uzbeks." *Problems of Communism* 40, no. 5(1991): 23–44.

Clark, Susan. "The Central Asian States: Defining Security Priorities and Developing Military Forces." In *Central Asia and the World: Kazakhstan, Uzbekistan, Tajikistan, Kyrgyzstan, Turkmenistan*, ed. Michael Mandelbaum. New York: Council on Foreign Relations Press, 1994.

Critchlow, James, *Nationalism in Uzbekistan: A Soviet Republic's Road to Sovereignty.* Boulder, CO: Westview Press, 1991.

Critchlow, James. "The Ethnic Factor in Central Asian Foreign Policy." In *National Identity and Ethnicity in Russia and the New States of Eurasia*, ed. Roman Szporluk. Armonk, NY: M.E. Sharpe, Inc., 1994a.

Critchlow, James. "Nationalism and Islamic Resurgence in Uzbekistan." In *Central Asia: Its Strategic Importance and Future Prospects*, ed. Hafeez Malik. New York: St. Martin's Press, 1994b.

Cullen, Robert. "Central Asia and the West." In *Central Asia and the World: Kazakhstan, Uzbekistan, Tajikistan, Kyrgyzstan, Turkmenistan*, ed. Michael Mandelbaum. New York: Council on Foreign Relations Press, 1994.

Dawisha, Karen and Bruce Parrott. *Russia and the New States of Eurasia: The Politics of Upheaval.* Cambridge: Cambridge University Press, 1994.

Ferdinand, Peter. "The New Central Asia and China." In *The New States of Central Asia and Their Neighbors*, ed. Peter Ferdinand. New York: Council on Foreign Relations Press, 1994.

Fierman, William, ed. *Soviet Central Asia: The Failed Transformation.* Boulder, CO: Westview Press, 1991.

Fierman, William. "Political Development in Uzbekistan: Democratization?" In *Conflict, Cleavage, and Change in Central Asia and the Caucasus*, ed. Karen Dawisha and Bruce Parrott. Cambridge: Cambridge University Press, 1997.

Fridman, Leonid A. "Economic Crisis As a Factor of Building Up Socio-Political and Ethnonational Tensions in the Countries of Central Asia and Transcaucasia." In *Central Asia and Transcaucasia: Ethnicity and Conflict*, ed. Vitaly V. Naumkin. Westport, CT: Greenwood Press, 1994.

Fuller, Graham E. *The Democracy Trap: The Perils of the Post-Cold War World.* New York: Dutton Publishers, 1991.
Fuller, Graham E. *Central Asia: The New Geopolitics.* Santa Monica, CA: RAND, 1992.
Fuller, Graham E. "From Eastern Europe to Western China: The Growing Role of Turkey in the World and its Implications for Western Interests." *RAND Corp.* (LC 93–19278), 1993.
Fuller, Graham E. "Central Asia and American National Interests." In *Central Asia: Its Strategic Importance and Future Prospects*, ed. Hafeez Malik. New York: St. Martin's Press, 1994a.
Fuller, Graham E. "Emerging Political Elites." In *The New Geopolitics of Central Asia*, ed. Ali Banuazizi and Myron Weiner. Bloomington: Indiana University Press, 1994b.
Fuller, Graham E. "Russia and Central Asia: Federation or Fault Line?" In *Central Asia and the World: Kazakhstan, Uzbekistan, Tajikistan, Kyrgyzstan, Turkmenistan*, ed. Michael Mandelbaum. New York: Council on Foreign Relations Press, 1994c.
Gankovsky, Yuri V. "Russia's Relations with the Central Asian States Since the Dissolution of the Soviet Union." In *Central Asia: Its Strategic Importance and Future Prospects*, ed. Hafeez Malik. New York: St. Martin's Press, 1994.
Garfinkel, Harold. *Studies in Ethnomethodology.* Englewood Cliffs: Prentice-Hall, 1967.
Ghorban, Narsi. "The Role of the Multinational Oil Companies in the Development of Oil & Gas Resources in Central Asia and the Caucasus." *Iranian Journal of International Affairs* 5 (1993): 1–15.
Gillis, John R., ed. "Memory and Identity: The History of a Relationship" In *Commemorations: The Politics of National Identity.* Princeton, NJ: Princeton University Press, 1994.
Gleason, Gregory. "Uzbekistan: From Statehood to Nationhood." In *Nation and Politics in the Soviet Successor States*, ed. Ian Bremmer and Ray Taras. Cambridge: Cambridge University Press, 1993.
Gleason, Gregory. *Indigenous Democracy in Central Asia.* Avaliable at: opher://gopher.soros.org:70/00/Affiliated_Orgs/OSI_NY/Tajikistan_Project/democracy 1.txt, 1996.
Gleason, Gregory. *The Central Asian States: Discovering Independence.* Boulder, CO: Westview Press, 1997a.
Gleason, Gregory. "Uzbekistan: The Politics of National Independence." In *New States, New Politics: Building the Post-Soviet Nations*, ed. Ian Bremmer and Ray Taras. Cambridge: Cambridge University Press, 1997b.
Goodman, Melvin. "*Perestroika*: Its Impact on the central Asian Republics and Their Future Relations with Moscow." In *Central Asia: Its Strategic Importance and Future Prospects*, ed. Hafeez Malik. New York: St. Martin's Press, 1994.
Haas, Michael. Private e-mail from the author, April 29, 1997.
Haghayeghi, Mehrdad. *Islam and Politics in Central Asia.* New York: St. Martin's Press, 1995.
Hale, Henry. "Islam, State-Building and Uzbekistan Foreign Policy." In *The New Geopolitics of Central Asia and Its Borderlands.* ed. Ali Banuazizi and Myron Weiner. Bloomington: Indiana University Press, 1994.

Handler, Richard. "Is Identity a Useful Cross-Cultural Concept?" In *Commemorations: The Politics of National Identity*, ed. John R. Gillis. Princeton, NJ: Princeton University Press, 1994.

Hauner, Milan. *What Is Asia to Us?: Russia's Asian Heartland Yesterday and Today.* Boston: Unwin Hymen, 1990.

Hiro, Dilip. *Between Marx and Muhammad: The Changing Face of Central Asia.* London: Harper Collins Publishers, 1995.

Honigmann, John J. "Tribe." In *A Dictionary of the Social Sciences,* ed. Julius Gould and William L. Kolb. New York: Free Press, 1964.

Hunter, Shireen T. *Central Asia Since Independence.* Westport, CT: Praeger Publishers, 1996.

Huskey, Eugene. "Kyrgyzstan: The Fate of Political Liberalization." In *Conflict, Cleavage, and Change in Central Asia and the Caucasus*, ed. Karen Dawisha and Bruce Parrott. Cambridge: Cambridge University Press, 1997a.

Huskey, Eugene. "Kyrgyzstan: The Politics of Demographic and Economic Frustration." In *New States, New Politics: Building the Post-Soviet Nations*, ed. Ian Bremmer and Ray Taras. Cambridge: Cambridge University Press, 1997b.

Hyman, Anthony. "Central Asia's Relations with Afghanistan and South Asia." In *The New States of Central Asia and Their Neighbors*, ed. Peter Ferdinand. New York: Council on Foreign Relations Press, 1994.

Islam, Shafiqul. "Capitalism on the Silk Route." In *Central Asia and the World: Kazakhstan, Uzbekistan, Tajikistan, Kyrgyzstan, Turkmenistan*, ed. Michael Mandelbaum. New York: Council on Foreign Relations Press, 1994.

Karimov, Islam. *Uzbekistan on the Threshold of the Twenty-First Century: Challenges to Stability and Progress.* New York, NY: St. Martin's Press, 1998.

Karimov, Islam A. Address by H.E. Mr. Islam Karimov, President of the Republic of Uzbekistan, at the 48th Session of the United Nations General Assembly (28 September). Tashkent: Uzbekistan, 1993.

Karimov, Islam A. *Uzbekistan: The Road of Independence and Progress.* Tashkent: Government of Uzbekistan, 1992.

Kaiser, Robert J. "Ethnic Demography and Intestate Relations in Central Asia." In *National Identity and Ethnicity in Russia and the New States of Eurasia*, ed. Roman Szporluk. Armonk, NY: M.E. Sharpe, Inc., 1994.

Karasik, Theodore. "Azerbaijan, Central Asia, and the Future Persian Gulf Security." *RAND Corp.* (N-3579–AF/A), 1993.

Karpat, Kemal H. "The Sociopolitical Environment Conditioning the Foreign Policy of the Central Asian States." In *The Making of Foreign Policy in Russia and the New States of Eurasia*, ed. Adeed Dawisha and Karen Dawisha. Armonk, NY: M.E. Sharpe, Inc., 1995.

Katz, Mark N. "Emerging Patterns in the International Relations of Central Asia." In *The Making of Foreign Policy in Russia and the New States of Eurasia*, ed. Adeed Dawisha and Karen Dawisha. Armonk, NY: M.E. Sharpe, Inc., 1995.

Konarovsky, Mikhail. "Russia and the Emerging Geopolitical Order in Central Asia." In *The New Geopolitics of Central Asia*, ed. Ali Banuazizi and Myron Weiner. Bloomington: Indiana University Press, 1994.

Koroteyeva, Victoria and Ekaterina Makarova. "The Assertion of Uzbek Identity." Available at: http://iias.leidenuniv.nl/iiasn/iiasn6/central/uzbek.html, 1996.

Krader, Lawrence. *Peoples of Central Asia*. The Hague: Mouton, 1963.

Lowenthal, David. "Identity, Heritage, and History." In *Commemorations: The Politics of National Identity*, ed. John R. Gillis. Princeton, NJ: Princeton University Press, 1994.

Lubin, Nancy. "Central Asia: Issues and Challenges for United States Policy." In *The New Geopolitics of Central Asia*, ed. Ali Banuazizi and Myron Weiner. Bloomington: Indiana University Press, 1994.

Makarova, Ekaterina. Private e-mail from the author, April 11, 1997.

Malik, Hafeez. "New Relationships Between Central and Southwest Asia and Pakistan's Regional Politics." In *Central Asia: Its Strategic Importance and Future Prospects*, ed. Hafeez Malik. New York: St. Martin's Press, 1994.

Manafi, Kambiz. "Refining, Oil Balances and Trade in the Black Sea, Transcaucasian and Central Asian Republics." *OPEC Bulletin* 24 (1993): 9–11.

Mandelbaum, Michael, ed. *Central Asia and the World: Kazakhstan, Uzbekistan, Tajikistan, Kyrgyzstan, Turkmenistan*. New York: Council on Foreign Relations Press, 1994.

Mesbahi, Mohiaddin. "Regional and Global Powers and the International Relations of Central Asia." In *The Making of Foreign Policy in Russia and the New States of Eurasia*, ed. Adeed Dawisha and Karen Dawisha. Armonk, NY: M.E. Sharpe, Inc., 1995.

Munro, Ross H. "Central Asia and China." In *Central Asia and the World: Kazakhstan, Uzbekistan, Tajikistan, Kyrgyzstan, Turkmenistan*, ed. Michael Mandelbaum. New York: Council on Foreign Relations Press, 1994.

Naumkin, Vitaly V. "Experience and Prospects for Settlement of Ethno-National Conflicts in Central Asia and Transcaucasia." In *Central Asia and Transcaucasia: Ethnicity and Conflict*, ed. Vitaly V. Naumkin. Westport, CT: Greenwood Press, 1994.

Nissman, David, "Legal Protections in the Central Asian Countries." Available at: http://www.jamestown.org/prism/072195/nissma.htm, 1995.

Nissman, David. "Turkmenistan: Just Like Old Times." In *New States, New Politics: Building the Post-Soviet Nations*, ed. Ian Bremmer and Ray Taras. Cambridge: Cambridge University Press, 1997.

Neubauer, Deane E. Private e-mail from author, July 7, 1997.

OGD. *The World Geopolitics of Drugs 1997/1998 Annual Report*. Available at: http://www.ogd.org/index_gb.html, 1998.

Olcott, Martha Brill. "Emerging Political Elites." In *The New Geopolitics of Central Asia*, ed. Ali Banuazizi and Myron Weiner. Bloomington: Indiana University Press, 1994.

Poliakov, Sergei P. *Everyday Islam: Religion and Tradition in Rural Central Asia*. London: M.E. Sharpe, 1992.

Red Apple Contraception Program. Available at: http://www.tfgi.com/projects/hl_5_97.htm.

Robillard, Albert. Private e-mail from author, June 3, 1997.

Schoeberlein-Engel, John. Private e-mail from the author, April 27, 1997

Sollors, Werner. *Beyond Ethnicity: Consent and Descent in American Culture*. Oxford: Oxford University Press, 1986.

Winthrop, Robert H. *Dictionary of Concepts in Cultural Anthropology*. Westport, CT: Greenwood Press, 1991.

Chapter 14

Conclusions and Assessments: Strategies in Center-Periphery Relations

Daniel R. Kempton and Terry D. Clark

DEMOCRACY AND OTHER MOTIVES FOR CHANGING CENTER-PERIPHERY RELATIONS

In much of the world, democratization has been accompanied by a significant devolution of powers and responsibilities from central ministries to regional and local governments. This has certainly been the case with the Soviet successor states analyzed in this volume. Each in its own way and at its own pace has had to determine both the specific powers and responsibilities to be devolved and the extent to which powers will be devolved or will remain with the center. To some degree there appears to be a natural relationship between the consolidation of democracy and the establishment of governmental accountability at the local and regional level. More succinctly, even in an age of advanced instantaneous communication, the only way to effectively make local political rule more accountable is to devolve power to government leaders and institutions at the local level. Local institutions provide citizens with their greatest degree of contact with government and the greatest possibilities for political participation. The ultimate success of democracy in the states of the former Soviet Union may well rest largely on their ability to contribute to a sense of political efficacy among the population.

As argued in Chapter 2, the devolution of power can reinforce democracy by providing minority groups an opportunity for greater political autonomy. While local autonomy may be of greatest importance for ethnic minorities, it may also be highly prized by cities, villages, and agricultural zones, which simply have economic, political or cultural interests that vary from the national norms. Thus regional or local interests may find or even create a greater degree of responsiveness in their local governments than they would likely receive from a central government. Ultimately, the devolution of power also gives more citizens opportunities to meaningfully participate in the governing process.

If the devolution of power contributes to, or is even necessary for, effective and responsive democratic government, then the states of the former Soviet Union are collectively starting from a major deficit. Despite its vast size and ethnic diversity, the Soviet Union was characterized by some of the most centralized center-periphery relations on the face of the globe. Thus, as stated in Chapter 1, each of the states of the former Soviet Union has had to develop its center-periphery relations *tabula rasa*. Despite their common heritage and shared center-periphery problems, the Soviet successor states vary greatly in size, population, ethnic distribution, distribution of resources, urbanization, and a variety of other resources. Thus, each has had to find its own solution to its center-periphery problems.

Despite the evident relationship between democracy and the devolution of power to regional and local governments there are other reasons for devolving power to periphery governments. The desire to increase economic and administrative efficiency with which governments deliver public goods and resources is a second reason for the devolution of power noted in the preceding pages. This can be accomplished by moving responsibility for implementing central government programs to lower levels of governance without providing those same levels of governance with either the authority or means to initiate their own programs and policies. Local and regional governments in this model are nothing more than field agencies of the central ministries. Center-periphery relations are marked by hierarchy and subordination of lower levels of governance to the center. This seems to come closest to describing what has occurred in Uzbekistan while in Lithuania the effort to turn local government into an arm of the center has thus far failed. Russia's efforts to control its regional governments have met with decidedly mixed results.

In Russia the motivation was not so much to improve efficiency, but to devolve those powers to the regions and republics (*subekty*) that the center simply was not capable of exercising. To some extent, particularly from 1991 until 1993, power was devolved to the Russian periphery because the *subekty* sought powers and the federal government was so internally divided that it was either unwilling or unable to stop the *subekty* from taking the powers they wanted. After the economic collapse, however, the *subekty* again assumed powers that the federal government simply could not afford to exercise.

There are rational reasons for elites and bureaucrats at the national level not to devolve decision-making authority and resources to lower levels of governance. By doing so, they necessarily empower autonomous units of governance from which their own authority can be challenged by regional and local elites. In the worst of cases, this can lead to fragmentation of the state. At a minimum, it can weaken the state as is evidenced in Ukraine and Russia where regionalism has undermined state power and authority.

Nonetheless, the Lithuanian case makes it clear that local autonomy need not lead to the weakening of the national state and the threat of fragmentation. When we compare the healthier state of center-periphery relations in Lithuania with that in Ukraine or Russia, and even Uzbekistan, the fundamental difference appears to be that in the former case there is a strong national identity to which all principal players (elites at the national, regional, and local levels) subscribe. This permits the debate over the contours of the center-periphery relations to occur within the framework of consensus on the larger issues concerning the boundaries of the state.

Regionalism in Russia, Ukraine, and Uzbekistan has impeded the emergence of a similar consensus. As a consequence, center-periphery debates frequently encompass differing views concerning the limits of the state and on occasion may even challenge its very existence. This seems to indicate, as a rough rule of thumb, that states that are large and regionally diverse are most likely to be threatened by the results of devolving power. The risks of devolving power are even greater when regional diversity is overlapped with ethnic diversity, as it is in all three of these cases. Ironically, however, it is in these same cases where the benefits of devolving power are greatest. The devolving of significant powers to regional and local governments may create sufficiently responsive governments to satiate powerful regional or ethnic concerns.

In essence, the transitions to democracy in Russia, Ukraine, and Uzbekistan are a good deal more complicated than that in Lithuania. In the latter, there are really only two challenges: the development of a free market and the creation of a democratic political order. Conversely, the three former states are faced with the challenge of accomplishing both of these tasks while simultaneously engaging in a state-building project. Hence, it should not be surprising that the impetus to deny autonomy to lower levels of governance would be stronger in such states. The effort to do so, however, has serious consequences for the success of democratization.

These consequences have been most readily apparent in the case of Russia. In Chechnya, and to a lesser extent Dagestan, Russian attempts to deny autonomy or take back autonomy already being exercised by the regional governments have twice escalated into armed conflict. While Chechnya is the most virulent example, Russia has carefully had to manage its center-periphery relations with a variety of *subekty* including Primorskii Krai, Tatarstan, Tuva, and many others. However, we do not conclude that the Russian experience with devolution is exceptional, and the more peaceful and consensual experience of Lithuania is the norm. The regional problems of Moldova, Azerbaijan, and Georgia all parallel in certain ways Russia's uncertain attempts to trade a devolution of power for greater acceptance of undivided state sovereignty.

National elites in the states of the former Soviet Union are understandably troubled by the political conflict to which the devolution of responsibilities and authority to regional and local governments give rise. Even more troubling are the inefficiencies that such political conflict entails. For this reason the Lithuanian central government has attempted to reverse some of the reforms in an effort to tighten control over local governments. However, the achievement of consensus by destroying the basis of political conflict is in and of itself undemocratic. What is achieved is consensus not only concerning the "the rules of the game" but consensus on the very details of policy, a consensus gained by denying voice to alternative views.

If democracy is nothing else, it is the institutionalization of political conflict. For democracy to work there must be competing elite views on policy. Consensus is necessary only as regards the legitimacy of the state and the democratic rules by which political differences will be resolved. Understood in these terms, autonomous regional and local governments are essential to democracy. They provide a base from which alternative elites can emerge and challenge ruling elites. It is this very phenomenon that Uzbekistan's Karimov has attempted to avoid by undermining the autonomy of regional and local governments.

Stability in Center-Periphery Relations

Logically the key to establishing stable center-periphery relations is creating a balance somewhere between the absolute centralization associated with Soviet totalitarianism and *de facto* autonomy for local and regional governments. This means on the one hand that local or regional governments must have significant powers devolved to them. On the other hand, it also means that the local governments remain sufficiently tied to the central government so that their increased autonomy does not become a first step on the road to independence. Let us first examine the devolution of power and the creation of local or regional autonomy.

Decentralization and Autonomy

The devolution of responsibilities from central ministries to regional and local governments, or decentralization, as evidenced in our case studies need not be associated with federalism as a constitutional choice. Indeed, it would appear that local governments in federal systems do not necessarily have greater local autonomy than those in unitary systems. There may even be cases where regional governments in unitary systems are granted more powers than the component governments in federal systems. Thus the differences between the functioning of federal and unitary governments are not so great as commonly thought. As B.C. Smith notes, the major difference relating to national-local links is that in federalism the structure of these relations can not be changed without adhering to a constitutional procedure involving the local governments in the decision. In unitary systems, changes can be made by a simple legislative act or government policy.[1] Put more frankly, it is not the relative distribution of power given to local or regional governments that separates federal and unitary systems. Rather, it is the inability of the central government to change the distribution of powers between center and periphery without the consent of the periphery that distinguishes federal and unitary systems. Therefore, whether a post-Soviet state has chosen a federal or unitary form of governance, in all cases some degree of decentralization has occurred. (It is also dangerous to assume that simply because a state declares itself a federal system, that it really is so.)

What distinguishes our case studies from each other is the degree of local autonomy that has emerged as a consequence of decentralization, and the specific powers that have been transferred to the local or regional levels. But what accounts for higher levels of autonomy in one system than another? Why have political elites at the local level in Lithuania or the regional level in Russia and Ukraine been more successful in defending their roles against the encroachments of the center than those in Uzbekistan? In short, what factors permit regional and local governments to maintain a non-trivial degree of autonomy? A number of factors emerged in the preceding cases.

The first factor, and the one most often cited in the literature, is financial autonomy. In particular, many specialists argue that a local or regional government's power to independently determine and collect revenues is critical to its maintenance of autonomy. Lacking such a financial base, local and regional governments are virtually prohibited from exercising any discretion in initiating or shaping local programs and policies. An independent revenue source is all the more critical if central bureaucrats are opposed to decentralization. This is frequently the case in that their power will be diluted by the introduction of local administration with the authority to act independently of the center.[2] Central bureaucrats can use the dependence of local and regional governments on central government grants to shape local programs. Indeed, they can go so far as to dictate how monies allocated in the central grants are to be used, thereby leaving local governments with little to no room for discretion.

At the same time, when the central government does not have the resources to meet even the most basic needs of the regional and local government, the central government's ability to maintain the centralization of power is significantly weakened. In Russia, for example, because the central government has not delivered on its promises of support to the regional and republican governments, those governments feel relatively free to ignore central policies in favor of domestic decisions. If the central government is already failing to meet a regional or local government's financial needs, the importance of threats of further financial cutbacks diminishes in importance.

Our case studies however generally agree with more recent arguments that regional and local government dependence on central grants is not enough to assure central control. Conversely, an independent revenue source is not in and of itself sufficient to guarantee autonomy to lower levels of governance. Concurrently, no matter how much financial control the center has, it is nonetheless dependent on the local level. The very fact that local politicians and administrators are the ones who execute central programs gives them an informal grant of discretion. Even under totalitarianism, there is simply no means available to the central government to guard against the infusion of local priorities into these programs. This is an even greater problem when the locality is further removed from the center geographically and when the local government exercises greater control over the actual expenditure of funds. Just as important is the fact that the central government is dependent on local government for information. Control over the information that the center must act on gives local officials extraordinary power to shape policies and programs at their level.[3]

A second factor promoting autonomy is the emergence of trained professional administration at the regional or local level. The development of center-periphery relations in Lithuania indicates that the absence of a trained professional administration will complicate efforts by local governments to plan and execute policy initiatives. Further, the lack of a core of administrators has impeded the efforts of locally elected politicians in lobbying and exerting pressure on central ministries to support local initiatives. There is a risk in the emergence of a well-trained, local professional administration, however. Local civil servants could become part of a national association with a unified, professional interest. In such cases, they could work at all levels of governance to undermine policies and programs legislated or decreed by democratically elected officials and supported by a majority of citizens. This is a particular threat in post-Soviet states newly emerging from bureaucratic rule under the tutelage of a single party and lacking any democratic traditions or patterns of behavior.

In Russia, the president has attempted to introduce a degree of Soviet-style centralization by making regional administrators directly responsible to Moscow. Central to this has been the battle to increase the powers of the presidential representatives, whose task it is to oversee the use of federal funds by regional governments. If Moscow has its way, central bureaucrats will oversee, if not control, the use of federally generated funds. Here too, the relative expertise and capability of the regional administrators will have a considerable effect on the autonomy of the regional governments. Well-trained and professional administrators will find more ways to use federal resources to accomplish regional objectives irrespective of the central government's attempts to direct regional policy.

A third factor that was critical for securing regional or local autonomy in all of our cases was the legitimacy of the regional or local government. When local or regional governments made policy choices that conveyed to their citizens the existence of an active civil society capable of mobilizing the public and holding elected officials accountable, then the public generally backed the local or regional government in its political struggles with the center.[4] A civil society comprising organizations uniting citizens at the grassroots level is able to support and sustain local initiatives against the opposition of the central government. Further, by holding politicians accountable, they serve as a buttress against the attempts of the center to co-opt local politicians and administrators.

A local political process, while in the early stages of development in all of the countries considered in this volume, clearly reinforces the efforts by local elites in Lithuania and regional elites in Ukraine and Russia to carve out an independent political space from the central government. While it would appear on first observation that formal, constitutional structures of local and regional governance in Uzbekistan have been undermined by the virtual non-existence of a similar political process in that country, further consideration leads to a contrary conclusion. Anthony Bichel's chapter in particular makes clear that a local political process is as alive there as elsewhere in the post-Soviet space. The *mahalla* are a clear expression of local citizens and elites working to achieve local interests. For this very reason, the central government has attempted to limit their more representative functions. Despite such efforts, however, the *mahalla* are likely to give rise to the emergence of a counter elite with a regional and local base of political support with which the center will ultimately have to negotiate, unless of course it is willing to exercise power with little to no effective means of legitimating itself with the vast majority of its citizens.

The preceding cases also suggest that local political party organizations strong enough to convey political information from citizens to the national level are a related fourth factor in promoting regional or local autonomy. If these parties have ties with national parties they will further assist in giving local politicians access to those at the center. However, there is a risk that if ties between national and local party organizations become too strong, then local party organizations would subordinate their interests to national policy goals.[5] In cases of great ethnic diversity, especially Russia, the relationship between regional and national parties has been tenuous at best. In such cases, local or regional parties can trade their support for a given national party for considerations that are of particular importance to the region or locality.

A fifth factor in promoting local autonomy is a popular regional or local leader. The effect of a popular dynamic leader in maintaining autonomy can be similar to that of a highly legitimate democratic government or a participatory political party. All three serve to coalesce local or regional attitudes into a more effective tool when bargaining with the national government. A popular charismatic leader, such as Shamiev in Tatarstan or Dudaev in Chechnya, may be particularly effective when negotiating with the central government. More precisely, if he can personally deliver regional votes or support to a national candidate or party, he will have considerable leverage when lobbying for local interests. Thus the cases provided numerous examples of *subekt* leaders trading their support for national leaders in exchange for benefits for their *subekt*. Conversely, there are serious drawbacks with associating local or regional political autonomy too closely with any particular individual. First, a charismatic populist leader is more likely to ignore significant minority groups within the locality or region than is a government whose legitimacy is based largely on its democratic basis. Thus, the early evidence suggests that charismatic leaders such as Dudaev in Chechnya or Nazdratenko in Primorskii Kraii are more likely to use their increased autonomy to openly challenge the central government. Put crassly, for these leaders, the greater the power the regional or local government can acquire, the greater their own power. Thus, charismatic leaders may be motivated to further expand local autonomy simply to increase their personal power, rather than because greater autonomy is in the interests of their constituents. A second problem is that while personalistic leaders can help accrue autonomy, the autonomy they accumulate is not institutionalized and may not survive them.

A sixth factor that helps maintain regional or local autonomy is a constitution, or other legal division of powers, which clearly institutionalizes the devolution of some powers to the regional or local level. For example if the national constitution explicitly gives local or regional governments the right to raise certain types of revenues or gives them clear jurisdiction in key policy areas, then the judicial system may emerge as an ally in the effort to protect local and regional autonomy. The bottom line is that the more difficult it is for either side to alter devolution of powers to the local or regional governments, the easier it is for the localities to maintain and exercise their autonomy.

A final factor that can help maintain regional or local autonomy is a political system that gives representatives an institutionalized role in the creation of national policy. As argued in Chapter 2 the representation of the regional or local governments is a necessary precondition of federalism. However, even in unitary systems, such as Lithuania, territorially based representation in national politics gives the local or regional governments the means to collectively protect their autonomy. In Russia, the Federation Council, the upper chamber of Russia's bicameral parliament, has given the regions a meaningful ability to guard their autonomy against encroachment by the national government. In Ukraine, regional governments have acquired substantial autonomy, so much so that they threaten to undermine the integrative capacity of the central government. In Uzbekistan on the other hand, the central government has denied all meaningful autonomy to local and regional governments. Only the *mahalla* hold the potential to redress this problem. Lithuania is the one non-Russian case surveyed in this volume where a balance between local autonomy and the central government has been achieved.

From Autonomy to Dismemberment

The other side of the balance in stable center-periphery relations is making sure that the increased autonomy for regional and local governments, which has occurred in all the Soviet successor states, does not become the first step on the road to independence. The initial concern of many specialists was, as stated in Chapter 1, that the breakup of the Soviet Union would unleash centrifugal forces with no predetermined or natural endpoint. From this perspective, the devolution of power to local and regional governments, which was intended both to increase economic efficiency and to satiate regionally concentrated minorities, could provide these regionally defined groups a natural base from which to advance claims for independence. Such has undoubtedly been the case in Crimea, and the Russian Caucuses. However, these cases have proven thus far to be the exception, rather than the rule. In a number of cases with problems similar to those of Chechnya, such as Tatarstan and Crimea, an all-out drive for political independence has been avoided.

What seems to be critical in such cases is the willingness of the national government to devolve sufficient cultural and economic power to the regions to satiate their demands for autonomy. Obviously, this is a delicate balance that likely differs from case to case. Therein lies the dilemma. Devolving key powers to Tatarstan may satiate the local government sufficiently to diminish any demands for independence, while the same powers may not satiate the government of Chechnya. In the latter case this devolution of power further empowers the government of Chechnya in its struggle for complete independence. Such varying reactions leads inevitably to the conclusion that no single model of center-periphery relations is universally applicable even in Russia, let alone for all the Soviet successor states.

SUCCESSFUL PATTERNS OF CENTER-PERIPHERY RELATIONS?

Clearly each of the Soviet successor states analyzed in this book has created its own pattern of center-periphery relations. In this final section we will analyze each of these patterns, and as promised in Chapter 1, provide a preliminary assessment of their effectiveness. Before considering our cases, however, a couple of cautionary notes are in order. First, keep in mind that the each of the Soviet successor-states may have different objectives, and may assign differing priorities to the same objectives. For example, avoiding ethnic resistance may be critical to Russia, moderately important to Ukraine, and largely unimportant in Lithuania. Second, our verbiage of creating patterns of center-periphery relations implies a conscious effort on the part of successor states. Indeed, each successor state has recognized the importance of center-periphery relations and made explicit attempts to create a constitutional pattern of relations. At the same time, this is misleading in that the actual pattern of center-periphery relations does not correspond precisely to the pattern laid out by the center. Instead, the pattern is heavily influenced both by demands coming from the periphery, and by de facto practices, which frequently violate the spirit if not the letter of center-periphery relations as laid out in the national constitution or other documents.

As discussed in Chapters 2 and 8, the pattern of Russian center-periphery relations is officially a federal one. Elazar defined federalism as "self rule plus shared rule."[6] Elsewhere he elaborates, "In the broadest sense, federalism involves the linking of individuals, groups, and polities in lasting but limited union in such a way as to provide for the energetic pursuit of common ends while maintaining the respective integrities of the parties."[7] Ultimately, federalism requires both that the regional or local governments are given significant powers and that they have the constitutional and real ability to prevent unilateral changes to the distribution of powers by the national government. Chapter 2 then laid out the necessary and beneficial conditions for the creation of federalism. In the substantive chapters the authors then sought to assess Russia's progress toward federalism.

The Russian chapters reached a number of important conclusions. First, Russian center-periphery relations have evolved significantly. As was demonstrated in all of the cases, both the powers legally assigned to the Russian *subekty*, and those actually exercised by the *subekty* have varied over time. In the late post-Soviet period, most of the *subekty* claimed far more powers than they were able to exercise. Yeltsin's initial conflict with Gorbachev, and his subsequent one with the Russian Soviet left the *subekty* relatively unchallenged to claim nearly any power they sought. Yeltsin's victory over Gorbachev, and later against the Soviet, ushered in brief periods of centralization, when the federal government sought to limit the devolution of powers, or even to reclaim powers—such as in Komi and Sakha. Some stability was created by the imposition of the 1993 constitution. Nonetheless, pressures for change continue. While many central administrators believe too much power has escaped to the *subekty*, the recent Russian financial collapse has forced many of the *subekty* to assume even greater powers and responsibilities.

Second, although Russia has vacillated between periods of increased autonomy for the *subekty* and periods of recentralization, the long-term trend has been one of increasing federalism. As concluded in Chapter 8, Russia now possesses more of the necessary and beneficial conditions for federalism than it has at any time in its past. Russia today possesses at least two levels of government, each of which has meaningful autonomy. This is in itself an important and remarkable change from a decade ago. At the same time, as specified in the Constitution and as seen in Part I, there are many issues over which Russia's component governments and federal government share power. The bottom line is that Russian governance today must be considered "shared rule." Moreover, as demonstrated in Chechnya, Kaliningrad, and Sakha, neither the central government, nor the *subekty* can easily change the distribution of powers in center-periphery relations. This has not prevented unilateral attempts to change the balance, most notably Chechnya's claim of independence and Yeltsin's attempts to reign in the government of Primorskii Krai. However, such attempts have been extremely costly and generally have not been successful. This leads to the tentative conclusion that the Russian model of federalism has brought some stability to Russian center-periphery relations.

A final conclusion is that the introduction of federalism to Russia has, at least partially served its major end. Federalism was chosen in Russia explicitly because it would allow the central government to deal flexibly with the varied levels of demands for political autonomy. While Tatarstan, Sakha, and Komi sought economic autonomy and considerable cultural autonomy, many of the territorially based *subekty* were less interested in cultural autonomy. Thus Russia has developed an asymmetrical form of federalism that allows it to deal with the varying demands and diverse capabilities of its *subekty*. Because of Russia's immense size and considerable diversity, the flexibility asymmetric federalism offers gives it significant advantages over other forms of center-periphery relations. Asymmetric federalism, as it is evolving in Russia, allows diverse *subekty*, many of whom were tied to the Soviet Union by force or the threat of force, to negotiate their divergent participation in the Russian Federation. This strategy has apparently succeeded in Sakha, Tatarstan, and Komi, among others. However, in Chechnya it has failed with catastrophic consequences. Moreover, it has had a more insidious effect on many of Russia's regions, which see asymmetrical federalism as placating the ethnically defined republics, while shifting an inordinate burden to the regions of the Russian heartland.

In sum, the shared governance inherent in federalism has given Russia highly conflictual center-periphery relations. However, this is neither completely surprising, nor entirely problematic. As previously argued, federalism is a system designed not to eliminate center-periphery conflict, but to channel it. With the notable exception of Chechnya, federalism has helped channel Russian center-periphery relations into the sphere of political struggle and negotiation. In this sense, Russia's unique form of federalism has helped Russia to manage, at least temporarily, many of its unique center-periphery problems. However, it is much too early to conclude that Russia has found a permanent solution to its center-periphery problems.

Ukrainian center-periphery relations are similar to the Russian case, particularly relations between Moscow and the national republics. An ethnic component undergirds and supports Ukraine's regions in negotiations with Kiev. As a consequence, the regions have been able to acquire a significant degree of autonomy vis-à-vis the center. However, the evolution of these center-periphery relations has thus far been in a more centrifugal direction weakening the integrative capacity of the young state. Nonetheless, the national politicians have thus far been careful not to aggravate regional tensions to the point that fragmentation ensues. Indeed, Kubicek's analysis leads to the more hopeful conclusion that the weakness of Ukrainian nationalism will ultimately permit Kiev and the regions to engage in a state-building project based on civic consciousness instead of national or ethnic identity. This will permit not only a more effective central government to emerge but regional and local governments as well. While the regions enjoy substantial autonomy, a weak center has precluded their being able to resolve a range of political, social and economic difficulties, the most serious of which require a coordinated response which only a strong center can induce.

The problems of center-periphery relations in Uzbekistan, and indeed in Central Asia, are the inverse of those in Ukraine. Here the center has denied any meaningful autonomy to the regions. Fearing that traditional regional identities might provide a base for the emergence of political rivals in the periphery, the office of the president has been used to amass personal power. This process has not only weakened the capacity of regional and local governments to address pressing social and economic problems, it has weakened the central government as well by focusing on the development of personal power at the expense of institutionalization of the political system. The consequent lack of an effective governing capacity and the threat of regime illegitimacy that this entails have forced the president to turn to traditional institutions of self-government to fill the vacuum. Nevertheless, even here the president has been careful not to invest these institutions with enough authority to undermine his own. The result has been a center-periphery pattern familiar to students of third world politics in which the central government becomes the prize in a "zero-sum game" between traditional regional elites. The leader of the current ruling elite uses the executive power to the benefit of a privileged region (more often the elites of that region rather than the region itself). Neither democratic politics nor an efficient economy can emerge until this pattern changes.

Lithuania demonstrates the healthiest pattern of center-periphery relations among those studied in this volume. Given both its relatively small size and ethnically homogenous population, the country has adopted a unitary government. Nonetheless, local governments have achieved a significant degree of autonomy permitting the emergence of a balanced relationship between them and the center. While the central government has attempted to recentralize, it has been impeded in doing so by its dependence on the efficient functioning of relatively strong local governments. The bargaining position of these local governments in relation to the center will continue to grow as local civil societies and local public administrations are strengthened. As a consequence, pressing social and economic problems have been engaged with a relatively greater degree of success as solutions to problems have been found at the most efficient level of governance.

It is thus clear that the collapse of the Soviet Union left all of the Soviet successor states a parallel problem. Each had to either recreate the totalitarian centralization of the Soviet Union, or create its own form of center-periphery relations. To this point none has opted for the extreme centralization of the Soviet period. However, although these states face similar problems in creating stable center-periphery relations *tabula rasa*, they do so with extremely varied conditions. They vary in history, size, ethnic diversity, external ties, and many other meaningful ways. Thus, each has sought to develop a form of center-periphery relations uniquely adapted to its conditions.

While it is too early to judge the ultimate success of these parallel experiments, it is worth noting that the terrifying trends discussed in Chapter 1 have not materialized. The 1991 collapse of the Soviet Union undoubtedly unleashed the centrifugal forces of ethnic nationalism, religious animosity, and regional self-interest. The twin principles of centralized rule and the immutability of borders were abandoned. These centrifugal forces had no predetermined or natural endpoint. The successor states and the borders they inhabited were often the result of the whims of Soviet tyrants. But to a large extent, Pandora's box has remained shut. Despite their serious social, economic and political problems, successor states have survived now for nearly a decade without disintegrating into political chaos or ever smaller parts. To some degree, this book helps to explain how.

NOTES

1. B.C. Smith, *Decentralization: The Territorial Dimension of the State* (London: George Allen and Unwin Ltd., 1985).

2. Joseph R.A. Ayee, "The Adjustment of Central Bodies to Decentralization: The Case of the Ghanaian Bureaucracy," *African Studies Review* 40 (September 1997): 37–57.

3. R.A.W. Rhodes, *Control and Power in Central-Local Government Relations* (Westmead, England: Gower Publishing Company Ltd., 1981); J.D. Stewart, "Grant Characteristics and Central-Local Relations," in *New Approaches to the Study of Central-Local Government Relationships,* ed. George Jones, pp. 10–17 (Westmead, England: Gower Publishing Company Ltd., 1980).

4. James S. Wunsch, "Decentralization, Local Governance and the Democratic Transition in Southern Africa: A Comparative Analysis," paper presented at the African Studies Association annual meeting in San Francisco, California, 23 November 1997 (revised 22 November 1997).

5. John Gyford, "Political Parties and Central-Local Relations," in *New Approaches to the Study of Central-Local Government Relationships,* ed. George Jones, pp. 28–39 (Westmead, England: Gower Publishing Company Ltd., 1980).

6. Elazar, 1987, p. 12 (italics in the original).

7. Elazar, 1987, p. 5.

Index

About the Contributors

JAMES ALEXANDER has been teaching at Northeastern State University in Oklahoma since 1997. He is the author of *Political Culture in Post-Communist Russia: Formlessness and Recreation in a Traumatic Transition* (2000) and has contributed to several edited volumes on regional issues—such as Komi political transition in a comparative perspective and regional democratization in Russia.

ANTHONY BICHEL is the Director of Teaching/Learning Technologies at Juniata College in Huntingdon, Pennsylvania, where he also teaches political science and information technology. He is the co-editor of the Central Asian volume of the forthcoming *Encyclopedia of Asia.* His publications include "Air Force One: The Cinematic Erasure of Central Asia," "Political Parties in Central Asian Republics" and *(Re)Discovering Central Asian Geopolitics: Critical Reflections on a Realist Space.*

HELGE BLAKKISRUD is the current Head of the Center for Russian Studies at the Norwegian Institute of International Affairs, where he has been a Research Fellow at the Centre for Russian Studies since 1995. He was also the Norwegian representative to the OSCE in Latvia 1994.

TERRY D. CLARK is an associate professor of political science at Creighton University where he is also the director of the graduate program in international relations (INR). He has published widely in major journals devoted to the study of post-communist Europe. His scholarship has won him considerable recognition, including several major grants supporting travel and research in the former Soviet Union from such agencies as the Fulbright Committee, the International Research and Exchanges Board (IREX), the MacArthur Foundation, and the Kennan Institute.

ROGER D. KANGAS is the Professor of Central Asian Studies for the College of International and Security Studies at the George C. Marshall Center in Garmisch, Germany. Prior to joining the Marshall Center, he was the Central Asian Course Coordinator for the U.S. Department of State's Foreign Service Institute and Adjunct Professor at Georgetown University.

DANIEL R. KEMPTON is an associate professor of political science and department chair at Northern Illinois University. He has published two books and more than twenty scholarly articles and book chapters. His articles have appeared in a wide variety of journals including *Slavic Review, Europe-Asia Studies, Journal of Modern African Studies, Journal of Southern African Studies* and *Africa Today*. He has been a Rhodes University Fellow (1991), a Fulbright Fellowship Recipient (South Africa, 1992), and a Pew Fellowship recipient at Harvard University (1993).

PAUL KUBICEK is an assistant professor of political science at Oakland University. He is the author of *Unbroken Ties: The State, Interest Associations, and Corporatism in Post-Soviet Ukraine* (2000).

INGMAR OLDBERG is an associate Director of Research at the Swedish Defense Research Establishment (FOA). He has published extensively on Russian defense policy, Russia's relations with its neighbors in the west, and on Russian regions, especially Kaliningrad. His most recent co-authored books include *At a Loss: Russian Foreign Policy in the 1990s* (1999) and *In Dire Straits: Russia's Western Regions between Moscow and the West* (2000).

ANN E. ROBERTSON is managing editor of *Problems of Post-Communism* and an adjunct professor in political science at the George Washington University. Her current research focuses on the utility of secession as a method of state-building in the Soviet and Yugoslav successor states.

LAWRENCE R. ROBERTSON is a Senior Social Science Analyst in the Bureau for Europe and Eurasia at the U.S. Agency for International Development. His recent publications include volume 26 of *Russia and Eurasia Facts and Figures Annual* and "The Constructed Nature of Ethnopolitics" in *International Politics*.